TEACHER'S RESOURCE MANUAL

THE
LATINO EXPERIENCE
IN U.S. HISTORY

CONSULTANTS

Pedro A. Cabán
Rutgers University

Bárbara Cruz
University of South Florida

José Carrasco
San Jose State University

Juan García
University of Arizona

GLOBE FEARON
EDUCATIONAL PUBLISHER
PARAMUS, NEW JERSEY

Paramount Publishing

ABOUT THE COVER

Illustrator Cindy Wrobel combined symbols and imagery from the root cultures of Latin America and from present-day Latino communities to create the cover design for *The Latino Experience in U.S. History.* Her design integrates these elements using vibrant colors that express the vitality, spirit, and diversity of Latino communities in the United States.

Executive Editor   Stephen Lewin

Senior Editor   Francie Holder

Editors   Bob Rahtz, Mindy DePalma

Art Director   Nancy Sharkey

Production Manager   Penny Gibson

Production Editor   June Bodansky

Production Coordinator   Nicole Cypher

Senior Product Manager   Elmer Ildefonso

Electronic Page Production   Northeastern Graphic Services, Inc.

Maps   Mapping Specialists Limited

Printed in the United States of America 1 2 3 4 5 6 7 8 9 10 98 97 96 95 94 93

ISBN: 835 90643 4

GLOBE FEARON
EDUCATIONAL PUBLISHER
PARAMUS, NEW JERSEY

Paramount Publishing

CONSULTANTS

Pedro A. Cabán is Associate Professor of Political Science and Chairperson of the Department of Puerto Rican and Hispanic Caribbean Studies at Rutgers University. He received his Ph.D. from Columbia University and has written and published on Puerto Rico's political economy and on multiculturalism in higher education.

José Carrasco is Chairperson of the Mexican American Studies Department at San Jose State University. He received his Ph.D. in Sociology of Education from Stanford University. He has worked in the social sciences with an emphasis on Mexican American Studies.

Bárbara Cruz is Assistant Professor of Social Science Education at the University of South Florida. She received her Ph.D. in Curriculum and Instruction from Florida International University. She has actively promoted both Latin American studies and global and multicultural studies at the secondary level of education.

Juan García is an Associate Professor of History and the Director of the University Teaching Center at the University of Arizona. He received his Ph.D. from the University of Notre Dame. The focus of his research is Mexican and Mexican American history, U.S. history, and ethnic studies.

REVIEWERS

Estella Acosta
Multicultual Education
Director
Orange County
Long Beach, California

John Arevalo
Social Studies Teacher
Harlendale High School
San Antonio, Texas

Theodore Bueno
Foreign Language,
Bilingual Education,
Red Program Administrator
and District Coordinator
Pueblo City School
District 60
Pueblo, Colorado

Mary García
Dean of Instruction
Pershing Middle School
Houston, Texas

Pilar de García
Bilingual Specialist
Albuquerque, New Mexico

Delores Gonzales Engelskirchen
District Superintendent
Chicago, Illinois

Lydia Hernández
Instructional Specialist
Cultural Heritage Center
Dallas, Texas

José E. Lebrón
Principal
Julia de Burgos
Middle School
Philadelphia, Pennsylvania

Albert Moreno
Bilingual Education
San Jose USD
San Jose ,California

Carrie Page
Social Studies Teacher
Sly Junior High School
Tampa, Florida

Manuel N. Ponce
Director of Mexican
American Education
Commission for Los
Angelels Unified School
District
Los Angeles, California

Carmen Idalia Sánchez
Assistant Principal of Social
Studies
South Bronx High School
Bronx, New York

Frank de Varona
Superintendent
Dade County Public
Schools, Region I
Hialeah, Florida

TABLE OF CONTENTS

Lesson Plans for *The Artist's View*   **94**

Testing Program

Answer Key for Testing Program   **144**

Activity Sheets

Answer Key for ESL/LEP Activity Sheets   243

About the Writing Process   248

Writing Process Evaluation Guides   250

Writing Workshops

Checklist for Writing a Research Paper   281

Using Outline Maps with *The Latino Experience in U.S. History*   283

▶ INTRODUCING THE PROGRAM

The Latino Experience in U.S. History is designed to meet the needs of students and teachers who want to learn the part people from Spain, Mexico, Central America, the Caribbean, and South America play in U.S. history. The many features in the student text and the Teacher's Resource Manual will help students read, comprehend, and think critically about the Latino experience. The structure of the text and the lesson plans enables teachers to use the program either as the core text in a Latino history course or as a supplement to a United States history course. The correlation (pp. 11–14 of this Manual) shows how to use the text as a supplement.

FEATURES OF THE STUDENT TEXT

Organization

Each unit of the student text opens with a six-page section called **The Big Picture**. It sets students in time and place with an overview of the events happening in the United States and in Latin America. **The Big Picture** gives a historical backdrop for the chapters.

A two-page timeline provides a visual cue for events that happened in the United States and in Latin America in the unit. Each chapter within a unit provides specific information about how Latinos participated in that period of U.S. history. The emphasis throughout the text is on individuals and on the actual stories and words of Latinos from their arrival in the Americas to the present. The writing style is narrative rather than expository. Students will be present in 1492 as Spanish explorers and adventurers land on a sandy beach of a Caribbean island; they will be there as the *tejanos* face disappointment when the independence they gained from Mexico only makes them feel like strangers in their own land—Texas; they will be there to share the dreams of immigrants like Jesús Garcia who crossed the border into the United States to find a better life; they will be there as César Chávez leads Latino migrant workers to victory, and a farmworkers' union is born.

All chapters of *The Latino Experience in U.S. History* have a time box called **Snapshot of the Times** that relates to the unit timeline and highlights key events in the chapter. Within each chapter, there are two or three sections. Each section begins with a purpose-setting question and ends with **Taking Another Look**. This section review asks students to demonstrate understanding of the material by answering two comprehension questions and one critical thinking question.

All **The Big Pictures** and chapters incorporate primary sources. A six-page list in the student text provides sources for all excerpts quoted in the text as well as a jumping-off point for research. The primary source materials are presented as written, with abridgments made only to eliminate extraneous material. If dialect was used in the original source, it has been retained. Difficult words are followed by synonyms or definitions within brackets.

Incorporated Biographies

Many history books isolate the accomplishments of individuals in tinted boxes set apart from the main text. *The Latino Experience in U.S. History* incorporates biographies of people—ordinary and extraordinary—within its running narrative. Photographs are included wherever possible so students see the real people.

Focus On . . . and Close Up

The Latino Experience in U.S. History ends each chapter with a **Focus On . . .** feature. Each one highlights some aspect of the chapter by making a past-to-present connection, by showing the Latino experience in a global context, or by emphasizing the arts or education. The feature appears at the end of the chapter so that the flow of student reading will not be interrupted.

The chapter review called **Close Up** provides a variety of review materials, higher-level thinking activities, and skills instruction and practice. The **Who, What, Where** of History and **Making the Connection** help students with their understanding of the important people, places, and events of a chapter as well as with the chronology of events discussed.

A section entitled **What Would You Have Done?** asks students to put themselves in someone else's place and analyze how they would have acted. This is a powerful tool in helping students develop empathy. Many of the exercises call for students to develop paragraphs, letters, advertisements, and other written communication.

Building Skills provides instruction and practice in one of 34 skills important for success in social studies. The activity sheets in this Manual provide additional practice in these important history skills.

The final section in each chapter review, **Express Yourself**, allows ESL/LEP students to demonstrate understanding of the facts and concepts of the chapters. While specifically designed for students whose first language is not English, these activities also serve as an alternative assessment opportunity for all students.

The illustration program uses a variety of maps, charts, graphs, photographs, lithographs, woodcuts, and so on, to help the Latino experience come alive for students. The illustration program also serves a teaching purpose. Every map, chart, and graph and many of the other illustrations have questions within captions that require students to study and analyze the illustration.

Maps, Charts, Graphs, and Illustrations

The Latino Heritage feature found in each unit supplies an additional dimension to Latino history through the poetry, letters, and stories of Latino writers spanning the period from the first encounter to contemporary times. Each selection or poem is presented in Spanish and in English with a short introduction in English about the writer. As students read and discuss the selections, they gain insight into the lives and thoughts of Latino people in U.S. history.

Latino Heritage

Too many history texts turn the discussion of the arts and sciences into laundry lists of people and their works. *The Latino Experience in U.S. History* departs from this approach in two ways. For a discussion of the arts and sciences of the 1900s, galleries provide photographs of key figures, explore the significance of those figures in the development of the arts, sciences, and technology, and cite representative works with reasons for their importance. For the arts of other periods, certain key individuals and their works are discussed in detail in the narrative.

Galleries

A full-color art section call **The Artist's View** shows representative works of art by African, Native American, Spanish, and Latino artists. Informative captions explain the influence that African, Native American, and Spanish works of art had on Latino artists and describe Latino folk art and professional Latino art. A special set of lesson plans in this Manual (pp. 94–99) provides information on the pieces and the artists as well as teaching suggestions and cooperative learning projects.

The Artist's View

Each component of the *Teacher's Resource Manual* was developed with the twofold use of the text in mind—as a core text in a Latino history course or as a supplement to a U.S. history course. The first section of the Manual provides a chart showing how *The Latino Experience in U.S. History* can be used as a supplement to U.S. history courses (pp. 11–14).

TEACHER'S RESOURCE MANUAL

The next section is a discussion of ways to integrate language arts into the teaching of history (pp. 15–19). The Manual includes a discussion of the use of the writing process in history classes (pp. 248–249), evaluation guides for assessing student writing (pp. 250–252), and a four-page **Writing Workshop** for each unit (pp. 253–280). The listing of resources in chapter lesson plans indicates where the **Writing Workshops** may be used. To help students in preparing and writing a report based on research, a **Checklist for Writing a Research Paper** has been included (pp. 281).

Incorporating Language Arts and the Writing Process

Lesson Plans

The largest portion of this Manual details lesson plan suggestions for teaching *The Latino Experience in U.S. History* (pp. 20–93). Each unit of lesson plans begins with an overview page describing the major concept of the unit and listing unit content themes. The overview presents a cooperative learning project for the unit that is excellent to use in classrooms with language-diverse populations. The overview also includes a list of resources for teachers and students.

The lesson plans for **The Big Picture** include a theme statement, an overview of the content, strategies for using the **Voices of the Times** quotation in the student text as well as the timeline, a **Focus Activity**, and teaching strategies for each section. If the text serves as a supplement, this organization allows the teacher to use just those portions of **The Big Picture** required for the curriculum. The teacher may also find that in such a situation, **The Big Picture** may be omitted because the core text has enough information to set the stage. If this is the case, the teacher could move immediately to the lesson plans for the chapters, picking and choosing as the course demands.

After an **Overview** of the chapter, a **Focus Activity** for the chapter, and a list of materials that may be used in developing chapter lessons, the lesson plans for each chapter are then divided by section. Each section lesson plan provides an objective tied directly to the teaching strategy. Many strategies contain primary source materials as the springboard for the lesson. Many sections also contain a **Historical Sidelight**, with additional information about a person, an event, or a topic from that text section.

The lesson plans for the chapters are followed by six pages of lesson plans for **The Artist's View** (pp. 95–99).

Evaluation

A **Testing Program** (pp. 100–143) with **Answer Key** (pp. 144–151) provides a two-page unit test for each unit, which may be used either as a pretest or as a posttest, and a one-page test for each chapter. The tests include matching, multiple choice, short answer, and essay questions. All answers are provided in the **Answer Key**, including guidelines for evaluating the essays.

Activity Sheets

Each chapter has an **Activity Sheet** of one or more pages (pp. 152–182). These sheets provide additional historical information as well as skill instruction. Primary sources, maps, charts, and graphs are used as vehicles for developing student understanding of content and skills.

ESL/LEP Teacher's Handbook

A short essay entitled **Teaching Strategies for ESL/LEP Students** introduces a section designed for teachers of ESL/LEP students. The essay (pp. 190–192) presents several strategies that are successful with ESL/LEP students. Lesson plans (pp. 193–205) for all chapter sections present specific teaching strategies to use in ESL/LEP classrooms. **The Big Picture**s and all chapters have **ESL/LEP Activity Sheets** (pp. 206–242) for students for whom English is a second language. These activity sheets were developed to increase ESL/LEP students' understanding of the text and help them become more efficient learners. However, because techniques for teaching language-diverse populations are basically good techniques for the general school population, many of the worksheets may be used effectively with all students. Answers for both types of activity sheets are provided (pp. 183–189 and pp. 243–247).

Geography

A one-page chart entitled **Using Maps with *The Latino Experience in U.S. History*** (p. 283) provides suggestions for emphasizing the five themes of geography in teaching the Latino experience. This is followed by outline maps (pp. 284–287) of the world, the United States, the Americas, and Latin America.

CORRELATIONS TO COURSES IN UNITED STATES HISTORY

The chart below is intended as an aid for teachers using *The Latino Experience in U.S. History* to supplement a course in United States History. The chart shows common divisions of year-long history courses and the parts of the book that apply to those divisions.

THE FIRST SETTLERS (PREHISTORY–1500s)

Unit Opener	Chapter		Special Features	
Unit 1 *The Big Picture*: Peopling the Americas, Enormous Empires, Peoples of the Southwest, East of the Mississippi	Chapter 1	Face to Face in the Americas: A Meeting in the Caribbean, Resistance and Conquest, Experiment in Empire Building, Out of Africa	Chapter 1	Focus On: Rethinking Columbus Day
			Chapter 2	Focus On: Rediscovering Aztlán
	Chapter 2	Struggle for an Empire	*The Artist's View* A2–A3	

THE ESTABLISHMENT OF EUROPEAN COLONIES (1500s–1700s)

Unit Opener	Chapter		Special Features	
Unit 1 *The Big Picture*: Africa the Homeland, African Empires of Gold, A New Spanish Nation, Race for Colonies, New World Rivalries	Chapter 3	New Ways of Life	Chapter 3	Latino Heritage: Sor Juana Focus On: The Gift of Maize
	Chapter 4	Reaching Out from the Caribbean	Chapter 4	Focus On: Cubans in Miami
	Chapter 5	The Spanish Borderlands	Chapter 5	Focus On: The Jémez Feast
			The Artist's View A1–A5	

THE ESTABLISHMENT OF THE UNITED STATES (1760s–1780s)

Unit Opener	Chapter		Special Features	
Unit 2 *The Big Picture*: The British Colonies in 1763, Roots of Conflict, A War for Independence, A New Law of the Land, In Latin America	Chapter 6	The Spanish and the American Revolution	Chapter 6	Focus On: The Heritage of New Orleans
			The Artist's View A7	

EXPANSION AND REFORM IN THE NEW NATION (1790s–1850s)

Unit Opener	Chapter		Special Features	
Unit 2 *The Big Picture*: An Expanding Nation, The War of 1812, The Monroe Doctrine, A Thriving Economy, In Latin America **Unit 3** *The Big Picture*	Chapter 7	The Road to Latin American Independence	Chapter 7	Focus On: The End of Slavery in South America
	Chapter 8	Life in the Mexican Borderlands	Chapter 8	Focus On: A Master Carver
		Life in New Mexico	*The Artist's View* A1–A5	
		Life in Mexican California	Latino Heritage: Ignacio Rodríguez Galvan	

WESTWARD EXPANSION (1840s–1880s)

Unit Opener	Chapter		Special Features	
Unit 3 *The Big Picture*	Chapter 8	Life in the Mexican Borderlands Changing Ways in Texas	Chapter 9	Focus On: *Tejano* Place Names
	Chapter 9	Revolt in Texas	Chapter 10	Focus On: Old Los Angeles
	Chapter 10	War Between the United States and Mexico	Chapter 11	Focus On: El Clamor Publico
	Chapter 11	Foreigners in Their Own Land	*The Artist's View* A1–A5	
Unit 4 *The Big Picture:* Settlement of the West			Latino Heritage: El Carroferril	

THE CIVIL WAR AND RECONSTRUCTION (1860s–1870s)

Unit Opener	Chapter		Special Features	
Unit 3 *The Big Picture* Unit 4 *The Big Picture:* A Bloody Civil War, Reconstruction	Chapter 12	Latinos in the U.S. Civil War (1861–1865)	Chapter 12	Focus On: A Latino Astronaut

ECONOMIC GROWTH IN THE UNITED STATES (1870s–1910s)

Unit Opener	Chapter		Special Features	
Unit 4 *The Big Picture:* A Network of Railroads, New Industries, A Flood of Immigrants	Chapter 13	A Changing World	Chapter 13	Focus On: La Placita
			The Artist's View A8	

THE UNITED STATES AS A WORLD LEADER (1890s–1920s)

Unit Opener	Chapter		Special Features	
Unit 4 *The Big Picture:* A New Expansionist Spirit, Expanding in the Pacific and Latin America	Chapter 14	The Cuban-Spanish-American War (1868–1898)	Chapter 14	Focus On: Guantanamo Bay
	Chapter 15	Puerto Rico and Cuba Under United States Control (1898–1920s)	Latino Heritage: José Martí	
			Chapter 15	Focus On: *El Morro*
Unit 5 *The Big Picture:* A Canal Across Panama, Policing Latin America	Chapter 16	The Mexican Revolution and New Patterns of Immigration (1900–1920)	Chapter 16	Focus On: Artists of the Revolution
	Chapter 17	Latinos and World War I (1914–1920)	Latino Heritage: Registro de 1918	
			The Artist's View A9	

AMERICA BETWEEN THE WORLD WARS (1910s–1940s)

Unit Opener	Chapter		Special Features	
Unit 5 *The Big Picture*: Prosperity and Progressivism, The Roaring Twenties, The Great Depression, The New Deal	Chapter 16	The Mexican Revolution and New Patterns of Immigration (1900–1920) From Boom to Depression (1920–1940)	Chapter 17	Focus On: Mutual Aid in Santa Barbara
	Chapter 17	Latinos and World War I, Growing Immigration, Moving North	Chapter 18	Focus On: Basques of the United States
			The Artist's View A10	
	Chapter 18	From Boom to Depression		

WORLD WAR II, THE COLD WAR, AND KOREA (1940s–1950s)

Unit Opener	Chapter		Special Features	
Unit 5 *The Big Picture*: World War II	Chapter 19	Latinos and World War II	Chapter 19	Focus On: The Pachuco Image
			Latino Heritage: Luis Polés Matos	
Unit 6 *The Big Picture*: The Cold War Begins, A New "Red Scare," In Latin America	Chapter 20	The Great Migration from Puerto Rico		

CHALLENGES AT HOME AND ABROAD (1940s–1980s)

Unit Opener	Chapter		Special Features	
			Chapter 4	Focus On: Cubans in Miami
			Chapter 14	Focus On: Guantanamo Bay
Unit 6 *The Big Picture*: The Fabulous Fifties, The Civil Rights Movement, the Vietnam War, 1968–a Violent Year, In Latin America	Chapter 20	The Great Migration from Puerto Rico (1945–1980)		
	Chapter 21	New Arrivals from the Caribbean	Chapter 20	Focus On: Religious Diversity
	Chapter 22	The Struggle for Equal Rights	Chapter 21	Focus On: Latino Jews
	Chapter 23	New Immigrants from Central and South America	Chapter 22	Focus On: A Changing Role for Latinas
	Chapter 24	A Growing Voice	Chapter 23	Focus On: The Tango
			Chapter 24	Focus On: A Voice for Latino Writers
			The Artist's View A11–A16	
			Gallery of Latino Writers	
			Gallery of Latino Artists	
			Gallery of Latino Performing Artists	

THE UNITED STATES TODAY (1970s–1990s)

Unit Opener	Chapter		Special Features	
Unit 7 *The Big Picture*: A Conservative Mood, the Prosperous 1980s, Controlling Immigration, Fighting Communism, The End of the Cold War, The End of Good Times, Action in Foreign Affairs, Hard Times and Violence, A New Direction, In Latin America	Chapter 24	A Growing Voice	Chapter 24	Focus On: A Voice for Latino Writers
	Chapter 25	Mexican Americans Today	Chapter 25	Focus On: Border Jumpers
	Chapter 26	Puerto Ricans Today	Chapter 26	Focus On: Puerto Rican Dance
	Chapter 27	Cuban Americans Today	Chapter 27	Focus On: The Calle Ocho Festival
	Chapter 28	Central Americans and Dominicans Today	Chapter 28	Focus On: The National Pastime
	Chapter 29	South Americans in the United States Today	Chapter 29	Focus On: Honoring Latin American Heroes
	Chapter 30	Toward a New Century	Chapter 30	Focus On: Se Habla Español
			The Artist's View A11–A16	
			Latino Heritage: Naomi Lockwood Barletta	
			Gallery of Latino Entrepreneurs	
			Gallery of Latino Scientists	

THE LATINO EXPERIENCE IN U.S. HISTORY • © Globe Fearon

▶ INTEGRATING THE LANGUAGE ARTS INTO
▶ THE TEACHING OF HISTORY

In recent years educators have become increasingly aware of the need to integrate the language arts into other subject areas. Usually when people think of the language arts, they think of reading and writing, but listening and speaking are equally important. Listening and speaking, like reading and writing, are essential elements in the communication of knowledge.

THE READING PROCESS

Every kind of reading material, no matter what the content area, has peculiarities that must be identified and mastered by the reader. History, for instance, has a specialized vocabulary, its own logic of organization, and its own kind of sentence structure.

An added complication is that students also bring a wide variety of skills to the task of reading history materials. Every teacher has faced the problem of having students who read quickly and with excellent comprehension in the same class with students who struggle to decode text.

As you know, prior experience is a significant factor in the comprehension of text; it is often more important than the student's ability to decode individual words. Since experience varies so much from student to student, it is important to have students share their understandings with one another—and correct their misunderstanding—before approaching the text. This sharing of information and perceptions is easily accomplished by using graphic organizers.

GRAPHIC ORGANIZERS

Graphic organizers are diagrams that illustrate the connections among ideas. Such organizers may take many forms, such as semantic maps, webs, timelines, and idea clusters. The point is to create a visual display of the associations or properties of topics. For instance, suppose that students are about to read a chapter from *The Latino Experience in U.S. History* that discusses the importance of Florida to the Spanish empire. Most students will have a limited knowledge of this subject. In order to prepare students to understand the chapter, you can help them share what knowledge they have in an idea cluster.

The students create an idea cluster by listing all the words and images that come to their minds when they hear the name of a topic, in this case, La Florida. You write these ideas on the chalkboard as students share them. One advantage of this technique is that all students are able to participate in, and learn from, this activity. As the students dictate their ideas, you will have an opportunity to introduce and use in context any unfamiliar vocabulary that students encounter in the text. Through discussion, you are also able to correct any information students may have that is incorrect or inaccurate.

A typical idea cluster might look like this:

```
  colonized by Spain      surrounded by water ──── Atlantic

                                    │           Caribbean

                          LA FLORIDA

  St. Augustine                                  Native Americans

  oldest U.S. city          pirates
```

Or like this:

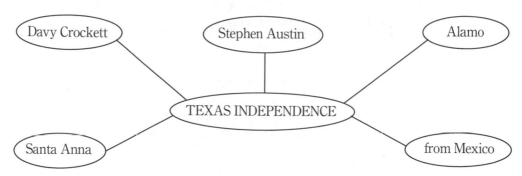

Such diagrams are pictures of the collective knowledge of the group about the topics. In order to develop the diagrams, the students had to draw upon their experience and generate meaning. As they read the chapters and learn additional relevant details, they can add to their graphic organizers, which then become visual representation of their new learning.

PREDICTION GUIDES

Another way of directing student attention and building needed background information is through the use of prediction guides. A prediction guide is merely a series of statements that students write concerning the material that they are about to read. The statements are written so that thinking is stimulated at the literal, interpretive, and applied levels.

Example:

Literal
Christopher Columbus first sailed from Palos, Spain.

I agree _____   I disagree _____

Inferential
Iron weapons and gunpowder gave Europeans an advantage over Native Americans of the Caribbean.

I agree _____   I disagree _____

Applied
The weapons of the Spaniards aided them in conquering the native people of the Caribbean.

I agree _____   I disagree _____

As the students respond to these statements, they are predicting what they will read. (The prediction guides should not be graded for accuracy.) This prereading focus gives students the chance to read with a purpose as they judge their preconceptions and change their ideas.

Vocabulary is another factor in understanding content-area material. All the research that has been done in the area of language acquisition reveals that unfamiliar words should always be taught in context if students are to retain their meaning. One way to teach new vocabulary is to give the students sentences in which the words are used in context and then require the students to infer the meaning. After students complete their inferences, they check their dictionaries for the correct meanings.

Example:
The Spanish used horses, dogs, and guns to subjugate the Taino of Hispaniola.

I think the word subjugate means _____.

Dictionary definition: _____

It is often necessary to focus the students' attention as they read. In *The Latino Experience in U.S. History,* the text itself provides purpose-setting questions to direct the reading experience. These questions appear at the beginning of each section of the chapter. Students should consider the questions before reading begins. Discussion should always follow silent reading. It is important that students be asked to provide information and opinions and that they be required to substantiate their opinions by reading pertinent text aloud. In whole-class lessons, it is important that students be encouraged to discuss their answers with one another as well as with you.

Another method of guiding silent reading encourages students to pose their own questions about events and ideas in the text. With this method, you preview the chapter with the students. Together, you examine the visuals that appear in the chapter. In discussing these images, you give the students a chance to predict what they are going to read. You may also wish to mention some key ideas or events covered in the test.

In another method, you divide the class into small discussion groups of five or six students and ask them to list questions about the text. Turning section heads into questions is a good study technique. Next, have students read to find the answers to their own questions.

Students who have difficulty reading text need to be taught comprehension-monitoring skills. Reading teachers refer to these skills as *metacognitive.* This terms means that students must develop awareness of themselves as readers. They must learn to think about how they process the text. Such students read aloud portions of the text that are difficult for them to decode and interpret during independent reading. They explain why portions of the text were hard to understand and demonstrate how they worked with the text to create meaning. Working with these students to recognize problems of text interpretation, you can lead them to identify their own strategies for getting meaning from print. As they deal with their reading difficulties, students benefit from using alternative sources of knowledge, particularly information learned from listening and speaking.

In this "information age," much of what students learn comes from listening. They listen constantly to radio and television. However, this is usually passive listening in which they are being entertained. Students are not listening for information, and often what they actually retain is incomplete or inaccurate. Ask any student about a current controversial public issue and you will frequently discover that the issue is poorly understood, at best.

To a great extent, this lack of listening comprehension can be attributed to the fact that few students are taught *how* to listen. Most people in the United States come from cultures that have rich oral traditions. Yet this emphasis on oral learning has been eclipsed by the availability of print materials. In our eagerness to teach students how to read, we have neglected to teach them how to listen.

One method of teaching listening skills to your students is to read a section of connected text to your class daily. After reading to them, ask your students to summarize what they have heard. If the students are typical, the information in their summaries will be disappointing at first. Once they begin to listen for who, what, when, where, why, and how—with a purpose, that is—the students will be able to report the content of what you have read more and more accurately.

Just as the development of listening skills has been neglected, the development of speaking skills has also been given little attention. Of course, most social studies classrooms are filled with discussion. However, the same students often seem to do most of the talking. Often the less articulate students sit silently. In addition, a student may talk freely and comfortably with his or her peers. However, when he or she stands up in front of a

DIRECTED READING

META-COGNITIVE SKILLS

LISTENING

SPEAKING

classroom filled with those very same peers, gasps, stammers, and many "uh's" and "uhm's" can be heard.

Speaking in front of a group does not seem safe to many people. That is why creating an environment in which students feel safe to speak is so important in the development of speaking skills. The first step in creating such an environment is to limit the number of people in the audience. Extremely inarticulate students may need to be paired with a single partner at first. Gradually, as the student becomes more confident, the number of participants may be increased.

The most nonthreatening situation for listening and speaking is the cooperative learning group. In this situation, all the students are equal. Properly monitored, a cooperative learning group can be effective in turning a fearful speaker into a confident one. The key to teaching the reluctant speaker is structure. Whereas being called upon to speak extemporaneously on an issue to the whole class might cause reactions of terror in some students, the task of reporting a piece of discrete and limited information to a small group does not seem so threatening. You can arrange the group assignments with this in mind. After a time, the students with stage fright will grow more confident and can be given more challenging assignments.

WRITING

The writing process has been treated elsewhere in this Manual (see pp. 248–249). However, writing should be an important part of every social studies lesson. Students learn to write the same way they learn to play the piano—by practicing. Just as practicing makes better pianists, it also makes better writers.

Writing also makes better readers. One way to increase your students' comprehension of written text is to make them write about a passage before they read it. This is a particularly effective way to prepare your students to read difficult primary source material. Students often struggle to read material written in previous centuries. Quite often the vocabulary is beyond them and the content does not seem relevant to their own lives. Writing is the way to make the connections for them.

Suppose, for example, that your students are about to read an excerpt from the writings of José Martí. This is challenging text, so it is advisable to work with students to create an idea cluster. Since the text concerns Martí's thoughts about what freedom means to a country and a people that have been controlled by Spain, students should think of what their feelings might be if they were in the same situation.

The resulting idea cluster might look like this:

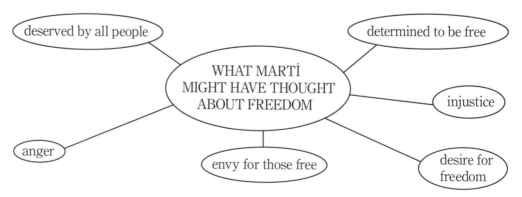

deserved by all people — determined to be free — WHAT MARTÍ MIGHT HAVE THOUGHT ABOUT FREEDOM — injustice — anger — envy for those free — desire for freedom

As soon as the students finish listing ideas, have them take out a piece of paper and write very quickly what ideas and arguments they think they will read about in the excerpt by Martí. Tell students that they will not receive a mark for their brief essay and that they should not worry about spelling or punctuation, since this is not for publication.

Be certain that everyone writes something down on paper. The important thing about this assignment is that it be strictly stream-of-consciousness; it is designed to rid students of writer's block that is often caused by fear of writing something inaccurate or "dumb."

After students have been writing for two or three minutes, tell them to put down their pens. Ask if anyone in the groups wants to share what he or she has written. You will find many students eager to share their efforts. Write their predictions about the Martí piece on the chalkboard. Tell the students that they should now read the text to verify the accuracy of their predictions. After students finish reading the text (this may be done silently or aloud), refer to the list of predictions on the chalkboard and discuss with the class which of their predictions were accurate.

This entire activity will take only 10 or 15 minutes of class time. Yet it will yield obvious dividends in reading comprehension, student interest, and student participation in the learning process.

▶ UNIT 1 Spain in the Americas
(pp. 2–65)

UNIT THEME
The meeting of the Spanish, Native Americans, and Africans in the Americas eventually created a new and distinctive Hispanic American culture.

UNIT CONCEPTS
- Thousands of years ago, people from Asia migrated to the Americas and spread out over the land, establishing new civilizations.
- In their search for a sea route to Asia in the late 1400s, Europeans encountered the Americas, where they raced to establish colonies.
- Spanish exploration of the Caribbean resulted in the conquest and enslavement of Native Americans and Africans in the Americas.
- Spanish conquest of Native American civilizations in what is now Mexico led the way to the creation of a vast Spanish empire.
- Reaching out from the Caribbean and Mexico, Spain extended its conquests into South America, spreading Spanish culture and religion.
- By conquering Florida and fortifying its island bases in the Caribbean, Spain sought to secure its empire in the Americas.
- Looking to the borderlands north of New Spain, the Spanish pushed into what are now Texas, New Mexico, and California, where they established settlements, built towns and missions, and created an Hispanic American culture that lasts to this day.

UNIT OVERVIEW
Unit 1 describes how the distinctive cultures of Native Americans, Africans, and Europeans intermingled in the Americas to create a new culture that combined elements of all three. *The Big Picture* and the five chapters in the unit describe the backgrounds of the cultures and (1) the first meeting of these cultures in the Caribbean, (2) Spain's conquest of a Native American empire in Mexico, (3) the development of new ways of life in Spain's American colonies, (4) the importance of Florida and the Caribbean in securing Spain's empire, and (5) the extension of Spain's empire north into what are now Texas, California, and New Mexico.

In teaching this unit, it is important to emphasize the impact of Spain's colonial empire on the North American continent. Stress that from the meeting of three cultures—Spanish, Native American, and African—a new and distinctive Hispanic American culture emerged.

COOPERATIVE LEARNING ACTIVITY
The following cooperative learning activity can be used for alternative assessment after study of the unit has been completed.

At the end of the unit, divide students into three groups, one representing Spanish colonists; one, Native Americans; and one, Africans. Have each group identify and list elements of its culture. Each group should present its list to the class and explain how its culture contributed to a new and distinct Hispanic American culture. In evaluating students' work, consider the cultural elements they have identified and their analysis of their group's cultural contributions to a new way of life in the Americas.

RESOURCES
Unit 1 Test (pp. 100–101)
Outline maps: The Americas, The World, Latin America (pp. 284, 285, 286)
Unit 1 Writing Workshop (pp. 253–256)
The Big Picture 1 ESL/LEP Activity Sheet (p. 206)

THE LATINO EXPERIENCE IN U.S. HISTORY • © Globe Fearon

Unit 1   THE BIG PICTURE (pp. 3–9)

Theme

Latinos are the descendants of Native Americans, Africans, and Spaniards, whose cultures mingled in the Americas to form a distinctive Hispanic American culture.

Overview

The Big Picture describes the arrival of three groups of people in the Americas. The earliest were people who migrated from Asia and spread throughout the continents. Laying claim to vast areas of the Americas, England, France, and Spain became fierce rivals as they raced to establish colonies, giving little thought to the people whose lands they had taken and to those whom they had enslaved. From the kingdoms of West Africa came unwilling people, Africans taken from their homelands and enslaved by Europeans, whose arrival in the Americas forever changed life on the continents.

Objectives

- To classify elements of a people's culture.
- To use a timeline to write a summary of events in the Americas from A.D. 300 through 1774.
- To understand cause and effect in the European conquest of the Americas.

Introducing *The Big Picture*

On the chalkboard, write the headings Agriculture, Trade, Food, Architecture, Religion, Writing, Art. Refer students to the text on pp. 3–6 describing Native American civilizations. Call on students to identify elements of these cultures and place them under the appropriate headings. Have students compare and contrast the cultures. Discuss with them possible reasons for the similarities and differences.

Using the Timeline

Divide the class into three groups. Assign one group Native Americans, one group Africans, and one group Europeans. Using the timeline on pp. 4–5, have each group draw up its own timeline summarizing events in its history from A.D. 300 to 1774. Students may skim *The Big Picture* and chapters in the unit to find additional information to add to their timelines. Have the groups present their timelines for class discussion. Ask which events the groups consider most important and why. Guide students to recognize connections among events in the three groups and ask them to explain these connections.

Teaching *The Big Picture*

Understanding Cause and Effect. Assign the text on pp. 7–9, beginning with "The Slave Trade." As students read, write the following events or issues (causes) on the chalkboard.

- Europeans set out on the Crusades.
- Europeans want to bypass Arab-Italian control of trade routes.
- The Portuguese mariner Diaz sails around the southern tip of Africa in 1488.
- The Spanish monarchs unite Spain in 1492.
- Columbus arrives in the Americas.
- In 1502, a Portuguese ship lands on the coast of West Africa.
- Cortés and Pizarro arrive in the Americas.
- England defeats the Spanish Armada in 1588.
- Spain, England, and France continue to claim more and more land in the Americas.

When students have finished the reading, explain that you have written on the chalkboard several events, or causes, leading up to and including the European conquest of the Americas. Ask students to copy the causes and then from their reading of the text, identify and write down the effects of each. Remind them that a cause can have more than one effect. Call on volunteers to read their effects aloud and discuss them with the class. Ask which causes and which effects students consider most significant in the European conquest of the Americas. What other effects can they think of?

For ESL/LEP students, see The Big Picture 1 ESL/LEP Activity Sheet, p. 206.

Review and Practice

Assign Taking Another Look, p. 9.

Answers to *Taking Another Look* (p. 9)

1. Peoples of Central and South America built cities, erected great pyramids, developed writing; people in Mexico established a huge empire, built great pyramids, gathered wealth from trade and tribute; southwestern people farmed, developed irrigation; while some built elaborate homes in cliffs, others lived in adobe villages; some were hunters and traders. **2.** through trade and collecting taxes in gold **3.** After years of warfare, Spain's monarchs drove out the Muslims and united the nation under one religion and one crown. **4. Critical Thinking** Possible answers may include the idea that conditions in the colonies were much different from those in the homeland, and that colonists would resent being exploited and their own needs ignored.

Chapter 1 Face to Face in the Americas (pp. 10–21)

Overview

In 1492, two very different worlds collided in the Caribbean. After Columbus's voyages, the Spanish quickly took possession of the land. Native American resistance was met by the iron weapons of the conquistadors, who wiped out huge numbers of Native Americans. Adding to the reduction in the Native American population were the diseases the Spanish brought with them. The remaining Native Americans were forced into the *encomienda* system. Under this system, Spanish settlers were given a grant of land and the use of Native American labor. As Native Americans continued dying from oppression and disease, Spain introduced African slavery to the Caribbean, forcibly shipping thousands of Africans to toil in the sugar cane fields and mills. In spite of brutal treatment, Africans endured, and their culture mixed with that of Native Americans and the Spanish to form a new Hispanic American culture.

Historical Sidelight

Rebellion and Escape. Many Africans in the Americas refused to accept their condition as slaves and continued to rebel and escape. The first recorded slave rebellion occurred in 1522 on Hispaniola, and was brutally suppressed. In 1537, Africans in Mexico City conspired to murder all Spaniards. But the plot was uncovered, and the revolt never took place. Escape was sometimes more successful. Fugitives could find refuge in remote regions and some established free settlements in several countries.

Resources

Chapter 1 Activity Sheet (p. 152)
Chapter 1 Test (p. 102)
Chapter 1 ESL/LEP Activity Sheet (p. 207)

Focus Activity

Have students consider what might happen when very different cultures meet for the first time. Have them draw up a list of possible events. When they have finished the chapter, ask them to go back over their lists and compare their speculations with what actually happened in the Caribbean.

Teaching Section 1: A Meeting in the Caribbean (pp. 11–12)

Objective

- To form a generalization about the first contacts between Spanish and Native Americans

Developing the Section

Forming a Generalization. After students have read Section 1, tell them they will be asked to form a generalization about how Spain's arrival in the Caribbean might affect the Native Americans. Ask the following questions: How did the Spanish present themselves to the Taino? (*in armor and with guns*) What was the first thing the Spanish did? (*took possession of the land and renamed it*) How did the Taino view the Spanish and how did they treat them? (*thought they might be from heaven, and brought them provisions*) What was included in the cargo Columbus sent to Spain? (*gold, birds, plants, Native American captives*) Now ask students what generalization they can form about the possible effect of Spain's arrival in the Caribbean on the Native Americans. (*The Taino were peaceful, unsuspecting people who might be enslaved by the Spanish in the future.*)

Review and Practice

Assign Taking Another Look, p. 12.

Answers to Taking Another Look (p. 12)

1. by taking possession of the island of Guanahani for Spain 2. handsome, well-built, peaceful; could be made slaves 3. **Critical Thinking** Answers may include claiming land for Spain and establishing a base from which Spain could create a vast empire.

Teaching Section 2: Resistance and Conquest (pp. 12–15)

Objective

- To understand the impact of Spain's conquest on the culture of the Caribbean people

Developing the Section

Making a Prediction. After students have read Section 2, have them reread the statement of Las Casas on page 13. Then ask them to write their own prediction of how the Spanish conquest will change the lives and culture of Caribbean peoples. Call on volunteers to read their predictions and explain the basis on which they made them.

Review and Practice

Assign Taking Another Look, p. 15.

Answers to Taking Another Look (p.15)

1. soldiers, priests, colonists 2. had superior weapons, brought European diseases that killed the people 3.

Critical Thinking from its strategic location guarding the other islands and the mainland

Teaching Section 3: Experiment in Empire Building (pp.15–17)

Objective
- To examine the role of the *encomienda* system in building Spain's empire.

Developing the Section
Writing a Report. Ask students to imagine that they have been appointed governor of Hispaniola. Have them write a report to Queen Isabella explaining the *encomienda* system they have established. Their reports should explain the organization and purpose of the system, the role of Native Americans, and how the system will help Spain build its empire.

Review and Practice
Assign Taking Another Look, p. 17.

Answers to Taking Another Look (p. 17)
1. first cathedral, hospital, university in the Americas 2. end conflict among settlers by giving grants of land and Native American labor, end Native American slavery but tie them to the land, convert Native Americans to Christianity 3. **Critical Thinking** stop the right of settlers to use Native American labor as they pleased, give fair wages and improve working and living conditions, allow Native Americans freedom of movement in their own land

Teaching Section 4: Out of Africa (pp. 17–19)

Objective
- To recognize the role of enslaved Africans in the history of the Caribbean

Developing the Section
Making an Outline. Have students copy the subheads in Section 4. Ask them to list under each subhead the main idea in each paragraph under that head. When they have finished the outlines, have them write a summary of the section explaining how Africans affected the history of the Caribbean.

Review and Practice
Assign Taking Another Look, p. 19.

Answers to Taking Another Look (p. 19)
1. needed more workers to plant, tend, and cut the cane and run the sugar mills 2. African population swelled, Africans contributed their traditions to make a new culture. 3. **Critical Thinking** Although the Spanish were the rulers, African ways greatly influenced the Caribbean.

Extending the Chapter
Researching Cultures. Divide students into three groups to research Spanish culture in the Americas, Native American Caribbean culture, and African culture in the Americas. Have them present their findings in oral reports, illustrations, or both.

Looking Ahead
After students have read Looking Ahead, p. 19, have them speculate on problems the Spanish might encounter on the mainland.

Answers to Close Up (pp. 20–21)

The Who, What, Where of History
1. Caribbean 2. African conquistador who served Spain 3. Taino leader who fled slavery to fight the Spanish 4. Santo Domingo 5. system of rule in which landowners forced Native Americans to work for them 6. priest who protested the oppression of Native Americans 7. Atlantic passage of enslaved Africans

Making the Connection
1. Diseases decimated Native Americans, making it easier to conquer them. 2. Growth of the sugar industry demanded more and more labor. 3. arrival of enslaved Africans

Time Check
1. 1492 2. First enslaved Africans arrived in the Americas.

What Would You Have Done?
1. might go for riches, land, glory, adventure; might not because of risks, uncertainty of gaining wealth or land, opposition to conquest of other people 2. injustices to Native Americans, no right to take their lands, un-Christian behavior

Thinking and Writing About History
1. Spanish official: land, riches, and a great empire for Spain. African: slavery, brutal treatment, endless toil Catholic priest: chance to spread Christianity, expand influence of Church. Native American: loss of homelands, disease, bondage, suffering 2. should include lands seized, villages destroyed, families enslaved or killed, death from European diseases

Building Skills
1. building open at the sides with roof of grass, clothing of women, women preparing and cooking food, different kinds of cooking utensils, different ways of preparing food 2. List should note kinds of structures built, little clothing necessary because of tropical cli-

mate, fact that women prepared and cooked food, the utensils used, foods included flat cakes cooked on griddles, other foods cooked in bowls. **3.** Paragraph is a secondary source since it is based on the study of a primary source, the drawing.

Chapter 2   Struggle for an Empire (pp. 22–33)

Overview

Lured by rumors of immense riches on the mainland of the Americas, one of the Spanish explorers who set out from the Caribbean to search for gold and land was Hernan Cortés. Spurred on by stories of gold and a vast empire to the west, he enlisted an army and sailed for Mexico. He marched inland to the seat of Aztec power, the great city of Tenochtitlán. Welcomed at first, the Spaniards' greed for riches soon angered the Aztec. In the ensuing struggle, Cortés massacred thousands of Aztec. Aided by a smallpox epidemic that swept the city, Cortés took Tenochtitlán and destroyed the Aztec empire.

Historical Sidelight

Malintzin. The young woman who guided Cortés to the heart of the Aztec empire had been stolen from her home as a child. When she was given to the Spanish as a gift, they promptly baptized her and renamed her Marina. In the Spanish chronicles of the conquest she is credited with great skill as a negotiator and diplomat. Some historians argue that her powers of persuasion helped convince the Aztec vassals as well as Motecuhzoma himself that the Spanish were gods and Cortés was the returned Quetzalcoatl, the Aztec principal god. It was said that if Marina had not been loyal to Cortés, she could have helped destroy his small army.

Resources

Chapter 2 Activity Sheet (p. 153)
Chapter 2 Test (p. 103)
Chapter 2 ESL/LEP Activity Sheet (p. 208)

Focus Activity

Have students examine the picture and caption on page 22. Ask what impressions they get about the Aztec from this picture and caption. What can they predict from these about the fate of the Aztec empire?

Teaching Section 1: Seeking Adventure and Gold (pp. 23–25)

Objective

* To recognize the motives of the Spanish in exploring the mainland of the Americas.

Developing the Section

Recognizing Motives. Based on their prior knowledge of Spanish aims in the Caribbean, ask students what might have motivated the Spanish to explore the American mainland. (*wealth, fame, adventure, new opportunities, spread Christian religion*) Of these, which do they think were most important to conquistadors like Cortés? Discuss how early encounters with Native Americans of Mexico affected the motives of adventurers like Cortés.

Review and Practice

Assign Taking Another Look, p. 25.

Answers to Taking Another Look (p. 25)

1. opportunities denied to them in Spain **2.** The Maya had large cities, gold, and would resist the Spanish. **3. Critical Thinking** Cortés knew more about Native Americans; he did not go to explore but to amass wealth and fame.

Teaching Section 2: Marching to Tenochtitlán (pp. 25–29)

Objective

* To draw conclusions based on visual sources

Developing the Section

Using Visual Sources. Have students study the pictures on pages 26 and 27. Ask them to find "facts" in the pictures. (*Spanish weapons, armored soldiers, horses, unarmed Aztec with offerings, Aztec clothing*) From the pictures, what conclusions might they draw about how Cortés gained entry into the Aztec empire?

Review and Practice

Assign Taking Another Look, p. 29.

Answers to Taking Another Look (p. 29)

1. had cannons and horses to strike fear into the Native Americans **2.** to cut off the possibility of his soldiers retreating and any choice but to win or die **3. Critical Thinking** He might have fought them in battle and even have defeated them. If so, there might have been no Spanish conquest of Mexico and no vast Spanish empire in the Americas.

Teaching Section 3: Toppling an Empire (pp. 29–31)

Objective
- To draw inferences about Aztec beliefs from a song

Historical Sidelight
Mystery of the Treasure. Just before the battle of *la noche triste*, Cortés and his men had gathered an enormous treasure in gold, silver, and jewels, which they abandoned when they retreated from the city. Upon their return, they found most of the treasure had disappeared. No one knew where to lay the blame. Some Spaniards insisted that the Aztec had removed it from Tenochtitlán before the siege began. Others believed the stories told by remaining Aztec that their leaders had thrown it in the lake rather than let the Spanish have it. Whatever the answer, it was never found.

Developing the Section
Drawing Inferences. Read aloud the following lines from an Aztec song:

We only came to sleep.
We only came to dream.
It is not true, no, it is not true
That we came to live on the earth.
We are changed into the grass of springtime.
Our hearts will grow green again
And they will open their petals,
But our body is like a rose tree:
It puts forth flowers and then withers.

Ask students what this song reveals about Aztec beliefs. (*Life of the spirit, the heart, is more important than physical life; though the body dies, the spirit lives.*) Discuss how this song might inspire the Aztec to resist the Spanish. (*Since the death of the body is inevitable, it is less important to die than for the spirit to live on.*)

Review and Practice
Assign Taking Another Look, p. 31.

Answers to Taking Another Look (p. 31)
1. splendid buildings, thousands of people, markets packed with merchandise and food, gold and precious stones, broad highways **2.** superior Spanish weapons, Spanish treachery, Native American allies of the Spanish who hated the Aztec, Motecuhzoma's indecision, smallpox **3. Critical Thinking** Mexicans are proud of his courage and the resistance of their ancestors and want to maintain their Aztec heritage.

Extending the Chapter
Researching Legends. Tell students that the Aztec had many legends to explain their past and the world around them. Divide students into groups to research some Aztec legends. Ask students to use the library to look for such legends as the creation of the world, the origins of the Aztec, the founding of their empire, and their religious beliefs and rituals. Discuss how the legends affected the Aztec way of life.

Looking Ahead
After students have read Looking Ahead, p. 31, ask them to consider how the conquest of the Aztec would affect other native people on the mainland of the Americas.

Answers to Close Up (pp. 32–33)

The Who, What, Where of History
1. Spanish province of Estremadura **2.** Native American woman who guided Cortés to the Aztec **3.** language of the Aztec **4.** emperor of the Aztec **5.** goods paid by people to their conqueror **6.** Tenochtitlán **7.** night in which hundreds of Spanish soldiers were killed by the Aztec **8.** last Aztec emperor

Making the Connection
1. They made conquered people convert to Roman Catholic religion; ended Native American religious rites and substituted Catholic shrines **2.** She translated for Cortés, led him to the Aztec, and warned him of an attack.

Time Check
1. Hispaniola, Cuba, Mexico **2.** last Aztec emperor surrendered to the Spanish

What Would You Have Done?
1. for punishment: Cortés's disobedience, his ambition could cause future problems for the crown; against punishment: he gained a foothold on the mainland, promised great riches for Spain. **2.** with Cortés: made them free of Aztec rule; too powerful to resist; with Aztec: Cortés would enslave them, had destroyed their religion, better to die than be conquered

Thinking and Writing About History
1. should reflect Cortés's conquests in Cuba, Yucatán, Mexico and the destruction of the Aztec empire. **2.** Note an island in a lake, causeways, emperor's palace, markets, zoo **3.** may reflect anger, grief, hatred of Spanish over destruction of religion and way of life

Building Skills
1. entirely destroyed **2.** Weep my people; The water has turned bitter, The food is bitter! **3.** Note the Aztec deserting the city and bitterness and grief over loss of homes, city, and nation. **4.** believed in a higher being

Chapter 3 New Ways of Life (pp. 34–45)

Overview

As Native Americans struggled to build a new city for their Spanish conquerors on the ruins of their own capital of Tenochtitlán, other conquistadors plunged into the rain forests and mountains of Central and South America searching for new empires to conquer. As they added new lands to Spain's growing empire, priests began to arrive on the mainland to spread the Roman Catholic faith. The priests began a mission system that brought a completely different way of life to native peoples. Through a growing trade with Europe, Asia, and Africa, Spain's colonies became a place where the peoples of Europe, Africa, and the Americas formed a new and different culture.

Historical Sidelight

Exports of the Americas. The goods that flowed from the Americas through the Columbian Exchange influenced the entire world. The medicinal plants used by Native Americans fought malaria, headaches, and dysentery. Potatoes helped stave off starvation in Europe. The lowly sunflower reached Russia to serve as a source of cooking oil. Chiles spiced the foods of India. Corn became a staple of peoples around the world.

Resources

Chapter 3 Activity Sheet (p. 154)
Chapter 3 Test (p. 104)
Chapter 3 ESL/LEP Activity Sheet (p. 209)

Focus Activity

Refer students to the illustrations and captions on pp. 34, 35, 37, 39, the feature on p. 41, and the Focus On feature on p. 44. Ask: What can you tell from these illustrations and features about the way of life in New Spain? *(roles of women, Native Americans, mestizos; religious ideas; crops grown)* Explain to students that the blend of Spanish, Native Americans, and Africans produced a new culture in the Americas. Have students speculate on how this new way of life might affect each group. After students have read the chapter, have them compare their speculations with the text.

Teaching Section 1: Extending Spain's Reach (pp. 35–37)

Objective

- To evaluate the qualities that made conquistadors search for new lands

Developing the Section

Evaluating. Ask students to identify some of the qualities of the conquistadors. *(courage, ambition, ruthlessness, greed)* Ask how these qualities enabled the conquistadors to explore and conquer new lands. Guide students to understand that the conquistadors forged an empire but did not necessarily rule as good governors.

Review and Practice

Assign Taking Another Look, p. 37.

Answers to Taking Another Look (p. 37)

1. performed the labor that built the city **2.** for glory and gold **3. Critical Thinking** because of the brutality of the conquests

Teaching Section 2: New Religious Voices (pp. 37–38)

Objective

- To understand that the mission system was both beneficial and harmful to Native Americans.

Developing the Section

Creating a Chart. Have students create a chart with two columns, one headed "Benefits of the Mission System" and the other "Harmful Effects of the Mission System." Ask them to identify and list the benefits and drawbacks under the appropriate heading. Call on volunteers to read their charts aloud. Lead a class discussion on the question of whether or not the benefits outweighed the harmful effects.

Review and Practice

Assign Taking Another Look, p. 38.

Answers to Taking Another Look (p. 38)

1. similarities between Christianity and the Native Americans' religion; failure of old deities to help them **2.** convert Native Americans and teach them new methods of farming, crafts **3. Critical Thinking** similar: forced Native Americans to work for them, limited freedom of movement; different: better working conditions, food, and clothing, treated more fairly

Teaching Section 3: The Columbian Exchange (pp. 38–40)

Objective

- To explore the relationship between trade and changing ways of life

THE LATINO EXPERIENCE IN U.S. HISTORY • © Globe Fearon

Developing the Section

Recognizing Relationships. Ask students to think of examples of things they use and foods they eat that are the products of another country. Guide them to understand that the exchange of goods, peoples, and ideas is the means by which cultures spread around the globe.

Review and Practice

Assign Taking Another Look, p. 40.

Answers to Taking Another Look (p. 40)

1. cattle, pigs, sheep, grain, great variety of fruits and vegetables 2. needed new labor as disease decimated the Native Americans and Spanish colonies on the mainland expanded 3. **Critical Thinking** Exchange of products, people, and ideas through trade spread aspects of different cultures around the globe.

Teaching Section 4: A Center of Spanish Culture (pp. 40–43)

Objective
• To understand how social divisions in New Spain led to inequalities in society

Developing the Section

Recognizing Inequalities. Divide students into groups representing the social classes of New Spain. Ask each group to write a paragraph describing its role in society. Have a spokesperson from each group read aloud its essay. Then lead a class discussion on the inequalities inherent in such a social division. You might ask students to speculate on how these inequalities might affect future developments in New Spain.

Review and Practice
Assign Taking Another Look, p. 43.

Answers to Taking Another Look (p. 43)

1. appointed royal representatives to rule, replacing conquistadors 2. *peninsulares*, settlers born in Spain; *criollos*, people born of Spanish parents in the Americas; *mestizos*, people of mixed Spanish and Native American ancestry; Native Americans; enslaved Africans; mulattoes 3. **Critical Thinking** kinds of clothing worn, kinds of structures, leisure activities, music

Extending the Chapter

Researching Literature. Have students research literature written in New Spain. You might have them work in groups to research areas such as poetry, novels, plays, and stories. Have students present their findings in oral reports.

Looking Ahead

After students finish reading Looking Ahead, p. 43, ask them if they had been settlers in New Spain would they have stayed in Mexico or would they have wanted to explore new lands and settle new colonies? After students have read Chapter 4, ask if they have changed their minds.

Answers to Close Up (pp. 44–45)

The Who, What, Where of History

1. Yucatán 2. conqueror of the Incas 3. in the Andes Mountains 4. Roman Catholicism 5. spread of culture form one region to another 6. poet of New Spain 7. *peninsulares, criollos, mestizos,* Native Americans, enslaved Africans, mulattoes 8. the forcing of people to work for wages so low that they became bound to owners of land

Making the Connection

1. Mexico City was built on the ruins of Tenochtitlán. 2. Colonization brought trade and the exchange of goods, people, and ideas.

Time Check
1. b, c, a 2. 1551

What Would You Have Done?

1. accept: escape disease and death, receive food, clothing, shelter, learn new skills that might bring new opportunities; reject: not free to move about, have to accept new religion and language, forced to give up own culture and accept Spanish ways 2. Answers should reflect conditions in the colony and the Church and the role of women in Spanish society. Attending the university dressed as a man: point out the dangers, but indicate the decision is hers. Stopping writing at the Church's demand: advise her to consider to what extent she thinks the Church has a right to control her life.

Thinking and Writing About History

1. Brochures should indicate silver fairs were held in Veracruz and Acapulco. Spain received great treasure while New Spain received a great variety of goods from Spain and the Philippines. 2. Essays should give examples of the new foods and present a generalization about how these foods changed diets around the world.

Building Skills

1. the exploitation of Native Americans to build unnecessary works for the clergy 2. such exploitation should be stopped 3. superfluous, sumptuous, grandiose 4. Monasteries are more elaborate than the royal court, great numbers of Native Americans work but receive no wages and little food.

Chapter 4   Reaching Out from the Caribbean (pp. 46–53)

Overview

For nearly 50 years after 1513, Spanish expeditions searched for wealth through an area that stretched north from Florida to Delaware Bay and west to northern Mexico. But they found no golden empires. Efforts to settle the area also were failures. The Spanish decided to give up further colonization efforts, but the threat of a French base in Florida spurred the Spanish into action again. In 1565, a Spanish force wiped out the French base and built an outpost they called St. Augustine. Here, the governor set up the first European code of laws in what is now the United States, and the little settlement grew to become an important part of Spain's defenses in the Caribbean. To further protect its treasure ships from English attacks, Spain fortified Puerto Rico and Cuba, entryways into the Caribbean.

Historical Sidelight

A Fountain of Youth? As the governor of Puerto Rico, Juan Ponce de León had heard of a Native American who claimed that his father had visited a place called Bimini and had returned home rejuvenated by a wonderful fountain of youth there. From this, a legend grew up that Ponce de León was searching for this fountain when he discovered Florida. It is more likely that tales of gold there inspired his voyages. Ponce de León found no gold or a magic fountain in Florida, but he did claim for Spain all the land north and east of the Gulf of Mexico.

Resources

Chapter 4 Activity Sheet (p. 155)
Chapter 4 Test (p. 105)
Chapter 4 ESL/LEP Activity Sheet (p. 210)

Focus Activity

Refer students to the map of Spanish colonies in Florida and the Caribbean on page 51. Ask why they think the location of these colonies was important to the security of Spain's empire in Mexico and South America. Remind them of the goods that flowed back and forth between Europe and New Spain. Point out that France and England were beginning to explore the Americas. Ask: How do you think Spain would respond to attempts by these nations to establish colonies on the mainland? (*might fortify the Caribbean, attack the newcomers, build new colonies on the mainland*) As students read the chapter, have them compare their answers to Spain's actual reaction.

Teaching Section 1: La Florida (pp. 47–48)

Objectives
- To understand how explorations by other European nations led Spain to build a settlement in Florida

Developing the Section

1. Evaluating an Issue. Ask students what Spain's major purpose was in its first attempts to explore and settle La Florida. (*to find new sources of gold*) Call on volunteers to state reasons why these attempts failed. (*natural disasters, disease, starvation*) What other reasons might there have been? (*lack of preparation, attacks by Native Americans*) Discuss with students why it might be that Spain's major purpose in exploring Florida (*the search for gold*) hindered attempts at settlement. What might Spain have done differently to encourage settlement?

2. Writing a Report. Have students imagine they are a Spanish official in the Caribbean concerned about the French threat to Florida. Ask them to write a report to the king of Spain explaining why it is important to build colonies in Florida.

Review and Practice
Assign Taking Another Look, p. 48.

Answers to Taking Another Look (p. 48)
1. north from Florida to Delaware Bay, west to northern Mexico **2.** to keep out the French **3. Critical Thinking** did not find gold, settlements failed, threats from the French

Teaching Section 2: Outposts of Empire (pp. 48–51)

Objective
- To analyze Spain's decision to fortify its island bases in the Caribbean

Historical Sidelight

Sir Francis Drake. As a sea dog, Sir Francis Drake carried on a relentless campaign against Spanish treasure ships and settlements. Although exploration was not Drake's major goal in the Americas, he was the first Englishman to circumnavigate the globe. On a 1577 voyage, he sailed through the Strait of Magellan, plundering the west coasts of South and North America and claiming for England what is now the West Coast of the United States. Drake can also take much of the credit for the defeat of the Spanish

Armada. The use of light, maneuverable ships with heavy cannon in attacking Spain's heavier, clumsier vesels was a technique Drake had perfected.

Developing the Section

Analyzing a Decision. Have students identify and list reasons why Spain decided to fortify its island bases. (*location as entryways to the Caribbean, continuing raids by privateers, more Spanish interest in gold and silver in New Spain and Peru than in farming the islands, islands as naval bases for treasure ships*)

Review and Practice

Assign Taking Another Look, p. 51.

Answers to Taking Another Look (p. 51)

1. decided to use them as a defense system **2.** threats from the English **3. Critical Thinking** would probably argue it was to secure all of Florida from attacks by the English

Extending the Chapter

Tracing Explorers' Routes. Divide students into small groups and provide each group with an outline map of the Caribbean and North America. Have each group choose an explorer discussed in the chapter and research the explorer's journey through La Florida. Have each group re-create on the map the route taken by the explorer. When the maps are completed, ask volunteers to create one large wall map showing all the explorations.

Looking Ahead

After students have read Looking Ahead, p. 51, ask them to discuss whether they, as Spanish leaders, would have decided to explore further in North America even though their colonization efforts in La Florida were not very successful.

Answers to Close Up (pp. 52–53)

The Who, What, Where of History

1. San Miguel de Guadalupe, Georgia **2.** discoverer of Florida **3.** Florida, Georgia, Carolinas, Tennessee, Alabama, Mississippi, Arkansas, Louisiana, Texas **4.** Pedro Menéndez de Aviles **5.** laws to guide the conduct of soldiers, first European code of laws enacted in what is now the United States **6.** San Juan **7.** St. Augustine

Making the Connection

1. St. Augustine was built near the site of Fort Caroline. **2.** A strong defense was needed to prevent England's expansion and secure Spain's claim to Florida.

Time Check

1. England defeated the Spanish Armada in a great battle in Europe. **2.** defeat of the Armada

What Would You Have Done?

1. go: chance for riches, adventure stay: too risky, already had land or wealth **2.** courage, resourcefulness, honesty, able to enforce discipline, traits needed to build a settlement

Thinking and Writing About History

1. Stories should include the who, what, where, when, and why of the event. **2.** Speech may include endurance of settlers, skill in building, importance of fort to Spain's defenses.

Building Skills

1. Spanish Harbor Defenses in the Caribbean, 1695 **2.** Acapulco and Veracruz, Mexico; Havana, Cuba; San Juan, Puerto Rico; Cartagena, New Granada **3.** Shipping routes **4.** city far from the Caribbean defenses

Chapter 5   The Spanish Borderlands (pp. 54–65)

Overview

Still dreaming of an empire of gold, Spanish explorers mounted expeditions into what is today the southwestern United States. Although their dreams were not realized, they claimed the region for Spain. Santa Fe became Spain's first important town in its conquest of the Southwes. In the early 1700s, alarmed by the expansion of the French into what is now East Texas, Spain took control and found the land ideal for grazing cattle. In the mid–1760s, reports of British and Russian ships along the Pacific coast prompted Spain to send soldiers and priests into Upper California. By the late 1700s, missions stretched all along the coast.

Historical Sidelight

The Mysterious Blue Lady. One of the tales the first explorers to march north into New Spain's borderlands heard was of a mysterious Blue Lady. In what is now Arizona, explorers came across some bands of Native Americans who knew about the Christian religion. They said that a mysterious woman dressed in blue had taught them the Europeans' faith. What was so bewildering to the Spanish was that in Spain there was a woman, Marie Coronel de Agreda, who headed a religious order whose members wore blue robes. In addition, the woman claimed to have visited Native Americans, whom she described accurately. Her claims were carefully examined, but no evidence was found that she had ever been out of Spain.

Resources
Chapter 5 Activity Sheet (p. 156)
Chapter 5 Test (p. 106)
Chapter 5 ESL/LEP Activity Sheet (p. 211)

Focus Activity
Have students read the chapter-opening story about Father Kino on pp. 54–55. Ask what motivated him to spend most of life journeying through the Spanish Borderlands. *(desire to convert new people, to map new lands)* What was Father Kino's ultimate goal? *(build a system of missions and trails reaching to the Pacific)* Ask students how they think the work of Father Kino would be important to future Spanish settlement.*(knowledge of a new region, maps to guide future expeditions)* Explain that in this chapter, they will learn what other factors motivated the Spanish to push into their northern borderlands.

Teaching Section 1: The Kingdom of New Mexico (pp. 55–58)

Objective
• To understand the reasons for New Spain's push into its northern borderlands

Developing the Section
Forming Questions. Before they read the section, have students draw up questions they would ask Spanish officials about the exploration of New Spain's northern borderlands and its first settlements. Then have students read the section and look for answers to their questions. Ask students to write a paragraph summarizing their questions and answers. Call on volunteers to read their summaries for discussion by the class.

Review and Practice
Assign Taking Another Look, p. 58.

Answers to Taking Another Look (p. 58)
1. Arizona, New Mexico, Texas, Oklahoma, Kansas **2.** to find new sources of silver, convert Native Americans **3. Critical Thinking** lands were taken, tribute demanded, punished if resisted

Teaching Section 2: Across the Rio Grande (pp. 58–61)

Objective
• To gather evidence to support a generalization about settlement in Texas.

Developing the Section
Gathering Evidence. Write the following generalization on the chalkboard: "Settlement of East Texas was influenced by the landscape of the region." Call on students to list evidence from the section to support the generalization. You might ask students to contrast the settlement of East Texas with that of Florida.

Review and Practice
Assign Taking Another Look, p. 61.

Answers to Taking Another Look (p. 61)
1. by opening a trade route to New Mexico **2.** by controlling the plains and launching deadly attacks against settlers **3. Critical Thinking** Their words, clothing, skill with horses were the basis for much of the way of life of later U.S. westerners.

Teaching Section 3: Along the Pacific Coast (pp. 61–63)

Objective
• To analyze how the missions and pueblos influenced the culture of California.

Developing the Section
Analyzing Influences. Ask students to write the following statements: "Missions changed the way of life of Native Americans in California"; "The mestizo culture of California grew out of the pueblos." Then have them identify supporting facts for each statement and write a statement explaining how missions and pueblos influenced California's culture.

Review and Practice
Assign Taking Another Look, p. 63.

Answers to Taking Another Look (p. 63)
1. to secure the land for Spain against possible British and Russian invasion **2.** Many were killed or died of European diseases; forced to give up their own ways and accept the Spanish religion and language; forced to labor for the missions. **3. Critical Thinking** Missions were established as stepping stones along an overland trade route.

Extending the Chapter
Writing a Chronicle. Have students write a class chronicle of the Spanish borderlands. It should include

THE LATINO EXPERIENCE IN U.S. HISTORY • © Globe Fearon

entries about political, social, and economic events. Divide students into research groups, and explain that each group will contribute an article on one of these phases of the history. When the articles are completed, have the groups combine them to form a class chronicle.

Looking Ahead

After students have read Looking Ahead, p. 63, ask them to speculate on how the struggle of English colonists might influence Spanish colonists to seek independence.

Answers to Close Up (pp. 64–65)

The Who, What, Where of History

1. northern lands of New Spain 2. Arizona, New Mexico, Texas, Oklahoma, Kansas 3. leader of the pueblo revolt 4. Caddo chief who acted as interpreter and negotiator for the Spanish with Native Americans 5. help in setting up missions to convert Native Americans 6. Spanish or Native American cattleherders 7. at San Diego

Making the Connection

1. Numerous Apache raids led the Pueblo people to agree to de Vargas's takeover and protection. 2. The possibility of French expansion led the Spanish to control Texas.

Time Check

1. 82 2. 1598

What Would You Have Done?

1. **accept:** avoid conflict with France, get help in setting up missions **reject:** French trade would be in competition with Spain's trade, would give France a foothold in New Spain 2. good farming land, towns growing up that would need workers, ranching, protection of presidios, opportunities for trade

Thinking and Writing About History

1. include descriptions of work, living conditions, treatment by priests, new religion, language, food, clothing 2. should reflect news, not opinion, give answers to who, what, where, when, why, how. 3. may include description of city, founders, work of those who built it, future prospects

Building Skills

1. for protection 2. The land is mostly desert and is very sparsely settled.

▶ UNIT 2 Toward Independence (pp. 66–103)

UNIT THEME

Because of the differences between the British and Spanish colonies in the Americas, their movements for independence took different forms and had different results.

UNIT CONCEPTS

- In the 1700s, Spain, Britain, and France fought a series of wars for empire that resulted in Spanish and British domination of the Americas.
- Conflict between Britain and its 13 colonies erupted into revolution and the founding of the United States.
- During the American Revolution, the Spanish colonies helped the Patriots gain independence from Britain.
- Revolutions of the late 1700s and early 1800s weakened Spain's control over its American colonies.
- Spanish policies and the influence of other revolutions led Mexico to rebel against Spain and win its independence.
- Revolution spread throughout Spain's colonies, and by 1825 all that remained of its empire were Cuba and Puerto Rico.
- Mexico's independence brought economic, political, and social change to its northern provinces.

UNIT OVERVIEW

Unit 2 traces the struggle for independence in the British and Spanish colonies in the Americas and explores the changes that resulted when colonies gained their freedom. *The Big Picture* and the three chapters in the unit describe the events and issues leading up to independence in North and South America and (1) the role of the Spanish in supporting the American Revolution, (2) the movement for independence in Spain's colonies, and (3) changes in Spanish colonies in what is now the United States under an independent Mexican government.

In teaching this unit, guide students to recognize the differences in economic, political, and social conditions between Spain's and Britain's former colonies. Lead them to understand how these differences led the independent colonies in different directions.

COOPERATIVE LEARNING ACTIVITY

The following cooperative learning activity can be used for alternative assessment after study of the unit has been completed.

Divide students into three groups and assign each group one of the following Mexican provinces: New Mexico, California, and Texas. Have the groups create brochures designed to attract settlers to their province. Brochures should describe the environment, social, political, and economic life, and opportunities for wealth and advancement, such as they were. Students might illustrate their brochures with maps and drawings. Have each group present its brochure to the class. In evaluating the presentations, consider students' creativity in preparing their work, their understanding of the qualities of their province, and the persuasiveness of their brochures in attracting settlers.

RESOURCES

Unit 2 Test (pp. 107–108)
Outline Maps: Latin America, The Americas (pp. 285–286)
Unit 2 Writing Workshop (pp. 257–260)
The Big Picture 2 ESL/LEP Worksheet (p. 212)

Unit 2 THE BIG PICTURE (pp. 67–73)

Theme

The successful struggle of Britain's American colonies to gain independence encouraged Spain's colonies to fight for their freedom.

Overview

The Big Picture explores revolutions in the British and Spanish colonies that led to independence and the building of new nations in the Americas. Although British colonists enjoyed a great deal of political freedom, they resented increasing British attempts to control their affairs, and in 1776 rebellion broke out. The colonists' victory over Britain led to the birth of an independent nation that began to expand its borders. Inspired by the American Revolution, the Spanish colonists rebelled and successfully threw off Spanish rule. The struggle for independence in Latin America lasted many years, and its results were very different from those of the American Revolution. With little political liberty under Spain, the new republics were inexperienced in self-government and, being separated by mountains and vast distances, had no practice in working together.

Although slavery was abolished, the old social order remained in place. The economic hardship caused by the long conflict made it even more difficult to create stability or unity. The 17 nations that emerged from Spain's empire faced a long period of political turmoil.

Objectives

- To interpret a quotation
- To use a timeline to understand the relationship between events
- To consider the results of revolution in two different societies

Introducing *The Big Picture*

Refer students to the statement by Pablo Vizcardo on p. 69. How does he compare English colonists with Spanish colonists? (*English bravely fought for liberty, Spanish do nothing to gain freedom from Spain.*) Why do you think Vizcardo made this comparison? (*wants Spanish colonists to be independent*)

Using the Timeline

Refer students to the timeline on pp. 68–69. Divide the class into groups and ask each group to select two events on the timeline that are connected. Have them write a paragraph explaining how the events are connected. They may skim *The Big Picture* and chapters in the unit for additional information.

Teaching *The Big Picture*

Speculating About Events. Assign The British Colonies in 1763 on pp. 67–68 and The Spanish Colonies in 1763 on pp. 71–72. Make two columns on the chalkboard with the headings Spanish Colonies and British Colonies. Under each, write subheads such as Head of Government, Form of Government, Patterns of Settlement, Forms of Labor, Social Structure, Opportunities, Freedoms, and Liberties. Students may suggest others. Call on students to fill in the columns and compare political and social factors and discuss differences. Have them speculate on reasons why with such different experiences, both societies eventually rebelled against their home countries.

Review and Practice

Assign Taking Another Look, pp. 71 and 73.

Answers to Taking Another Look (pp. 71 and 73)

p. 71: **1.** heavy taxes, limited power of colonial governments **2.** Louisiana Territory **3. Critical Thinking** creation of Constitution, acquisition of Louisiana, War of 1812, Monroe Doctrine p. 73: **1. Spanish:** tight control by Spanish government, rigid social classes, mixing of ethnic groups **British:** largely self-governed, movement within social classes, little ethnic mixing **2.** Spain was weakened by Napoleon's conquest. **3. Critical Thinking succeed:** independent nations formed, slavery abolished, Spain no longer a power in the Americas **fail:** division among the nations, old social system retained, economic hardship, political turmoil

Chapter 6   The Spanish and the American Revolution (pp. 74–83)

Overview

As a result of the French and Indian War in the mid–1700s, Spain gained control of the vast Louisiana Territory. Now Spain and Britain were the two great rival empires in the Americas. When the English colonists, the Patriots, began their revolution, Spain grasped the opportunity to weaken British power by aiding the Patriot cause. Particularly important in this effort was the Mississippi River. Controlled by Spain, the river provided a highway for supplying the Patriots. The Spanish *rancheros* of Texas also indirectly aided the Patriots by driving their cattle to Louisiana to supply Spanish armies, which came into open conflict with the British. Aware that the British were planning an invasion of Louisiana, the Spanish moved to protect the Mississippi Valley and to regain Florida. In the fighting that followed, Spain triumphed and, by the end of the American Revolution in 1783, had secured Louisiana and reconquered Florida.

Historical Sidelight

A Forgotten Negotiator. As a merchant in New Orleans, Oliver Pollack was instrumental in negotiating for money and supplies from the Spanish for the Patriot cause. He was particularly influential in getting aid for the campaigns of George Rogers Clark, the commander of Virginia's military forces who defended and finally conquered the northwestern frontier. Pollack also persuaded Governor Bernardo Gálvez advance thousands of dollars from Gálvez's own secret fund. Pollack personally advanced more than $136,000 to the campaigns of Clark. Despite his tireless efforts in the Patriot cause, the future state of Virginia refused to reimburse him, and he was bankrupted. Ten years passed before Pollack received his money from Virginia and the new U. S. government.

Resources

Chapter 6 Activity Sheet (p. 157)
Chapter 6 Test (p. 109)
Chapter 6 ESL/LEP Activity Sheet (p. 213)

Focus Activity

Have students read the chapter introduction on text pp. 74–75. Then refer them to the map of Spanish contributions to the Patriot cause on p. 78. Remind students of the importance of the Mississippi River as a route for trade and of New Orleans as a port. After students have studied the map, ask them to write a paragraph explaining how the Spanish aided British colonists in the American Revolution.

Teaching Section 1: Supplying the Patriot Side (pp. 75–77)

Objective

- To understand the importance of Spain's contribution to the Patriot cause

Developing the Section

Writing Letters. Ask students to work in pairs or small groups to compose two letters: one from a Patriot official asking for Spanish help and explaining why it is important; the other from a Spanish official answering the request, explaining the aid Spain will give and how it will help the Patriot cause. Call on volunteers to read the requests and responses to the class.

Discuss the impact of Spain's help and what might have happened if Spain had refused or had decided to back the British.

Review and Practice

Assign Taking Another Look, p. 77.

Answers to Taking Another Look (p. 77)

1. linked widely scattered British and Spanish settlements **2.** enabled Patriots to get weapons and supplies they needed, weakened British power by limiting their use of New Orleans and protecting Patriot ships **3. Critical Thinking** Helping the Patriots weakened Britain and helped secure Spain's hold on its territories.

Teaching Section 2: Joining the Fight (pp. 77–80)

Objective

- To evaluate the role of Bernardo de Gálvez in securing Spain's northern territories

Developing the Section

Writing a Biography. Have students write a biography of Bernardo de Gálvez. Explain that the biographies should include the qualities that made him a leader and his role in helping to secure Spain's territories. The biographies should also assess Gálvez's accomplishments and draw conclusions about his influence on the outcome of the American Revolution and on Spain's continued presence in the Americas.

Review and Practice

Assign Taking Another Look, p. 80.

Answers to Taking Another Look (p. 80)

1. captured British forts along the Mississippi River, going as far north as Lake Michigan **2.** key posts in retaking Florida from the British **3. Critical Thinking** Patriots might have lost their struggle, Britain would have remained as a great power in the Americas, Spain might have become a stronger power.

Teaching Section 3: The First Cattle Drives (pp. 80–81)

Objective
- To recognize the relationship between the early cattle drives from Texas and the outcome of the American Revolution

Developing the Section
Creating a Flow Chart. On the chalkboard write Texas Rancheros Owned Great Herds of Cattle. Tell students that they are going to create a flow chart of events to show the role played by Texas in the outcome of the American Revolution.

Call on volunteers to state events in sequence, and write these under the heading on the chalkboard. (Examples: Gálvez needed food for his army, Louisiana did not produce enough food, Gálvez went to the Texas ranchers, cattle were rounded up.) Lead students to the understanding that getting food for Gálvez's army enabled that army to fight the British, thus aiding the Patriots and influencing the outcome of the American Revolution.

Review and Practice
Assign Taking Another Look, p. 81

Answers to Taking Another Look (p. 81)
1. great herds of cattle there could supply his army with food 2. constant warfare with Native Americans 3. **Critical Thinking** By supplying food, Texas helped feed Spanish armies, enabling them to continue aiding the colonists by fighting the British.

Extending the Chapter
Writing a Story. Using material in the text and further library research, have students write a fiction story about a cattle drive from Texas to Louisiana. Encourage students to choose a main character, the

historical setting, and events that took place on the drive. Call on volunteers to read their stories aloud.

Looking Ahead
After students have read Looking Ahead, p. 81, ask them to speculate on how Spain, which appeared to be stronger after the American Revolution, would find itself in a weakened condition and in danger of losing its empire in the Americas.

Answers to Close Up (pp. 82–83)

The Who, What, Where of History
1. Mississippi 2. governor of Louisiana who aided the Patriots and fought the British 3. shipped supplies to Patriots, protected Patriot ships on the Mississippi, limited British use of the river 4. Spanish ranch owners 5. Texas

Making the Connection
1. linked settlements together, provided route for trade and transportation 2. Spain helped the Patriots win independence by fighting the British and weakening their power.

Time Check
1. 1777 2. 2 3. 1779

What Would You Have Done?
1. defeat the British, strategic importance of the port, would help regain all of Florida 2. **help:** would weaken British power and protect Spain's territory **neutral:** would disrupt trade with British, might lead to defeat and loss of territory

Thinking and Writing About History
1. Paragraphs should include importance of the river as a link between eastern and western British colonists and a highway for moving supplies, and New Orleans as an important stopping point on the river, and center for trade. 2. Reports should include weakening of Spain's chief rival in the Americas, possibility of regaining lost territories.

Building Skills
1. a.I, b.I, c.R 2. a.I, b.R, c.R 3. a.R, b.I, c.I

Chapter 7 The Road to Latin American Independence (pp. 84–93)

Overview
At the end of the American Revolution, events in the new United States and in Europe rose to challenge the Spanish empire. U.S. expansion to the west and south drove more and more settlers into Florida and

Louisiana. As wars in Europe drained its resources, Spain gave up trying to defend those territories. By 1819, all of Spain's lands east of the Mississippi were part of the United States. Only two years later, Spain lost Mexico as it became independent. Leaders in South

America led the fight for independence. By 1825, South America was free. Only Puerto Rico and Cuba in the Caribbean remained as Spain's colonies in the Americas.

Historical Sidelight

An Unlikely Revolutionary. Father Miguel Hidalgo y Castilla, often called the Torchbearer of the Revolution, seemed to be unsuited for the role of revolutionary. He was an untiring advocate of farming and industrial projects, and he loved to read technical and scientific books. Hidalgo was very fond of music and taught it to the Native Americans of his parish. His generosity toward Native Americans won him great admiration among the people. Hidalgo was 57 years old when he raised the torch of revolution. His courage and unwavering dedication to the independence of Mexico transformed what began as a revolt of dissatisfied *criollos* into an uprising of all Mexicans.

Resources

Chapter 7 Activity Sheet (p. 158)
Chapter 7 Test (p. 110)
Chapter 7 ESL/LEP Activity Sheet (p. 214)

Focus Activity

Refer students to the section titles of the chapter on pp. 85, 88, and 89. Ask them to turn these headings into questions and write them down. Tell them to use these questions as a guide as they read each section. When they have finished the chapter, have them answer each question with a brief summary.

Teaching Section 1: Challenges in the North (pp. 85–87)

Objective

• To gather information in order to discuss Spain's loss of Florida and Louisiana

Developing the Section

Gathering Information. When students have completed the section, write the following statements on the chalkboard:

• Spanish policies helped slow the growth of Florida.
• Newcomers were encouraged to settle in Louisiana, but trade was restricted.
• Events in Europe and pressure from the United States forced Spain to give up its territory in Florida and Louisiana.

Have students use examples from the section to support the statements. Discuss Spain's policies and the problems it faced.

Review and Practice

Assign Taking Another Look, p. 87.

Answers to Taking Another Look (p. 87)

1. recruiting settlers from Europe and the United States, increasing trade, offering free land 2. Spain's resources were drained by taking part in wars in Europe 3. **Critical Thinking** Most students will say probably not. It was the strict enforcement of trading and immigration laws and tight control of businesses that helped keep the provinces from prospering.

Teaching Section 2: Independence for Mexico (pp. 88–89)

Objective

• To compare points of view about the Mexican revolution

Developing the Section

Comparing Points of View. Divide the class into two groups, one to summarize and support the views of Mexican revolutionaries, and one to summarize and support the views of settlers in the provinces who did not join in the rebellion. Have the groups write their arguments and compare them. Then discuss why settlers in the provinces did accept the new government.

Review and Practice

Assign Taking Another Look, p. 89.

Answers to Taking Another Look (p. 89)

1. *Criollos* wanted to be free of *peninsulare* rule. 2. split over future of Texas, defeat by Spanish troops 3. **Critical Thinking** protection by Spain from attacks of Native Americans and foreigners. Many, however, would want to be free of strict Spanish rule as the provinces were growing and expanding.

Teaching Section 3: Changes in Spanish America (pp. 89–91)

Objective

• To analyze the differences in the responses of Spanish colonists to revolution

Developing the Section

Writing Letters. Have students work in pairs, one student to represent a *criollo* revolutionary in South America, the other to represent a *criollo* planter in Cuba. Have each write a letter to a friend in Spain explaining his or her support of or opposition to rebellion. Call on volunteers to read their letters aloud and discuss the reasons given, for and against. Ask how location, economy, slavery affect responses.

Review and Practice
Assign Taking Another Look, p. 91.

Answers to Taking Another Look (p. 91)
1. encouraged them to revolt **2.** made them afraid slaves would revolt, so looked to Spain for protection **3. Critical Thinking** Louisiana and Florida had many settlers from Europe and the United States and were trying to build up their economies. They were not much affected by far-off revolutions. *Criollos* of Mexico wanted to be rid of *peninsulare* domination. In Latin America, liberties were limited. Colonists in Cuba and Puerto Rico feared slave rebellions and wanted Spain's protection.

Extending the Chapter
Preparing Biographies. Divide students into pairs. Ask one to research Simón Bolívar and the other José de San Martín and prepare biographies. Ask students to present their biographies to the class and compare the lives and work of these two leaders.

Looking Ahead
After students have read Looking Ahead, p. 91, ask them to imagine what it would be like to suddenly have a new government about which they knew very little. Discuss with them how their lives might be changed.

Answers to Close Up (pp. 92–93)

The Who, What, Where of History
1. American, French, Haitian **2.** governor of East Florida who promoted immigration to the province **3.** tar, pitch, turpentine **4.** northern border of Florida with the United States **5.** Mexico **6.** priest who set off the Mexican revolution **7.** revolutionary leader who helped free colonies in South America **8.** Boyaca **9.** Cuba, Puerto Rico **10.** Toussaint L'Ouverture

Making the Connection
1. Revolutions inspired Spanish colonists to fight for their freedom **2.** When Mexico became independent, those provinces became part of Mexico **3.** Cuba and Puerto Rico feared that slave uprisings would occur in those colonies.

Time Check
1. The United States won its freedom from Britain **2.** 1819 **3.** 11

What Would You Have Done?
1. agree that encouraging settlement and trying to build trade and economy were beneficial, but Spain's business and trade restrictions and delays in getting things done hindered development **2. stay:** possible new opportunities under new government, fewer restrictions **leave:** little protection now from attack, new government too far away to give help

Thinking and Writing About History
1. recruit new settlers from Europe and the United States, ease restrictions on trade and building new businesses **2.** Paragraphs should include: planters in Haiti are killed or flee from revolution and sugar market collapses, giving an opportunity to planters in Puerto Rico and Cuba to increase their own sugar industry; increased production demanded more labor, and more slaves were imported; Haitians took over Santo Domingo, increasing fears of slave uprisings in Cuba and Puerto Rico; slaves rebelled on those islands so planters needed more protection from Spain; Puerto Rico and Cuba did not want independence from Spain

Building Skills
1. The Road to Latin American Independence **2.** Challenges in the North, Independence for Mexico, Changes in Spanish America **3.** a. 3 b. 1 c. 2 d. 2 e. 1 **4.** pressures from the United States, restrictive business and trade policies, wars in Europe draining Spain's resources; took little part in revolution, were concerned about protection, but joined new Mexican nation; inspired revolts throughout South America which resulted in many independent nations, but Cuba and Puerto Rico remained loyal to Spain because they needed protection and were becoming prosperous from sugar industry

Chapter 8 Life in the Mexican Borderlands (pp. 94–103)

Overview
An independent Mexico now controlled New Mexico, California, and Texas. Encouraged by Mexico's government, settlers moved into New Mexico, where farming, sheep ranching, and trade expanded. Although some opportunities existed for those at the bottom of society, a system of peonage held many in bondage. In California, mission lands were taken from the Church and given to cattle ranchers. A flourishing trade in hides and tallow brought prosperity but also increased the gap between rich and poor. Growing unrest by Native Americans trapped in peonage led to frequent conflicts. With little protection from Mexico, California's ties to Mexico weakened.

Texas was unattractive to most Mexicans because of raids by Native Americans. The province remained sparsely settled until Mexico offered large grants of land to U.S. citizens. By 1830, Anglos in Texas outnumbered Mexicans, and Mexican officials grew concerned.

Historical Sidelight

The First Anglo Trader. In 1821, William Becknell of Franklin, Missouri, was in trouble. A farmer and a speculator, Becknell was bankrupted by the depression that hit the United States in 1819. Fleeing his creditors, he headed west with a pack train of goods to trade with trappers and Native Americans. Along the way, Becknell heard of Mexico's revolt against Spain and changed his course for Santa Fe, New Mexico. Five months later he was back in Franklin, where he stunned the townspeople by opening sacks of silver and dumping their contents on the ground. Becknell returned to Santa Fe with a wagon train of goods, and other Anglo traders followed as goods flowed between Missouri and Santa Fe.

Resources

Chapter 8 Activity Sheet (p. 159)
Chapter 8 Test (p. 111)
Chapter 8 ESL/LEP Activity Sheet (p. 215)

Focus Activity

Open the chapter by asking students what qualities they think people would need to live and work in a remote territory far from their homelands. As they read the chapter, have them find examples of these qualities among the settlers in Mexico's northern provinces.

Teaching Section 1: Life in New Mexico (pp. 95–98)

Objective

- To evaluate the effects of the peonage system on the society of New Mexico

Developing the Section

Writing an Essay. Divide the class into groups and have each group write an essay on the question, Why is equality of opportunity important in a society? They should consider how New Mexico was settled, the accomplishments of New Mexicans in their far-off province, the strengths of New Mexican society and its weaknesses, and the effect of the way it was governed on people of all classes.

Review and Practice

Assign Taking Another Look, p. 98.

Answers to Taking Another Look (p. 98)

1. People had a spirit of independence from their government but depended upon one another for defense, goods, and their livelihood. **2.** In return for taking care of a rancher's herd, a villager received some of the livestock and cash in the form of a loan. **3. Critical Thinking** join the military, marry a wealthy woman, engage in trade, work for a sheep rancher and build up a herd

Teaching Section 2: Life in Mexican California (pp. 98–99)

Objective

- To dramatize changes that occurred in Mexican California

Developing the Section

Creating a Skit. Assign a group of students to prepare a skit in which the following people take part: a priest whose mission has been secularized, a wealthy ranch owner, a trader in hides and tallow, a Native American under the peonage system. Have them discuss the changes that have taken place under the Mexican government. Have students suggest other possible ways in which life changed in California.

Review and Practice

Assign Taking Another Look, p. 99.

Answers to Taking Another Look (p. 99)

1. brought wealth to many, widened gap between rich and poor and brought conflict between them, strengthened California's ties to the United States. **2.** resentment and anger among Native Americans because of treatment by wealthy Californians. **3. Critical Thinking a.** large ranches established, growing trade, wide gap between rich and poor **b.** New Mexico mostly at peace with Native Americans, conflict in California with Native Americans; little or no contact with foreigners in New Mexico, much trade with foreigners in California

Teaching Section 3: Changing Ways in Texas (pp. 100–101)

Objective

- To evaluate a plan for settlement and speculate on its effects

Developing the Section

Writing an Editorial. Have students work in pairs to write an editorial on the Texas plan of settlement, one from the point of view of an Anglo settler, one from that of a Mexican official. Students should

THE LATINO EXPERIENCE IN U.S. HISTORY • © Globe Fearon

speculate about the plan's effects on the development of Texas.

Review and Practice
Assign Taking Another Look, p. 101.

Answers to Taking Another Look (p. 101)
1. danger from Native Americans, far from home 2. could not get enough settlers from Mexico or Europe 3. **Critical Thinking** far from home, continuous raids by Comanche Native Americans, little trade, opportunities limited mostly to cattle raising on huge, isolated ranches

Extending the Chapter
Preparing Documentaries. Divide students into three groups to gather illustrations about life in New Mexico, Texas, and California. Have each group write a narration for its materials and make an oral presentation to the class.

Looking Ahead
After students have read Looking Ahead, p. 101, write the phrase *Manifest Destiny* on the chalkboard. Explain that in the 1800s this was the idea that the United States should expand its territory and influence throughout North America. Ask students to consider how this might affect Mexico's northern provinces.

Answers to Close Up (pp. 102–103)

The Who, What, Where of History
1. governor of a town in New Mexico who provided defense and cared for the people 2. Taos 3. poor young man in New Mexico who rose to the top to become governor of the province 4. hides, tallow 5. Mexican settlers in Texas 6. on the Brazos

Making the Connection
1. They were trapped in the peonage system and their anger led to unrest. 2. Huge land grants attracted growing numbers of U.S. settlers.

Time Check
1. When Mexico became independent (1821) 2. 1848.

What Would You Have Done?
1. **support:** gave opportunities to poor people to build a herd of livestock, gave them a chance to become wealthy; **oppose:** if times became hard, person would become indebted and might never be able to repay loan, system kept people in bondage, widened the gap between rich and poor 2. **yes:** flourishing trade with Anglos, many Anglos settled and married Mexicans, the United States would give better protection; **no:** way of life could change, the United States could impose restrictions, might do away with peonage system

Thinking and Writing About History
1. must help defend community, keep peace with Native Americans, grow or make things needed, exchange with others items you don't produce, share timber land and grazing land with community craftsworkers: weaver, carpenter, blacksmith, potter, wood carver, tailor, shoemaker, brickmaker 2. Article may include reactions to working and living conditions, freedom of movement, feelings about ranch owners, opportunities for a better life 3. Ad may stress land good for cotton growing, water plentiful on the Brazos, opportunities for cattle raising and trade, Mexican government far away, *empresario* in charge

Building Skills
1. Vallejo had specific ideas for protecting the province. 2. It was based on barter.

▶ **UNIT 3** A Time of Upheaval (pp. 104–141)

UNIT THEME

The continuing expansion of the United States and the struggle of Latin American nations to form lasting governments brought change and unrest to North and South America.

UNIT CONCEPTS

- Political rivalries in Mexico led to deep divisions within the nation, which affected the future of its northern provinces.
- In response to Mexico's attempts to stop the flood of Anglo settlers into Texas, revolt broke out and Texas gained its independence.
- U.S. recognition of an independent Texas set off a conflict with Mexico that ended in the United States annexing Texas.
- In the war with Mexico, the United States achieved its goal of expanding to the Pacific by acquiring all of Mexico's northern territories.
- Mexicans who found themselves U.S. citizens faced loss of their lands and prejudice and discrimination.
- Although Mexican Americans were treated as foreigners in their own land, they tried to adjust by holding on to their own way of life but adapting it to the reality of their situation.

UNIT OVERVIEW

Unit 3 describes how expansionism in the United States led to war with Mexico and explores the changes that occurred in Mexico's northern territories when they became part of the United States. *The Big Picture* and the three chapters in the unit describe events and issues in the United States and Latin America that led to change and upheaval and: (1) the revolt in Texas that led to its independence, (2) the U.S. acquisition of Mexico's northern territories following the war with Mexico, and (3) the changes and problems that Mexican Americans faced in a land that was part of a new country.

In teaching this unit, you might emphasize the importance of the changes in the United States at this time and their impact on Mexico and Latin America. As students proceed through the unit, ask them to consider how the future of the United States and Latin America were influenced by events and issues that occurred in the period between 1830 and 1860.

COOPERATIVE LEARNING ACTIVITY

The following cooperative learning activity can be used for alternative assessment after study of the unit has been completed.

Divide the students into three groups and have each group create a television program about the U.S. war with Mexico and its political, social, and economic impact on both nations. The broadcast should reflect the point of view of three groups: the U.S. government, Mexican officials, and Mexican Americans who became citizens in a different land. Have each group select writers, reporters on the scene, and an anchorperson. Writers and reporters should focus on particular stories, and anchors should supply commentary and continuity.

RESOURCES

Unit 3 Test (pp. 112–113)
Outline Maps: The United States, The Americas (pp. 285, 287)
Unit 3 Writing Workshop (pp. 261–264)
The Big Picture 3 ESL/LEP Activity Sheet (p. 216)

THE LATINO EXPERIENCE IN U.S. HISTORY • © Globe Fearon

Unit 3 THE BIG PICTURE (pp. 104–111)

Theme

Unrest and conflicts in the United States and Latin America led to upheaval and change in the early and mid–1800s.

Overview

The Big Picture traces the events and issues that led to change in the United States and Mexico in the early to mid–1880s. Progress and Manifest Destiny, the spirit of expansionism in the United States, led the young republic to think more and more of Mexico's northern provinces as part of its territory. Determined to reach the Pacific, the United States went to war with Mexico and achieved its goal when it acquired all the northern territories. But expansion proved to be a mixed blessing. Gaining new land only brought division and heightened the conflict in the United States over the question of slavery. By 1860, the debate over the slavery issue had reached a point where the United States was on the brink of civil war. Mexico and other Latin American lands abolished slavery but, plagued by political and economic problems, were struggling to form stable governments. Unrest and conflict marked their attempts, but by 1860, reform movements had brought progress and economic development.

Objectives

- To analyze a quotation
- To use a timeline to categorize events
- To debate the pros and cons of U.S. expansionism

Introducing *The Big Picture*

Refer students to the quotation from Voices of the Times on p. 105. Ask how General Mier y Terán views the United States *(as a conqueror)*. Recall with students Spain's conquest of the Americas and how it had affected the lives of the people living there. Ask: Would the general probably view Spain's actions differently from those of the United States? *(because the Spanish tradition was part of his heritage, he might be inclined to view Spain's actions from a different perspective than he would those of the United States)* Discuss with students how his point of view might affect Mexico's future relations with the United States. *(would intensify the already tense relations between the two countries)*

Using the Timeline

Refer students to the timeline on pp. 106–107. Ask them to suggest several headings under which entries on the timeline could be grouped. *(industry, transportation, conflict, expansion, reform)* Write the headings on the chalkboard and call on volunteers to list events under the appropriate heading.

Teaching *The Big Picture*

Debating an Issue. After students have read *The Big Picture*, assign two teams to debate the following issue: Resolved: The expansionist goals of the United States made war with Mexico inevitable. While the teams plan their arguments, have the rest of the class make two columns on a sheet of paper and head them Pro and Con. Ask them to record the pro-and-con arguments in the appropriate columns as the debate is carried on. After the debate, gather the appropriate arguments onto a large class chart and discuss the validity of each argument.

Review and Practice

Assign Taking Another Look, pp. 109 and 111

Answers to Taking Another Look, pp. 109 and 111

p. 109: **1.** in transportation, industry, trade **2.** to avoid further division over slavery by making the number of slave states equal to the number of free states **3. Critical Thinking** Gold brought settlers and wealth to California but heightened the dispute over slavery in the rest of the United States p. 111: **1.** with bitterness and hatred but also with a spirit of nationalism that brought reforms and progress in Mexico **2.** The centralized government controlled Mexico's states, and their loss of power led to dissension and revolt. **3. Critical Thinking** Years of war with Spain, economic turmoil, political divisions within the nation, loss of territories, foreign invasions, all brought upheaval, which made it difficult to get rid of dictators who could take control under such conditions.

Chapter 9 Revolt in Texas (pp. 112–121)

Overview

Following independence, Mexico was in political turmoil as its leaders became divided over the nation's form of government. Their rivalry encouraged the rise of strong military leaders who promised to restore order and protect Mexico's borders. Events in Texas were of special concern to Mexico as Anglo settlers poured into the territory, vastly outnumbering *tejanos*, the Mexican settlers. Mexico imposed restrictions on immigration and trade, which brought protests from Anglos as well as *tejanos* and led to open rebellion. When the war was over, Texas had become an independent republic that now looked to the United States for protection.

Historical Sidelight

A Clash of Cultures. Anglos in Texas confronted an old, established culture that few of them understood. They openly expressed contempt for the *tejanos'* Catholic religion and practiced their own Protestant faith in defiance of Mexican law. Anglos also broke Mexican law by bringing in enslaved African Americans.

Resources

Chapter 9 Activity Sheet (p. 160)
Chapter 9 Test (p. 114)
Chapter 9 ESL/LEP Activity Sheet (p. 217)

Focus Activity

Have students read the introduction on pp. 112 and 113. Ask them the purpose of General Mier y Terán's journey to Texas. (*look into conditions*) What did he find? (*Anglos ignored Mexican law, ran their own affairs, few Mexican officials to enforce the law*) What did he advise? (*occupy Texas*) Have students speculate on how these findings might affect future relations between Mexico and Texas.

Teaching Section 1: A Time of Unrest (pp. 113–114)

Objective

• To understand how political divisions in Mexico led to the rise of military leaders

Developing the Section

Writing an Editorial. Have students work in pairs to write editorials, one favoring a federalist government for Mexico and one supporting a centralist government. Each editorial should explain why the type of government it favored would be best for Mexico and the kind of leadership it needed. Call on volunteers to present their editorials to the class.

Review and Practice

Assign Taking Another Look, p. 114.

Answers to Taking Another Look (p. 114)

1. *Tejanos* lived mostly in towns, Anglos in rural settlements; each group kept its own ways; Anglos felt superior to *tejanos*. **2.** liberal federalists wanted states to share power with the central government, end special privileges, reduce Church power, protect freedom of the press; conservative centralists wanted a strong central government, the wealthy and the Church in power, and press censorship in force **3. Critical Thinking** viewed as a strong leader who would end turmoil, restore order, and protect Mexico from outside invaders, also very clever and shrewd politician

Teaching Section 2: Alarms in Texas (pp. 114–117)

Objective

• To analyze Mexico's concern over Anglo expansion in Texas

Developing the Section

Analyzing an Issue. Have students write a brief paragraph explaining why Mexico needed to be concerned over the expansion of Anglos in Texas. To begin, you might read the following words by an expansionist writer, John L. O'Sullivan: [It is] "the fulfillment of our manifest destiny to overspread the continent allotted by Providence for the free development of our yearly multiplying millions."

Review and Practice

Assign Taking Another Look, p. 117.

Answers to Taking Another Look (p. 117)

1. to stop the flood of Anglos who they feared would take over Texas **2.** refused to obey them, asked for statehood within Mexico, skirmished with Mexican troops **3. Critical Thinking agree:** defied Mexico's laws, could be encouraged by the United States, which wished to acquire Texas, attacked Mexican soldiers, talked of rebellion and independence **disagree:** did not want revolution but freedom from strict laws and regulations; petitioned for reform and statehood; were divided between independence and statehood within Mexico

Teaching Section 3: Texas Gains Independence (pp. 117–119)

Objective

- To create a leaflet calling on *tejanos* to support independence and join Sam Houston

Developing the Section

Writing a Leaflet. Have students work in pairs or small groups to write a call to arms urging *tejanos* to support independence and join Houston. The leaflet should appeal to *tejanos'* dislike of Mexican rule, Santa Anna's revenge if rebellion fails, loyalty to province rather than central government, and tell advantages of freedom and independence.

Review and Practice

Assign Taking Another Look, p. 119.

Answers to Taking Another Look (p. 119)

1. second siege of the Alamo, Texas declaration of independence, battle of San Jacinto 2. Many took part in fighting against Mexico and leaders signed the Texas declaration of independence. 3. **Critical Thinking for:** freedom from strict Mexican laws, chance for trade and business, might become part of U.S. **against:** opposition to slavery, loss of lands, continued Anglo discrimination, domination by Anglos

Extending the Chapter

Writing a News Article. Write the following headlines on the chalkboard: Alamo Overcome, Defenders Killed, Historic Meeting of Texas Delegates Declares Independence, Sam Houston Victorious at San Jacinto. Divide students into three groups and assign one headline to each group. Have the groups write a news article for the headline. Have students present their articles orally to the class for discussion.

Looking Ahead

After students have read Looking Ahead, p. 119, ask them to consider how Mexico's refusal to recognize Texas independence might lead to war with the United States.

Answers to Close Up (pp. 120–121)

The Who, What, Where of History

1. Mexican general who warned of Anglo expansion 2. in San Antonio and Goliad and towns around them 3. military leader and president of Mexico who was defeated by Texans 4. Anglo *empresario* who organized an army against Mexico 5. *tejano empresario* who urged Anglos to oppose Santa Anna's government 6. Mexican general who surrendered the Alamo to the Texans 7. besieged by Santa Anna, overcome, and its defenders killed 8. at the San Jacinto River 9. suffered discrimination and fled to Mexico

Making the Connection

1. In moving away from reform and imposing a strong central government, he incited unrest and rebellions that finally led to war. 2. Both the Republic of Texas and the United States wanted Texas to be part of the United States, but admission as a state was opposed by the United States for fear of war with Mexico and because of the slavery issue.

Time Check

1. Austin's arrest in Mexico City 2. 1836 3. about a month and a half

What Would You Have Done?

1. **support:** constitution is law of Mexico, Texas is part of Mexico, should work for reform within the constitution **declare independence:** constitution not valid anymore because of dictatorships, *tejanos* will have more freedom in an independent Mexico 2. **join:** add land with opportunities for business, trade, market for goods; if a Southerner, would welcome support of a slave state **not join:** opposition to slavery, Texas too vast to control, could mean war with Mexico

Thinking and Writing About History

1. Student's diaries may describe scene before the Alamo, feelings about serving under Santa Anna and about the defenders, or thoughts about how the battle will end. 2. Letters may tell about the surprise attack, the Mexican lack of preparation, the charge into the camp, the fighting in revenge for Santa Anna's cruelty, or the capture of Santa Anna. 3. Some may support a trial as punishment for his cruelty and as an example for others who might try to invade Texas; others may suggest his return to Mexico, which would bring his disgrace and downfall as a dictator.

Building Skills

2, 3, 5, 6

Overview

In 1837, the United States recognized an independent Texas. But incidents along the Texas-Mexican border and Texas's claim to lands as far west as California alarmed the United States. To forestall a Texas empire, the government finally annexed Texas in 1845. In the face of Mexico's fury at the move, President James K. Polk prepared for war, which began in May of 1846. More than a year of fighting followed. The treaty that ended the war did not end the suspicion and distrust between the United States and Mexico.

Historical Sidelight

Opposition to War. Not everyone in the United States supported the war with Mexico. A distinguished public servant, 86-year-old Albert Gallatin, who had been secretary of the treasury and minister to both Great Britain and France, voiced his opposition to the war. Gallatin wrote a pamphlet called "Peace with Mexico" in which he claimed the war was unjustly begun by the United States. He wrote, "At this time the claim [that Americans were superior to Mexicans] is but a pretext for covering and justifying unjust usurpation [seizure] and unbounded ambition."

Resources

Chapter 10 Activity Sheet (p. 161)
Chapter 10 Test (p. 115)
Chapter 10 ESL/LEP Activity Sheet (p. 218)

Focus Activity

Read aloud the following statement by U.S. Secretary of State James Buchanan in 1846: "Destiny beckons us to hold and civilize Mexico." As they read the chapter, have students consider how this statement reflected the attitude of many people in the United States.

Teaching Section 1: Background to War (pp. 122–125)

Objective

- To understand the relationship between U.S. expansionism and the war with Mexico

Developing the Section

Understanding Relationships. List the following events on the chalkboard: **1.** The United States officially recognized Texas as an independent nation in 1837. **2.** Texas and Mexico disagreed over the southern border of Texas. **3.** In 1842, Texans and Mexicans were involved in armed skirmishes. **4.** In 1842, Texas claimed the lands reaching as far as California. **5.** In 1845, the United States annexed Texas. **6.** In 1846, the United States ordered soldiers to build a fort along the Rio Grande. Have students write a paragraph explaining the relationship between expansionism and the war with Texas.

Review and Practice

Assign Taking Another Look, p. 125

Answers to Taking Another Look (p. 125)

1. land along the Rio Grande **2.** fear that Texas would ally itself with Great Britain and build a huge empire **3. Critical Thinking Mexico:** fired on U.S. soldiers at the Rio Grande; **U.S.:** precipitated war by invading what Mexicans considered their soil

Teaching Section 2: Mexico and the United States at War (pp. 126–128)

Objective

- To create maps showing the U.S. strategy in the war with Mexico

Developing the Section

Creating Maps. Divide students into three groups to create maps showing the U.S. three-pronged attack on Mexico: invasion and occupation of northern Mexico, taking of California and New Mexico, and the invasion and march to Mexico City. When maps are completed, you might have students draw up a class map showing all three strategies.

Review and Practice

Assign Taking Another Look, p. 128

Answers to Taking Another Look (p. 128)

1. the short-lived independent republic of California **2.** for their brave defense of Chapultepec Castle in Mexico City **3. Critical Thinking** Anglo settlers were increasing in California, not enough Mexican troops to defend it, U.S.-aided takeover by Anglos

Teaching Section 3: Aftermath of War (pp. 128–129)

Objective

- To interpret a quotation concerning the future of the Mexican people in the lands taken over by the United States

Developing the Section

Interpreting a Quotation. Refer students to the statement by a Mexican diplomat on p. 127. What does he mean when he says that the people will have to wander in search of hospitality? (*Anglos will not welcome them.*) Why does he say North Americans hate Mexicans? (*They are descended from Native Americans.*) Discuss with students why the diplomat feels this way and whether or not they agree with him.

Review and Practice

Assign Taking Another Look, p. 129.

Answers to Taking Another Look (p. 129)

1. present-day California, New Mexico, Nevada, Utah, and parts of Colorado and Wyoming 2. gave the people a choice of whether to return to Mexico or stay as U.S. citizens 3. **Critical Thinking** difficult to uproot families and lose farms or businesses, more freedom under the United States, more economic opportunities

Extending the Chapter

Judging a Leader. As President, James K. Polk achieved nearly every one of his goals, among them the acquisition of Mexican territory. Have students write an essay about Polk that responds to this question: Should a leader be judged on the success of achieving his or her goals or on his or motives? Call on volunteers to read their essays for class discussion.

Looking Ahead

After students have read Looking Ahead, p. 128, ask them to list reasons why they think Mexicans in the United States would now face difficulties. Have them save their lists and compare their responses to the conditions of Mexicans described in Chapter 11.

Answers to Close Up (pp. 130–131)

The Who, What, Where, of History

1. southwestern Texas 2. Rio Grande 3. south and west of the Nueces River 4. Mexican president forced to resign by the military 5. on the Rio Grande 6. Mexican commander who sent troops across the Rio Grande to drive back U.S. soldiers 7. short-lived independent republic of California 8. U.S. forces were drawn into a trap by Mexican troops and defeated 9. just outside Mexico City

Making the Connection

1. The annexation of Texas broke a U.S.-Mexico treaty, and Mexico prepared for war, which was precipitated by U.S. move along the Rio Grande. 2. Anglos declared a republic in California and received help from invading U.S. forces.

Time Check

1. 1841 2. 1 year 3. first clash between Mexican and U.S. soldiers at the Rio Grande; U.S. declaration of war against Mexico; creation of Bear Flag Republic; battle of San Pascual

What Would You Have Done?

1. Proposals may include closely watching U.S. moves, possible negotiations with Texans to recover some land, direct invasion; responses should reflect realities of the situation. 2. may include equal civil rights, right to practice own religion, follow own way of life, own land, hold political office 3. **leave:** fear of domination by Anglos, may be denied equal opportunities, might lose land and cattle, escape prejudice **stay:** hard times in Mexico after the war, own the ranch and land, been in California for generations, guaranteed protection by U.S. Constitution, possibility of bigger profits from the Gold Rush

Thinking and Writing About History

1. should tell the facts of what happened and express feeling as a Mexican 2. should be told in first person and give facts of the skirmish; may extol the bravery and strategy of the *californios* 3. should show an understanding of the heroism of the young men and how Mexicans feel about them

Building Skills

1. The equipment of the two armies was far from equal. U.S. weapons were superior to those of the Mexicans. 2. Under the Treaty of Guadalupe Hidalgo, Mexicans who lived in California, Texas, and New Mexico were guaranteed protection.

Chapter 11   Foreigners in Their Own Land (pp. 132–141)

Overview

The Mexican people who lived in what was now the southwestern part of the United States faced uncertain prospects. But most hoped to benefit from new opportunities. California's gold-rush boom proved profitable for ranchers and merchants and provided many jobs. Old Mexican families retained political influence in New Mexico and Arizona, where the Anglo population grew slowly. In California, their power diminished as Anglos poured in. Eager for land, Anglos urged the government to examine land grants that had been held by Mexicans for generations. During the examination process, which often took years, Anglos grabbed up a great deal of land. Despite injustices and discrimination, Mexican Americans adjusted by keeping their own ways while living in an Anglo world.

Historical Sidelight

A Legendary Hero. According to the story, Joaquín Murieta was a mild-mannered young man whose transformation into the terror of California began when he was driven off his gold-mining claim by Anglo thugs. He turned to dealing cards in a saloon, but a drunken crowd lynched his brother and nearly beat Murieta to death for allegedly stealing a horse. The young man vowed revenge and set out on his career as a bandit. A popular legend tells that a miner walked into a saloon one day with a bag of gold dust and offered to bet that he could kill Murieta the first time he laid eyes on him. A young Mexican in the saloon took the bet, then grabbed the bag of gold dust and disappeared through the door before anyone realized the young man was Murieta himself. He had won the bet and got his gold without firing a shot.

Focus Activity

Refer students to the Snapshot of the Times, on p. 136. Then read aloud the question at the beginning of the chapter: What were some results of the U.S. takeover of Mexican lands? Ask students to form some answers to the question and list them. Have students add to or modify their lists as they read through the chapter.

Teaching Section 1: Living Under a New Flag (pp. 133–135)

Objective
• To compare the changes experienced by former Mexicans in different areas of the Southwest

Developing the Section
Comparing Changes. Divide students into two groups. Have one group identify changes Mexican Americans experienced in California; the other, changes in New Mexico and Texas. Ask a spokesperson from each group to read its list aloud. Then lead a class discussion comparing similarities or differences and explaining reasons for them.

Review and Practice
• Assign Taking Another Look, p. 135.

Answers to Taking Another Look (p. 135)
1. population increased much more rapidly 2. a. New Mexico, southern California b. Anglo populations in these areas grew slowly; *ricos* outnumbered Anglos, allowing them to keep their influence. 3. **Critical Thinking** classified as foreigners so they could be taxed; violence against them in the gold fields; vagrancy laws applied unjustly against people of Spanish descent.

Teaching Section 2: Land Claims and Courts (pp. 135–137)

Objective
• To understand the effects of the land claims law on Mexican Americans

Developing the Section
Creating a Courtroom Scene. Have students set up a courtroom scene in which a Mexican American is tried for throwing squatters off his land. Ask students to play the roles of the rancher, judge, prosecutor, defense attorney, squatters, and witnesses. Let the class act as the jury. Allow time for student preparation. When all the evidence has been presented and arguments heard, have the jury make its decision. Lead a class discussion about the verdict.

Review and Practice
Assign Taking Another Look, p. 137.

Answers to Taking Another Look (p. 137)
1. Treaty of Guadalupe Hidalgo promised them their land. 2. said land not being put to productive use; deeds and documents often missing or boundaries uncertain 3. **Critical Thinking** Strictly speaking it did fulfill its treaty obligation in that the majority of claims were upheld. But Mexicans were forced to spend time and money in appeals, and many left their lands.

Teaching Section 3: Looking for Justice (pp. 137–139)

Objective
• To draw conclusions about the role of the social bandits in Mexican American life

Developing the Section
Writing Editorials. Refer students to the feature about Cortina on p. 139. Have them work in small groups to write an editorial for a Mexican American newspaper about Cortina and his exploits. Remind students that an editorial expresses an opinion. Call on volunteers to read their editorials and discuss why legends grew up around men like Cortina.

Review and Practice
Assign Taking Another Look, p. 139.

Answers to Taking Another Look (p. 139)
1. harshly discriminated against and treated as inferiors 2. social bandits acted on behalf of people who were oppressed, ordinary bandits acted on their own behalf 3. **Critical Thinking** did not want to leave their homes and land, wanted to live peacefully, may not have had a better alternative

Extending the Chapter
In Their Shoes. Ask students to imagine that they are ordinary Mexican Americans in the United States in the mid–1800s. Have them write letters to relatives in Mexico telling about their lives and work. Ask them to end their letters by encouraging or discouraging their relatives to come north.

Looking Ahead
After students have read Looking Ahead, p. 139, ask them how they as Mexican Americans might have felt over the slavery issue. Ask how they think the slavery conflict would have affected their lives.

Answers to Close Up (pp. 140–141)

The Who, What, Where of History
1. northern Mexico 2. a wealthy Mexican American 3. those dealing with property, water, mineral rights 4. tax on foreigners who mined for gold, which was applied to Mexican Americans who were U.S. citizens 5. ranch owner near San Francisco whose lands were taken by Anglo settlers 6. illegal settler 7. set up a commission to examine land grants in California 8. well-known and respected *mestizo* landowner and politician in California who was denied the right to testify in a court 9. outlaws who claim to act on behalf of oppressed people 10. legendary Texas social bandit who was never caught 11. social bandit around whom many legends grew

Making the Connection
1. Newcomers swelled the population, making it eligible for statehood 2. Examining titles under the law took so long that squatters settled on lands and often grabbed them up.

Time Check
1. 4 years 2. 1850, 1912 3. Texas; *empresarios* held most grants and had sold land to settlers, keeping better records.

What Would You Have Done?
1. Arguments may include: well-known and respected landowner, county official, signed the state's constitution, U.S. citizen with citizen's rights under the Constitution 2. **yes:** he was helping the people and avenging wrongs done to them, would not rob the rancher; **no:** is a lawbreaker even though he helps the people

Thinking and Writing About History
1. Letter may include chance to strike it rich, become a merchant or obtain other kinds of work, little work in Mexico, more freedom in California. 2. should tell who, what, where, when, and why and show understanding of Anglo attitudes toward Mexicans. 3. may include need for Mexican Americans to have a fighter for their rights, articles in Spanish would keep them informed about events in the world, show understanding of their needs, motivate them to become literate. 4. show understanding of all aspects of civil rights all U.S. citizens are entitled to enjoy (voting, freedom of religion and speech, right to keep property, and so forth).

Building Skills
Check that students carry out the instructions provided and do so correctly. Possible responses for section statements: **Section 1:** Mexicans who became U.S. citizens found their lives changed. Although the California Gold Rush brought opportunities for Mexicans, Anglos poured into the territory, lessening Mexican influence and discriminating against them. **Section 2.** When the United States took possession of the Southwest, many Mexicans lost their lands. Because Anglos wanted more land, the U.S. government began to examine the land grants held by Mexicans in the Southwest, and during the lengthy process of settling claims, Anglos grabbed up much Mexican land. **Section 3:** Mexican Americans found ways to respond to the prejudice and discrimination they faced in the United States. In response to discrimination, some Mexicans fought as outlaws for the benefit of their people, but most kept their old ways while trying to adapt to the new situation.

▶ UNIT 4 A Time of Growth
(pp. 142–193)

UNIT THEME

Latinos made numerous significant contributions to the growth and development of the United States in the late 1800s and early 1900s.

UNIT CONCEPTS

- During the Civil War, gaining control of the New Mexico Territory was important to both the Union and the Confederacy.
- Thousands of Latinos participated in the Civil War, many of whom assumed significant roles.
- Immigrants from Spain, Puerto Rico, and Cuba played a major part in the growth and expansion of the United States.
- In the New Mexico Territory, the influx of settlers brought by the railroads upset the way of life of the *nuevomexicanos*.
- By the late 1800s, Cuba and Puerto Rico were all that remained of Spain's vast colonial empire in the Americas.
- A revolution began in Cuba in 1895, launched by Cuban immigrants living in the United States.
- U.S.-Spanish relations became strained over the issue of Cuba; many in the United States called for war.
- Spain was defeated in the Cuban-Spanish-American War. Under the terms of the peace treaty, Cuba was granted independence; control of Puerto Rico was given to the United States.
- Contrary to the expectations of the Puerto Rican people, the U.S. government did not bestow independence on Puerto Rico.
- Under the Platt Amendment, the United States retained a measure of control in Cuba.
- Most Cubans and Puerto Ricans resented U.S. control.

UNIT OVERVIEW

Unit 4 highlights Latino influence in the United States in the late 1800s and early 1900s. *The Big Picture* and the four chapters in the unit describe: (1) the role of Latinos in the Civil War, (2) the part immigrants from Spain, Puerto Rico, and Cuba played in the growth of the United States and the effect on *nuevomexicanos* as the country grew, (3) the causes and results of the Cuban-Spanish-American War, and (4) the effect of U.S. control on Puerto Rico and Cuba.

In teaching this unit, stress the variety of roles Latinos played and the importance of Latino contributions. Emphasize, too, how the role of the United States changed significantly as a result of the Cuban-Spanish-American War. With Puerto Rico as a possession and Cuba as a protectorate, the United States became a colonial power.

COOPERATIVE LEARNING ACTIVITY

The following cooperative learning activity can be used for alternative assessment after study of the unit has been completed.

At the end of the unit, ask groups of students to create a mural-sized collage illustrating highlights of the unit. The collage should contain words, pictures, and other images that summarize the major ideas of "Latinos in the Later 1800s." In evaluating students' work, consider visual appeal, organization, thoroughness, and originality.

RESOURCES

Unit 4 Test (pp. 117–118)
Outline Maps: The United States, The Americas, Latin America (pp. 285, 286, 287)
Unit 4 Writing Workshop (pp. 265–268)
The Big Picture 4 ESL/LEP Activity Sheet (p. 220)

Unit 4 THE BIG PICTURE (pp. 142–149)

Theme

In many ways, the late 1800s was a time of great change for the United States. The years after the Civil War saw the nation grow and expand and eventually become a colonial power. Latinos played an important role in bringing about many of these changes.

Overview

The Big Picture treats four pivotal features of U.S. history in the late 1800s: the Civil War and Reconstruction, immigration, the growth of railroads and industry, and the country's expansion. After the Civil War, with the Union still intact, the country entered a period of unparalleled growth. During the late 1800s, Latin America was also changing. Mexico, Argentina, and Chile were among the countries trying to achieve a stable government as well as economic growth.

Objectives

- To analyze the significance of growth and change in the United States in the late 1800s and early 1900s
- To use a timeline to categorize events
- To brainstorm about the effects of expansion on the United States
- To gather evidence about the role other countries played in Latin American affairs

Introducing *The Big Picture*

On the chalkboard, write the words "Growth" and "Change." Ask students how these words applied to the United States in the period covered in this unit. Record the responses on the chalkboard. As a follow-up activity, have students create a visual or verbal picture comparing the United States in the early 1800s to the United States in the early 1900s.

Using the Timeline

Divide the class into three groups. Ask each group to review the events on the timeline on pp. 144 and 145. Have them choose four events from the timeline that had a lasting effect on the United States and four events that had a lasting effect on Latin America. They should be prepared to explain their selections. Students may skim *The Big Picture* and the chapters in the unit for additional information. Ask: Which events are on both lists? Of all the events mentioned, which one do you think had the greatest effect? See if the class can reach a consensus on this.

Teaching *The Big Picture*

Brainstorming. Ask students what pictures come to mind when they think of the expansion of the United States. *(covered wagons, building railroads, acquiring territory, treatment of Native Americans)* List their responses on the chalkboard. Encourage them to think not only in terms of expansion across the continent—from the Atlantic to the Pacific—but also of overseas expansion.

Gathering Evidence. After students have read the section "In Latin America," ask them to find at least five examples of the influence of the United States and European countries on Latin American affairs. Summarize their findings on the chalkboard, listing the countries involved and the role they played in Latin America.

Review and Practice

Assign Taking Another Look, pp. 146 and 149.

Answers to Taking Another Look (pp. 146 and 149)

p. 146: **1. a.** The 13th, 14th, and 15th amendments freed enslaved African Americans, made them citizens with equal rights under the law, and gave African American males the right to vote. **b.** Most Southern states passed Jim Crow laws to segregate the African Americans and to keep them in an inferior position. **2.** They wanted to increase the nation's power and influence. U.S. industry wanted to find new markets for goods and cheap sources of raw materials. **3. Critical Thinking** Justified: students might cite the Monroe Doctrine or the national interest of the United States. Disagree: students might argue that U.S. involvement violated the sovereignty of other American nations. p. 149: **1. a.** When Mexico could not pay its foreign debt, Napoleon III sent French troops into Mexico City and named a French ally Mexico's new emperor. **b.** Continued Mexican resistance, arms supplied by the United States after its Civil War was over, and the withdrawal of the French troops led to the empire's collapse. **2.** Latin American nations relied on foreign investors for the money to develop their natural resources. The economies of the Latin American countries, therefore, depended on the prosperity of the industrial nations. **3. Critical Thinking** The economies of the Central American countries, like those of Argentina and Chile, depended on foreign investors. However, the principal products of Central American nations were mostly agricultural.

Chapter 12 Latinos in the U.S. Civil War (1861–1865) (pp. 150–159)

Overview

During the years 1861 to 1865, a civil war divided the United States. Ten thousand Latinos took up arms in the conflict. In the New Mexico Territory, a Confederate attack prompted many Latinos who had been uncommitted to enlist in the Union army. The daring exploits of such men as Manuel Chaves did much to aid the Union. Other Latinos aided the Confederate cause. Among them were Santos Benavides, Lola Sánchez, and Loreta Janeta Velázquez. Perhaps the most famous Latino to fight in the Civil War was David Farragut, the hero of the battles of New Orleans and Mobile Bay. Another hero of the North was Cuban-born Fedèrico Fernández Cavada.

Historical Sidelight

Capturing New Orleans. When David Farragut was given command of a fleet of 24 ships and ordered to capture New Orleans, he relished the assignment. The task, however, would not be easy. In order to reach New Orleans, Farragut had to get past Forts Jackson and St. Philip and the line of hulks that stretched between them. After six days of unsuccessfully bombarding the forts, Farragut devised another plan. His ships would sail under cover of darkness! Unfortunately for Farragut, the moon rose, revealing his fleet, and the Confederates began to fire. He later wrote, "It seemed as if all the artillery of heaven were playing upon the earth." Somehow, the ships managed to survive the shells and explosions—all but four successfully passed the forts—and New Orleans surrendered without firing a shot. Farragut's plan had worked and he was hailed as a hero.

Resources

Chapter 12 Activity Sheet (p. 163)
Chapter 12 Test (p. 119)
Chapter 12 ESL/LEP Activity Sheet (p. 221)

Focus Activity

Have students read the story about Loreta Janeta Velázquez at the beginning of Chapter 12. Ask: What risk was Velázquez taking? What would her attitude be about her cause to prompt her to take such a risk? Can you think of a cause you would be willing to take a similar risk for?

Teaching Section 1: The Civil War in the U.S. Southwest (pp. 151–154)

Objective
- To explain the significance of the New Mexico Territory to the Confederacy

Developing the Section
Writing a Report. Have students assume the role of a Confederate officer in the Civil War. You have been ordered to write a report to be sent to your superiors explaining why it is imperative for the Confederacy to win control of the New Mexico Territory. Reports should be both factual and persuasive.

Review and Practice
Assign Taking Another Look, p. 154.

Answers to Taking Another Look (p. 154)
1. an attack on New Mexico by Confederates from Texas **2.** He led 490 New Mexico volunteers on a daring raid. They lowered themselves down a 200-foot (60-meter) mountain to capture the Confederates' supply train. Then they destroyed the wagons and burned all the supplies. **3. Critical Thinking** Possible answer: Fighting for the United States made them feel they were part of the country.

Teaching Section 2: Fighters for Two Flags (pp. 154–157)

Objective
- To understand why Latinos fought in the Civil War
- To evaluate the contributions Latinos made in the Civil War

Developing the Section
Role Playing. Have students choose one of the men or women discussed in Section 2. They should assume the role of that person and explain to the class what part he or she played in the Civil War and the reasons for his or her action. This activity can also be done as "Who Am I?" Students would role play, describing their activities during the Civil War, and the class would try to identify the historical figure each person is describing.

Review and Practice

Assign Taking Another Look, p. 157.

Answers to Taking Another Look (p. 157)

1. "Damn the torpedoes! Full speed ahead!" He made it clear that he was not about to turn back. 2. sent aloft in hot air balloons to sketch what he observed of the enemy's movements 3. **Critical Thinking** Students should support their choices with specifics from the chapter.

Extending the Chapter

Doing Research. Have students research the life of one of the Latino men or women highlighted in this chapter or the life of another Latino man or woman who played a part in the Civil War. Students can present their findings to the class in the form of oral or written reports.

Looking Ahead

After students have read Looking Ahead, p. 157, have a volunteer read the last sentence aloud, "The United States took a growing interest in Latino lands to the south." Ask them to speculate about whether this growing U.S. interest would be beneficial or harmful to the Latino lands to the south.

Answers to Close Up (pp. 158–159)

The Who, What, Where of History

1. lieutenant colonel who led New Mexico volunteers against the Confederates at Glorieta Pass 2. at Glorieta Pass 3. a cavalry regiment of Mexican Americans who fought for the South 4. Cuban-born woman who spied for the South 5. in the battle for New Orleans 6. His sketches of enemy troop movements made from the air helped the Union forces in battle. 7. Costa-Rican born astronaut who spoke in Spanish from a spaceship to North and South America.

Making the Connections

1. The invasion brought the war to New Mexico, threatening people's homes. No longer indifferent to who won the war, many New Mexicans enlisted as volunteers in the Union army. 2. Farragut's attack weakened Vicksburg, enabling General Grant to capture it a year later.

Time Check

1. Sibley's invasion of New Mexico 2. in November 1863

What Would You Have Done?

1. **in favor:** the Confederate cause needed all the help it could get, especially from such a brave woman; **opposed:** a woman should not take an active part in the fighting but could serve the cause in other ways. 2. Possible answer: by supporting the Union army against the Confederacy and possibly by enlisting in the Union army

Thinking and Writing About History

1. Check articles for accuracy. 2. **supporter of Confederacy:** defend homeland from invasion, personal reasons, sympathy on part of wealthy Latino landowners for Confederacy, belief in Confederate cause; **supporter of Union:** opposition to slavery, enmity between Latinos and Anglo Texans, Confederate attack on New Mexico 3. Report should cover the events as described in the chapter.

Building Skills

Implied main idea: Farragut was very brave.

Chapter 13   A Changing World (1860s–1912) (pp. 160–171)

Overview

During the late 1800s and early 1900s, many new groups of people came to the United States and many people moved within thc United States. Among the settlers who came to the United States were immigrants from Spain seeking better opportunities. At first Spaniards were drawn to areas where Spanish culture was strong, but in time they settled in other areas as well. Puerto Ricans and Cubans came to the United States in growing numbers in the late 1800s. Many of them were fleeing rebellions in their countries. Often these immigrants dreamed of returning to their homes when independence was won. In time, however, they developed strong ties to their new communities. During this same period, many Anglo settlers moved into the U.S. Southwest. There they came into conflict with the *nuevomexicanos* who had lived therc for many years. As New Mexico's population grew, there were increased calls for statehood. By 1912, the states of New Mexico and Arizona had been admitted to the union.

Historical Sidelight

The Government and Railroad Building. The inclusion of that part of the present-day United States that constituted the Gadsden Purchase from Mexico shows the close connection between the building of railroads and the U.S. government. The semiarid desert land was not attractive for settlement. But to Secretary of War Jefferson Davis, it provided the easiest route across the Southwest for a projected southern transcontinental railroad to the Pacific. Through Davis's influence, the U.S. minister to Mexico, James Gadsden of South Carolina, was ordered to make an offer to Mexico to buy the territory. On June 30, 1854, a treaty was signed under which the United States paid Mexico $10 million for 19 million acres (7.7 million hectares). The original treaty also gave the United States the right to build a highway or a railroad across Mexico's isthmus of Tehuantepec. However, before the U.S. Senate ratified the treaty, it eliminated this provision and limited the treaty to the region that would satisfy the need for a railroad. During the Civil War, the U.S. government took an even more serious step to encourage railroad building when, in 1862, it offered to give railroad companies 20 square miles (5,480 hectares) for every mile (1.6 kilometers) of track they laid. Companies seized the opportunity and soon railroads crisscrossed the nation.

Resources
Chapter 13 Activity Sheet (p. 164)
Chapter 13 Test (p. 120)
Chapter 13 ESL/LEP Activity Sheet (p. 222)

Focus Activity
Ask students to draw a picture of the city of Tampa, Florida, as it is described in the chapter opener. Allow students to study their classmates' pictures. Then ask: How would you react if you were brought to such a place? What could possibly motivate people to settle in a place "filled with dangers and discomforts"? *(economic opportunity, hope for a better life, escaping from something worse)* List responses on the chalkboard.

Teaching Section 1: New Spanish Immigration (pp. 161–162)

Objective
- To re-create the experience of Spanish immigrants to the United States

Developing the Section
Writing a Letter. Students should imagine that they are immigrants from Spain to the United States in the late 1800s or early 1900s. Have them write a letter to a friend or family member explaining why they chose to come to the United States and describing what their life is like there.

Review and Practice
Assign Taking Another Look, p. 162.

Answers to Taking Another Look (p. 162)
1. in New York City, California, Louisiana, and later in Florida, Hawaii, and Idaho **2.** sheep and cattle herding **3. Critical Thinking** Latin America's language and culture were less foreign to them than those of the United States.

Teaching Section 2: Newcomers from Puerto Rico and Cuba (pp. 162–166)

Objective
- To describe the experience of immigrants from Puerto Rico and Cuba

Developing the Section
Creating Leaflets. Tell students to read the description on p. 165 of the company town established by Vicente Martínez Ybor. Then tell them to imagine that they have been hired by Ybor to create illustrated leaflets describing the company town at Ybor City. The purpose of the leaflets is to portray the town in the best possible light in order to encourage people to settle and work there.

Review and Practice
Assign Taking Another Look, p. 166.

Answers to Taking Another Look (p. 166)
1. Rebellions against Spanish rule led to fighting and hardship in Puerto Rico and Cuba. **2.** He read to the workers as they made cigars. Some *lectores* also encouraged their listeners to become involved in strikes or in political activities. **3. Critical Thinking** Possible answer: materials from or about Cuba, political writings, romantic stories

Teaching Section 3: New Mexico (pp. 166–169)

Objective
- To evaluate a quotation
- To express an opinion regarding the activities of the *nuevomexicanos* reacting to the cattle boom

Developing the Section
Analyzing a Quotation. Direct students to read the quotation from Judge James O'Brien on p. 167. Have them write a paragraph explaining the background of the judge's remarks and what his decision meant. In a second paragraph, students should agree or disagree with the judge's statement and give reasons for their position.

Review and Practice
Assign Taking Another Look, p. 169.

Answers to Taking Another Look (p. 169)
1. They disagreed about how the land should be used; neither understood the other's culture, customs, and traditions. **2.** Members of Congress did not want to admit New Mexico while most of its people were Spanish-speaking Roman Catholics of Mexican descent. **3. Critical Thinking** Calling out federal troops would cause greater friction between *nuevomexicanos* and Anglos and promote violence.

Extending the Chapter
Writing an Editorial. Ask students to reread the paragraphs that discuss *las Gorras Blancas.* Then have them write an editorial advocating a particular course of action that might have appeared in an Anglo newspaper and another editorial that might have appeared in a newspaper for *nuevomexicanos.*

Looking Ahead
After students have read Looking Ahead, p. 169, have them try to predict the outcome of the struggle by Cuba and Puerto Rico to free themselves from Spanish rule. To provoke discussion, you might remind them that the two islands were all that remained of what had once been an immense Spanish colonial empire in the Americas.

Answers to Close Up (pp. 170–171)

The Who, What, Where of History
1. California and Louisiana had been part of Spain's colonial empire and elements of Spanish culture still existed there. **2.** in parts of the U.S. West, especially Idaho **3.** On "the Day of the Homeland," Christmas Eve, 1893, workers in the Puerto Rican cigar factories in New York City donated a day's pay to be given to the island's independence movement. **4.** a leading Cuban cigar manufacturer who set up a company town near Tampa, Florida, in the late 1800s **5.** a person in a cigar factory who read to the workers while they made cigars **6.** groups of *nuevomexicanos* who cut fences, wrecked rail lines, and destroyed Anglo property in an attempt to protect their lands and homes

Making the Connection
1. As revolts against Spanish rule broke out in Puerto Rico and Cuba, thousands of people fled to the United States to escape the fighting and the hardship. **2.** The railroad brought to the Southwest large numbers of Anglo settlers and businesspeople whose ideas of progress, culture, and traditions conflicted with those of the *nuevomexicanos.*

Time Check
1. between 1900 and 1910 **2.** 1912

What Would You Have Done?
1. in California; its people, language, and culture would have been familiar and its climate would have been not too different from that of Spain. **2.** fenced in their property and used any means short of violence to protect *nuevomexicano* lands and way of life; some might have joined *las Gorras Blancas.*

Thinking and Writing About History
1. Might describe similarities between Tampa and Cuba, work in a cigar factory, interest in independence for Cuba **2.** Speech might dwell on cruelty of the Spanish and hard life on the island and importance of having a free and independent Puerto Rico. **3. Anglo rancher:** cattle boom will bring great prosperity to the region, tremendous expanses of land are needed for grazing, barbed-wire fences are essential for protecting a herd; *nuevomexicano* **farmer:** ranchers are often guilty of stealing *nuevomexicano* land; the fences, railroads, and large ranches are destroying their simple way of life.

Building Skills
Generalizations: sentences 1, 2, 5, 6

Chapter 14 The Cuban-Spanish-American War (pp. 172–183)

Overview
By the late 1800s, Spain's colonial empire had been reduced to the two Caribbean islands of Cuba and Puerto Rico. Independence movements sprang up in the face of Spain's reluctance to give up its last two colonies. Cuban rebels fought a Ten Years' War from 1868 to 1878. Another uprising began in 1895. By 1898, relations between Spain and the United States were strained over the issue of Cuba. Tensions escalated, and many in the United States called for war. After the explosion in Havana harbor of the U.S. battleship *Maine,* the United States declared war on Spain. At the end of the Cuban-Spanish-American War, Spain granted independence to Cuba and turned additional territories, including Puerto Rico, over to the United States.

Historical Sidelight

Mobilizing for War. When the United States declared war on Spain, the country was poorly prepared, especially for fighting on land. The U.S. Army numbered 28,000 largely inexperienced troops compared to 155,000 veteran Spanish troops in Cuba. Spain also possessed superior arms and equipment. For U.S. forces, there were not enough rifles, uniforms, or food.

Before the war, Secretary of War Russell Alger had been asked by President McKinley, "How soon can you put an army in Cuba?" Alger replied, "Forty thousand men there in ten days." In fact, it was seven weeks before the first U.S. troops arrived in Santiago.

Resources

Chapter 14 Activity Sheet (p. 165)
Chapter 14 Test (p. 121)
Chapter 14 ESL/LEP Activity Sheet (p. 223)

Focus Activity

Ask students to write a letter to a friend in another country explaining what independence means and why it is important to them. List some of their key ideas on the chalkboard. Ask: Do you think independence means more to someone who has had to fight for it? Why or why not?

Teaching Section 1: Background to Revolution (pp. 173–174)

Objective
- To examine the pros and cons of Cuba's status as a colony of Spain

Developing the Section
Debating. Debate the following: "Spain should have granted independence to Cuba after the Ten Years' War." Assign several students to represent Spain's point of view; others, Cuba's. When the debate is over ask the class which side presented more convincing arguments.

Review and Practice
Assign Taking Another Look, p. 174.

Answers to Taking Another Look (p. 174)
1. Spain was determined not to give up the last of its colonial possessions. In addition, Cuba was a source of wealth for Spain. **2.** The Cuban desire for independence reminded people in the United States of their own nation's struggle for freedom. **3. Critical Thinking** Spain was determined to do whatever was necessary to end the rebellion. The Cubans did not have the resources to fight a much stronger Spain.

Teaching Section 2: The War of 1895 (pp. 174–178)

Objective
- To identify key issues in Martí's plea for support for the Cuban revolution

Developing the Section
Writing a Speech. Have students write a speech Martí might have given asking people to support the rebels in Cuba in their fight for independence. Remind them that Martí was an electrifying—and extremely successful—speaker. Volunteers might want to deliver their speeches in class.

Review and Practice
Assign Taking Another Look, p. 178.

Answers to Taking Another Look (p. 178)
1. He wrote and gave electrifying lectures in support of Cuban independence. **2.** The rebels fought a guerrilla war. General Weyler launched a brutal campaign that included martial law, the forced relocation of people from the countryside to towns and cities, and burning the countryside to starve out the rebels. **3. Critical Thinking** His speeches and his writings show a concern for the peoples of all the Americas.

Teaching Section 3: Uncertain Victory (pp. 179–181)

Objective
- To give examples of yellow journalism

Developing the Section
Identifying Propaganda. Ask students to find examples of reporting in newspapers that is not as objective as they think it should be. Have volunteers share their findings with the class. Discuss what is meant by "yellow journalism." Have students evaluate the samples they collected to decide whether they would be considered yellow journalism. Then have students write news accounts of the Cuban-Spanish-American War (or of a current events topic) that are examples of yellow journalism.

Review and Practice
Assign Taking Another Look, p. 181.

Answers to Taking Another Look (p. 181)
1. the de Lôme letter and the sinking of the U.S. battleship *Maine* **2.** control of Wake, Guam, Puerto Rico, and the Philippines **3. Critical Thinking in favor:** the United States helped restore normal conditions and prepare for free elections; **opposed:** the

United States was more concerned with the economic interests of U.S. companies than with the right of the Cuban people to rule themselves.

Extending the Chapter

Analyzing a Quotation. Copy the following quotation on the chalkboard: "I think . . . possibly the President could have worked out the business without a war, but the current was too strong, the demagogues [leaders who appeal to emotion rather than reason] too numerous, and the fall elections too near." (Senator John C. Spooner) Ask students to read Spooner's quotation and to answer these questions: Do you think Senator Spooner supported the war? Explain. What does he mean when he says, "The current was too strong"? From what you have read in this chapter, do you think his opinions are justified?

Looking Ahead

After students have read Looking Ahead, p. 181, have them try to predict how the people of Cuba and Puerto Rico will react to the strong U.S. role in their countries. To provoke discussion, you might remind students that France had come to the aid of the U.S. colonies in their war for independence from Great Britain. Ask how the colonists would have reacted if, after the revolutionary war, France had acquired control of the former British colonies.

Answers to Close Up (pp. 182–183)

The Who, What, Where of History

1. sugar, tobacco, and coffee produced wealth for Spain 2. leaders in the Ten Years' War for independence from Spain 3. a tax on goods being brought into a country 4. a Cuban who fought for his country's independence and inspired others to do the same 5. raised money for the Cuban independence movement and even sold their home to contribute to the cause 6. in Havana harbor 7. a Cuban rebel commander who helped coordinate the U.S. military's role in the Cuban-Spanish-American War

Making the Connection

1. Both represented attempts to rid the islands of the control of Spain and become independent. 2. Cuban Americans responded to pleas from leaders like José Martí by donating the money needed to buy guns and ammunition for the rebels.

Time Check

1. 1868 2. 57 years (1821 to 1878) 3. 1898

What Would You Have Done?

1. Students who agree with Martí's decision should cite his deep commitment to the cause of Cuban independence and his desire to do whatever was necessary to achieve it. Those who disagree should mention how effective—and irreplaceable—he was in gaining support for the independence movement. 2. Possible answer: with mixed feelings—joy that Spain had granted Cuba its independence and dismay at the military government being set up on the island by the United States

Thinking and Writing About History

1. For Martí, the central idea of freedom was liberty and opportunity for *all* people. 2. One example of sensationalism in reporting is the *Journal* headline "Destruction of the War Ship *Maine* Was the Work of an Enemy." Students may cite supermarket tabloids as examples of sensationalism in present-day journalism. 3. If newspaper accounts are believed, the editorial might urge going to war against Spain. If the accounts are treated with skepticism, the editorial might urge caution and an impartial investigation of the explosion.

Building Skills

1. Generalizations: sentences 1, 3, 4 2. The destruction of the *Maine* and the conviction on the part of most Americans that Spain was somehow responsible for it was the most significant factor in the U.S. decision to declare war on Spain. 3. Emotion rather than reason was the main element in supporting the decision to go to war.

Chapter 15   Puerto Rico and Cuba Under United States Control (pp. 184–193)

Overview

After the Cuban-Spanish-American War, Cuba was granted its independence from Spain. Puerto Rico, too, was free of Spanish control. In the years that followed, however, the United States acted to limit the independence of the two island nations, making Puerto Rico a U.S. possession and Cuba, a protectorate. As a result, Cubans and Puerto Ricans viewed the United States with suspicion.

Immediately after the war, the people of Puerto Rico thought the United States would help them gain full independence and complete democracy. But by 1900, with the passage of the Foraker Act, the U.S. government had acted to restrict Puerto Rico's autonomy. Over time, Puerto Ricans achieved a greater share in the governing of their island, but not the complete independence many of them sought.

In Cuba, too, the United States acted to protect its interests, especially U.S. business interests. The Platt Amendment, added to the Cuban constitution at the insistence of the United States, gave the United States the right to intervene in Cuba to preserve order and to establish naval bases on the island. Many Cubans were unhappy with the Platt Amendment and accepted it reluctantly as the price of independence.

Historical Sidelight

U.S. Citizenship. Dissatisfaction with the status of Puerto Rico under the Foraker Act was intense and talk of independence widespread. In 1911, Secretary of War Henry L. Stimson visited the island and was made aware of Puerto Ricans' feelings. He suggested that the problem could be solved by binding Puerto Ricans even more closely to the United States by offering them the opportunity to become U.S. citizens. This idea was contained in the Jones Act, which took effect on March 2, 1917. Only 288 of Puerto Rico's people chose not to accept U.S. citizenship.

Resources

Chapter 15 Activity Sheet (p. 166)
Chapter 15 Test (p. 122)
Chapter 15 ESL/LEP Activity Sheet (p. 224)

Focus Activity

Have students read the chapter opener. Ask: How did the U.S. takeover in Cuba and Puerto Rico turn out differently from what the people there had expected?

Teaching Section 1: The United States and Puerto Rico (pp. 185–188)

Objective

• To compare the Foraker and the Jones acts

Developing the Section

Making a Chart. Have students make a chart with two columns and three rows. Label the columns "Foraker Act" and "Jones Act." Label the three rows "Provisions," "Advantages," and "Disadvantages." Have them complete the chart based on the information in Section 1.

Review and Practice

Assign Taking Another Look, p. 188.

Answers to Taking Another Look (p. 188)

1. According to the Foraker Act, the U.S. President appointed the upper house of Puerto Rico's legislature and the island's governor. Puerto Rico's legislation was reviewed by the U.S. Congress. Puerto Rico's representative in the U.S. House of Representatives could not vote. 2. He worked with Spain and later with the United States to gain self-government for Puerto Rico. He founded the newspaper *La Democracia*, served as Puerto Rico's representative in Congress, and worked tirelessly for six years to change the Foraker Act. 3. **Critical Thinking** A patriot would have resented the U.S. occupation, preferring self-rule for Puerto Rico.

Teaching Section 2: The Republic of Cuba (pp. 188–191)

Objective

• To explore how the Cuban people felt about the U.S. role in their country

Developing the Section

Drawing a Cartoon. Discuss the features of political cartoons. Ask students to draw a political cartoon that a Cuban might have drawn to show how he or she regarded the U.S. role in Cuba.

Review and Practice

Assign Taking Another Look, p. 191.

Answers to Taking Another Look (p. 191)

1. It gave the United States the right to intervene in Cuba to preserve order and to establish naval bases on the island. 2. It was a blessing in that it became the backbone of Cuba's economy. During the boom years, landowners and sugar mill owners grew fabulously rich. It was a curse because the country's economy was so dependent on a single crop. When sugar prices dropped, Cuba's entire economy suffered. 3. **Critical Thinking** Possible answer: Cubans had no experience with self-government and were easily fooled by those who promised reform.

Extending the Chapter

Collecting Political Cartoons. Remind students that the U.S. role in Puerto Rico and Cuba continues to be controversial. Ask them to try to find (or to draw) political cartoons concerning this topic as it applies today.

Looking Ahead

After students have read Looking Ahead, p. 191, ask them to predict ways in which the people of both islands "tried . . . to become masters of their own homelands." To provoke discussion, you might ask, "What would you have done?"

Answers to Close Up (pp. 192–193)

The Who, What, Where of History
1. kept Puerto Rico under the political control of the United States 2. Puerto Rican nationalist who served as the island's representative in the U.S. Congress 3. law that gave Puerto Ricans a greater role in governing their island 4. Puerto Rican labor leader and head of the Puerto Rican Socialist party 5. measure that gave the United States the right to intervene in the affairs of Cuba 6. Guantanamo Bay 7. elected president of Cuba in the mid–1920s who pledged reform and promised to reject the Platt Amendment but who was corrupt and came to rule as a dictator

Making the Connection
1. The island's location at the entrance to the Caribbean was important to the defense of the United States and its interests in the region. 2. granted U.S. citizenship to all Puerto Ricans who wanted it. 3. believed that statehood would give Puerto Rico more control over its economy and allow it to improve conditions there 4. U.S. business interests owned Cuba's profitable sugar mills and made sugar the backbone of the island's economy.

Time Check
1. 17 years 2. passage of the Platt Amendment; U.S. base established at Guantanamo Bay; revolt of the Cuban Liberal party; José Miguel Gómez becomes president of Cuba 3. 1912

What Would You Have Done?
1. **Yes:** could use the position to push for greater self-government for Puerto Rico. **No:** Puerto Ricans could not even vote in Congress, an indication of how little influence the Puerto Rican representative would have. 2. Possible answer: would resent having to agree to the Platt Amendment, which limited the freedom Cuba had won

Thinking and Writing About History
1. Letters will probably reflect a belief that the United States planned on helping Puerto Rico gain full independence. 2. **Disagree:** would remind Coolidge of the U.S.'s own struggle for independence and stress the importance of true democracy and self-government. **Agree:** mention the benefits of U.S. rule and argue that Puerto Rico had more freedom than it had enjoyed under Spanish rule 3. Speech would call for support in opposing the Platt Amendment, in ending corruption, and in instituting reform.

Building Skills
1. Possible generalization: The United States thought it should control Puerto Rico. 2. Possible generalization: The United States was not willing to give Cuba complete independence.

► UNIT 5 Changes in a New Century (pp. 194–247)

UNIT THEME

The 1910 revolution in Mexico uprooted thousands of Mexicans, who emigrated to the United States, where great social and economic changes occurred.

UNIT CONCEPTS

- During the long revolutionary struggle in Mexico, thousands of Mexicans entered the United States.
- Living in the United States changed the lives of the Mexican immigrants.
- Drawn by the demand for labor during World War I, Mexican and other Latino immigrants moved in increasing numbers to the United States.
- In the Great Depression of the 1930s, Latinos organized to fight for their rights.
- Thousands of Latinos served in the U.S. armed forces in World War II, and other thousands swelled the labor force as Mexicans were encouraged to emigrate to the United States.
- Latinos faced discrimination during World War II, which sometimes escalated into violence and riots.

UNIT OVERVIEW

Unit 5 describes the years from the 1910 Mexican revolution through World War II, during which hundreds of thousands of Mexicans emigrated to the United States. Along with the rest of the population, Latinos in the United States experienced two world wars and the Great Depression. Because of prejudice and racism, they organized to fight for their rights. When war came, they served with distinction in the U.S. armed forces. *The Big Picture* and the four chapters in this unit describe the industrial and foreign expansion of the United States and the effects on Latin America and: (1) the growth of immigration from Mexico to the United States, (2) the role of Latinos in World War I and its effect on their lives, (3) the struggle of Latinos to survive the economic hardships of the depression, and (4) changes in the lives of Latinos as a result of World War II.

COOPERATIVE LEARNING ACTIVITY

The following cooperative learning activity can be used for alternative assessment after study of the unit has been completed.

Divide the class into groups and have each group survey the unit to find evidence to support the following propositions: During the first half of the 20th century, Latinos in the United States faced racism, discrimination, and injustice. Despite economic and social hardships, Latinos found more opportunities in the United States than were possible in Latin America. When groups have finished gathering their evidence, ask spokespersons to report on each group's findings. Have students use the evidence they have gathered to write a paragraph answering this question: Why were thousands of Latinos determined to remain in the United States despite the conditions they faced? In evaluating students' work, consider how they have used the evidence to support their conclusions.

RESOURCES

Unit 5 Test (pp. 123–124)
Outline Maps: The Americas, the United States, the World (pp. 284, 285, 287)
Unit 5 Writing Workshop (pp. 269–272)
The Big Picture 5 ESL/LEP Activity Sheet (p. 225)

Unit 5 THE BIG PICTURE (pp. 194–201)

Theme

Industrial and foreign expansion by the United States in the first half of the 1900s had a significant impact on Latin America.

Overview

The Big Picture explores the economic and political changes occurring in the United States in the early to mid–1900s and their impact on Latin American nations that were struggling with social and economic problems. Industrial expansion in the United States brought prosperity to the nation and encouraged the large-scale immigration of Latinos as well as Europeans. Prosperity was accompanied by the expansion of U.S. economic interests in Latin America as the United States assumed the role of policeman of the Americas and repeatedly interfered in Latin American affairs. Following World War I and the prosperity of the 1920s, the United States was plunged into the Great Depression, which did not end until World War II. In Latin America, nations struggled to cope with political upheavals and social problems while faced with the growing power of the United States. In the 1930s, changing U.S. policies toward Latin America helped bring about better relations, and Latino support for the United States in World War II brought the hope that Latinos would gain economic opportunities and a better life in the United States.

Objectives

- To use a quotation to understand the impact of U.S. foreign expansion on Latin America
- To use a timeline to classify events in the United States and Latin America
- To express an opinion on the role of the United States in Latin America

Introducing *The Big Picture*

Write on the chalkboard the following statement by Senator Albert Beveridge of Indiana, spokesperson for U.S. commercial expansion in the early 1900s: "Ah! As our commerce spreads, the flag of liberty will circle the globe, and the highways of the ocean–carrying trade to all mankind–. . . be guarded by the guns of the republic." Ask: What is Beveridge's main point? (*U.S. expansion will bring liberty to others and will be guarded by guns if necessary.*) Ask: How do you think Latin Americans might have reacted to this idea? (*resentment, concern over U.S. economic domination and possible political domination*)

Using the Timeline

Divide students into small groups and refer them to the timeline on pp. 196–197. Ask each group to pick a decade and study the events listed. Have them classify the events in their decades under the headings Political, Economic, Social. Have groups report on their classifications and explain their reasons for the classification.

Teaching *The Big Picture*

Expressing an Opinion. Divide students into two groups, one to represent the views of U.S. leaders, and the other, the views of Latin American leaders on the role of the United States in Latin American affairs. Students may express their opinions in the form of letters, speeches, editorials, or reports. Have each group present its work to the other for class discussion.

Review and Practice

Assign Taking Another Look, pp. 199, 201.

Answers to *Taking Another Look* (pp. 199, 201)

p. 199: **1.** encouraged Panamanian revolution in Colombia and signed a treaty with independent Panama to build the canal **2.** claimed they were taking needed jobs from U.S. citizens **3. Critical Thinking** tremendous U.S. business investments in Latin America, need for cheap labor of Mexican immigrants by U.S. agriculture p. 201: **1.** redistribute land, build schools, support unions, nationalize industries, labor reform, extend voting rights, increase industrialization **2.** foreign investment dropped, shrinking demand for its exports resulted in less money to buy foreign goods, purchase of raw materials cut back **3. Critical Thinking** glad to be rid of foreign domination, perhaps better pay and working conditions under own government, better chance to organize unions

Chapter 16   The Mexican Revolution and New Patterns of Immigration (pp. 202–211)

Overview

In 1910, the people of Mexico were under the rule of dictator Porfirio Diáz. Although Diáz modernized Mexico in many ways, no opposition was allowed to his harsh, corrupt rule, which impoverished the majority of Mexicans. The revolution that followed was a time of chaos as bands of revolutionaries and soldiers fought back and forth and presidents rose and fell. By the time the revolution ended in the late 1920s, nearly a million Mexicans had died and thousands of others had fled to the United States. A source of cheap labor for U.S. industry, Mexicans worked at the lowest-paying jobs in factories and on farms. Many lived in crowded *barrios* in the cities; others became migrant workers.

Historical Sidelight

Crossing the Border. For Mexican immigrants, the journey north was a terrible ordeal. Most could not afford the train fare, so they walked. A young woman named Elisa Recinos traveled on foot for more than four months with her husband and child, heading for Texas. They lived on food they got from farmers along the way, and sometimes were able to sell bird cages they had made. Most of the time, they slept outdoors. If Mexican immigrants were lucky, they could pay the $8 head tax and pass the medical exam that finally allowed them to cross the border.

Resources

Chapter 16 Test (p. 125)
Chapter 16 Activity Sheet (p. 167)
Chapter 16 ESL/LEP Activity Sheet (p. 226)

Focus Activity

Read aloud the following quote by a Mexican immigrant about conditions caused by the revolution in Mexico: "I looked for work for a long time but everything had stopped, factories, mills, everybody was without work. With the farms burned there weren't even any tortillas left to eat."

Ask students what they might do under such circumstances. (*emigrate to the United States*) Have them speculate on what kinds of changes this would bring to the United States and to Mexicans who made their homes in the United States.

Teaching Section 1: Background to Revolution (p. 203)

Objective
- To gather evidence concerning the reasons for revolution in Mexico

Developing the Section
Gathering Evidence. Have students write down the motto of the dictator Porfirio Diáz: "little politics, much administration." Have them work in pairs or small groups to find evidence in the section that Diáz based his administration on this motto. Ask students to use the evidence they have gathered to give reasons why revolution began again in Mexico.

Review and Practice
Assign Taking Another Look, p. 203.

Answers to Taking Another Look (p. 203)
1. left them as poor as ever 2. jailed his opponent 3. **Critical Thinking** realized there was no way other than violence to win

Teaching Section 2: A Long Struggle (pp. 204–206)

Objective
- To evaluate the success or failure of revolutionaries like Villa and Zapata

Developing the Section
Writing Essays. Ask students to write an essay on the activities of the leaders Pancho Villa and Emiliano Zapata. The essays should cover the goals of Villa and Zapata and how successful they were in achieving them. Have students present their essays and discuss them. Ask which of the leaders they think had the most significant impact on the revolution.

Review and Practice
Assign Taking Another Look, p. 206.

Answers to Taking Another Look (p. 206)
1. redistribute land, improve education, limit influence of Church, recognize labor unions 2. arrest of

U.S. sailors, refusal of Mexican government to salute U.S. flag **3. Critical Thinking similar:** both backed revolution, both began with ideas of reform **differences:** Madero too weak to carry out reform; Carranza stronger, approved a constitution with reforms in it

Teaching Section 3: North from Mexico (pp. 206–209)

Objective
• To analyze changes in the way of life of Mexican Americans in the United States

Developing the Section
Role Playing. Have a group of students assume one of the following roles as a Mexican American: a migrant worker, a miner, a farmer, a store owner, a factory worker, a union organizer, a person who has returned to Mexico several times. Have students tell about themselves, their conditions of living and working, how they hope to better themselves, their relationships with Anglos, and why or why not they intend to remain in the United States. Ask them to talk about how their situations are similar or different and how their lives in the United States are different from their lives in Mexico. Then lead a class discussion on how the lives of Mexican Americans changed in the United States.

Review and Practice
Assign Taking Another Look, p. 209.

Answers to Taking Another Look (p. 209)
1. turmoil and chaos of the Mexican revolution **2.** farming, mining, factory work, as migrant workers **3. Critical Thinking** continuing revolution in Mexico, wages low but still better than in Mexico, security and help in the *barrios*, possibility of owning their own businesses

Extending the Chapter
Investigating the Present. Divide the class into groups and assign them to research present conditions of Mexican Americans. Topics may include: *barrio* life, working conditions, job opportunities, equality of rights, conditions of migrant workers, people in the arts, political and educational leaders. Have groups present their reports to the class and discuss how conditions have changed or how they have remained the same.

Looking Ahead
After students have read Looking Ahead, p. 209, ask them to suggest what influences they think the growing Mexican American community would have in the United States.

Answers to Close Up (pp. 210–211)

The Who, What, Where of History
1. more modernization but impoverishment for the majority and oppressive and corrupt government **2.** leader who called on Mexicans to revolt but who was too weak to carry out reforms **3.** revolutionary leader who worked for land reform **4.** invasion of Mexico to capture Villa **5.** escape revolutions, promise of a better life, excitement and adventure **6.** section of a city with large Latino population

Making the Connection
1. The significant factor in bringing about revolution was the farmers' lack of land, most of which was owned by relatively few rich people. **2.** The turmoil and chaos of the revolution led people to emigrate to escape its horrors.

Time Check
1. 1910 **2.** 1914.

What Would You Have Done?
1. Responses may include to immediately bring about land reform, make no compromises with his opponents, reduce the power of his opponents by controlling the military, stick to his principles of reform. **2.** Letters should show an understanding of the situation in Mexico and the problems faced by Mexicans in the United States and give reasoned answers for the writer's viewpoint.

Thinking and Writing About History
1. enduring and hardy, short of food, know how to escape and hide themselves **2.** well supplied with arms, stronger than Villa's forces **3.** Essay should reflect the fact that the United States was ill prepared for the pursuit, had no support among the people.

Building Skills
b. was given at the time events happened **d.** was written by a person who saw what happened **f.** document written at the time of the events **g.** photo taken at the time of the march

Chapter 17 Latinos and World War I (pp. 212–223)

Overview

The entry of the United States into World War I in 1917 had a significant impact on the Latino community. Thousands served in the war despite the fact that they were viewed with hostility and suspicion. While many Latinos were proving their loyalty in the fighting, others were contributing to the war effort on the home front. The need for workers created thousands of new jobs for Mexicans who moved to the United States. Mexican Americans also gained new opportunities as they moved into higher-paying and more skilled jobs, many of which they found in the cities of the Midwest and the North. Yet most Latinos still lived in poverty and were still the victims of racism and prejudice.

Historical Sidelight

The Oldest State Capital. Founded in 1609, Santa Fe, New Mexico, is the oldest of the 50 state capitals.. The plaza where Spanish, Mexicans, Anglos, and Native Americans once traded is still a center for bargaining and buying, and the Palace of the Governors is now a museum that reminds visitors of the city's Spanish roots. Festivals continually celebrate the people's Spanish heritage and, in the words of the Archbishop of Santa Fe, the people "wish to be identified correctly as longtime Americans by birth and nationality."

Resources

Chapter 17 Activity Sheet (p. 168)
Chapter 17 Test (p. 126)
Chapter 17 ESL/LEP Activity Sheets (p. 227)

Focus Activity

Have students read the chapter introduction on pp. 212–213. Ask them what Marcelino Serna accomplished. *(captured enemy soldiers singlehandedly.)* What was his reward? *(received some honors but not the highest U.S. honor)* Ask students what they think their attitudes might be toward the United States if they had been Serna. As students read the chapter, have them note examples of discrimination and the reactions of Latinos.

Teaching Section 1: Going to War (pp. 213–214)

Objective
• To find relevant facts to support a statement about the role of Latinos in the U.S. armed forces in World War I

Developing the Section

Finding Relevant Facts. Write the following statement on the chalkboard: "In spite of hostility and prejudice, Latinos served with courage and distinction in World War I." Ask students to look for at least four relevant facts in Section 1 to support this statement and list them on the chalkboard. Have the students write a paragraph using the statement as a topic sentence. Call on volunteers to read their statements and discuss them.

Review and Practice
Assign Taking Another Look, p. 214.

Answers to Taking Another Look (p. 214)
1. suspicious of their loyalty because of German intrigue in Mexico, Villa's raid, strike in California **2.** Serna: captured German soldiers; Lucero: destroyed two German machine gun positions **3. Critical Thinking yes:** to prove loyalty, to show courage; **no:** not want to serve because of prejudice against Latinos, American hostility, often kept at training camps and not allowed to fight

Teaching Section 2: Growing Immigration (pp. 214–219)

Objective
• To create questions about the increase in immigration from Mexico and its effect on the lives of Mexican Americans

Developing the Section

Creating Questions. When students have read Section 2, have them work in pairs or small groups to write a question for each subhead that relates to the effect of increased immigration on Mexican Americans. *(Example: How did new jobs in the United States provide opportunities for Mexican immigrants?)* Ask students to read their questions to the class and discuss them.

Review and Practice
Assign Taking Another Look, p. 219.

Answers to Taking Another Look (p. 219)
1. violence and disorder in Mexico, increased job opportunities in the United States **2.** *colonias:* communities of Mexican agricultural workers in villages and towns near their work; *barrios:* Latino neighbor-

hoods in cities **3. Critical Thinking** through mutual aid societies that gave help in civil rights matters, aided the sick, served as labor organizations, sponsored social and cultural activities, kept alive Mexican heritage

Teaching Section 3: Moving North (pp. 219–221)

Objective

- To write a letter summarizing conditions Mexican Americans faced in the North

Developing the Section

Writing to Congress. Divide students into small groups to write letters to their Congressional representatives about conditions faced by Mexican Americans in a northern city. Have them propose at least one law they think would help improve conditions. Have students read the letters aloud and discuss them.

Review and Practice

Assign Taking Another Look, p. 221.

Answers to Taking Another Look (p. 221)

1. wanted a better life than as farmworkers and expanding industry of the North promised better jobs and a better life **2.** Most found unskilled jobs in steel mills, stockyards, factories, railroads, restaurants, hotels **3. Critical Thinking advantages:** improved economic conditions because of better pay; **disadvantages:** cities strange, treated with hostility and prejudice, regarded as inferiors, treated harshly by authorities

Extending the Chapter

Investigating Conditions. Have students work in groups to further investigate working conditions in cities in the early 1900s. Have them research and report on Latino women in the work force, working conditions for European immigrants, problems of African American workers, workers' attempts to form labor unions. Ask them to present their reports orally for class discussion.

Looking Ahead

After students have read Looking Ahead, on p. 221, write the term *Great Depression* on the chalkboard. Point out that the Great Depression occurred in the United States in the 1930s. Call on students to suggest a definition of a depression. Lead them to understand that it was a period of hard economic times for all Americans. Discuss the effects it would have had on Latinos.

Answers to Close Up (pp. 222–223)

The Who, What, Where of History

1. Mexican American soldier in World War I whose bravery earned him honors but not the highest U.S. honor **2.** moved into higher-paying, skilled jobs, more work for women in factories **3.** Southern California **4.** Mexican American farming communities in small towns and villages **5.** provided aid in civil rights matters, helped the sick, promoted social and cultural life **6.** United Workers Union of Mexicans in California **7.** better-paying jobs, economic improvement

Making the Connection

1. The Jones Act granted Puerto Ricans U.S. citizenship so they could then serve in the military. **2.** Many more workers were needed, and Mexicans were encouraged to emigrate in great numbers to work in agriculture and industry. **3.** Living in the Southwest for generations, Latinos often resented newcomers who might increase competition.

Time Check

1. 1917 **2.** 1916

What Would You Have Done?

1. Almanzán: work is too hard for low pay, is not worth it to work with people who are so prejudiced. **Sepulveda:** has rights as a U.S. citizen and as much right to a job as an Anglo, is from Arizona, can fight back against discrimination **2. Southwest:** established Mexican communities with same language and religion, can work in industry or agriculture **New Mexico:** center of Mexican culture and gaining political power, cities in the North strange **Middle West or Northeast:** promise of better work with higher pay in expanding Northern industries, chance to rise economically

Thinking and Writing About History

1. extol bravery of Serna, question action and attitude of government, give reasons why Serna should have the medal **2.** point out strength in working together, support for individuals who need help, withholding labor is an effective weapon since employers need workers, but could be violence against union members, employers could fire them **3.** Letters may reflect outrage at the prejudice shown, support for Sepulveda's standing up to the baker; show understanding of what it is like to be discriminated against.

Building Skills

1. A fact is something that actually happened or is true. An opinion states a person's views that may or may not be based on facts. **2. facts:** form colonies; **opinion:** are unsettled, move readily from place to place, forming colonies and living in a clannish manner are unfavorable characteristics **3.** no; although Mexican Americans formed colonies, that in itself is not an unfavorable fact, only the writer's opinion; not all Mexican Americans move from place to place, not all are unsettled, and many lease or acquire land. **4.** more research into people's conditions **5.** would suspect writer's bias against Mexican Americans

Chapter 18   From Boom to Depression (pp. 224–235)

Overview

In the 1920s, the United States sharply curtailed immigration, except from Mexico. The economic boom of the period demanded more workers for U.S. farms and industries. Mexicans moved north in growing numbers. But dreams turned sour as the Great Depression gripped the United States in the 1930s. Production slowed dramatically, creating massive unemployment and pushing Latinos into even deeper poverty. Anger and resentment by Anglos at the loss of jobs were directed toward Mexicans, and thousands were forcibly returned home. Hope was revived when the New Deal created many programs of relief and recovery. Forced to struggle for survival, Latinos organized unions and formed groups across the country to fight for their rights.

Historical Sidelight

Repatriation. Jorge Acevedo lived in a Mexican American area of Los Angeles in the 1930s. Although a U.S. citizen, he was forcibly returned to Mexico in the 1930s. When rounded up, people were piled into trucks and vans. Families were often separated, and many drivers refused to stop for food or water. At the border, the people were simply dumped. Determined to return to the United States, Acevedo slipped across the border and, traveling at night and avoiding main roads, made the 2,500-mile (4,000-kilometer) journey back to Los Angeles. Acevedo later became a community leader and in 1967 was appointed director of the federal government's War on Poverty program in Santa Clara County.

Resources

Chapter 18 Activity Sheet (p. 169)
Chapter 18 Test (p. 127)
Chapter 18 ESL/LEP Activity Sheet (p. 228)

Focus Activity

Direct students to read the introduction to the chapter on pp. 224–225. Then ask them to write down the quote on p. 224, "Tell the people in the camp to organize. Only by organizing will they ever have decent places to live." As they read the chapter, have students find evidence to support or refute this advice. When the chapter is completed, ask them to write an essay explaining why this was or was not good advice.

Teaching Section 1: Boom Times of the 1920s (pp. 225–227)

Objective

• To write about the effects of the 1920s on Mexicans and Mexican Americans

Developing the Section

Writing Feature Articles. Write these headlines on the chalkboard: "Congress Passes Immigration Act of 1924," "Debate Rages Over Immigration from Mexico," "*Mutualistas* Grow as Latinos Organize," "Texas Latinos Form Civil Rights Group Called LULAC." Divide students into four groups, each to write a feature article using a headline above. Call on a spokesperson to read each group's article aloud to the class.

Review and Practice

Assign Taking Another Look, p. 227.

Answers to Taking Another Look (p. 227)

1. They needed workers. **2.** provided loans to begin businesses **3. Critical Thinking wise:** wanted to prepare Mexican Americans to be U.S. citizens first, Mexican Americans second;. **unwise:** would eventually cause Mexican Americans to lose their heritage

Teaching Section 2: Hard Times and the New Deal (pp. 227–230)

Objective

• To debate the issue of repatriation

Developing the Section

Debating an Issue. Divide the class into two teams to draw up arguments supporting or refuting this proposition: The United States was justified in repatriating Mexicans. Ask two students to list the pro and con arguments on the chalkboard, and conclude by having the class vote on the issue.

Review and Practice

Assign Taking Another Look, p. 230.

Answers to Taking Another Look (p. 230)

1. unemployment because of depression, usually gave available jobs to Anglos, heightened discrimination because of hard times **2.** Mexicans deported to Mexico because of claims they took jobs from Anglos **3. Critical Thinking** gave some relief in cash payments, at first got jobs on public works programs, later were barred if not U.S. citizens, got less in cash payments than Anglos; New Deal gave some relief, but policies discriminated; Latinos probably got less help than Anglos.

Teaching Section 3: Organizing for Strength (pp. 230–233)

Objective

- To understand how the treatment of Latinos led to organizing for their rights

Developing the Section

Analyzing a Primary Source. Read aloud this account by a government official who tried to intimidate a union organizer in New Mexico.

> Attempts were made by my office to intimidate Pallares [the union organizer] by withholding relief and by inventing reasons by which he could be removed from relief jobs. . . . Threats were made to starve his family in order to involve him in an argument which the relief agency hoped would give rise to violence on his part.

Divide students into small groups to prepare a paragraph or two explaining what effect they think the official's actions would have on Pallares and how Pallares might react. Guide students to understand how such treatment led to organizing and the uniting of Latinos to fight for their rights.

Review and Practice

Assign Taking Another Look, p. 233.

Answers to Taking Another Look (p. 233)

1. supply of workers larger than available jobs, so easy to replace workers who quit, national unions gave no support **2.** Confederation of Unions of Farm Workers and Mexican Workers **3. Critical Thinking** Violence toward workers made it difficult to organize them; working for civil rights would help unite all Latinos.

Extending the Chapter

Preparing Biographies. Assign groups of students to prepare biographies of union organizers and civil rights leaders of the 1930s. Allow time for library research. Have them present their biographies in a form similar to that used in the text.

Looking Ahead

After students have read Looking Ahead, p. 231, recall with them the experiences of Latinos in World War I. Discuss whether things might be the same or different for Latinos during World War II.

Answers to Close Up (pp. 234–235)

The Who, What, Where of History

1. 1921: set a temporary limit on immigration from outside Western Hemisphere; **1924:** lowered limits, making them permanent, cut off Asian immigration completely **2.** clubs organized by LULAC to teach English to preschoolers **3.** Confederation of Mexican Workers **4.** Return of Mexicans to their country during the Great Depression **5.** California **6.** Mexican American civil rights worker **7.** Congress of Spanish-Speaking Peoples.

Making the Connection

1. Limiting immigration from outside the Western Hemisphere made labor scarce, so employers hired more Mexicans. **2.** Massive unemployment caused people to blame Mexicans for taking jobs, so thousands of Mexicans were deported to leave jobs open for U.S. citizens.

Time Check

1. 4 **2.** 1938

What Would You Have Done?

1. yes: by learning English at an early age, would be able to cope better in U.S. society **no:** would be separated from Mexican heritage. **2. yes:** stronger with others, get better working conditions, higher pay; **no:** could not afford to lose wages if went on strike, could be violence and brutal treatment

Thinking and Writing About History

1. Responses should reflect happiness among friends or family, familiar ways of life, no prejudice or racism; yet miss friends in Chicago, times hard in Mexico

Building Skills

Population patterns: Latino population grew in northern states; many Mexicans repatriated in 1930s; U.S. Mexican population declined in depression **Work:** Efforts to organize Mexican farmworkers grew in 1920s; farmworkers staged many strikes in 1930s; new kinds of farm machinery reduced need for seasonal workers **Relations with Non-Latinos:**

Anglos took many jobs from Mexicans in 1930s; in the depression, Anglos claimed Mexicans took away their jobs; Mexicans formed new civil rights groups to fight for equal rights. Paragraphs should give reasonable, logical explanation for choice.

Chapter 19 Latinos and World War II (pp. 236–247)

Overview

Half a million Latinos served in the armed forces during World War II, fighting with distinction. Service in the war opened up new horizons. After the war Latino veterans took advantage of government benefits that offered educational and economic opportunities. As U.S. industry expanded for war, employers desperately looked for workers. Puerto Ricans and Mexican Americans worked in factories and on farms. To meet the labor shortage, the government began the controversial *bracero* program that brought in Mexican laborers to harvest crops and work on the railroads. The war brought many economic gains to Latinos but did not end racism and prejudice, which sometimes erupted into violence and riots.

Historical Sidelight

The Sleepy Lagoon Case. In August 1942, police found the body of a young man near the Sleepy Lagoon swimming hole in the Los Angeles *barrio*. They immediately arrested 300 Mexican American teenagers. Although there were no witnesses to the alleged crime, 22 young men were tried, of whom 12 were convicted of murder and sent to prison. At a pretrial hearing, the attitudes of the Los Angeles police toward Mexican Americans were revealed when an officer declared that "Crime is a matter of race," and therefore "race must be punished." Mexican Americans formed a defense committee to work for an appeal through a national campaign. The committee succeeded, and the verdict was reversed in 1944.

Resources

Chapter 19 Activity Sheet (p. 170)
Chapter 19 Test (p. 128)
Chapter 19 ESL/LEP Activity Sheet (p. 229)

Focus Activity

Make two columns on the chalkboard headed Problems and Progress. Ask students to consider problems Latinos might encounter during World War II and what progress they might make. Write these under the appropriate headings. As students read the chapter, have them modify the lists.

Teaching Section 1: Latinos in the Armed Forces (pp. 237–239)

Objective
- To write generalizations about Latinos in the armed forces in World War II

Developing the Section
Writing Generalizations. Have students work in small groups to write a generalization with two or more supporting facts for each of the four subheadings in the section. Have them read their reports for a class discussion on the question "What was military service like for Latinos during World War II?"

Review and Practice
Assign Taking Another Look, p. 239.

Answers to Taking Another Look (p. 239)
1. Mexican Americans, Puerto Ricans 2. benefits for job training and education 3. **Critical Thinking** patriotism, chance to prove oneself, expand experiences, gain new skills and benefits

Teaching Section 2: The Home Front (pp. 239–242)

Objective
- To analyze the controversy surrounding the *bracero* program

Developing the Section
Writing Letters. Divide students into small groups to represent one of the following: Mexican American farmer, Anglo farmer, union official, Mexican government official. Have them write a letter to the agency in charge of the program explaining their position on the *bracero* program and make recommendations for changes, if any, they would like to see made.

Review and Practice
Assign Taking Another Look, p. 242.

Answers to Taking Another Look (p. 242)
1. many more skilled jobs available and chance to gain economically 2. to bring Mexican laborers into the United States temporarily to work on farms and railroads; begun to meet labor shortage because of war 3.

THE LATINO EXPERIENCE IN U.S. HISTORY • © Globe Fearon

Critical Thinking advantages: guaranteed minimum wage, government protection from discrimination, could save some money; disadvantages: away from family, backbreaking work with long hours, poor housing and food

Teaching Section 3: Facing Prejudice (pp. 242–245)

Objective
- To recommend actions that might have been taken to avoid the riots in Los Angeles.

Developing the Section
Finding Alternatives. Divide the class into small groups and ask each to suggest at least three courses of action they would recommend that might have prevented the riots in Los Angeles. Remind them to consider the results of each suggestion. Have each group make its recommendations and encourage students to challenge one another's suggestions. Discuss which of the recommendations students think would have been most effective and why.

Review and Practice
Assign Taking Another Look, p. 245.

Answers to Taking Another Look (p. 245)
1. attacks against Mexican Americans in 1943 that began in Los Angeles and spread to other cities 2. encouraged riots by saying zoot-suiters needed a lesson 3. Critical Thinking a. a badge of honor and pride b. symbol of a gang youth who should be attacked and beaten

Extending the Chapter
Researching Political Progress. Explain to students that one result of World War II was a new awareness by Latinos that political action was necessary to gain their rights. Divide students into groups and have them research grass-roots political organizations, focusing on their goals and achievements. Groups include Unity Leagues, the Community Service Organization, the Council of Mexican American Affairs. Have students present their findings in oral reports and discuss how the organizations helped increase Latino political power.

Looking Ahead
After students have read Looking Ahead, p. 245, ask them to consider new courses of action Latinos could take to guarantee equality in political, social, economic, and educational areas.

Answers to Close Up (pp. 246–247)

The Who, What, Where of History
1. Mexican American soldier denied burial in his hometown in Texas 2. Philippines 3. New Mexican unit that laid railroad tracks across North African desert 4. Japanese-speaking Latino marine who persuaded more than 1,000 Japanese to surrender 5. provided educational and economic benefits to veterans 6. group that fought for equal treatment of Latino veterans in postwar life 7. agency created to guarantee equal treatment of workers in any industry that held government contracts 8. Mexican American historian and scholar who served as member of FEPC 9. Mexican laborers hired by U.S. employers to harvest crops and work on railroads 10. Mexican American teenagers in Los Angeles who adopted a certain style of dress as a badge of pride and honor

Making the Connection
1. Forum was established as a response to the discrimination against Longoria when he was denied burial in his hometown. 2. To make it possible for Latinos and African Americans to have skilled and semiskilled jobs needed for wartime industry, the FEPC was formed to bar discrimination against them.

Time Check
1. 4 2. 1943

What Would You Have Done?
1. Responses should show understanding of the benefits available under the bill. 2. yes: guaranteed minimum wage, protected from discrimination, can return home, save some money; no: long hours and very hard work, away from family, poor housing and food 3. Responses may include: leave, stay and insist on rights as a citizen, report it to local veterans' group, point out that you fought for your country, decide to form a group to fight for equality.

Thinking and Writing About History
1. Memos may discuss kind of work, wages made, coworkers, discrimination or not, chances for advancement. 2. Editorial should show understanding of facts of the system, why established, with opinion based on reasonable arguments.

Building Skills
1. a, b 2. a, c 3. b, c

▶ UNIT 6 A Changing Postwar World
(pp. 248–319)

UNIT THEME

Since World War II, nations of the Western Hemisphere have undergone political, economic, and social changes that have caused large numbers of Latinos from South and Central America to seek a new homeland in the United States.

UNIT CONCEPTS

- Puerto Ricans in large numbers left their island for the mainland to seek jobs.
- Many challenges faced the Puerto Rican migrants and Latino immigrants in the United States.
- Political upheavals and persecution in the Caribbean nations and Central and South America caused many people to emigrate.
- Latino organizations developed to help the Spanish-speaking immigrants overcome the difficulties of living in a new country.
- Latinos were encouraged by the Civil Rights Movement of the 1960s and 1970s to organize to improve their lives.
- Latino groups have sought to encourage the development of national and cultural pride.
- Latinos have enriched many aspects of the cultural life of the United States.

UNIT OVERVIEW

Unit 6 describes the movement of Spanish-speaking people to the United States since the 1950s, the challenges they faced, and the impact they have had on life in the United States. *The Big Picture* and the five chapters in this unit describe (1) movement of people from the Caribbean nations, (2) the struggle of Latinos to gain equal rights, (3) immigration from Central and South America, and (4) the impact of Latinos on U.S. culture.

In introducing this unit, you might want to examine contributions from various Latino cultures. You might have students listen to recordings of Latin music and note unusual rhythms and instruments. You might give each student a copy of Corky Gonzalez's poem *"Yo Soy Joaquín,"* to read, followed by a discussion of the poem in class. Other possibilities include the reading of a Puerto Rican folktale or a showing of one or two episodes of the "I Love Lucy" TV program. Whatever the choice, explain to the students that they will be studying about the various Latino cultures, the reason why people came here, the hardships they faced, and the contributions they have made to U.S. society.

COOPERATIVE LEARNING ACTIVITY

The following cooperative learning activity can be used for alternative assessment after study of the unit has been completed.

Divide the students into groups and assign each group one of the countries that is mentioned in the unit. Ask students to prepare a "Puerto Rican (or Dominican, Cuban, etc.) Culture Display" in which they present information about their particular country. They should include examples of the following: art, music, literature, graphs, charts, pictures, history, geography, food, costumes, customs, and leaders. You might ask each group to decorate a section of the classroom for its presentation. Photograph or videotape the presentations to show to other classes or invite other classes to see the presentations.

RESOURCES

Unit 6 Test (pp. 129–130)
Outline Maps: The Americas, Latin America, the United States (pp. 285, 286, 287)
Unit 6 Writing Workshop (pp. 273–276)
The Big Picture 6 ESL/LEP Activity Sheet (p. 230)

UNIT 6: THE BIG PICTURE (pp. 248–255)

Theme

The Cold War, the Civil Rights Movement, and political unrest in Central and South American nations during the years following World War II impacted the movement of Latinos to the United States and their lives here.

Overview

The Big Picture of Unit 6 deals with developments in the United States after World War II that affected Americans politically, socially, and economically. Following the war, the United States emerged as a world power challenged by the Soviet Union. A bitter Cold War developed between the two powers. In the United States, a great fear of communism developed, and some Americans were suspected of being Communist sympathizers. This fear of communism influenced U.S. foreign policy in Central and South America. The United States supported anti-Communist leaders and was often involved in the overthrow of left-wing and liberal regimes there. Most Latinos did not share in the economic boom that followed World War II. They were often treated like second-class citizens. Since they were among the newest arrivals in the United States and spoke little English, most of the new Latino residents lived together in urban *barrios* where conditions were often crowded. Some social progress was made, however, when African Americans led by Dr. Martin Luther King, Jr., began to press for their civil rights. Their gains benefited Latinos and Native Americans as well.

Objectives

- To understand the Cold War and the two instances when fighting developed
- To prepare an emotional anti-Communist speech that might have been given during the anti-Communist days in the United States
- To write a letter protesting U.S.-involvement in the affairs of a Central or South American nation
- To use a timeline to organize events that affected Latino movement to the United States

Introducing *The Big Picture*

Ask students to speculate on what might cause a Latino family to move from their country to the United States. List the reasons on the board and have the students copy them. The list might include: employment, home/community life, education, escape from religious and/or political persecution, join other family members, hope for a better future. Discuss the ease or difficulty of newly arrived Latinos' achieving any of the above. Tell students that they will be reading a section that will mention some of the reasons they listed. Ask them to put a check mark beside any they find and note the page number. After reading, go over their findings with them.

Using the Timeline

On the chalkboard, draw a timeline beginning with 1945/end of World War II and ending with 1970/overthrow of the Somoza family in Nicaragua. Ask the students to go back to the text and find other events that affected either Latino movement to the United States or Latino life in the United States. Have them copy the completed timeline.

Teaching *The Big Picture*

1. Preparing a Speech. Discuss first the Red Scare and its impact on Americans. Then discuss the components of an emotional speech *(does not need to be factual, plays on people's fears, seeks to persuade to the speaker's point of view)*. Divide the class into four groups, each with the task of preparing an emotional anti-Communist speech that might have been given to students like them during the Red Scare. Have them select one student from the group to deliver the speech after it has been cooperatively written.

2. Writing a Letter. After students have read the "In Latin America" section, have them write a letter to the President of the United States in which they protest U.S. intervention in their country. Have the students read their letters aloud or post them on a bulletin board.

Review and Practice

Assign Taking Another Look, pp. 253 and 255.

Answers to Taking Another Look (pp. 253 and 255)

p. 253: **1.** Korea and Vietnam **2.** charge people with political disloyalty with little or no evidence **3. Critical Thinking a.** Their gains benefited Latinos. **b.** nonviolent protests—sit-ins, mass marches. p. 255 **1.** Guatemala, Cuba, Dominican Republic, Chile, Nicaragua **2.** Socialist government nationalized many industries; reopened relations with Cuba **3. Critical Thinking** No, the United States wanted allies and did not want communism in the Western Hemisphere.

Chapter 20 The Great Migration from Puerto Rico (pp. 256–267)

Overview

Puerto Rico's political status changed after World War II from a colony to a commonwealth of the United States. As a commonwealth, it became a self-governing country with its own constitution, elected officials, flag, and national anthem, and with political and economic ties to the United States. Although conditions in Puerto Rico continued to improve during the 1950s and 1960s, many Puerto Ricans migrated to the United States, where wages were higher and jobs more plentiful than on the island. However, on the mainland they discovered prejudice against non-English-speaking people, job and housing discrimination, and limited educational opportunities. To help Puerto Ricans overcome these difficulties, community organizations were formed.

Historical Sidelight

Fish and Factories. Leticia Roman was known to all her neighbors near the Puerto Rican city of Ponce as Doña Licha. Every day for years, at five o'clock in the morning Doña Licha would go out in her boat for the day's catch of fish. Hundreds of boats would cover the water "like crabs on a beach," she recalls and adds sadly, "That was before the factories came." Now the giant chemical plants that sprouted in the region discharge hot water into the sea and foul the air with thick black smoke. The fish die by the thousands and are washed up on the beach as the tide recedes. Now Doña Licha relies on food stamps to help her buy food. "The Americans send the food stamps and we eat from them," she remarks. "But if it weren't for their factories and that smoke, I would be living from my boat and fish. So I suppose they owe me this. Anyway, they benefit from the smoke; I benefit from the stamps. We end up even. That's the American way of doing things." Doña Licha was content to remain on the island. Thousands of other Puerto Ricans, not willing to live on food stamps, left for the mainland in the years after the 1950s.

Resources

Chapter 20 Activity Sheet (pp. 171–172)
Chapter 20 Test (p. 131)
Chapter 20 ESL/LEP Activity Sheet (p. 231)

Focus Activity

Read to the students a short quote or a poem by or about a Puerto Rican, such as "AmeRican" by Tato Laviera (see *Tapestry: A Multicultural Anthology,* Globe Book Company, 1993, p. 357), that expresses strong feeling about being in the United States. Ask students for their reactions to the quoted material. Explain that their reactions may be similar to those of the Puerto Rican immigrants to the United States.

Teaching Section 1: A New Form of Government (pp. 257–260)

Objective

- To gather data and list the differences between a colony and a commonwealth

Developing the Section

Listing Differences. Tell students to divide their paper into two columns. Title one column "Colony" and the other "Commonwealth." Under each have them write information gathered from the section that pertains to each. This could be done as an individual, small group, or whole class activity.

Review and Practice

Assign Taking Another Look, pp. 259–260.

Answers to Taking Another Look (pp. 259–260)

1. World colonial empires broken up; the United States moved to liberate its own colonies. **2.** allowed Puerto Rico to have its own constitution **3. Critical Thinking** Either PPD, PIP, or PNP; reasons for choice based on text explanations of platforms.

Teaching Section 2: Meeting New Challenges (pp. 260–262)

Objective

- To write a letter home explaining challenges faced in the United States

Developing the Section

Writing a Letter. Have students use the information in the section about numbers of immigrants, where they settled, and how they encountered prejudice to write a letter to friends or relatives in Puerto Rico. The letter should either encourage or discourage emigration. Post the letters on a bulletin board.

Review and Practice

Assign Taking Another Look, p. 262.

Answers to Taking Another Look (p. 262)

1. through foreign investment change from agricultural to industrial society **2.** adjustment to climate,

THE LATINO EXPERIENCE IN U.S. HISTORY • © Globe Fearon

prejudice because of language, limited job and educational opportunities **3. Critical Thinking** They were U.S. citizens but were not treated as such.

Teaching Section 3: Lending a Helping Hand (pp. 262–265)

Objective
- To evaluate programs designed to help Puerto Ricans

Developing the Selection
Making an Evaluation. Divide the class into groups with each responsible for covering a support group developed to assist immigrants: the Office of the Commonwealth, Aspira, Puerto Ricans of All Ages, and one group to include the Puerto Rico Merchants Association, Puerto Rican Family Institute, and Puerto Rican Forum. Each group should prepare to tell the rest of the class what their organization did and evaluate whether or not it was successful.

Review and Practice
Assign Taking Another Look, p. 265.

Answers to Taking Another Look (p. 265)
1. established the Office of the Commonwealth **2.** promote educational achievement, develop sense of pride, make libraries more accessible to Spanish-speaking immigrants **3. Critical Thinking** help develop sense of pride by telling traditional folktales

Extending the Chapter
Producing a Puppet Show. Divide the class into groups. Have each group find a folktale from a different culture. Have them construct puppets (from very simple finger puppets to elaborate fabric puppets, as time allows) that will "tell" the folktale.

Looking Ahead
After students have read Looking Ahead, p. 265, have them speculate on what cultural richness the Puerto Rican migrants and those from other Spanish-speaking nations brought to the United States.

Answers to Close Up (pp. 266–267)

The Who, What, Where of History
1. South Bronx section of New York City **2.** small grocery stores **3.** governor of Puerto Rico when it became a commonwealth **4.** *Partido Popular Democratico* **5.** self-governing nation with political and economic ties to the United States **6.** Puerto Rican Independence Party, New Progressive Party **7.** peasants **8.** period from 1940 to 1970 when nearly 1.4 million people of Puerto Rican descent lived in the United States **9.** New Jersey farms **10.** employment service, translator, and guide to city services **11.** language barrier, high dropout rates, low-paying jobs **12.** co-founder of Puerto Rican Forum and Aspira **13.** library project aimed at reaching Spanish speakers in South Bronx **14.** director of South Bronx project

Making the Connection
1. The law allowed creation of the commonwealth. **2.** encouraged U.S. companies to build factories in Puerto Rico to provide jobs **3.** Cheap transportation to the United States became available.

Time Check
1. became a commonwealth **2.** PPD **3.** 1950s, 1960s

What Would You Have Done?
1. Answers should show an understanding of the purpose of Operation Bootstrap. **2.** Answers should reflect major problems faced by Puerto Ricans such as the language barrier, limited job or educational opportunities. **3.** Answers should reflect knowledge of the South Bronx Project.

Thinking and Writing About History
1. Story should include: Luis Muñoz Marín; becoming a commonwealth; July 25, 1952; fortress guarding San Juan harbor; celebration of becoming self-governing; passage of Public Law 600. **2.** Skit should reflect knowledge of Operation Bootstrap.

Building Skills: Interpreting Historic Statistics
1. South Bronx area of New York City **2.** 182,964 **3.** increase because of increase in first-generation Puerto Ricans **4.** increase, continue trend **5.** with increase in newcomers, growing need for assistance; immigrants moving to other cities

Chapter 21   New Arrivals from the Caribbean (pp. 268–281)

Overview
Political upheavals in the island nations of Cuba and the Dominican Republic produced many changes.

In Cuba the overthrow of Fulgencio Batista by Fidel Castro was greeted at first with great joy by the Cubans. However, within a year some Cubans were objecting to Castro's policies and his movement toward communism. Thousands of Cubans fled to Miami, Florida, as political exiles. In 1961, a plan to invade Cuba and overthrow Castro failed. By 1973, when Castro stopped granting exit permits, about 10 percent of Cuba's population had emigrated, mostly to Florida. In the Dominican Republic the assassination of President Rafael Trujillo led to government instability and uncertainty. Many Dominicans left the country for the United States. Most settled in New York City.

Historical Sidelight

U.S. Troops in the Dominican Republic. Because of the Dominican Republic's strategic location and business investments, the United States has sent its troops to the Caribbean republic several times. The first took place in 1916, when U.S. Marines were dispatched to create a National Guard to fight against guerrilla bands. The marines stayed until 1924. Rafael Trujillo was an ardent supporter of the U.S.-occupation force. He developed the National Guard into his own power base and used it to maintain control from 1930 to 1961.

Resources

Chapter 21 Activity Sheet (p. 173)
Chapter 21 Test (p. 132)
Chapter 21 ESL/LEP Activity Sheet (p. 232)

Focus Activity

Ask students what they think of when they hear the word *dictator*. List their responses on the board. Tell them that in this chapter they will read about some dictators and the effect the dictators had on their countries.

Teaching Section 1: Upheaval in Cuba (pp. 269–273)

Objective
- To list the impact of a dictatorial government on a country

Developing the Section
Listing Effects. After reading Section 1, make two columns on the chalkboard, one headed Positive, the other Negative. Have students volunteer information about Cuba under the dictatorships of Machado, Batista, and Castro to fill in under each heading.

Review and Practice
Assign Taking Another Look, p. 273.

Answers to Taking Another Look (p. 273)
1. instituted Communist regime with state ownership of land and businesses, increased taxes on foreign investors, state control of the economy, road and education improvements 2. to live in a country without the political and economic restrictions placed on Cuba by Castro 3. **Critical Thinking** Most Cubans in the United States now realized they would never return to Cuba to live.

Teaching Section 2: A Growing Cuban Presence (pp. 273–277)

Objective
- To depict the different waves of emigration from Cuba

Developing the Section
Depicting Emigration. Divide the students into three groups and give each a sheet of construction paper and colored pencils. Have each group draw pictures showing how the various groups of emigrants left Cuba. Group 1: 1962–1965, Group 2: 1965–1973, Group 3: 1974–present. Have students indicate the dates and encourage creative captions about their pictures.

Review and Practice
Assign Taking Another Look, p. 277.

Answers to Taking Another Look (p. 277)
1. banned flights, had to go through other countries or come on small boats across choppy seas 2. was losing its human resources 3. **Critical Thinking similar:** both very intelligent, helped Cubans living in Dade County, were successful in their careers; **different:** much more difficult for Miguel to come to the United States

Teaching Section 3: Turmoil in the Dominican Republic (pp. 277–279)

Objective
- To write a letter in agreement or disagreement with American intervention in Dominican affairs

Developing the Section
Writing a Letter. Have students read the section, paying careful attention to the involvement of U.S. Marines in 1965 and 1966. Discuss the reasons that President Lyndon Johnson may have had for sending them there and why Latin American nations objected. Then have the students write a letter to their members

of Congress either supporting the use of U.S. troops or attacking it.

Review and Practice
Assign Taking Another Look, p. 279.

Answers to Taking Another Look (p. 279)
1. supporters of Trujillo were threatened, confused political situation 2. to keep it from coming under Communist rule 3. **Critical Thinking** racial prejudice, language, environment

Extending the Chapter
Writing a Biography. Divide the class into groups of four. Each group must invent a biography about a fictional typical Cuban or Dominican immigrant to the United States. Biographies should include when, why, how subjects came to the United States; where they settled; what life in the United States was like for them; what obstacles they had to overcome; what contributions they have made to their community. One person from each group should read the biography to the rest of the class.

Looking Ahead
After students have read Looking Ahead, p. 276, have them speculate on the civil rights issues that would be important to U.S. Latinos.

Answers to Close Up (pp. 280–281)

The Who, What, Where of History
1. Communist leader of Cuba 2. broke them up into communes 3. one who leaves a home country for political reasons 4. Miami, Florida 5. Cuban exiles trained by CIA for armed invasion of Cuba 6. jungles of Guatemala 7. U.S. citizen of Cuban descent, first Cuban American officer in WAC, U.S. counterintelligence agent during World War II 8. dictator of Dominican Republic 1930–1961 9. welcomed immigrants, feared Communist takeover of Dominican government 10. New York City

Making the Connection
1. both dictators of Caribbean nations who had made themselves wealthy at the expense of their nation 2. left Cuba when Castro's government became Communist 3. The United States did not want another Communist nation in Caribbean.

Time Check
1. 1959: Castro overthrew Batista; 1961: failed Bay of Pigs invasion; 1962: October Crisis; 1965: agreement between Cuba and the United States to allow immigration 2. Cuban Missile Crisis 3. 1961

What Would You Have Done?
1. Answers should show an understanding of how Cuba had changed under Castro and communism and whether individual would be willing to live under these circumstances or flee. 2. Answers should reflect feelings of patriotism Cubans felt for their homeland as opposed to possibility that the attack would fail.

Thinking and Writing About History
1. Skits should convey Cubans' sense of despair at loss of life and realization that they would probably never be able to return to Cuba to live. 2. Speech should include his pride in his heritage and the difficulties that he had to overcome. 3. Letter might note cold climate, tall buildings, school, language, racial difficulties.

Building Skills
1. great pride in Cuban contributions 2. any points from second paragraph 3. as an important link between the United States and Latin American nations 4. The facts cited lead to this conclusion.

Chapter 22   The Struggle for Equal Rights (pp. 282–295)

Overview
The decades of the 1950s, 1960s, and 1970s were turbulent times for ethnic groups in the United States who were seeking their civil rights. This chapter tells about the struggles primarily of Mexican Americans to obtain better working conditions, to regain land lost by the Mexican Americans after the Treaty of Guadalupe Hidalgo, to create self-help groups, and to gain political strength. It also tells of the achievements of several prominent leaders in these struggles and their desire to instill cultural pride in the Mexican American people.

Historical Sidelight
Identity. This poem (which will be used in teaching Section 1) was written by Julio Noboa Polanco, who was born in the Bronx of Puerto Rican parents. The poem expresses the idea of individual strength and freedom, an idea that formed the basis of the struggles of many Latinos in the United States.

Identity

Let them be as flowers,
always watered, fed, guarded, admired,
but harnessed to a pot of dirt.

I'd rather be a tall, ugly weed,
clinging on cliffs, like an eagle
wind-wavering above high, jagged rocks.

To have broken through the surface of stone,
to live, to feel exposed to the madness
of the vast, eternal sky.
To be swayed by the breezes of an ancient sea,
carrying my soul, my seed, beyond the mountains
    of time
or into the abyss of the bizarre.
I'd rather be unseen, and if
then shunned by everyone, than to be a pleasant-
    smelling flower,
growing in clusters in the fertile valley,
where they're praised, handled, and plucked
by greedy, human hands.

I'd rather smell of musty, green stench
than of sweet, fragrant lilac.
If I could stand alone, strong and free,
I'd rather be a tall, ugly weed.

Resources

Chapter 22 Activity Sheet (p. 174)
Chapter 22 Test (p. 133)
Chapter 22 ESL/LEP Activity Sheet (p. 233)

Focus Activity

Ask students what rights they think are the most important ones they or their parents enjoy in the United States. List them on the chalkboard. Ask students to think about what they might do if they were part of a group living in the United States that did not have these rights. Discuss their ideas and then tell them they will be reading about what Mexican Americans have done to gain their civil rights.

Teaching Section 1: La Causa (pp. 283–287)

Objective

• To interpret poetry and relate it to social and political struggles

Developing the Section

1. Interpreting and Relating Poetry. After reading Section 1, have students meet in small groups. Each group should make a chart with the following headings: Leader, Cause, Outcome, Additional Infor-

mation. Have them go through the section and complete the chart. (You may want to divide the section into smaller parts and assign each group one of the parts.) When they have completed this assignment, give each student a copy of the poem by Polanco (see the Historical Sidelight for this chapter) and have them read it silently. Ask them to write down their first reaction/feeling to the poem. Then ask them to write why this poem might appeal to any of the people whom they have listed on their chart. Read the poem orally and discuss the idea of conformity versus independence and one's identity. Tie this discussion into the ideas in Section 1.

Review and Practice

Assign Taking Another Look, p. 287.

Answers to Taking Another Look (p. 287)

1. to organize migrant farmworkers to obtain better wages and working conditions **2.** strike, boycott, march to Sacramento, fast against violence **3. Critical Thinking** Answers should show understanding of the conditions of the migrant workers and why it was important to organize in order to bring about changes. Yet some migrant workers might not join because they could not afford to be without an income during a strike and they feared reprisals by farm owners.

Teaching Section 2: A Time for Action (pp. 287–293)

Objective

• To list ways in which activists can achieve change

Developing the Section

Listing Activist Tactics. Put the following list on the board: Luis Valdez, Rubén Salazar, Reies López Tijerina, Rodolfo "Corky" Gonzales, José Angel Gutiérrez, MALDEF, The Young Lords. Have the students read the section and write down the methods used by each of the listed individuals or groups to achieve its goals. Have them list any other methods used that were mentioned in Section 1. Then divide the students into small groups and have each group develop a plan for obtaining a particular goal, for example, better working conditions, health benefits, voter turnout, educational opportunities, or any other appropriate goal. Remind them that their first effort may not meet with success. What will be their follow-up plans? Have each group report its plan.

Review and Practice

Assign Taking Another Look, p. 293.

Answers to Taking Another Look (p. 293)

1. instill pride, gain full civil rights 2. did not reflect U.S. citizenship 3. **Critical Thinking** Answers should reflect knowledge of gains of Latino rights movements: cultural pride, political representation, unionization of farmworkers, public awareness of unjust laws and conditions, emergence of self-help groups, educational assistance (bilingual programs), improved health care.

Extending the Chapter

Conducting an Interview. Pair students and have them do further research on any one of the people mentioned in the chapter or any other prominent Latino leaders currently in the news. Then direct them to prepare a television interview with that person. The interviewer should ask probing, interesting questions that will allow the student taking the role of the interviewee to relate anecdotes to the audience.

Looking Ahead

After students have read Looking Ahead, p. 293, have them speculate on the differences newly arrived Latinos today might find compared to those who came to the United States prior to the 1960s.

Answers to Close Up (pp. 294–295)

The Who, What, Where of History

1. farmworkers' union 2. strike 3. DiGiorgio Corporation vineyard in Delano, California 4. cofounder of NFWA 5. name of farmworkers' movement to gain improved working conditions and civil rights. 6. Mexican American political activist, founder of *La Cruzada Para la Justicia* 7. party aimed at gaining political control for Chicanos 8. organization of young Puerto Ricans in New York City who fought for rights

Making the Connection

1. *La Causa* was formed in part to overturn the law that allowed farm owners to hire *braceros*. 2. The successes of the Civil Rights Movement and support from its leaders encouraged Mexican American leaders to move forward in their organization of the migrant farm workers. 3. Chicanos protested the high death rate of Mexican Americans in a war that was draining off funds that could have been used to help Mexican Americans in the United States.

Time Check

1. 1965 2. *La Causa*, 1962

What Would You Have Done?

1. Answers should reflect the goals of the unionization movement and the risks that workers took in joining. 2. Answers should reflect either the idea that many looked upon the term *Chicano* in a negative manner because it did not reflect U.S. citizenship, or Rubén Salazar's definition of *Chicano*. 3. Answers should reflect the idea of civil disobedience and how far students feel it should be taken.

Thinking and Writing About History

1. Students should include a physical description of Chávez, Robert Kennedy's and Ethel Kennedy's participation, the sharing of bread, and the statement written by Chávez. 2. The *acto* should poke fun at vineyard owners and promise victory for the farmworkers. 3. The timeline should include items listed in Snapshot of the Times, p. 287, as well as the end of the *bracero* program (1964), the NFWA strike against DiGiorgio vineyard (1965), farmworkers' march to Sacramento (1966), Chávez's fast (1968).

Building Skills

1. writer's father, a farmworker 2. great respect for their difficult labor 3. Father cannot write, but he can make straight furrows, indicating pride in his work, difficult working conditions (heat), father's contribution is as good as anything written. 4. to remind himself of importance of individual farmworkers and how valuable what they produce is to the whole world

Chapter 23 New Immigrants from Central and South America (pp. 296–303)

Overview

Immigration from South and Central America increased dramatically after the 1960s. Most of the newcomers left their homes because of political and economic instability or repressive governments. This chapter looks at causes for immigration from Guatemala, El Salvador, Nicaragua, Argentina, Colombia, Uruguay, and Chile. It also tells about U.S. involvement and support of anti-Communist governments.

Historical Sidelight

Operation Peter Pan. In 1959, shortly after the Castro takeover, rumors spread that the Cuban government was planning to issue *Patria Potestad* ("Paternal

Authority"), a decree to take children away from their parents. Immediately, the Catholic Bureau set to work. It organized a save-the-children project known as Operation Peter Pan. This consisted of an underground network that provided parents with passports and false visas to allow them to send their children out of the country. Parents who faced prison because of their political beliefs were willing to send their children away from the growing oppression. Until the operation ended in 1962, it is estimated that over 14,000 children left Cuba without their parents and lived with foster families in other countries.

Resources
Chapter 23 Activity Sheet (p. 175)
Chapter 23 Test (p. 134)
Chapter 23 ESL/LEP Activity Sheet (p. 234)

Focus Activity
Give the students a map of Central and South America and help them locate and outline the following countries: Guatemala, El Salvador, Nicaragua, Argentina, Colombia, Uruguay, and Chile. On the chalkboard also list the names of the countries and tell students that in this chapter they will be studying about events in recent years in these countries and why so many people have left their homes to come to the United States.

Teaching Section 1: Struggle for Democracy in Central America (pp. 297–299)

Objective
• To link history and geography in Latin America

Developing the Section
Linking History and Geography. After reading the section, divide the students into three groups representing Guatemala, El Salvador, Nicaragua. Give each group a sheet of butcher paper or construction paper. Have students draw a large map of their country showing latitude and longitude, mountains, rivers, lakes, major cities. Then have them research each country for the population, the distribution of wealth, the major agricultural and industrial products, the type of government and its current leaders. Direct the students to arrange this information on the sheet with the map and have them present it to the rest of the class. (A similar activity could also be used with Section 2 of the chapter, which includes Argentina, Colombia, Uruguay, and Chile.)

Review and Practice
Assign Taking Another Look, p. 299.

Answers to Taking Another Look (p. 299)
1. to turn land over to peasants 2. political unrest, economic inequality, encouragement by rebel leaders in one country to other countries to take up arms, policies of Roman Catholic Church calling for "social justice" for the poor, TV and newspaper coverage of human rights abuses 3. **Critical Thinking In favor:** helped eliminate a system that would place severe restrictions on political and economic freedom; **opposed:** just another example of U.S. intervention in Central America, plus the fact that the United States regarded every attempt at liberal reform as Communist or Communist inspired.

Teaching Section 2: New Voices from South America (pp. 299–301)

Objective
• To explore the cultural richness of South American countries

Developing the Section
Exploring Cultural Richness. After students read this section, divide the class into four groups representing Argentina, Colombia, Uruguay, and Chile. Have each group research the cultural traditions (music, folklore, literature, dance, art, clothing, festivals) of each country. Each group should present its findings to the class using both audio and visual aids in the presentation.

Review and Practice
Assign Taking Another Look, p. 301.

Answers to Taking Another Look (p. 301)
1. because of the terror of "the dirty war" 2. **Colombia:** government repression, banditry, guerrilla warfare; **Uruguay and Chile:** government coups followed by repressive regimes 3. **Critical Thinking similarities:** language, escaped harsh political regimes, mostly middle-class; **differences:** cultural traditions of each country, ethnic backgrounds of immigrants

Extending the Chapter
Making a Mural. Divide the class into seven groups: Guatemala, El Salvador, Nicaragua, Argentina, Colombia, Uruguay, and Chile. Give each group a length of butcher paper to design a mural representing its country. Pictures may be drawn or cut from magazines. Students can add graphs, charts, and maps—anything that will help tell their country's story. Hang the murals in the classroom and invite other classes in to see them.

Looking Ahead

After reading Looking Ahead, p. 301, have the students name as many Latino artists, writers, and entertainers as they can. List them on the board and tell students that they will have an opportunity to study about some of these people in the next chapter.

Answers to Close Up (pp. 302–303)

The Who, What, Where of History

1. sudden overthrow of the government 2. help landless peasants and improve conditions in Guatemala 3. Roman Catholic leader in El Salvador who was assassinated 4. group that overthrew Somoza in Nicaragua 5. waged by military leaders in Argentina against anyone who opposed them 6. Colombia 7. Chilean author and teacher

Making the Connection

1. The United States was determined to keep Soviet influence and communism out of the Western Hemisphere 2. Military leaders in Argentina kidnapped any who opposed the government; those never seen again became known as the *desaparecidos* (disappeared ones). 3. Political repression and instability led to increased immigration.

Time Check

1. CIA intervention in Guatemala 2. killing of Father Rutilio Grande, who was working for reform, focused world attention there

What Would You Have Done?

1. Answers should focus on repressive governments, human rights violations, economic changes as well as risks to life and family safety 2. Answers should reflect knowledge of conditions within the country, risks involved in staying, and hopes for the future 3. Probably none because military and police were so strong; however, some might mention work in underground movements or reform movements sponsored by Catholic Church.

Thinking and Writing About History

1. The editorial should tell about human rights violations and suggest that the United States cease all aid to and trade with Guatemala. 2. The eulogy should mention efforts made by Romero or Grande to stop terror and repression in El Salvador and how he was stopped by assassination 3. U.S. government would support Somoza regime as being preferable to communism or socialism. The Cuban government would urge the overthrow of Somoza. The Sandinistas would stress their pride in the leadership of Augusto Sandino, who led peasant army against U.S. Marines in 1926. 4. The skit should include pride in culture (folklore, music, dance) 5. The petition should stress human rights violations and the terror felt by citizens.

Building Skills

The propaganda might describe Arbenz's reforms as radical and Communist inspired, influenced by the Soviet Union.

Chapter 24   A Growing Voice (pp. 304–319)

Overview

Beginning in the 1950s and continuing into the 1990s, Spanish-speaking people came to the United States in increasing numbers. By the early 1980s the United States had become the fourth-largest Spanish-speaking nation in the world. These people brought cultural richness and diversity and blended it into the overall pattern of U.S. culture. This chapter examines the contributions of Latino writers, artists, and entertainers who have had an impact on U.S. life.

Historical Sidelight

Latino Readers and Viewers. The host of Latinos of long standing and the flood of newer Spanish-speaking people have created a new market for Spanish reading material and for the broadcasting industry. Over 100 Spanish-language newspapers are published in addition to magazines such as *Regenera-*cion and *La Raza*. A newer English-language magazine for Hispanic women, *Latina*, provides articles about health, fashion, films, and cooking and is typical of the many women's magazines for the general audience. The English-language magazine *Hispanic* tracks trends and developments in the Latino community. By 1980, there were countless Spanish-language radio stations. The fact that 23 commercial Spanish-language television stations can operate profitably is an indication of the growing economic importance of Latinos in the United States. Because of the size of the Latino market, television is a major Latino business enterprise.

Resources

Chapter 24 Activity Sheet (p. 176)
Chapter 24 Test (p.135)
Chapter 24 ESL/LEP Activity Sheet (p. 235)

Focus Activity

Give students a list of names of the people who appear in this chapter. Explain that they are all writers, entertainers, and popular figures in the Latino community. Pronounce the names with the students, and then tell them to make brief notations about each as they read about them in the chapter.

Teaching Section 1: New Cultural Perspectives (pp. 305–315)

Objective
- To understand the impact Latino writers and artists have had in sharing their culture in the United States

Developing the Section
Understanding the Impact of Writers and Artists. Tell students to read Section 1. But before beginning they are to divide a sheet of paper into three columns, headed Writer/Artist, Cultural Origin, Impact/Message. As they come across a reference to a writer, a group of writers, or an artist in their reading, they should note it on their charts and fill in the columns. Then they should compare their charts with those of other students.

Review and Practice
Assign Taking Another Look, p. 315.

Answers to Taking Another Look (p. 315)
1. encouraged creative expression, helped promote Puerto Rican culture on mainland, increased Puerto Rico's cultural independence, encouraged pride in national identity 2. writers struggled with idea that they were now exiles, and those who had supported the revolution felt betrayed; felt caught between two cultures. 3. told of struggles faced by Mexican Americans and urged them to cling to their culture

Teaching Section 2: Reshaping Popular Culture (pp. 315–317)

Objective
- To interview a famous Latino entertainer or sports figure

Developing the Section
Preparing an Interview. Pair the students and have pairs prepare questions they might ask one of the Latino entertainers or popular figures mentioned in the section in an interview. After further research, one student in each group should assume the role of the interviewee and answer the questions. As a final step, students might write a news article based on the information of the interview.

Review and Practice
Assign Taking Another Look, p. 317.

Answers to Taking Another Look (p. 317)
1. music with an African-Caribbean beat and dances such as the mambo and the cha-cha-cha 2. Number of Latinos in the United States grew, and more went into entertainment fields. 3. **Critical Thinking** increase awareness of Latino culture, showcase talents of Latino artists

Extending the Chapter
Preparing a Game. Divide students into groups of four. Each group should research prominent Latino writers, artists, or entertainers not mentioned in the textbook and prepare a brief biography of that person.

Looking Ahead
After students have read Looking Ahead, p. 317, point out that according to the 1990 census, the Latino population in California constituted about 25 percent of the total population of the state. Over half were between the ages of 24 and 35. Ask the students to predict the growth of the Latino population in the United States over the next 10 to 20 years and describe the changes that might occur because of this growth.

Answers to Close Up (pp. 318–319)

The Who, What, Where of History
1. Puerto Rican painter, helped promote Puerto Rican culture in the United States 2. New York businessperson who founded Puerto Rican Heritage Publications to publish literary works by Puerto Rican writers 3. center for creative artists in Puerto Rico 4. New York City 5. urged Mexican Americans to cling to their culture and not surrender it to the Anglo way of life 6. Judith Baca, Los Four, the Royal Chicano Airforce, and *Las Mujeres Muralistas* 7. mambo, cha-cha-cha, merengue, bombas, plenas, salsa 8. musician known for adding African Caribbean drums and rhythms to rock-and-roll 9. baseball legend from Puerto Rico

Making the Connection
1. The Instituto encouraged a cultural renaissance and national identity for Puerto Ricans. 2. Cuban writers exiled in the United States found their ties to home cut by the revolution, and their writing reflected the struggle of being an exile holding on to dreams of returning home one day. 3. Movement increased pride in their Mexican heritage, encouraged writers to look to their Mexican past, and led to great outpouring of literature.

THE LATINO EXPERIENCE IN U.S. HISTORY • © Globe Fearon

Time Check
1. 1960s 2. *El Movimiento* 3. 1984

What Would You Have Done?
1. Answers should include reference to national pride and cultural renaissance. 2. possibly a movie for a broad audience but showcasing Latino artists

Thinking and Writing About History
1. Review should refer to Puerto Rican poets who show special pride in their African Caribbean heritage 2. Poem should reflect love of home and desire to return someday. It could also reflect feeling of betrayal of ideals of the revolution. 3. Poster should be colorful, mural-like, reflecting pride in heritage. 4. Mention should be made of Latin dances and rhythmic music.

Building Skills
1. a name he chose 2. negative opinion 3. suggests cultural independence 4. too extreme, shows no tie to United States

⊵ UNIT 7 Latinos Today
(pp. 320–391)

UNIT THEME

    Latinos are the fastest-growing ethnic group in the United States, and their influence on society, culture, and politics is increasing. Many Latinos are recent arrivals in the United States, having left their own countries because of economic and political turmoil. Many of the already established Latino communities in the United States help the newcomers adjust to their new homes.

UNIT CONCEPTS

- Mexican Americans have grown as a political force.
- U.S.-Mexico trade relations are undergoing review in connection with the North American Free Trade Agreement.
- Migration patterns of Puerto Ricans are changing.
- Cuban Americans are the most successful Latino group in terms of income and social status.
- Central Americans have fled violence and persecution in their native countries.
- A wide network of agencies has helped Central American refugees in the United States.
- Dominicans come to the United States to escape from the poverty of their homeland.
- South Americans seek economic opportunities and political freedom in the United States.
- The Latino population in the United States is increasing faster than any other group.
- Poverty is the primary problem facing many Latinos.
- Latino influence on U.S. politics, society, and culture has grown markedly.

UNIT OVERVIEW

    Unit 7 deals with the present status of Latinos in the United States. The chapters outline the reasons why people from South and Central America migrate north and describe their new lives in the United States. Latino communities across the nation have set up self-help networks. U.S. government policies became conservative in the 1980s, and social spending was cut. Support for civil rights and the plight of those fleeing oppressive regimes was not a priority of the government.

    In teaching the unit, you might discuss with students the question of social responsibility. Ask students what they think about protecting those who cannot fight for their own cause. Have students consider protection and violation of human rights. Ask what students think of the use of sanctions against countries with a history of human rights abuses.

COOPERATIVE LEARNING ACTIVITY

    A cooperative learning project that can be carried out with this unit involves the creation of a survival guide for life in the United States. Such a guide might consist of the names of people and local and national agencies that people in need of help can contact, as well as practical down-to-earth suggestions as to what they can do in case of emergencies. Outline the project with the class in order to agree on the focus the project should have and what the responsibilities of the cooperative groups should be. Encourage the use of library resources to find the names and addresses of foreign embassies, national and international aid organizations, and watchdog groups such as Amnesty International.

RESOURCES

Unit 7 Test (pp. 136–137)
Outline Maps: The Americas, Latin America, United States (pp. 285–287)
Unit 7 Writing Workshop (pp. 277–280)
The Big Picture 7 ESL/LEP Activity Sheet (p. 236)

Unit 7 The Big Picture (pp. 321–327)

Theme

The United States and the countries of Latin America are forging new ties as the United States changes its policies from intervention in the affairs of these countries to respect for the governments' ability to cope with their problems.

Overview

During the 1980s under the Reagan administration, while the country was undergoing a prolonged period of prosperity, the United States became more conservative. Spending for social programs was cut while the military budget mushroomed. As the Cold War with the Soviet Union continued, the United States sought to make sure that the governments of Latin American countries would be pro-United States and anti-Communist. But, with the waning of the Cold War in the late 1980s and a recession at home, the U.S. government began to lose interest in policing the internal affairs of Latin American countries. This shift allowed Latin American countries to try to work out their problems without interference from the United States. In a number of countries, democratic governments replaced military dictatorships. Economic hardship, however, still plagued the region. Several countries began to work together to create economic stability. Still, the effects of the violence and inflation that marked the 1980s continued to be felt into the 1990s, and there was no lessening of large-scale migration to the United States, both legal and illegal.

Objectives

- To redefine the United States as something other than a melting pot
- To understand that U.S. relations with countries of Latin America changed from one of control to one of respect
- To bring the history of Latinos up to date

Introducing *The Big Picture*

Read the section "In the United States." Ask if any students have encountered the term *melting pot*. Share responses. Ask them to consider what the melting-pot image implies for the individual cultural groups in the United States. Then have students discuss whether the melting pot is an accurate metaphor for the United States. Ask them to come up with other images or metaphors that they believe may represent the cultural and ethnic mix of the country more accurately. Ask students to draw pictures or cartoons of the images that seem suitable. Share these with the class.

Using the Timeline

Divide the class into small groups. Have each group choose a different event on the timeline on pp. 322 and 323. Have each group explain how the event it selected might have affected the lives of Latinos in the 1980s.

Teaching *The Big Picture*

Developing Background Information. Write the names of Latin American countries on the chalkboard. If you have space, list all the countries named in the unit. Divide the class into research groups. Each group is to choose a country or group of countries and provide background information about the countries and their relations with the United States. Each group should cover the geographic location, type of government, the nature of the economy, and the racial or ethnic makeup. Have a member of each group present its findings to the class.

Review and Practice

Assign Taking Another Look, pp. 325 and 327.

Answers to *Taking Another Look*

p. 325: **1.** cut spending on social programs, opposed affirmative action, increased military spending **2.** invaded Panama to overthrow President Manuel Noriega, fought Operation Desert Storm in Kuwait **3. Critical Thinking** Possible answers: introduce new foods, influence popular music and culture, provide cheap labor p. 327: **1.** developed a peace plan to end the fighting between Sandinistas and Contras in Nicaragua **2.** heavy debts to the U.S. and Europe, slump in oil prices, global recession **3. Critical Thinking** reduced inflation, paid off debts to other countries, developed new industries

Chapter 25   Mexican Americans Today (pp. 328–337)

Overview

Mexican Americans have moved from rural areas into cities such as San Antonio and Los Angeles. Many Mexican Americans who have entered the United States illegally live in fear of deportation. In 1986, the United States passed the Immigration Reform Act, which granted amnesty to undocumented workers who could prove they had been in the United States since 1982. Since 1965, U.S. companies have built assembly plants on the Mexican side of the U.S.-Mexico border. These plants have brought employment to poor towns, but the wages are low and the plants have caused a great deal of pollution. It is expected that when the North American Free Trade Agreement (NAFTA) goes into effect, Mexico will benefit from the establishment of the world's largest free-trade region.

Historical Sidelight

NAFTA. The idea for the North American Free Trade Agreement (NAFTA) began in the early 1980s. It is an attempt to combine the 370 million people of the United States, Mexico, and Canada into a single free-trade zone with a six-trillion-dollar economy. Mexico initially viewed the idea suspiciously. It seemed like another "gringo" trick to cheat Mexico. "Poor Mexico—so far from God, so close to the United States!" has been a popular Mexican saying for years. But as the Mexican economy grew more stable, the idea took hold. One objection to the treaty raised in the United States is that the country would lose many manufacturing jobs to low-wage factories in Mexico. Mexico looks at the problem from another point of view. It fears that Mexico would be a source of low-paying unskilled labor but that jobs requiring higher skills would remain in the United States or Canada. To help solve this problem, community colleges in the United States have created the Internal Consortium for Educational and Economic Development to help Mexico provide the education and training that would upgrade its workers.

Resources

Chapter 25 Activity Sheet (p. 177)
Chapter 25 Test (p. 138)
Chapter 25 ESL/LEP Activity Sheet (p. 237)

Focus Activity

Have the students read the introduction to this chapter and reread the section "Mojados in Texas" on p. 240 of Chapter 19. The class should list the differ-ences between the sections. Students should note that in Chapter 19 the Mexican Americans were shown as victims, while Chapter 25 depicts Mexican Americans as a political force to reckon with. Have students discuss or write about why they think this change came about.

Teaching Section 1: A Tale of Three Cities (pp. 329–332)

Objective

- To compare the cities of New York, San Antonio, and Los Angeles as homes of Mexican Americans

Developing the Section

Comparing and Contrasting. After reading the section, divide the class into three groups, each representing one of the three cities. Each group should prepare a digest of how Mexican Americans in the city live, including reasons why they think so many chose to settle in that city. Have a member of each group read its report. Then conduct a discussion of what the three cities have in common and how the Mexican American communities there are different.

Review and Practice

Assign Taking Another Look, p. 332.

Answers to Taking Another Look (p. 332)

1. 48 percent of population of Mexican descent, *tejano* music heard on radio, Mexican weather map printed in the newspaper **2.** Mexican music, food, and art styles; wide use of Spanish language **3. Critical Thinking Agree:** because of family here, possibility for better income than in home country. **Disagree:** NAFTA will provide better incomes in Mexico, penalties to U.S. employers who hire illegal immigrants, continuing prejudice against Mexican Americans

Teaching Section 2: The Lure of *El Norte* (pp. 332–335)

Objective

- To understand the purposes of the North American Free Trade Agreement

Developing the Section

Using Library Sources. Divide the class into four groups and have students research the North American Free Trade Agreement Zone in the periodical section of the library. One group should focus on reasons why it was considered necessary; another, on

THE LATINO EXPERIENCE IN U.S. HISTORY • © Globe Fearon

why some people opposed it; a third group, on its history; and another, on its regional impact. Either have students present their findings to the class or have them debate whether the agreement should go into effect.

Review and Practice
Assign Taking Another Look, p. 335.

Answers to Taking Another Look (p. 335)
1. granted amnesty to undocumented aliens who had been in the United States since 1982, raised penalties for employers who continued to hire undocumented aliens 2. no, since there are so many ways to cross the border 3. **Critical Thinking** Because the possibility of success is greater than the fear of being caught; also, even if caught and deported, one can always try again.

Extending the Chapter
Examining Tourism. Mexicans are not the only border crossers. U. S. citizens like to travel to Mexico. Have students examine a map of Mexico to identify popular tourist spots. Then have them come up with reasons why people would travel there. Some possibilities are: Cozumel—beaches; Tijuana—shopping, easy access to the United States; Yucatán—Mayan ruins; Mexico City—museum, ballet, architecture.

Looking Ahead
After students have read Looking Ahead on p. 335, ask them what they know now about Mexican Americans that they did not know before they read the chapter. Ask them whether they think the experience of Puerto Ricans in the United States, whom they will read about in the next chapter, will be different.

Answers to Close Up (pp. 336–337)

The Who, What, Where of History
1. Mothers of East Los Angeles 2. Mexican music with roots in the *cantina*. 3. Latino who was mayor of San Antonio and a member of President Bill Clinton's

cabinet 4. Los Angeles 5. first Latina to win a seat on the Los Angeles County Board of Supervisors 6. border guards 7. border between Mexico and the United States 8. amnesty for illegal aliens, fines for employers 9. pardon. 10. assembly plants on the Mexican side of the border 11. agreement among Mexico, the United States, and Canada to make North America a tariff-free zone

Making the Connection
1. A strong sense of family builds a strong community. 2. physical connections: river, bridges, roads; others: culture, language, music, ethnic background, history. 3. provides opportunities for U.S. citizenship 4. NAFTA is expected to increase the amount of manufacturing done in the *maquiladoras*. 5. With increased U.S.-Mexico trade, Mexican Americans will be needed to serve as expeditors.

Time Check
1. Immigration Act 2. 1960s 3. 1991 4. 1980s

What Would You Have Done?
1. **For:** protection of undocumented workers, more accurate census counts. **Against:** it sends message that entering the United States illegally is OK, employers would have to pay workers more. 2. **Support:** tariff-free goods would be cheaper, more business coming through El Paso. **Against:** workers in El Paso could lose their jobs, cutting owner's business 3. Answers should refer to climate, history, culture, and politics of the city.

Thinking and Writing About History
1. Petition should be polite and contain factual arguments against the building of the prison and the incinerator. 2. Ballads might express sorrow, excitement, and/or fear of the experience.

Building Skills
1. **Invalid:** Mexico alone accounted for 69.9 percent. 2. **Invalid:** over 80 percent were Spanish speakers. 3. **Valid:** Mexicans accounted for 69.9 percent. 4. **Valid:** 12 percent from Central America, 1.8 percent from Caribbean

Chapter 26 Puerto Ricans Today (pp. 338–347)

Overview
Puerto Ricans in the United States have settled into the rainbow culture of the United States. Their cultural and political activities are a part of life in the many cities in which they now live. Still, problems such as poverty, the high school dropout rate, and gangs persist. Some Puerto Ricans move from the *barrios* back to the island. There they find that the island has

undergone vast changes. They soon find out that the Spanish they speak is not the Spanish of the islanders. They also note the differences that divide the political parties.

Historical Sidelight

Violence in Politics. Politics in Puerto Rico have sometimes taken a violent turn. In 1978, two *independentistas*, Carlos Soto and Arnoldo Rosado, were killed in a police ambush. The police claimed the two were on their way to blow up a television transmitter and shot first. The U.S. Justice Department cleared the police. But hearings in the Puerto Rican Senate in 1983 and 1984 showed that Soto and Rosado were shot after surrendering. It turned out that the police were members of a death squad trained by the FBI and armed by a U.S. marshall. These so-called "Defenders of Democracy" committed acts of violence in the name of antiterrorism. Once the Defenders disbanded, information about what they had really done was made public, and in 1990 FBI director William Sessions sent a letter of apology to the Puerto Rican Senate for not having conducted an official investigation into the deaths of Soto and Rosado.

Resources

Chapter 26 Activity Sheet (p. 178)
Chapter 26 Test (p. 139)
Chapter 26 ESL/LEP Activity Sheet (p. 238)

Focus Activity

Ask students to name festivals and parades they are familiar with. Why are these held? Who benefits? Besides being fun to attend, could they also serve a political purpose, to gain exposure and acceptance for their sponsors? After this discussion, have students read the introduction to the chapter. Discuss reasons why the kind of festival described would be important to Puerto Ricans.

Teaching Section 1: On the Mainland (pp. 339–342)

Objective

- To explore the age distribution of the Puerto Rican population

Developing the Section

Reading a Population Pyramid. Tell the class that a good deal can be learned about a group of people by analyzing how many people there are in each age group and the ratio of men and women. Ask the class to study the graph of Puerto Rican population distribution on p. 340. From the shape of the graph, students should be able to understand why

it is called a population pyramid. They should understand from the graph that Puerto Ricans are a comparatively young people, with both a high birth rate and death rate. Also, there is an almost equal number of men and women at each age level. You might ask how the graph would look if many men were killed in wars. *(The percentage of adult women would be higher.)* Ask the students to speculate about what the graph would look like if the birth rate and the death rate were lower, as is true of the United States as a whole. *(The graph would look less like a pyramid and more like a rectangle.)*

Review and Practice

Assign Taking Another Look, p. 342.

Answers to Taking Another Look (p. 342)

1. more skilled immigrants, do not necessarily settle in New York, many return to Puerto Rico. **2.** more politically active, growth in community pride, better educated **3. Critical Thinking** possible to bring about needed change and improvements by electing Puerto Ricans to political office

Teaching Section 2: Ties to the Home Island (pp. 343–345)

Objective

- To define the difference between commonwealth and statehood in terms of what it means to be a citizen of either

Developing the Section

Research and Debate. Divide the class into three groups. One group should research debate techniques and forms in order to inform the other two groups about these topics. One of these groups will argue in favor of statehood, the other, commonwealth. Encourage role playing by having students take on identities such as the U.S. President, Puerto Rican governor, and senators from both the United States and Puerto Rico, as well as various person-in-the-street identities.

Review and Practice

Assign Taking Another Look, p. 345.

Answers to Taking Another Look (p. 345)

1. more political activity, difference in the way Spanish is spoken, building of roads and housing projects **2.** Puerto Rico's political status, environment, bilingual education **3. Critical Thinking Benefits:** trade protection, federal money for various programs, equal representation in Congress, more acceptance for Latinos all over the United States. **Drawbacks:** loss of Puerto Rican identity and language, inability to make political decisions that benefit just the island, loss of special tax status

Extending the Chapter

Library Research and Public Display. The class may create a portrait gallery of Puerto Rican artists (or of another segment of society, such as political leaders). Have students, working individually or in groups, first research the person selected and then write a brief biography. Encourage them to draw portraits of their subjects. Display these around the room.

Looking Ahead

After students have read Looking Ahead, on p. 345, ask them to guess how many students there are in their school and school district. Ask them if the numbers change every year, and brainstorm about why they change or do not change. Then ask them what would happen if 13,000 new students showed up one day in their school district. What if these new students did not speak English? How would schools absorb these students? Then tell them that this is what happened to the Dade County Schools after the Mariel Boatlift in 1980.

Answers to Close Up (pp. 346–347)

The Who, What, Where of History

1. New York City, Chicago, Philadelphia, Los Angeles, other cities 2. second-generation Puerto Rican who is born on the mainland and who speaks English 3. to get people to register to vote 4. first Puerto Rican woman in Congress 5. serve as community centers for the Puerto Ricans of New York City 6. a musical newspaper 7. a summer theater in East Harlem, New York City 8. in East Harlem 9. buildings in mainland style 10. PDP: peasant hat; PNP: blue palm tree

11. continue as a commonwealth, become a U.S. state, or become independent 12. PNP candidate elected governor of Puerto Rico in 1992 13. vote of the people on a particular issue

Making the Connection

1. With fewer unskilled jobs, people with more skills are the ones who come to the United States. 2. Higher Puerto Rican voter participation results in more Puerto Rican representatives. 3. If Puerto Rico becomes a state, Puerto Ricans will learn to speak English as well as Spanish. 4. Rapid industrialization tends to harm the environment, and environmental groups try to protect natural resources such as water, land, and plant and animal life.

Time Check

1. 1987 2. 1992

What Would You Have Done?

1. Possible arguments: a community gathering spot means fewer people on the streets, less chance of violence, greater community spirit and control, more money spent in the district. 2. Choice of party should be based on its platform as explained in the text.

Thinking and Writing About History

1. Answers should list foods, games, music, and crafts that are mentioned in the chapter. 2. Essay should stress the idea that a second-generation Puerto Rican would participate in two cultures, with two languages. 3. Letter could touch on damage to animal and plant life, loss of island's beauty, and pollution and other environmental hazards.

Building Skills

1. 0–4 2. smaller 3. They are about equal in each age category. 4. 0, 29

Chapter 27 Cuban Americans Today (pp. 348–357)

Overview

The Cuban American community is strong and active, with a tradition of working together. In 1980, 125,000 Cubans arrived in Florida as part of the Mariel Boatlift that Fidel Castro initiated. Slowly, the refugees were assimilated into the existing culture. Today, Cuban Americans are the most successful of all Latino groups in terms of jobs and income.

Historical Sidelight

Radio Martí. Cubans continue to risk their lives by building crude rafts in order to float to the coast of Florida. The Cuban government has accused the U.S. government of provoking people to take these risks through the broadcasts of the U.S. Information Agency's Radio Martí, a 50,000-watt radio station that beams news to Cuba. Radio Martí broadcasts news of successful escapes and tide and weather information. Cuba unsuccessfully demanded that the United States stop broadcasting this information. Radio Martí says that although it does broadcast stories of successful escapes, it also warns Cubans of the dangers of sharks, sunburn, dehydration, and exposure.

Resources
Chapter 27 Activity Sheet (p. 179)
Chapter 27 Test (p. 140)
Chapter 27 ESL/LEP Activity Sheet (p. 239)

Focus Activity
After students read the introduction to the chapter, ask them how they think an organization like Centro Mater and the Cuban community in Miami in general might respond to a sudden unexpected influx of thousands of Cuban refugees. Explain that such an influx occurred in 1980 in what came to be called the Mariel Boatlift. Discuss whether the community would try to help the refugees or whether it would resent their coming as an unwelcome burden on its resources. Tell the students that the way the community reacted, which they will read about in Section 1, will tell much about the attitudes of the Cuban Americans who live in Miami.

Teaching Section 1: New Waves of Refugees (pp. 349–351)

Objective
- To help students understand how Cuban refugees find their way to the United States

Developing the Section
Writing a Diary. Divide the class into three groups. Have students in one group play the role of a refugee on the Mariel Boatlift and write diary entries of the experience from the time he or she first heard of the possibility of leaving Cuba to arrival in Miami. Students in the second group should write diary entries of a Cuban who comes to the United States on a homemade raft. Students in the third group should write diary entries of a Cuban who travels to the United States on Flight 8506. When the diaries have been written, discuss them in class, noting what experiences all have in common and which were the more risky. Ask students how they think the refugees might fare in their new country.

Review and Practice
Assign Taking Another Look, p. 351.

Answers to Taking Another Look (p. 351)
1. Cubans seeking refuge in Peruvian embassy led to more Cubans demanding visas. Castro became angry and advertised that anyone wishing to leave Cuba could do so. 2. hasty refugee camps, financial burden, school overload, shift to blue-collar work force, people working together for a common cause 3. **Critical Thinking Yes:** It is home and worth rebuilding. **No:** United States has become home, is no longer a Cuban but an American, and there is more economic opportunity here.

Teaching Section 2: A Strong Cuban American Presence (pp. 352–355)

Objective
- To visualize the characteristics of the Cuban American community

Developing the Section
Illustrating a Book. Have students examine the illustrations in Section 2 of Chapter 27. Tell them that they are to edit a new book on the topic of this section that has many more pages than the textbook. Assign them the task of writing descriptions of four additional illustrations for the section topic. The illustrations must support visually the content of the section. When the students have completed their descriptions, evaluate them in class as to whether they illustrate the main points of the section. Some students may wish actually to draw the several of the illustrations described.

Review and Practice
Assign Taking Another Look, p. 355.

Answers to Taking Another Look (p. 355)
1. As a lawyer, she can communicate with both English- and Spanish-speaking clients. 2. They have turned Miami into a center of Latin America. 3. **Critical Thinking** It is the "gateway to Latin America," has a booming economy and a strong Latin American community.

Extending the Chapter
Elected Officials. Have the students find out which Cuban Americans hold elective positions in Miami today. Have them choose one of them and do research for a biography similar to the one of Xavier Suárez on p. 354.

Looking Ahead

After the students have read Looking Ahead on p. 355, tell them that the next chapter deals with other groups of refugees from Latin America. Have the students look up the meaning of the words *refugee, political prisoner, exile, sanctuary, coup, asylum.* Ask them to write a paragraph that explains what the first three terms have in common and how they differ.

Answers to Close Up (pp. 356–357)

The Who, When, Where of History

1. daycare center for Cuban American children 2. limited the number of refugees to the United States from any one nation to 50,000 3. Havana, at the Peruvian embassy (or at the port of Mariel) 4. Miami 5. Cuban refugee, arrived on Mariel Boatlift, operations manager of Miami's Spanish-language TV channel 6. twice daily flight from Havana to Miami 7. Union City, NJ 8. companies that do business in several countries 9. first Cuban American mayor of Miami 10. Miami

Making the Connection

1. The Mariel Boatlift was in conflict with the Refugee Act, as the number of refugees exceeded the allotment and they were not in grave danger. The people of the boatlift were denied refugee status. 2. The former Soviet Union had provided vital economic support to Cuba that was no longer supplied after the breakup.

3. Miami's location near the Caribbean and Central America makes it attractive to multinationals, since the Latino community provides a base for branching out to Latin American countries.

Time Check

1. 1980 2. since 1960

What Would You Have Done?

1. **Yes:** to pick up family and friends. **No:** because you are now an American, it might be a trick, the trip might be too dangerous. 2. **Yes:** because of home and family ties and the chance to create a new Cuba. **No:** because home is now in the United States, and Cuba would be in political turmoil.

Thinking and Writing About History

1. Editorial could point out that less than 20 percent of Mariels had been prisoners and many of these had been political prisoners. 2. **1959:** exiles, middle class, welcomed, Miami a sleepy town, Cubans planned to stay only until Castro could be overthrown. **1980:** Miami now a bustling city, Mariel refugee, a blue-collar worker, refugees not welcomed by U.S. government.

Building Skills

1. Cubans 2. about 75 students or 7.4 percent 3. The largest groups are from Cuba and Central America. 4. Students from other countries now make up over 60 percent of Centro Mater children.

Chapter 28   Central Americans and Dominicans Today (pp. 358–367)

Overview

Military coups and widespread violence made many people seek refuge in the United States, where they could live without fear. Part of the violence was because of U.S. intervention trying to unseat socialist and Communist regimes. When the U.S. government refused to accept refugees from Nicaragua, the Cuban American community in Miami rallied to help Nicaraguans, and churches across the United States created the Sanctuary Movement to provide refuge. People from the Dominican Republic, on the other hand, have come to the United States to seek economic stability and educational advancement.

Historical Sidelight

Refugees and the Law. The Sanctuary Movement did not consist only of churches. Nineteen cities, one Methodist seminary, and 11 universities also were members. Another member was the entire state of New Mexico, under an order by Governor Tony Anaya. The Immigration and Naturalization Services (INS) prosecuted people in the movement. In 1985, the INS prosecuted 18,000 cases of smuggling illegal aliens. The most famous trial, which gained a great deal of attention for the movement, took place in Tucson, Arizona, in 1986. After 6 months in court and 50 hours of jury deliberation, 8 of 11 defendants were found guilty of smuggling Salvadorans and Nicaraguans. INS Commissioner Alan Nelson said, "No groups, however well meaning and highly motivated, can arbitrarily violate the laws of the United States." The INS's star witness had been paid $21,000 to attend church meetings and gather evidence with a hidden tape recorder. This move led to a countersuit against the government since the evidence had been obtained without a search warrant. Other lawsuits stated that the United States was violating the 1980 Refugee Act. Said Jim Corbett, who was one of the three persons acquitted in Tucson, "We will continue to provide sanctuary services openly and go to trial as often as necessary to establish . . . that the protection of human rights is never illegal."

Resources

Chapter 28 Activity Sheet (p. 180)
Chapter 28 Test (p. 141)
Chapter 28 ESL/LEP Activity Sheet (p. 240)

Focus Activity

Read the introduction and discuss with the class the Central Americans who were coming to the United States. What were they like and what were their dreams and expectations?

Teaching Section 1: Leaving Central America (pp. 359–360)

Objective
- To obtain information through the use of interviews
- To explore how U.S. intervention in Central America contributed to political turmoil there

Developing the Section
Interviews. After students have read the section, have them interview parents, teachers, and adults about what they remember about the Iran-Contra scandal and the U.S. presence in Central America. As a class, prepare a list of questions to ask and review note-taking techniques before the interviews. Then have students present their findings to the class.

Review and Practice
Assign Taking Another Look, p. 360.

Answers to Taking Another Look (p. 360)
1. *La violencia* from internal struggles and coups, civil war in Nicaragua, death squads in Guatemala, human rights abuses 2. by helping Central American refugees find shelter 3. **Critical Thinking Yes:** because of U.S. funding of antigovernment factions in civil wars **No:** violence was not started by the United States, was long part of the history of the countries.

Teaching Section 2: A Growing Central American Presence (pp. 360–362)

Objective
- To continue to explore reasons why Central Americans left their countries

Developing the Section
Tracing History. Have students select a topic to research related to the violence in Central America. Topics might include the Iran-Contra scandal, death squads, the murder of Jesuit priests in El Salvador, and the Sanctuary Movement. Have students conclude their findings with a statement about the present political or social situation of the country.

Review and Practice
Assign Taking Another Look, p. 362.

Answers to Taking Another Look (p. 362)
1. The Cuban American community offered help. 2. lack of knowledge of English, lack of immigration documentation, jobs, schools, finding shelter 3. **Critical Thinking** because it protected the children of immigrants and provided a way for children to learn about the United States outside the community of refugees

Teaching Section 3: Dominicans in the United States (pp. 362–365)

Objective
- To survey a Dominican neighborhood in the United States

Developing the Section
Planning a TV Feature Report. Explain to the class that they are to form teams to plan a TV feature on the Dominican neighborhood in Washington Heights described in the text. Each team is to prepare a plan for what the TV production team is to film. Using the material in the text, the teams should describe places the crew should film, the people they should interview, and other highlights that will give a balanced picture of the community. Have teams read their reports in class. If time permits, combine the reports into one general report.

Review and Practice
Assign Taking Another Look, p. 365.

THE LATINO EXPERIENCE IN U.S. HISTORY • © Globe Fearon

Answers to Taking Another Look (p. 365)

1. because of economic opportunities that are so much greater in the United States than in the Dominican Republic 2. Washington Heights in New York City 3. **Critical Thinking** Possible answers: they used to think they could return to the Dominican Republic, but now returning is not feasible; better life in the United States; opportunities for education

Extending the Chapter

Getting Information Through Art. Find songs and poems about living in exile or being an alien. Two examples of songs from this period are Genesis's "It's No Fun Being an Illegal Alien" (from a 1983 album) and Sting's "They Dance Alone" (from his album "Nothing Like the Sun"; he also released an EP of the same songs, sung in Spanish). Poems by Juan Felipe Herrera are also a possibility. After listening to the recordings, discuss the works with students. Ask them what they learned from the songs.

Looking Ahead

After students have read Looking Ahead, p. 365, have them predict what problems the South American immigrants referred to might face and what qualities they would need to cope successfully with these problems.

Answers to Close Up (p. 366–367)

The Who, When, Where of History

1. winner of Nobel Peace Prize 2. violence in Central America resulting from political turmoil 3. group of churches and others that defied U.S. law by providing aid and shelter to Central American refugees 4. Miami 5. children of immigrants, regardless of legal status, have a right to attend public school 6. South Central Los Angeles 7. human rights group helping Central American refugees settle in the United States 8. bankrupt nation, low wages, lack of economic opportunity, inflation, unemployment

Making the Connection

1. When attempts at land reforms were ended by a military takeover in 1954, many landowners (ladinos) joined the Maya to wage guerrilla war on the government. 2. Trujillo bankrupted his country, so Dominicans seek economic opportunities elsewhere.

Time Check

1. 1982 2. 11 (1979–1990)

What Would You Have Done?

1. **Yes:** it's humane, you have the space, you believe the government is wrong. **No:** you don't believe in breaking the law, even though you disagree with it, you don't think people should enter the country illegally 2. **Apply again:** with legal status, it's easier to find work, don't have to fear deportation, and with student visa you could go to school. **Risk the trip:** might never get a visa, if caught can always try again

Thinking and Writing About History

1. Speeches should include reasons why the work was important (saving lives, creating a better world for children) 2. Interview should include fear of violence and death, how he or she traveled, who helped.

Building Skills

1. Kanjobal from Guatemala 2. Possible answers: U.S. citizenship, growing old, political situation in Guatemala, finding work, saving money 3. is a worthy person, having worked and paid taxes, Guatemala is "unstable and dangerous" 4. They want peace and stability.

Chapter 29 South Americans in the United States Today (pp. 368–375)

Overview

Like many Central Americans, South Americans come to the United States to escape violence and economic hardship. Their number is growing and is expected to reach 1 million early in the next century.

Historical Sidelight

Mothers of the Plaza de Mayo. During the 1970s and 1980s, the Argentine military government abducted and killed tens of thousands of "political enemies." When parents were abducted, the children were often taken with them. After the parents were killed, relatives would never hear of the children again. This led to the creation of a group called Mothers of the Plaza de Mayo, a human rights activist group that continually fought to get information about the children who had disappeared. In 1983, when the military government was replaced, the Mothers of the Plaza de Mayo petitioned the civilian government for help. The government then set up the National Bank of Genetic

Data, to which relatives of the missing children could donate blood samples to aid in the genetic identification of any of the children who might be located.

Resources
Chapter 29 Activity Sheet (p. 181)
Chapter 29 Test (p. 142)
Chapter 29 ESL/LEP Activity Sheet (p. 241)

Focus Activity
Have the class read the introduction and part of Section 1, through Florencia's statements about fear, at the bottom of the first column on p. 370. Read her statement to the class. Ask about the fear she is talking about. Have students freewrite for a few minutes about what might happen to people who live with that sort of fear. Share insights.

Teaching Section 1: The Lure of Freedom (pp. 369–371)

Objective
• To understand South America's long road to stability

Developing the Section
Timelines. Have students prepare reports on individual countries. Each report should consist of a timeline that notes the transition from military governments (in most cases) to more democratic governments. If possible, the "peak experience," either in terms of violence or of resolution, should be highlighted on the timeline. For example, Brazil reinstituted the right of habeas corpus in the late 1970s. Argentina shifted from a military to a civilian government in 1983. When sharing timelines, have students consider the question, "Why were military governments so prevalent?"

Review and Practice
Assign Taking Another Look, p. 371.

Answers to Taking Another Look (p. 371)
1. political freedom, economic opportunity, escape from economic crises and violence **2.** that the number of people from South America in the United States will top 1 million by the early 2000s. **3. Critical Thinking** She encounters prejudice as well as kindness, meets other Latinos (who help her), grows comfortable in her new community and makes it home.

Teaching Section 2: Building New Lives (pp. 371–373)

Objective
• To identify the differences among Latino groups

Developing the Section
Comparing and Contrasting. Write Latino and Latin American on the board. Ask students, "What do you think of when you hear these words?" and write responses on the board. Then ask for subgroups—Cubans, Central Americans, and others—and have students supply information about these groups. Call students' attention to the similarities and differences among the groups. Use the data to have the students develop compare/contrast essays about different groups, or reflective essays about how stereotypes can limit understanding about the particular characteristics of a group that set them apart from other, similar groups. Ask students to create a list of famous people from particular groups.

Review and Practice
Assign Taking Another Look, p. 373.

Answers to Taking Another Look (p. 373)
1. from many countries—see the last paragraph of the section **2.** It has the largest number of South Americans living there, as witnessed by its restaurants and availability of South American periodicals. **3. Critical Thinking** different histories, experiences in the United States, personal and political reasons for coming to the United States

Extending the Chapter
South Americans Through the Arts. Show the movie *Stand and Deliver*. If this is not possible, choose a short story to read by a South American author such as Jorge Amado, Isabelle Allende, or Gabriel García Márques.

Looking Ahead
After students have read Looking Ahead, p. 373, ask them to note any evidence of Latino or South American influence they have personally seen or seen on TV. Ask whether they agree with the prediction of greatly increasing Latino influence in the United States. Have them give reasons for their answers.

Answers to Close Up (pp. 374–375)

The Who, When, Where of History
1. peasant farmer **2.** dictator of Paraguay **3.** rapid rise in the cost of living **4.** Lima, Peru **5.** Bolivian-born math teacher who worked with Latino students

in Los Angeles **6.** Colombians of African, Native American, and Spanish descent **7.** Queens, New York City

Making the Connection
1. During a period of inflation, people earn relatively less and less so that it costs more and more just to survive. Some people get angry and, sometimes, violent, leading to instability in the government. People often leave the country to avoid the violence, as happened in many South American countries. **2.** Many different Latino groups move to the United States. Jackson Heights becomes home to a variety of Latino cultures.

Time Check
1. 1980 **2.** 1992

What Would You Have Done?
1. Students need to state which country they are from. **Pros:** greater freedom, stable government, bet-ter employment opportunities. **Cons:** need to learn a new language, difficulty of finding a congenial setting in which to live, facing anti-Latino prejudice. **2. Yes:** find people of similar background and a network. **No:** too easy not to learn English and assimilate.

Thinking and Writing About History
1. Include a description of the differences in political climate, but be careful not to use words that would get her parents in trouble if the censors read the letter. **2.** Possibilities: justify the importance of advanced math, re-create his skills as a teacher

Building Skills
1. Santiago, Chile **2.** new government, social spending to reduce poverty **3.** 1990 **4.** new government **5.** end of military government **6.** tax increases free market growth, social spending **7.** hard, deals with facts

Chapter 30   Toward a New Century (pp. 376–391)

Overview
The 1990 U.S. census showed that the Latino population had risen over 50 percent since 1980. It is now almost 10 percent of the total population. Latinos are the fastest-growing ethnic group in the United States. The census showed that Latinos as a group are young, that many live in poverty and are in a state of transition between the culture of their ancestors and that of the United States as a whole.

Historical Sidelight
Chicano Studies. In the spring of 1993, students began to demonstrate at the University of California at Los Angeles. Their demand: that the university create a Chicano Studies Department, since Latinos make up 40 percent of Los Angeles's residents. Subjects making up Chicano studies had been taught in a number of different departments at the university starting over 20 years before, but they had never been concentrated in one department. Chancellor Charles Young refused to meet with the students and announced that Chicano Studies would not be elevated to department status. He cited the lack of funds and a declining student enroll-ment as the reason. It was unfortunate that Chancellor

Young announced his decision the day before César Chávez's funeral. Perhaps in memory of the Chicano leader, students then began to occupy a faculty lounge. The police were called in and 99 students were arrested. Labor groups and Chicano activists moved to support the students, and State Senator Art Torres held up an appropriation of $838,000 that was to be used to build an addition to the university library.

Resources
Chapter 30 Activity Sheet (p. 182)
Chapter 30 Test (p. 143)
Chapter 30 ESL/LEP Activity Sheet (p. 242)

Focus Activity
Brainstorm with students about Latino influence on and contributions to U.S. society. Cite architecture, art, literature, food, clothes, words, and other contributions. Using magazines, drawings, and labels (such as food wrappers), create a collage of Latino goods and ideas.

Teaching Section 1: Latinos in the 1990s (pp. 377–381)

Objective
- To explore how the 1992 disturbance in Los Angeles affected Latino communities there
- To consider whether violence is a viable option in trying to change society

Developing the Section
Using Research Tools. Have students do research on the 1992 disturbances in Los Angeles. If possible, have them interview friends and family who remember the incident that brought on the disturbances and what their reactions were. Encourage library use for more data, particularly the background of the people who took part in the incident. Have students work in small groups to answer the question "How does news of violence in one community affect other communities?" Have students share answers, referring to the text. Then ask them to respond individually to the question, "Is violence an effective way to create social change?" Have them support their answers with examples from the textbook, the news, and possibly their own experiences.

Review and Practice
Assign Taking Another Look, p. 381.

Answers to Taking Another Look (p. 381)
1. young, growing percentage of population, poor 2. poverty, high school drop out rate 3. **Critical Thinking** revealed unrest and poverty in society, need for people to work together to address these problems

Teaching Section 2: The Growing Reach of Latino Culture (pp. 381–389)

Objective
- To see how perceptions of Latinos have changed

Developing the Section
Comparing and Contrasting. Compare Manuel Sotomayer's words with those of César Chávez (see Chapter 22) and Elías Sepúiveda (see Chapter 17). Write or discuss possible answers to the questions What has changed? What does the future look like for Latinos?

Review and Practice
Assign Taking Another Look. p. 389.

Answers to Taking Another Look (p. 389)
1. more registered voters leading to a greater political voice and more Latinos in office 2. increase in number of Latino-owned businesses and a rise of Latinos at the middle-management level of large corporations 3. **Critical Thinking** takes hard work, a sense of the past, hope for the future, and giving back to the community to succeed

Extending the Chapter
Survival Guides. Finish the survival guides begun in Unit 7 Cooperative Learning Activity. Ask students to describe how they think or hope the guide will need to change in the year 2000.

Looking Ahead
After students have read Looking Ahead, p. 389, ask them to look back over what they have learned. Encourage a free-writing session, asking students to share something that they have learned or something that they thought was important in studying the Latino experience.

Answers to Close Up (pp. 390–391)

The Who, When, Where of History
1. Latinos of Mexican descent 2. South Central Los Angeles 2. more programs to help end poverty, community effort to rebuild 4. first Latina in Congress 5. Lucille Roybal-Allard, Nydia Velázquez 6. Former mayor of San Antonio, member of cabinet in the Clinton administration 7. people willing to take risks in business

Making the Connection
1. immigration the major cause of the 53-percent jump in the Latino population 2. Larger population and increased interest in politics have led to more political power. 3. more Latino influences on food, music, literature

Time Check
1. 1980s 2. 1989

What Would You Have Done?
1. invest in jobs, education scholarships, community centers, and community crime watch 2. protection

against (repeal of) English-only laws, more political power to dictate policies

Thinking and Writing About History

1. might show reasons why business should support the trip—pride in community, better community atmosphere that would result in better business **2.** cite census and information from brainstorming session **3.** use TV, music, books

Building Skills

1. year, number of Latinos, percent of U.S. population, percent of change in Latino population **2. a.** 4.7 **b.** 9.0 **3.** increase of almost 8 million, or 1.9 percent of the population, but a drop of 17.6 in percent of change **4. a.** 6,346,000 **b.** 14,608,000 **5.** steadily increasing **6. for increase:** number of Latinos and percent of U.S. population both increase; **for decrease:** the percent of change is slowing down.

LESSON PLANS FOR *THE ARTIST'S VIEW*

The Artist's View insert, following p. 244 of the student text, contains full-color illustrations by artists and artisans who have contributed to the Latino artistic heritage. Additional information about these works and suggested strategies for teaching *The Artist's View* are given below.

THE ROOTS OF LATINO ART

Works in this category appear on pp. A2–A3 of *The Artist's View.*

OVERVIEW

Latino art reflects the rich cultural diversity of the Latino people themselves. It draws upon influences that reach from North America into the Caribbean and down through much of Central and South America. The historic works shown in *The Artist's View* represent only a very small sampling of the outpouring of creative efforts by the many peoples who have in some way been touched by and contributed to the Latino heritage of the Americas. The works on pp. A2–A3 were created by the three main groups who helped shape this heritage: Native Americans who first claimed the Americas as home, Spaniards who tried to wrestle the lands from them, and Africans who arrived in the Americas as enslaved people.

When Columbus set foot in the Americas in 1492, Native American artists worked with a variety of materials—wood, shells, clay, stone, gems, animal skins, paints, feathers, quills, and soft metals such as gold, silver, and copper. Artistic works honored nobility and deities (see p. A2) or celebrated the history of a people (see p. A3). Even today, many people in Puerto Rico and Mexico look back with pride at the artistic accomplishments of the Taino and the Aztec, the two early groups highlighted on pp. A2–A3 of *The Artist's View.*

The Spanish mixed political conquest with cultural conquest. Spanish priests and missionaries followed upon the heels of the conquistadors. In missions and churches, Native Americans learned about the customs and beliefs of their conquerors. They also came in contact with new materials and new methods for creating artistic works and crafts. The silver chalice on p. A2 is an example of the church art introduced to the Americas by Spanish priests and missionaries. Works on other pages in *The Artist's View* show how artists in the Americas took Spanish styles and created whole new forms of art. (For an example, see the *santos* on p. A8.)

Yet another aspect of Latino culture traveled to the Americas aboard slave ships. Although robbed of their freedom, enslaved Africans clung to memories of their African heritage. Using materials found in the Americas, Africans from dozens of cultures created works that reminded them of their homeland. The bronze head on p. A2 depicts the creative talents of the Benin—just one of the West African peoples who contributed to the blend of cultures that came together in the Americas.

FOCUS ACTIVITY

Write the phrase Roots of Latino Art on the chalkboard. Then direct students to study the artistic works and captions on pp. A2–A3 of *The Artist's View.* With this information, challenge students to write a short paragraph on this topic. (You may want ESL students to write the paragraph in their primary language and then have them translate it into English with the help of "student tutors" or a dictionary.)

TEACHING STRATEGY

Read aloud the following description of Taino chairs. Tell students it was written by Columbus in 1492.

These were most peculiar chairs. Each was made in one piece and in a strange shape, resembling a short-legged animal with a tail as broad as the seat. This tail lifted up to make a back to lean against. These seats are called *dujos* or *duchos* in their language.

Ask: How accurately did Columbus describe the chair? Which words show that these chairs were quite different from those of Europe? (*peculiar, strange*) Next, assign students to rewrite the description of the chair from the point of view of an archaeologist, or scientist who studies ancient peoples. Caution students to avoid all value-laden words. Ask: What might an archaeologist conclude about the Taino from this chair? Have students prepare similar "archaeological studies" of the other three works on pp. A2–A3.

COOPERATIVE LEARNING ACTIVITY

Divide the class into small groups and have each team research the early art of one of the present-day nations once ruled by Spain. The places may include Mexico, Puerto Rico, Cuba, the Dominican Republic, and countries in Central and South America. Direct students to locate pictures of works that show Spanish, Native American, and/or African influence. Have students attach these pictures or copies of the pictures to a large posterboard. Help students develop captions similar to those used in *The Artist's View*. Allow time for each group to present its findings to the class in a short oral report.

MADE IN THE AMERICAS
· ·
Works in this category appear on pp. A4, A5, and A8 of *The Artist's View*.

OVERVIEW

As settlers pushed into the Spanish borderlands, they founded far-flung outposts. Missions, presidios (forts), and pueblos (towns) dotted an area that stretched from what is now Texas to California. Here people fashioned clothing, dishware, furniture, and other items for everyday use. The Spanish and Native Americans borrowed from one another, producing new styles unique to the Americas. An example of this cultural diffusion is the Navajo jewelry eagerly sought by many people today. The Navajo learned Spanish silver-making techniques and designs and then fashioned necklaces, bracelets, rings, and belts in traditional Navajo styles. Another example of cultural melding is the cup shown on p. A5 of *The Artist's View*. The cup, excavated at a pueblo in New Mexico, was fashioned by a 17th-century artisan using Native American pottery methods to create European-style tableware.

Such a mixing of cultures showed up in nearly all items crafted in the borderlands—even in the presidios built to house Spanish soldiers. In Europe, soldiers often used iron armor and shields. But in the borderlands, where ironworking was rare, soldiers had to turn to rawhide, or the tough skins of cattle, for their protective wear. For defensive purposes, a typical soldier wore a cumbersome leather coat *(cuera)* and leather leggings *(botas)*. Most soldiers also carried a leather shield *(adarga)* like the one shown on p. A5. Such shields were found in the Palace of the Governor after Popé drove the Spanish out of Sante Fe in 1680.

Spanish settlers also filled their homes with handmade local crafts. They favored painted furniture such as the great cupboard, or *trastero*, on p. A4. Today, this *trastero* can be found in an elegant 19th-century room located at the Museum of New Mexico in Sante Fe. Besides painted furniture, the room displays all types of crafts typical of the borderlands—hand-woven blankets and rugs, embroidered woolen cloths called *colchas*, and more than a dozen *santos*, the Spanish word for "holy images."

Santos formed an important part of religious life in the Spanish colonies. People often treated the figures as members of the family, housing them in special glass cases called *santuarios* (sanctuaries). The *santeros*, or image makers, enjoyed great respect. They carved figures such as those on p. A8 out of pine or the dried root of a cottonwood tree.

They fashioned bodies out of one piece and attached arms and heads with wooden pegs. Today *santos* can be found in both the Southwest and Puerto Rico.

FOCUS ACTIVITY

Refer students to the map of Spanish outposts in the borderlands on p. 57 of the student text. Ask: What geographic facts on the map help explain why Spanish settlers in the borderlands developed a rich tradition of crafts? Lead students to understand the effect of distance from Mexico City and Spain.

TEACHING STRATEGY

Tell students, working individually or in small groups, to imagine that they are part of the staff at the Museum of New Mexico in Santa Fe. Challenge them to write a brochure for visitors that examines each of the crafts shown on pp. A4, A5, and A8. Encourage students to illustrate each brochure. If possible, allow students to research additional items to include in their brochures.

COOPERATIVE LEARNING ACTIVITY

Divide the class into small groups. Tell students to imagine that they are merchants in one of the borderland communities mentioned in Chapter 4 of the student text. These merchants hope to encourage people in Mexico and Spain to buy handmade goods produced by local artisans such as the *santeros*. Have students design posters or broadsheets that the merchants might use to advertise crafts from the borderlands. Encourage them to use Spanish words or phrases, if possible.

HISTORY THROUGH ART

Works in this category appear on pp. A1, A6, A7, and A16 of *The Artist's View*.

OVERVIEW

The historic development of Latino art spans more than 500 years. The art created by various people in various places and at various times provides a valuable source of information about the cultural evolution of the Spanish-speaking peoples of this hemisphere.

The representative historic works chosen for *The Artist's View* show how four artists from the past and present have tried to capture the Latino experience in U.S. history. The mission depicted on p. A1 and the sculpture of a sodbuster on p. A16 both reflect artistic efforts to reconstruct the past. The scene from the Civil War (p. A6) represents an eyewitness interpretation of a major battle of the war, while the portrait of the bishop of New Orleans (p. A7) was painted from life as a tribute to the high church official. The materials and styles shown in these four works range from traditional oil painting to contemporary fiberglass sculpture.

FOCUS ACTIVITY

Review the skills feature for Chapter 1 on p. 21 of the student text. Then refer students to the four works on pp. A1, A6, A7, and A16 of *The Artist's View*. Ask: Which of these works could be considered a primary source of information about the past? (*the Civil War scene and the portrait of the bishop*) Why? (*because they were done by artists contemporary with the subjects*) Which of these works would be considered a secondary source of information about the past? (*the pictures of the mission and the sodbuster*) Why? (*because they were done by artists from another time period*)

TEACHING STRATEGY

Divide the class into small groups and assign each group one of the works on pp. A1, A6, A7, and A16 of *The Artist's View*. Challenge students to develop short biographical sketches in which the various artists describe their works. After students have presented their sketches, ask: What does each of these artists want you to know about the past? What details in the painting or sculpture support your answer?

Assign teams of students to select a topic, a person, or an event from the Latino experience that interests them. For ideas, suggest that they skim through the student text, paying particular attention to the items mentioned in the Snapshot of the Times features. Challenge each team to create a work of art that presents information or conveys an opinion or feeling about the historic subject chosen. To highlight the variety of approaches open to students, remind them of the contrasting styles in the Civil War scene (p. A6) and the sodbuster (p. A16). If the students cannot create the work of art, you may wish to have them select a subject for a work and then describe the finished product in detail.

COOPERATIVE LEARNING ACTIVITY

VISIONS FROM THE ISLANDS

Works in this category appear on pp. A10, A12, A14, and A15 of *The Artist's View.*

OVERVIEW

Groups of Puerto Ricans, Cubans, and Dominicans have lived in the United States since the late 1800s and early 1900s. But, in the post-World War II era, their numbers boomed. In the 1950s, widespread air travel led to a brisk traffic between Puerto Rico and the mainland. In 1959, the Cuban Revolution sent the first of several waves of Cuban political exiles to the United States. Since the 1960s, political and economic upheavals in the Dominican Republic have spurred thousands of Dominicans to head to Puerto Rico or to U.S. cities such as New York. (For more on these immigration patterns, see relevant chapters in Units 6 and 7 of the student text.)

Artists who trace their ancestry to the Caribbean have added new visions to Latino art in the United States. Signs of Spanish influence and European training can still be seen in the works of some painters, but the strongest influence by far is what Puerto Rican artist Antonio Martorell calls the Afro-Caribbean heritage born on the islands themselves. The imprint of African culture on the Caribbean can be seen in the work of artists such as Dominican painter Adolfo Piantini (p. A15). Among the many forces that have shaped his work, Piantini cites a need to capture "the myths and stories of our African origins."

The works of artists from the Caribbean have also been shaped by the region's unique geography and by events that have affected the people on each island. In *Hurricane* (p. A14), Cuban-born artist Julio Larraz captures the storm-tossed Cuban landscape through an open window. Larraz has kept links to the island by depicting events that brought Cubans and other Caribbean refugees to the United States. Remarked Larraz in a 1991 interview:

I have painted lifeboats many, many times. Boats carrying refugees that have left not only my country [Cuba] but many countries in search of freedom, facing the unknown, the ocean, at the mercy of the elements.

The paintings on pp. A10, A12, A14, and A15 give the flavor of some of the works created by Latino artists from the Caribbean. For additional background on artistic styles that have come out of this region, see Chapter 24 of the student text.

FOCUS ACTIVITY

Using an opaque projector, show students the works of art on pp. A10, A12, A14, and A15. Be sure to block out the captions on each work. Tell students that the artists who created these works all come from the same general region in Latin America. Challenge students to guess the region. Ask: Do you think the artists come from Mexico, Central America, South America, or the Caribbean? Call on volunteers to explain how they arrived at their answers.

TEACHING STRATEGY

Have students, working in small groups, prepare mock television broadcasts on the accomplishments of Latino artists from the Caribbean. Refer students to the information in Chapter 24, the Gallery of Latino Artists, on pp. 310–311, and the pictures and captions on pp. A10, A12, A14, and A15. Encourage students to include at least one interview with one of the artists mentioned in these pages.

COOPERATIVE LEARNING ACTIVITY

Divide students into cooperative learning groups. As a creative-writing assignment, have them write poems to accompany *Hurricane* (p. A14), *Niña* (p. A15), or *Ciqua* (p. A10). Encourage students to share their poems with the class as a whole.

VISIONS FROM THE CONTINENTS

Works in this category appear on pp. A9, A11, and A13 of *The Artist's View*.

OVERVIEW

As the United States expanded across the North American continent, it came in contact with the Mexican heritage of the present-day Southwest. The influence of Mexican culture on the United States has grown steadily ever since that time. Today Mexican immigrants and people of Mexican ancestry constitute the largest Latino group in the nation.

The Artist's View shows two paintings that underscore the Mexican American presence in the United States. In *Afternoon in Piedmont* (p. A9), Xavier Martínez paints a Mexican American version of the traditional painting by James McNeill Whistler of his mother. Martínez uses his own Mexican American wife as the model and depicts her looking out at a hilly California landscape. The second work, *Empanadas* (p. A13), by Carmen Lomas Garza, reflects the outpouring of cultural pride during *El Movimiento*. (For more on *El Movimiento,* see Chapters 22 and 24 in the student text.)

The remaining two works in *The Artist's View*, on p. A11, reflect the increased immigration from the Spanish-speaking nations south of Mexico of recent years. The artistic styles and themes brought to the United States by these new arrivals are as varied as the nations from which they come. These two works represent contributions by artists from Colombia and Uruguay.

FOCUS ACTIVITY

Refer students to *Empanadas* on p. A13. After students have read the caption, ask them to write a diary entry that one of the children in the painting might have recorded at the end of the day. Entries should touch on some of the traditional activities depicted in the painting. (ESL students may write the entry in their primary language and then translate it into English with the help of "student tutors" or a dictionary.)

TEACHING STRATEGY

Divide the class into small groups and assign each group one of four paintings on pp. A9, A11, A13. Next, write the following incomplete sentence on the chalkboard: From (name of painting), I learned that _____. Call on students to read their statements aloud, recording their answers on the chalkboard. Repeat this exercise until each group has completed statements for all four works.

COOPERATIVE LEARNING ACTIVITY

Request volunteers to use the *Readers' Guide to Periodical Literature* to compile a list of recent articles on Latino art or artists in the 1990s. (The magazine *Hispanic* is a good source of information. It includes regular features on Latino art.) Then assign research teams to locate as many of these articles as possible in their school or community library. Next, assign groups of students to prepare short oral reports summarizing the information in each article. If possible, arrange to have an opaque projector available for students to present examples of art included in the various articles.

BRINGING ART INTO THE CLASSROOM

The following cooperative learning activities can be used for alternative assessment in conjunction with *The Artist's View,* either in their entirety or throughout the course at appropriate times.

Designing a Book. Divide the class into groups. Assign each group one of the unit-opening pages from *The Latino Experience in U.S. History.* Direct the groups to research and design a new illustrated unit-opening page using works by Latino artists or groups who have contributed to the Latino heritage. Tell students that their pages should reflect the content and themes of chapters within each unit. Ask them to use photographs of sites or people mentioned in the unit if works by Latino artists pertinent to the period are not available. In evaluating the designs, consider how closely the chosen art reflects the subject matter within the unit.

Selecting Representative Art. Divide the class into groups and assign each group to research one of the units in the book. Direct students to research the art created by the Latinos mentioned during the period covered by the unit. They are to select, as a group, one piece of art that seems most representative of the period under consideration. Students should obtain illustrations showing the art they have selected and present oral reports to the class in which they describe the work and the reasons they selected it. In evaluating the reports, consider thoroughness of research, organization of presentation, and appropriateness of selection.

Name _____ Date _____

UNIT 1 TEST: Spain in the Americas

I.   **MATCHING** Decide which definition in the right column best explains a term in the left column. Then write the letter of that definition in the space next to the term.

_____ 1. *encomienda* system   **a.** cattle herders

_____ 2. *vaqueros*   **b.** the use of warships to protect Spain's silver galleons

_____ 3. missions   **c.** northern lands of New Spain

_____ 4. convoy system   **d.** grant of land given to Spanish settlers

_____ 5. Spanish borderlands   **e.** settlements devoted to converting Native Americans to Christianity

II.   **UNDERSTANDING TIME** Read the following list of events. Then number the events from 1 to 6 in the order in which they happpened.

_____ Two Spanish expeditions arrive in Alta California.

_____ Juan de Oñate's group of 500 settlers reaches New Mexico.

_____ Columbus leads a second expedition to the Americas.

_____ Cortés completes the destruction of the Aztec empire.

_____ Menéndez builds a fort at St. Augustine in Florida.

_____ Pizarro conquers the Inca empire.

III.   **MULTIPLE CHOICE** Choose the answer that best completes the sentence or answers the question. Then write the letter of your choice in the space to the left.

_____ 6. Spain controlled the Native Americans and used their labor to build its empire by: **a.** using the Columbian Exchange. **b.** sending a huge army. **c.** developing the *encomienda* system. **d.** defeating the British and French.

_____ 7. Spanish rulers regarded New Spain as the most important part of their empire in the Americas because: **a.** it protected the Caribbean islands. **b.** it had gold and silver. **c.** it had been conquered by Cortés **d.** it was nearest to Spain.

_____ 8. Over many years, Spanish, Native American, and African ways of life mixed to produce news ways of life among the peoples of the Americas. This is an example of: **a.** cultural bias. **b.** cultural diffusion. **c.** the mission system. **d.** the *encomienda* system.

_____ 9. Which one of the following was *not* one of the features of Spanish rule in the Americas? **a.** Native Americans were converted to Catholicism. **b.** A rigid class system was set up. **c.** Native Americans tried to resist. **d.** *Criollos* were the largest landowners.

_____ 10. Coronado, de Vaca, and de Narváez led early *entradas*, or expeditions, into: **a.** La Florida. **b.** the Inca empire. **c.** the Spanish borderlands. **d.** the Aztec empire.

_____ 11. Native Americans' resistance to the Spanish conquest was broken by: **a.** Spanish weapons and diseases. **b.** treaties of friendship. **c.** the Spanish Armada. **d.** resettlement.

     THE LATINO EXPERIENCE IN U.S. HISTORY • © Globe Fearon

IV. **COMPLETING THE IDEA Choose the item from the list below that best completes each of the following sentences. Then write it in the space provided.**

Texas	vassals	peonage system
Menéndez	Christianity	Hispaniola
missions	social divisions	Las Casas

12. _____ was the Spanish priest whose protests against the harsh treatment of Native Americans caused Spain to end the *encomienda* system.

13. Roman Catholic friars set up _____ in the Spanish borderlands as communities where Native Americans lived and worked under strict discipline.

14. Some of the Native American peoples who served as _____ of the Aztec aided Cortés's army of conquest.

15. Priests and friars of the Roman Catholic Church came to the Americas to convert Native Americans to _____.

16. Under the Spaniards, the peoples who lived in the Americas were organized in strict _____ _____ based on their race, place of birth, and positions of power in society.

17. The island of _____ became the model for Spain's empire in the Americas.

18. King Felipe II sent _____ to drive the French out of Florida and to build a fort at St. Augustine.

19. To protect _____ from Apache and Comanche attacks, Spaniards set up *ranchos* that later grew into towns.

20. Under the _____, Native Americans were forced to work for such low wages that they were always poor and in debt to the *hacienda* owners.

V. **ESSAY Choose one of the following topics. Then write your answer in paragraph form on a separate sheet of paper.**

A. How did Spain's conquests in the Americas affect the cultures of the Native Americans?

B. Which Spanish explorer or conquistador do you think made the greatest contribution to establishing Spain's new empire? Explain your choice.

Name _____ Date _____

CHAPTER 1 TEST: Face to Face in the Americas

I. MATCHING Decide which definition in the right column best explains a term in the left column. Then write the letter of that definition in the space next to the term.

_____ 1. presidio   **a.** enslaved Africans' journey across the Atlantic

_____ 2. *encomiendas*   **b.** governors who ruled Spanish settlement

_____ 3. *adelantados*   **c.** Spanish fort

_____ 4. Middle Passage   **d.** Spanish settlers who received large land grants

_____ 5. *encomenderos*   **e.** grants of land given Spanish settlers with the right to use the labor of Native Americans

II. MULTIPLE CHOICE Choose the answer that best completes the sentence or answers the question. Then write the letter of your choice in the space to the left.

_____ 6. Columbus believed that the islands he landed on, called the Indies by Europeans, were located in: **a.** Africa. **b.** North America. **c.** Asia. **d.** South America.

_____ 7. The Spanish settlement that became the model for Spain's empire in the Americas was: **a.** Cuba. **b.** Santo Domingo. **c.** Jamaica. **d.** Puerto Rico.

_____ 8. The largest forced migration of human beings in world history was the forced shipment across the Atlantic of: **a.** Native Americans. **b.** conquistadors. **c.** Africans. **d.** Indians.

_____ 9. The crop that became the greatest source of Spanish wealth on the Caribbean islands was: **a.** cotton. **b.** tobacco. **c.** gold. **d.** sugar cane.

_____ 10. The explorer-soldiers sent by Spain to the Americas were known as: **a.** *captivos.* **b.** *hidalgos.* **c.** *asientos.* **d.** conquistadors.

_____ 11. Bartolomé Las Casas was a Spanish priest and former *encomendero* who devoted his life to protesting the injustice of: **a.** enslaving Africans. **b.** the Middle Passage. **c.** the *encomienda* system. **d.** the presidio system.

_____ 12. The Taino leader who fled Hispaniola rather than become a slave was: **a.** Hatuey. **b.** Juan Garrido. **c.** Nicolás de Ovando. **d.** Gonzalo de Vedosa.

_____ 13. By 1496, hunger and disease nearly wiped out the first Spanish settlement in: **a.** Cuba. **b.** Hispaniola. **c.** Puerto Rico. **d.** Jamaica.

_____ 14. Which of these events made the year 1505 a turning point in the history of the Americas? **a.** Columbus made his first expedition. **b.** La Isabella was founded. **c.** Las Casas became a priest. **d.** Enslaved Africans arrived.

_____ 15. Over time, African, Spanish, and Native American ways of life mixed to produce the culture found today in: **a.** Puerto Rico, Cuba, and the Dominican Republic. **b.** Jamaica and the U.S. Virgin Islands. **c.** San Salvador. **d.** Key West.

III. ESSAY Choose one of the following topics. Then write your answer in paragraph form on a separate sheet of paper.

A. The Spanish and the Native Americans viewed the arrival of Columbus's expeditions in very different ways. Explain why you agree or disagree with this statement, using evidence from the text.

B. Explain how Las Casas's struggle to protect Native Americans against harsh treatment by the Spanish led to another great evil—the enslavement of Africans.

     THE LATINO EXPERIENCE IN U.S. HISTORY • © Globe Fearon

▶ CHAPTER 2 TEST: Struggle for an Empire

I. **MATCHING Decide which definition in the right column best explains a term in the left column. Then write the letter of that definition in the space next to the term.**

_____ 1. *caciques*

_____ 2. vassals

_____ 3. *hidalgos*

_____ 4. tribute

_____ 5. *la noche triste*

a. minor Spanish nobles

b. leaders of the Tabascans

c. subject people, such as those ruled by the Aztec

d. "the night of sorrow," when many Spanish soldiers died at Tenochtitlán

e. goods and produce paid by a conquered people to their conqueror

II. **MULTIPLE CHOICE Choose the answer that best completes the sentence or answers the question. Then write the letter of your choice in the space to the left.**

_____ 6. In 1511, Cortés went with Velázquez on the expedition that conquered: **a.** Mexico. **b.** Hispaniola. **c.** Cuba. **d.** Santo Domingo.

_____ 7. After Cortés conquered the Maya and the Tabascans, they were: **a.** put in prison. **b.** sent to Spain. **c.** forced to convert to the Roman Catholic religion. **d.** executed.

_____ 8. Because of the Aztec belief that Quetzalcoatl would return in the year One Reed, Motecuhzoma: **a.** welcomed Cortés. **b.** sent an army to attack Cortés. **c.** imprisoned Cortés. **d.** became a Roman Catholic.

_____ 9. As Cortés and his army marched inland into Mexico, they were supported by Native Americans there who were the Aztec's: **a.** allies. **b.** priests. **c.** vassals. **d.** rulers.

_____ 10. The center of the Aztec Empire was in: **a.** Cozumel. **b.** the Valley of Mexico. **c.** Veracruz. **d.** Tabasco.

_____ 11. The Native American woman who told Cortés bout the Aztec religion and wealth, and translated their language for him was: **a.** Malintzin. **b.** Aguilar. **c.** Tenochtitlán **d.** Alvarado.

_____ 12. After Motecuhzoma was killed, the Aztec noble who became emperor was: **a.** Alvarado. **b.** Diaz. **c.** Cuauhtémoc. **d.** Marina.

_____ 13. Cortés gave his soldiers only one choice—to conquer the Aztec or die—when he: **a.** sank his ships. **b.** destroyed his horses. **c.** retreated to Veracruz. **d.** set fire to the Aztec capital.

_____ 14. Spanish soldiers regarded Tenochtitlán and Tlatelolco, the twin cities of the Aztec capital, as: **a.** Catholic shrines. **b.** small, dirty towns. **c.** vassal cities. **d.** equal to European cities.

_____ 15. The Spaniards' success in capturing Tenochtitlán was due to their superior arms and: **a.** poor Aztec military leaders. **b.** the arrival of more Spanish soldiers. **c.** the death of many Aztec from smallpox. **d.** their use of horses.

III. **ESSAY Choose one of the following topics. Then write your answer in paragraph form on a separate sheet of paper.**

A. Explain the main reasons why the Spanish were able to conquer the Aztec empire.

B. One historian has written, "Gold, religion, and ambition led Cortés into Mexico." Explain the meaning of this statement, using evidence from the text.

Name _____ Date _____

▶ CHAPTER 3 TEST: New Ways of Life

I. **MATCHING Decide which definition in the right column best explains a term in the left column. Then write the letter of that definition in the space next to the term.**

_____ 1. friars

_____ 2. mission

_____ 3. *congregaciones*

_____ 4. Columbian Exchange

_____ 5. cultural diffusion

a. communities run by religious orders

b. exchanges among peoples of different cultures during the 1500s

c. settlement devoted to spreading Christianity

d. spread of cultures across global regions

e. priests who belong to religious orders

II. **MULTIPLE CHOICE Choose the answer that best completes the sentence or answers the question. Then write the letter of your choice in the space to the left.**

_____ 6. What new name did the Spaniards give to the former Aztec capital? **a.** Veracruz **b.** New Spain **c.** Acapulco **d.** Mexico City

_____ 7. Cortés sent Alvarado into southern Yucatán to search for: **a.** the Inca empire. **b.** the Aztec empire. **c.** the Maya empire. **d.** New Spain.

_____ 8. The conquistador who conquered the Inca empire, which became Spain's South American colony, was: **a.** Pizarro. **b.** Villalobos. **c.** Mendoza. **d.** Quiroga.

_____ 9. The friars worked to convert many Native Americans to: **a.** religious orders. **b.** the *congregaciones* system. **c.** the Columbian Exchange. **d.** the Roman Catholic religion.

_____ 10. Two of the most important foods from the Americas in the Columbian Exchange were: **a.** wheat and oats. **b.** potatoes and corn. **c.** quinine and lemons. **d.** grapes and oranges.

_____ 11. The Spanish king, Carlos V, took the responsibility for governing New Spain away from the conquistadors and gave it to: **a.** viceroys. **b.** *peninsulares*. **c.** *criollos*. **d.** mulattoes.

_____ 12. What was the most important product in New Spain's economy? **a.** corn **b.** beans **c.** silver **d.** wheat

_____ 13. By 1542, the *encomienda* system of labor and land ownership in New Spain was being replaced by: **a.** slavery. **b.** the peonage system. **c.** manufacturing. **d.** missions.

_____ 14. The strict class divisions set up by the Spaniards among the peoples who lived in New Spain were based on: **a.** jobs. **b.** the New Laws. **c.** wealth and power. **d.** religion.

_____ 15. One result of the mission system was that the largest landowner in New Spain was the: **a.** Roman Catholic Church. **b.** *peninsulares*. **c.** viceroys. **d.** Native Americans.

III. **ESSAY Choose one of the following topics. Then write your answer in paragraph form on a separate sheet of paper.**

A. Describe some of the effects of the Columbian Exchange on the lives of Native Americans.

B. If you had been a *criollo* in New Spain, how might you have felt about the *peninsulares*? Give your reasons.

Name _____ Date _____

CHAPTER 4 TEST: Reaching Out from the Caribbean

I.   **MATCHING Decide which definition in the right column best explains a term in the left column. Then write the letter of that definition in the space next to the term.**

_____   **1.** convoy system

_____   **2.** *piratas*

_____   **3.** privateer

_____   **4.** St. Augustine

_____   **5.** Ordinances of Governance

    a. pirates

    b. first code of European laws enacted in what is now the United States

    c. method of using warships to protect Spain's galleons carrying silver

    d. first Spanish fort in La Florida

    e. a privately owned ship used as a warship

II.   **MULTIPLE CHOICE Choose the answer that best completes the sentence or answers the question. Then write the letter of your choice in the space to the left.**

_____   **6.** In 1521, Ponce de León and 200 Spanish soldiers and settlers landed on the coast of: **a.** Cuba. **b.** Puerto Rico. **c.** Mexico. **d.** Florida.

_____   **7.** King Felipe II sent Pedro Menéndez to Florida to: **a.** retake it from the English. **b.** destroy the French base of Fort Caroline. **c.** rescue Spanish colonists there. **d.** set up a shipbuilding center.

_____   **8.** Spain regarded its Caribbean islands as important mainly for their use as: **a.** sources of gold and silver. **b.** naval bases. **c.** manufacturing centers. **d.** sources of corn and potatoes.

_____   **9.** Castillo de San Marcos, the fort the Spanish built at St. Augustine: **a.** lasted only a few years. **b.** was renamed San Miguel de Guadalupe. **c.** was effective in helping to protect Spain's claim to Florida. **d.** was captured by the English in 1695.

_____   **10.** England began to attack Spain's Caribbean islands after the English navy defeated the Spanish Armada in: **a.** 1607. **b.** 1588. **c.** 1513. **d.** 1561.

_____   **11.** Pánfilo de Narváez, Hernando de Soto, and Tristán de Luna y Arellano were all Spanish: **a.** *piratas*. **b.** soldier-explorers. **c.** sea dogs. **d.** privateers.

_____   **12.** Spain's two main forts on Puerto Rico and Cuba were attacked and burned by: **a.** the French navy. **b.** Dutch privateers. **c.** Sir Francis Drake. **d.** the Armada.

13. Spain built forts and naval bases in the Caribbean to: **a.** protect sea routes to Peru and New Spain. **b.** defend Native Americans. **c.** prepare attacks on French warships. **d.** assemble the Spanish Armada.

14. After the English began to settle colonies in North America in 1607, Spain's fort at St. Augustine was: **a.** never completed. **b.** destroyed by the French. **c.** strengthened to defend Florida. **d.** captured by sea dogs.

15. The Puerto Rican city of San Juan was set afire in 1598 by: **a.** French privateers. **b.** Native American warriors. **c.** English sea dogs. **d.** the Spanish navy.

III.   **ESSAY Choose one of the following topics. Then write your answer in paragraph form on a separate sheet of paper.**

    A. Why was England's defeat of the Spanish Armada thousands of miles from the Caribbean so important to Spain's power in the Americas?

    B. Explain the dangers faced by the settlers at St. Augustine in the late 1500s and early 1600s.

Name _____ Date _____

CHAPTER 5 TEST: The Spanish Borderlands

I.   MATCHING Decide which definition in the right column best explains a term in the left column. Then write the letter of that definition in the space next to the term.

_____ 1. Spanish borderlands   **a.** small farms

_____ 2. *entradas*   **b.** cattle herders

_____ 3. *ranchos*   **c.** civilian settlers from New Spain

_____ 4. *vaqueros*   **d.** northern region of New Spain

_____ 5. *poblanos*   **e.** expeditions

II.   MULTIPLE CHOICE Choose the answer that best completes the sentence or answers the question. Then write the letter of your choice in the space to the left.

_____ 6. From his home base in what is now the Mexican state of Sonora, Father Kino started 25 missions in: **a.** Los Angeles. **b.** San Antonio. **c.** the Spanish borderlands. **d.** Mexico City.

_____ 7. A Caddo woman named Angelina helped strengthen Spanish rule in what part of the Spanish borderlands? **a.** New Mexico **b.** Baja California **c.** Texas **d.** Alta California

_____ 8. The first governor of the Kingdom of New Mexico was: **a.** Cabeza de Vaca **b.** Juan de Oñate. **c.** Estevánico. **d.** Coronado.

_____ 9. The Native Americans who provided Oñate's expedition with food and shelter began to resist when the Spanish: **a.** discovered gold. **b.** sent a new *adelantado*. **c.** set out toward the Pacific. **d.** tried to convert them to Christianity.

_____ 10. The Zuñi, Hopi, and Acoma regained control of the northern borderlands in 1680 after: **a.** Coronado's expedition. **b.** Popé's revolt. **c.** the Apache attacks. **d.** French traders arrived.

_____ 11. In 1540, Coronado began his expedition into the Spanish borderlands in search of: **a.** emeralds, turquoise, and gold. **b.** Cabeza de Vaca. **c.** Zuñi villages **d.** Louisiana.

_____ 12. The Spanish king sent 200 farm families from the Canary Islands to Texas in an effort to: **a.** tighten Spain's control. **b.** begin herding mustangs. **c.** recapture San Antonio. **d.** defeat the Hopi.

_____ 13. Spanish interest in settling New California was renewed by: **a.** the discovery of gold there. **b.** reports of British and Russian ships off the coast. **c.** Native American revolts. **d.** overcrowding in Baja California.

_____ 14. Because Native Americans in California preferred hunting, fishing, and farming, and disliked the harsh discipline, Spanish missions: **a.** were not established. **b.** were moved to Texas. **c.** grew at a slow rate. **d.** used enslaved Africans as labor.

_____ 15. By the early 1800s, the population of Los Angeles and other California pueblos consisted largely of: **a.** *poblanos.* **b.** *criollos.* **c.** people of mixed ancestry. **d.** *vaqueros.*

III.   ESSAY Choose one of the following topics. Then write your answer in paragraph form on a separate sheet of paper.

A. Explain the reasons that led the pueblo peoples to revolt in 1680 and describe the outcome of the revolt.

B. "The missions brought new ways of life to the Native Americans in the Spanish borderlands." Explain what this statement means, citing evidence from the text.

Name _____ Date _____

◆ UNIT 2 TEST: Toward Independence

I.   MATCHING Decide which definition in the right column best explains a term in the left column. Then write the letter of that definition in the space next to the term.

_____   1. *californios*   **a.** Spanish-speaking settlers in California

_____   2. *rancheros*   **b.** persons who governed and helped defend a town

_____   3. *patrones*   **c.** owners of ranches

_____   4. secularize   **d.** Mexican settlers in Texas

_____   5. *tejanos*   **e.** remove from religious ownership or control

II.   UNDERSTANDING TIME Choose the time in which each of the events listed below took place. Then write the date in the space to the left.

          1777   1819   1821   1825   1836

_____   6. Mexico wins its independence from Spain.

_____   7. Gálvez secretly begins to aid the Patriots in the Revolutionary War.

_____   8. The Republic of Gran Colombia is established.

_____   9. The missions in California are secularized by Mexico.

_____   10. Stephen Austin leads American settlers into Texas.

III. MULTIPLE CHOICE Choose the answer that best completes the sentence or answers the question. Then write the letter of your choice in the space to the left.

_____   11. During the American Revolution, Spain succeeded in helping the Patriots and also: **a.** defeating France. **b.** protecting its colonies. **c.** forming an alliance with Britain. **d.** ending the pueblo revolt.

_____   12. One of the most important contributions of the Spanish to the American cause was: **a.** the defeat of the British navy. **b.** control of the Mississippi River. **c.** the invasion of Jamaica. **d.** the recapture of Texas.

_____   13. In the Adams-Onis Treaty of 1819, the United States gave up its claim to Texas, and Mexico recognized what territory that was now part of the United States? **a.** California **b.** Puerto Rico **c.** New Mexico **d.** East and West Florida

_____   14. In 1821, Texas, California, and New Mexico, which had been the northern provinces of New Spain, became: **a.** Spanish borderlands. **b.** U.S. borderlands. **c.** part of Mexico. **d.** independent provinces.

_____   15. Unrest between wealthy *californios* and poor ranch workers slowly tied the ranch owners closer to: **a.** the United States. **b.** Mexico. **c.** the *patrones*. **d.** *genizaros*.

_____   16. By the 1830s, Mexico began to worry that what province might very soon be taken over by the United States?: **a.** California **b.** Texas **c.** New Mexico **d.** Santa Fe

IV. COMPLETING THE IDEA Choose the item from the list below that best completes each of the following sentences. Then write it in the space provided.

Texas	American Revolution	hides and tallow
partido	Puerto Rico and Cuba	*patrones*
missions	American settlers	Gálvez

17. During the American Revolution, _____ won back East and West Florida for Spain.

18. Spain supplied food for its soldiers fighting in the _____ by using cattle herds driven from Texas.

19. Spain offered free land to try to stop the flood of _____ into the Mississippi Valley.

20. During the wars of independence, _____ were the two Spanish colonies that remained loyal.

21. *Nuevomexicano* families lived in villages and small towns governed by _____.

22. Under the _____ system, poor herders tended cattle for the *ricos*.

23. When the _____ in California were taken from the friars, they ended up in the hands of government officials.

24. The main goods traded by *californios* were _____.

25. Stephen Austin brought 300 American families to _____ in 1825.

V. ESSAY Choose one of the following topics. Then write your answer in paragraph form on a separate sheet of paper.

A. Explain some of the problems Mexico faced in trying to govern New Mexico.

B. Explain why the Mexican government removed the missions from the control of the Franciscan friars.

CHAPTER 6 TEST: The Spanish and the American Revolution

I.   MATCHING Decide which definition from the right column best explains a term in the left column. Then write the letter of the definition in the space next to the term.

_____   **1.** neutral

_____   **2.** *vaqueros*

_____   **3.** Patriots

_____   **4.** *rancheros*

_____   **5.** Anglo Americans

a. cowhands who herded cattle

b. owners of ranches

c. people of non-Spanish descent

d. not supporting either side

e. British colonists fighting for independence

II.   MULTIPLE CHOICE Choose the answer that best completes the sentence or answers the question. Then write the letter of your choice in the space to the left.

_____   **6.** To support the Patriots against the British, the Spanish governor of Louisiana: **a.** blockaded Charleston, South Carolina. **b.** supplied 10,000 pounds (4,500 kilograms) of gunpowder. **c.** had Gálvez lead his army in an attack. **d.** supplied several warships.

_____   **7.** When the American colonies declared their independence in 1776, Louisiana was controlled by: **a.** France. **b.** Great Britain. **c.** Spain. **d.** Mexico.

_____   **8.** The main highway for travel and transportation west of the Appalachians was the: **a.** Pacific Ocean. **b.** Gulf of Mexico. **c.** Mississippi River. **d.** Atlantic Ocean.

_____   **9.** During the American Revolution, Gálvez won back Spain's control of: **a.** East and West Florida. **b.** New Orleans. **c.** Fort Pitt. **d.** Cuba.

_____   **10.** The Spanish victories against the British at Fort Bute, Baton Rouge, Natchez, and St. Joseph gave Spain total control of: **a.** the Appalachians. **b.** the Mississippi Valley. **c.** the Ohio Valley. **d.** the Bahamas.

_____   **11.** The problem of supplying food to Spanish troops was solved by driving herds of cattle from: **a.** Florida to Louisiana. **b.** New Orleans to St. Louis. **c.** Texas to Louisiana. **d.** New Orleans to Mobile.

_____   **12.** Gálvez tried to strengthen Spain's control over Louisiana by: **a.** inviting settlers from the British colonies. **b.** driving out Native Americans. **c.** siding with France. **d.** ending the French and Indian War.

_____   **13.** Texas *rancheros* drove over thousands of head of cattle from the missions to Nacogdoches through lands held by: **a.** the Comanche. **b.** Menchaca. **c.** British. **d.** Patriots.

_____   **14.** Gálvez's strategy was to aid the Patriots and at the same time: **a.** protect Spain's colonies. **b.** seek support from Britain. **c.** encourage revolution in Texas. **d.** defeat France's army.

_____   **15.** After the last battle between the British and the Patriots in 1781, Spain: **a.** called off further action against the British. **b.** attacked Native Americans in Florida. **c.** continued to fight the British. **d.** asked the Patriots to pay for the aid it had given them.

III.   ESSAY Choose one of the following topics. Then write your answer on a separate sheet of paper.

   A. Explain some ways that Spain helped the Patriots win the American Revolution.

   B. In what ways did Bernardo de Gálvez display great skill in protecting Spain's colonies?

Name _____ Date _____

▶ CHAPTER 7 TEST: The Road to Latin American Independence

I.   MATCHING Decide which definition in the right column best explains a term in the left column. Then write the letter of that definition in the space next to the term.

_____ 1. *californios*   **a.** tar, pitch, and turpentine

_____ 2. Republic of Gran Colombia   **b.** present-day Venezuela and Colombia

_____ 3. Dolores   **c.** settlers in New Mexico

_____ 4. *nuevomexicanos*   **d.** settlers in California

_____ 5. naval stores   **e.** Place where Mexican struggle for freedom started

II.   MULTIPLE CHOICE Choose the answer that best completes the sentence or answers the question. Then write the letter of your choice in the space to the left.

_____ 6. The governor who tried to build Florida into a stronger Spanish colony was: **a.** Fatio. **b.** Zéspedes. **c.** Miró **d.** Vicario.

_____ 7. The small number of Spanish settlers, strict trade policies, and events in Europe forced Spain to: **a.** slowly retreat from North America. **b.** fight to keep Louisiana. **c.** give Louisiana to the United States. **d.** seize Texas.

_____ 8. To deal with the flood of Anglo American settlers into the Mississippi Valley, Spain offered them: **a.** low taxes. **b.** special laws. **c.** gold. **d.** free land.

_____ 9. Spain's hold on Florida and Louisiana was threatened by: **a.** the presence of U.S. troops. **b.** the migration of many *criollos* to Mexico. **c.** a rapid increase in Anglo American settlers. **d.** the difficulty in supplying the region with food.

_____ 10. In 1819, Spain agreed to give East and West Florida to the United States, which gave up its claim to Texas, in the: **a.** Louisiana Purchase. **b.** Adams-Onis Treaty. **c.** French Revolution. **d.** Haitian Revolution.

_____ 11. Father Hidalgo and Leona Vicario were leaders in the fight for independence in: **a.** New Granada. **b.** Santo Domingo. **c.** Mexico. **d.** Cuba.

_____ 12. During the wars of independence, which two colonies remained loyal to Spain? **a.** Venezuela and Colombia **b.** Haiti and Santo Domingo **c.** Cuba and Puerto Rico **d.** Cuba and Haiti

_____ 13. Many of the leaders of the revolution in Latin America who fought for the right to govern themselves were: **a.** *criollos*. **b.** mestizos. **c.** Anglo Americans. **d.** *peninsulares*.

_____ 14. When Mexico won its independence in 1821, what happened to Texas and the northern provinces of New Spain? **a.** They joined the United States. **b.** They became part of Mexico. **c.** They became independent. **d.** They formed a new nation.

_____ 15. The demand for slave labor in Cuba and Puerto Rico grew rapidly after what event? **a.** the Mexican Revolution **b.** the battle of Boyacá **c.** the Louisiana Purchase. **d.** the slave revolt in Haiti.

III.   ESSAY Choose one of the following topics. Then write your answer in paragraph form on a separate sheet of paper.

A. If you had been a Native American living in the province of Texas in 1815, would you have supported Gutiérrez's rebels? Give your reasons.

B. Explain why Spain slowly was forced to give up its colonies bordering the United States.

► CHAPTER 8 TEST: Life in the Mexican Borderlands

I.   MATCHING Decide which definition in the right column best completes a term in the left column. Then write the letter of that definition in the space next to the term.

_____ 1. secularize

_____ 2. *tejanos*

_____ 3. *empresarios*

_____ 4. *partido* system

_____ 5. *patrón*

a. governor of a town who also provided for its defense

b. agents who recruited settlers

c. Mexican settlers in Texas

d. remove missions from religious ownership or use

e. system in which villagers herded cattle for landowners

II.   MULTIPLE CHOICE Choose the answer that best completes the sentence or answers the question. Then write the letter of your choice in the space to the left.

_____ 6. Because Native Americans raided the countryside, most *nuevomexicano* families lived in: **a.** villages and towns. **b.** *ranchos*. **c.** pueblos. **d.** missions.

_____ 7. A big trading fair was held each fall at: **a.** Chihuahua. **b.** Taos. **c.** Santa Fe. **d.** El Paso.

_____ 8. Under the *partido* system, many villagers: **a.** lost their land. **b.** learned how to carve wooden statues of saints. **c.** lived their lives in debt to *ricos*. **d.** formed labor unions.

_____ 9. New taxes levied on New Mexican villagers by the governor in 1837 led to: **a.** Apache raids. **b.** conflict with the United States. **c.** war with Mexico. **d.** rebellion.

_____ 10. The Mexican government removed the California missions from the control of the Franciscan friars because: **a.** missions were hindering economic growth. **b.** the Catholic Church requested it. **c.** the missions could not protect Native Americans. **d.** the mission system had been replaced by the *partido* system.

_____ 11. The growing trade in hides and tallow by *californios* increased their ties to: **a.** Mexico. **b.** New Mexico. **c.** the United States. **d.** France.

_____ 12. Few Mexicans wished to settle in Texas because: **a.** they had no means of getting there. **b.** Texas was very far away and was dangerous. **c.** they preferred to move to California. **d.** they knew they would have to work for Americans there.

_____ 13. The Mexican government gave Stephen Austin a land grant in Texas in order to: **a.** raise more cotton in Texas. **b.** teach *tejanos* how to become ranchers. **c.** increase the number of settlers in Texas. **d.** protect it from Native American raids.

_____ 14. Many Americans settled in Texas because: **a.** they were promised gold. **b.** they hoped to raise cotton. **c.** slavery was outlawed there. **d.** they were Catholics.

_____ 15. The Mexican government failed in its attempt to persuade which group to settle in Texas? **a.** Europeans **b.** Canadians **c.** South Americans **d.** Asians

III.   ESSAY Choose one of the following topics. Then write your answer in paragraph form on a separate sheet of paper.

A. Explain why *patrones* played such an important role in the settlement of New Mexico.

B. "By the 1840s, California was a land of large ranches with growing unrest between rich and poor." Give evidence from the text that this is a true statement.

UNIT 3 TEST: A Time of Upheaval

I.   MATCHING Decide which definition in the right column best explains a term in the left column. Then write the letter of that definition in the space next to the term.

_____   1. secularize   a. peace treaty between Mexico and the United States

_____   2. discrimination   b. illegal settlers

_____   3. Alamo   c. unjust treatment of people

_____   4. squatters   d. mission in San Antonio

_____   5. Treaty of Guadalupe Hidalgo   e. remove from religious control

II.   UNDERSTANDING TIME Read the following list of events. Then number the events in the order in which they happened. Note that two events happened in the same year.

_____   6.   The United States annexes Texas.

_____   7.   The United States and Mexico sign the Treaty of Guadalupe Hidalgo.

_____   8.   Mexican army defeats Texas defenders at the Alamo.

_____   9.   The United States declares war against Mexico.

_____   10. Discovery of gold in California.

_____   11. California is admitted as a state of the United States.

III.   MULTIPLE CHOICE Choose the answer that best completes the sentence or answers the question. Then write the letter of your choice in the space at the left.

_____   12. The two cultures that grew up in Texas were: **a.** centralist and federalist. **b.** *tejano* and Anglo. **c.** *tejano* and *rico*. **d.** *rico* and Anglo.

_____   13. The Mexican leader whose strong rule started uprisings in the Mexican borderlands was: **a.** Zavala. **b.** Cos **c.** Santa Anna. **d.** Travis.

_____   14. The United States did not annex Texas when it became independent in 1837 because: **a.** Anglos in Texas were opposed to it. **b.** Mexico opposed it. **c.** Northerners in the United States were against adding a slave state. **d.** President Polk was against it.

_____   15. The main cause of the war between the United States and Mexico was: **a.** Mexico's opposition to slavery. **b.** Taylor's invasion of Mexico. **c.** the Treaty of Guadalupe Hidalgo. **d.** U.S. expansionist policies.

_____   16. Although Mexican soldiers lost the battle of Chapultepec, it is remembered by Mexicans today because of: **a.** the six heroes. **b.** the death of Santa Anna. **c.** General Scott's entrance into Mexico City. **d.** Travis's defeat at the Alamo.

_____   17. The Mexican Americans in California, New Mexico, and Texas became foreigners in their own land when: **a.** Mexico sold this territory to the United States. **b.** Santa Anna betrayed them. **c.** the United States gained this territory by treaty. **d.** Mexico invaded it.

IV. **COMPLETING THE IDEA Choose the item from the list below that best completes each of the following sentences. Then write it in the space provided. Not all the choices will be used.**

bandit	Stephen Austin	territory
New Mexico	Anglos	Texas
tax	Santa Anna	*tejanos*
William B. Travis	Lorenzo de Zavala	Guadalupe Hidalgo

18. The discovery of gold in California resulted in a flood of _____ into this Mexican territory.

19. The Mexican leader who switched sides from supporting the liberals to supporting the conservatives was _____.

20. _____ at first believed that Texas should be a separate state in Mexico.

21. The Mexican American population of _____ remained larger than the Anglo population for many decades after the United States took over this territory.

22. In the Treaty of _____, Mexico lost nearly half of its territory to the United States.

23. One clear example of discrimination against Mexican Americans was California's foreign miners' _____ of 1850.

24. Juan Nepomuceno Cortina was a Mexican American _____ who became a hero to many of his people.

25. Most landowners in _____ were able to prove their titles to their lands.

V. **ESSAY Choose one of the following topics. Then write your answer in paragraph form on a separate sheet of paper.**

A. Why were Cortina and other Mexican American bandits considered heroes by their people?

B. Explain why the Battle of San Jacinto was the turning point in Texas's fight for independence.

▶ CHAPTER 9 TEST: Revolt in Texas

I. MATCHING Decide which definition in the right column best explains a term in the left column. Then write the letter of that definition in the space next to the term.

_____ 1. centralism

_____ 2. Alamo

_____ 3. *caudillos*

_____ 4. federalism

_____ 5. San Jacinto

a. battle in which Houston defeated Santa Anna

b. military leaders of Mexico's government

c. system in which power is shared by states and the central government

d. abandoned mission in San Antonio

e. system in which power is concentrated in the central government

II. MULTIPLE CHOICE Choose the number that best completes the sentence or answers the question. Then write the letter of your choice in the space to the left.

_____ 6. The *tejano* culture in Texas was centered around the: **a.** Alamo. **b.** Catholic Church. **c.** Protestant churches. **d.** *empresarios.*

_____ 7. Mexican liberals who wanted to reduce the power of the Catholic Church, protect freedom of the press, and end special privileges, supported what kind of government? **a.** centralism **b.** monarchy **c.** federalism **d.** statehood

_____ 8. Mexico's law of 1829 freeing enslaved people was aimed at: **a.** *caudillos.* **b.** *tejanos.* **c.** federalists. **d.** Anglo slave owners in Texas.

_____ 9. In 1834, Santa Anna's shift from supporting liberal reforms toward strong rule led to: **a.** revolts in Mexico's borderlands. **b.** his overthrow. **c.** war with the United States. **d.** Zavala's return to the Yucatán

_____ 10. *Tejanos* were undecided whether to support a centralist government they disliked or the Anglos who: **a.** were equal in number to them. **b.** outnumbered them by a large margin. **c.** would probably give them an equal role in a new government. **d.** might drive them out of Texas.

_____ 11. At first, Stephen Austin believed that Texas should be: **a.** independent. **b.** a separate state in Mexico. **c.** a state of the United States. **d.** controlled by *tejanos.*

_____ 12. The "war party" in Texas among the Anglos was headed by: **a.** Stephen Austin. **b.** Lorenzo de Zavala. **c.** William B. Travis. **d.** Gregorio Esparaza.

_____ 13. The first battle at the Alamo in 1835 ended in defeat for: **a.** the Mexicans. **b.** the Anglos. **c.** Austin. **d.** Travis.

_____ 14. In the second battle at the Alamo in 1836, Travis and his men: **a.** surrendered. **b.** were killed. **c.** defeated Santa Anna. **d.** escaped at night.

_____ 15. The final decisive battle in Texas's revolt against Mexico took place in 1836 at: **a.** San Jacinto. **b.** San Antonio. **c.** the Alamo. **d.** Goliad.

III. ESSAY Choose one of the following topics. Then write your answer in paragraph form on a separate sheet of paper.

A. If you had been a *tejano* living in Texas during the revolt, what facts would you have considered before making your decision as to which side to support?

B. Describe some actions Mexico took to tighten its control of Texas and explain their results.

Name _____ Date _____

CHAPTER 10 TEST: War Between the United States and Mexico

I.   MATCHING Decide which definition in the right column best explains a term in the left column. Then write the letter of that definition in the space next to the term.

_____   1. Nueces River

_____   2. *el desierto muerto*

_____   3. annex

_____   4. *los niños héroes*

_____   5. Treaty of Guadalupe Hidalgo

a. to take over territory and add it to a nation

b. six Mexican cadets who died at Chapultepec

c. ended the war between Mexico and the United States

d. southern border of Texas claimed by Mexico

e. the "dead desert" south and west of the Nueces

II.   MULTIPLE CHOICE Choose the answer that best completes the sentence or answers the question. Then write the letter of your choice in the space to the left.

_____   6. Many Mexicans believed the Texas revolt in 1836 was part of a U.S. plot to steal: **a.** California and Florida **b.** Texas and Florida **c.** New Mexico and California **d.** Colorado

_____   7. The United States recognized the Republic of Texas in: **a.** 1837. **b.** 1847. **c.** 1821. **d.** 1845.

_____   8. After Texas became independent, it faced a showdown with Mexico because Texas: **a.** claimed the land south of Rio Grande. **b.** voted to annex New Mexico. **c.** claimed the land south and west of the Nueces. **d.** allied with Britain.

_____   9. Mexico was outraged by President Polk's proposal to: **a.** annex California. **b.** buy New Mexico and California. **c.** withdraw from Fort Texas. **d.** buy Texas.

_____   10. Many Mexicans favored a war with the United States because it would: **a.** give Mexico a chance to win back Texas and halt U.S. expansion. **b.** show its strength. **c.** allow Santa Anna to show he was a good general. **d.** lead to a period of prosperity in Mexico.

_____   11. The Bear Flag Republic in California was set up by: **a.** Mexican immigrants. **b.** *californios*. **c.** Anglos. **d.** General Stephen W. Kearny.

_____   12. Soon after Santa Anna's army was defeated by General Winfield Scott at the battle of Buena Vista early in 1847, the United States: **a.** ended the war. **b.** landed forces at Veracruz. **c.** sent General Kearny to California. **d.** annexed Texas.

_____   13. The last Mexican soldiers to die at Chapultepec were: **a.** the boy heroes. **b.** Santa Anna's guard. **c.** the survivors of Buena Vista. **d.** the survivors of San Pascual.

_____   14. Under the Treaty of Guadalupe Hidalgo, all of the following took place **except**: **a.** The U.S. paid Mexico $25 million. **b.** The U.S. paid off $3.25 million Mexico owed U.S. citizens. **c.** Mexico lost almost half of its territory to the United States. **d.** Mexico recognized the Nueces River as Texas's southern border.

_____   15. At the end of the war, most *californios* and *nuevomexicanos* decided to: **a.** move to Mexico. **b.** become *vaqueros*. **c.** remain in their lands. **d.** emigrate to South America.

III.   ESSAY Choose one of the following topics. Then write your answer in paragraph form on a separate sheet of paper.

A. Describe the three main aims of the United States in the war with Mexico and explain how they were achieved.

B. One historian has written, "After Texas gained its independence, war between Mexico and the U.S. was inevitable [could not be avoided]." Cite evidence from the text in support of this statement.

► CHAPTER 11 TEST: Foreigners in Their Own Land

I. **MATCHING Decide which definition in the right column best explains a term in the left column. Then write the letter of that definition in the space next to the term.**

_____ **1.** Land Law of 1851   **a.** illegal settlers

_____ **2.** title   **b.** set up commission to examine California land titles

_____ **3.** discrimination   **c.** unjust treatment of people

_____ **4.** social bandit   **d.** claim to ownership of land

_____ **5.** squatters   **e.** outlaw who claims to act on behalf of oppressed groups

II. **MULTIPLE CHOICE Choose the number that best completes the sentence or answers the question. Then write the letter of your choice in the space to the left.**

_____ **6.** In 1848, Anglos poured into California because: **a.** oil had been discovered. **b.** the United States had annexed California. **c.** gold had been discovered. **d.** land was cheap.

_____ **7.** California laws that treated Latinos as "foreigners" were examples of: **a.** title claims. **b.** discrimination. **c.** commissions. **d.** squatter laws.

_____ **8.** California was admitted to the United States as a state long before New Mexico because: **a.** most of the people there were Anglos. **b.** California was richer than New Mexico. **c.** New Mexico had no constitution. **d.** New Mexico was harder to reach from the nation's capital.

_____ **9.** Which one of these statements was true of the former Mexican borderlands? **a.** Latinos were a majority in California. **b.** Latinos were a majority in New Mexico. **c.** Latinos were a majority in California and New Mexico. **d.** All *californios* were *ricos*.

_____ **10.** In New Mexico, *ricos* tried to keep their influence by: **a.** rewriting the constitution. **b.** passing the Land Law of 1851. **c.** favoring their workers. **d.** joining with Anglos in local governments.

_____ **11.** Which of the following protected *californios* in their right to own land and to be treated justly? **a.** The constitution of 1849. **b.** The Land Law of 1851. **c.** Antidiscrimination laws. **d.** The Foreign Miners' Tax of 1850.

_____ **12.** The unjust treatment of Mexican Americans was a violation of: **a.** the Kansas-Nebraska Act. **b.** the Treaty of Guadalupe Hidalgo. **c.** squatters' rights. **d.** the U.S. Constitution.

_____ **13.** Latino landowners in California and New Mexico had problems because: **a.** they had no titles to their lands. **b.** *ricos* abandoned their estates. **c.** Anglos wanted the land. **d.** the land was cheap.

_____ **14.** Many Mexican Americans viewed social bandits as heroes because they were: **a.** avenging wrongs done to their people. **b.** reclaiming land taken from them illegally. **c.** fighting to return the land to Mexico. **d.** writing stories like those of the English Robin Hood.

_____ **15.** Because landowners in California and New Mexico were forced to spend so much time and money defending their land claims, their *ranchos* and estates often were: **a.** occupied by *vaqueros*. **b.** taken over by squatters. **c.** seized by bandits. **d.** seized by Native Americans.

III. **ESSAY Choose one of the following topics. Then write your answer in paragraph form on a separate sheet of paper.**

A. What evidence is there to show that although *californios* no longer were as powerful as they had been before California became a U.S. territory, they still had considerable influence there?

B. Explain the difficulties Mexican Americans faced as they tried to adjust to being U.S. citizens.

Name _____ Date _____

▼ UNIT 4 TEST: Latinos in the Later 1890s

I. MATCHING Decide which definition in the right column best explains a term in the left column. Then write the letter of that definition in the space next to the term.

_____ 1. *tabaqueros*

_____ 2. *insurrectos*

_____ 3. U.S. Civil War

_____ 4. yellow journalism

_____ 5. Platt Amendment

a. gave United States the right to intervene in Cuba

b. sensational newspaper reporting that influenced U.S. decision to go to war with Spain

c. rebels seeking independence of Cuba

d. cigar makers

e. struggle between the Union and the Confederacy

II. UNDERSTANDING TIME From the list below, choose the date or time period in which each of the events listed took place. Then write the letter of the date or period in the space to the left. (A letter may be used more than once.)

| a. 1862 | b. 1868 | c. 1868–1878 |
| d. 1898 | e. 1900 | f. 1901 |

_____ 6. Puerto Ricans in town of Lares rebel against Spain.

_____ 7. Cuba agrees to add the Platt Amendment to its constitution.

_____ 8. Cuba and Spain fight the Ten Years' War.

_____ 9. The Cuban-Spanish-American War is fought.

_____ 10. Farragut leads Union navy in the capture of New Orleans.

_____ 11. The Foraker Act sets up government in Puerto Rico controlled by the United States.

III. MULTIPLE CHOICE Choose the answer that best completes the sentence or answers the question. Then write the answer of your choice in the space at the left.

_____ 12. The Union army in New Mexico scored an important victory in 1862 that ended Confederate efforts to take New Mexico in a battle that was fought at: **a.** Glorieta Pass. **b.** Mobile Bay. **c.** Santa Fe. **d.** Albuquerque.

_____ 13. As a result of Cuba's Ten Years' War against Spain, most of the Cubans who fled to the United States settled in: **a.** New York City. **b.** Tampa. **c.** Key West. **d.** Miami.

_____ 14. In the later 1800s, as railroads were built and many Anglo settlers arrived in the Southwest, *nuevomexicanos* suffered because: **a.** Anglos formed cartels. **b.** Congress passed the Homestead Act. **c.** Mexican forces invaded New Mexico. **d.** Anglos took much of their land.

_____ 15. The leader of Cuban nationalism in the late 1800s who was killed by Spanish troops in the War of 1895 was: **a.** Gomez. **b.** Martí **c.** de Lôme. **d.** Maceo.

_____ 16. Cuban rebels in 1896 tried to force Spain to give up control of Cuba by: **a.** burning Havana. **b.** burning the sugar fields. **c.** assassinating de Lôme. **d.** sinking the battleship *Maine*.

_____ 17. Under the terms of the Foraker Act, Puerto Rico no longer was a Spanish colony but now was: **a.** ruled by the U.S. Army led by General Wood. **b.** given full home rule. **c.** controlled by the United States. **d.** made a state.

IV. COMPLETING THE IDEA Choose the item from the list below that best completes each of the following sentences. Then write it in the space provided.

las Gorras Blancas	*lectores*	guerrilla war
Weyler	blockaded	Cuban-Spanish-American War
protectorate	Ten Years' War	

18. After the end of the _____, Cuba and Puerto Rico were no longer colonies of Spain.

19. Farragut commanded the Union navy when it _____ the Confederate ports along the Gulf of Mexico.

20. *Nuevomexicanos* formed _____ to protect their lands against the Anglo ranchers during the cattle boom in the 1880s.

21. _____, who read to Cuban workers in U.S. cigar factories, helped strengthen Cuban nationalism.

22. The cruel actions of General _____ in Cuba helped stir up U.S. feeling against Spain.

23. The _____ was the uprising by Cubans against Spanish rule.

24. Many Cubans were unhappy about the Platt Amendment because it made Cuba a _____ _____ of the United States.

25. Because Gomez and Maceo's Cuban rebel forces were so greatly outnumbered by the Spanish army, they decided they had to fight a _____.

V. ESSAY. Choose one of the following topics. Then write your answer in paragraph form on a separate sheet of paper.

A. Suppose you were Jose Martí speaking to a crowd of Cuban Americans in 1891 about Cuba's struggle for independence. Describe the things you would stress.

B. "In 1900, Puerto Ricans feared U.S. cultural imperialism as much as U.S. political and economic control." Explain what this statement means and give evidence to show that this fear was or was not carried out.

Name _____ Date _____

◢◣ CHAPTER 12 TEST: Latinos in the U.S. Civil War

I.   MATCHING Decide which definition in the right column best explains a term in the left column. Then write the letter of that definition in the space next to the term.

_____   1. secede   **a.** closing off a port

_____   2. blockading   **b.** the North

_____   3. the Union   **c.** the South

_____   4. U.S. Civil War   **d.** to withdraw from the Union

_____   5. the Confederacy   **e.** struggle between the Union and the Confederacy

II.   MULTIPLE CHOICE Choose the answer that best completes the sentence or answers the question. Then write the letter of your choice in the space to the left.

_____   6. One of the main reasons New Mexico was important to the South during the Civil War was that: **a.** it was a source of gold. **b.** Latinos there were sympathetic to its cause. **c.** it could lead to the control of the Gulf of Mexico. **d.** if it were taken it could open the road to the gold mines of California.

_____   7. The wealthy Latino landowners of New Mexico had much in common with: **a.** Anglo Texans. **b.** Southern slave owners. **c.** Northern businesspeople. **d.** Californians.

_____   8. The main struggle in the Southwest took place in: **a.** California. **b.** Utah and Colorado. **c.** Texas. **d.** the New Mexico Territory.

_____   9. Many Latinos who lived in New Mexico changed their minds about not being loyal to either side in the Civil War when: **a.** President Lincoln issued the Emancipation Proclamation. **b.** the South was defeated at Mobile Bay. **c.** the battle of Glorieta Pass was fought. **d.** General Sibley captured Albuquerque and Santa Fe.

_____   10. The victory of the Union army at Glorieta Pass in 1862 was important because it: **a.** sealed off Santa Fe. **b.** ended Confederate efforts to move on to California and Colorado. **c.** weakened the North. **d.** caused Texas to secede.

_____   11. Admiral Farragut, one of the war's great heroes, was a Latino who commanded the Union navy at the naval battle of: **a.** Norfolk. **b.** New Orleans. **c.** Charleston. **d.** Gettysburg.

_____   12. The Confederates tried to protect the port of Mobile against an attack from the Union navy by using: **a.** floating torpedoes. **b.** a blockade. **c.** long-range cannons **d.** submarines.

_____   13. Federico Fernández Cavada provided important information about the South by using: **a.** the newly invented camera. **b.** binoculars. **c.** hot-air balloons. **d.** carrier pigeons.

_____   14. Two Cuban-born women, Lola Sanchez and Loreta Velázquez, served as spies for: **a.** the Confederacy. **b.** New Spain. **c.** the Union. **d.** New Mexico.

_____   15. The victory of Colonel Benavides's Mexican American regiment over Union troops at Laredo in 1863 helped the South because it: **a.** blocked Chivington's advance. **b.** ended the Union threat to Texas. **c.** freed New Orleans. **d.** caused riots in the North.

III.   ESSAY Choose one of the following topics. Then write your answer in paragraph form on a separate sheet of paper.

  A. If you were a Latino living in New Mexico, which side, if any, in the Civil War would you have supported?

  B. Of the men and women mentioned in this chapter, whom would you choose as being the one who ran the greatest risk of losing his or her life in the war? Explain your answer.

► CHAPTER 13 TEST: A Changing World

I.   MATCHING Decide which definition in the right column best explains a term in the left column. Then write the letter of that definition in the space next to the term.

_____   1. constitutional convention   **a.** grocery stores

_____   2. *bodegas*   **b.** group of *nuevomexicanos* who fought Anglo ranchers

_____   3. *las Gorras Blancas*   **c.** cigar makers

_____   4. *tabaqueros*   **d.** meeting to write new basic laws for a government

_____   5. *lector*   **e.** a person who read to cigar workers as they worked

II.   MULTIPLE CHOICE Choose the answer that best completes the sentence or answers the question. Then write the letter of your choice in the space to the left.

_____   6. Most of the Spanish settlers who came to the Americas in the late 1800s settled in: **a.** Bolivia and Brazil. **b.** Paraguay and Uruguay. **c.** Argentina and Cuba. **d.** Puerto Rico and Cuba.

_____   7. Many of the Spanish immigrants who had raised cattle and sheep in the Basque region of northern Spain settled in what part of the United States? **a.** the West **b.** the East **c.** the South **d.** the North

_____   8. In 1868, people of the town of Lares rose up against Spanish rule in: **a.** the Dominican Republic. **b.** Puerto Rico. **c.** Cuba. **d.** Mexico.

_____   9. Many of the Puerto Ricans in the United States in the late 1800s lived in New York City and worked in: **a.** garment factories. **b.** sugar factories. **c.** railroad yards. **d.** cigar factories.

_____   10. Most of the Cubans who came to the United States in the late 1800s fled here after: **a.** the Cuban-Spanish-American War. **b.** the failure of the 1868 revolt. **c.** Spain granted Cuba independence. **d.** the United States acquired Cuba.

_____   11. In the early 1880s, the center of Cuban nationalism in the United States was: **a.** Miami. **b.** Key West. **c.** New York City. **d.** Tampa.

_____   12. Many Cubans moved to mainland Florida in the 1880s and 1890s because: **a.** cigar factories were built at Tampa and other towns. **b.** Ybor offered workers good wages. **c.** unions relaxed their rules. **d.** the weather was like Spain's.

_____   13. The lives of Latinos in the Southwest began to change rapidly as Anglo settlers flooded in, brought by: **a.** stagecoaches. **b.** airplanes. **c.** ships. **d.** railroads.

_____   14. In 1910, when New Mexicans met at Santa Fe to write a new constitution for New Mexico: **a.** all the members were Anglos. **b.** the U.S. Congress banned *nuevomexicanos* from the meeting. **c.** all the members were *nuevomexicanos*. **d.** one third of the members were *nuevomexicanos*.

_____   15. The cattle boom in New Mexico harmed *nuevomexicanos* because: **a.** Anglos slaughtered too many cattle. **b.** Anglos took much of their land. **c.** Congress gave their land to Native Americans. **d.** cattle prices fell sharply.

III.   ESSAY Choose one of the following topics. Then write your answer in paragraph form on a separate sheet of paper.

A. Suppose you were one of the Latino delegates to New Mexico's constitutional convention in 1910. What would your goals have been in drafting this document?

B. Explain why *lectores* were important in strengthening Cuban nationalism in the United States.

Name _____ Date _____

▶ CHAPTER 14 TEST: The Cuban-Spanish-American War

I. **MATCHING Decide which definition in the right column best explains a term in the left column. Then write the letter of that definition in the space next to the term.**

_____ 1. materialism   **a.** sensational newspaper reporting

_____ 2. guerrilla war   **b.** rebels seeking independence of Cuba

_____ 3. yellow journalism   **c.** use of surprise attacks to avoid pitched battles

_____ 4. *insurrectos*   **d.** love of money and wealth

_____ 5. martial law   **e.** military control of a country

II. **MULTIPLE CHOICE Choose the answer that best completes the sentence or answers the question. Then write the letter of your choice in the space to the left.**

_____ 6. By the mid–1800s, Spain's empire in the Americas included only: **a.** Central America. **b.** Cuba and Puerto Rico. **c.** South America. **d.** Mexico.

_____ 7. In 1868, Gomez and Maceo led the Cuban uprising known as the: **a.** Ten Years' War. **b.** Cuban-Spanish-American War. **c.** Hundred Years' War. **d.** Ten Weeks' War.

_____ 8. Cuban Americans supported Martí's struggle for Cuba's independence by: **a.** donating one tenth of their weekly wages. **b.** demanding that the United States send troops. **c.** waging a guerrilla war in Cuba. **d.** strikes and boycotts in the United States.

_____ 9. Although Martí admired the U.S. democratic system of government, he criticized the United States because of its: **a.** opposition to Spain. **b.** racial prejudice and materialism. **c.** trade policies. **d.** support of Spain.

_____ 10. One of the first Cubans to die in the War of 1895 was: **a.** Gomez. **b.** Maceo. **c.** Weyler. **d.** Martí

_____ 11. The Cuban rebels in 1896 determined to force the Spanish to give up control of Cuba by: **a.** calling an international peace conference. **b.** burning the sugar fields. **c.** sinking the Spanish navy at Havana. **d.** kidnapping Weyler.

_____ 12. Relations between Spain and the United States grew strained after the publication of: **a.** Spain's demand for a truce. **b.** de Lôme's letter. **c.** McKinley's diary. **d.** Weyler's secret report.

_____ 13. The two New York publishers whose newspapers stirred up hatred toward Spain after the *Maine* sank in Havana harbor were: **a.** Shafter and Sampson. **b.** Roosevelt and Luna. **c.** Pulitzer and Hearst. **d.** Dewey and Miles.

_____ 14. The ten-week Cuban-Spanish-American War took place in: **a.** 1898. **b.** 1895. **c.** 1900. **d.** 1885.

_____ 15. When the war ended, Cuba was freed of Spanish rule, but it was now controlled by a military government set up by: **a.** Britain, France, and the United States. **b.** the United States. **c.** American oil companies. **d.** Britain and Mexico.

III. **ESSAY Choose one of the following topics. Then write your answer in paragraph form on a separate sheet of paper.**

A. If you had fought with Gomez's rebel forces in the war for Cuba's freedom in 1895, describe the military tactics you would have used.

B. Explain why José Martí's dream of a new Cuba aroused such strong and passionate support among Cuban Americans.

► CHAPTER 15 TEST: Puerto Rico and Cuba Under
► United States Control

I. **MATCHING** Decide which definition in the right column best explains a term in the left column. Then write the letter of that definition in the space next to the term.

_____ 1. home rule   **a.** gave the United States the right to intervene in Cuba

_____ 2. protectorate   **b.** workers on the sugar and tobacco plantations

_____ 3. Foraker Act   **c.** country controlled by a stronger power

_____ 4. Platt Amendment   **d.** set up U.S.-controlled government for Puerto Rico

_____ 5. *jíbaros*   **e.** self-government

II. **MULTIPLE CHOICE** Choose the answer that best completes the sentence or answers the question. Then write the letter of your choice in the space to the left.

_____ 6. When the United States launched its invasion of Puerto Rico in 1898, Spain had just granted autonomy to: **a.** Puerto Rico. **b.** Cuba. **c.** Cuba and Puerto Rico. **d.** Guantánamo Bay.

_____ 7. One reason why the United States was interested in Puerto Rico was that: **a.** it believed there were large sources of gold there. **b.** its men could be drafted into the army in case of war. **c.** its location was important to the defense of the United States. **d.** the island could be used as a tourist attraction for Americans.

_____ 8. Its one-crop economy made Puerto Rico dependent on selling its sugar to: **a.** Cuba. **b.** Britain. **c.** the United States. **d.** Spain.

_____ 9. Under the Foraker Act, Puerto Rico was: **a.** granted independence. **b.** controlled by the United States. **c.** given home rule. **d.** governed by General Leonard Wood.

_____ 10. The Puerto Rican nationalist who opposed the Foraker Act and later served as Puerto Rico's first representative to the U.S. Congress was **a.** Mario García Menocal. **b.** José Miguel Gómez **c.** Luis Muñoz Rivera. **d.** Tomás Estrada Palma.

_____ 11. Santiago Iglesias was the Puerto Rican labor leader and head of the Socialist party who favored having Puerto Rico become: **a.** a protectorate. **b.** a state of the United States. **c.** a commonwealth. **d.** a colony.

_____ 12. At the end of the Cuban-Spanish-American War, Cuba was ruled by a U.S. military government headed by: **a.** Carlos Juan Finlay **b.** Walter Reed. **c.** General Nelson Miles. **d.** General Leonard Wood.

_____ 13. In 1902, Cuba became a new nation, but its independence was restricted by: **a.** the terms of the peace treaty. **b.** the Jones Act. **c.** the Platt Amendment. **d.** Spain.

_____ 14. During Cuba's first two decades of independence, Cubans were disappointed in the quality of their: **a.** political leaders. **b.** military men. **c.** businesspeople. **d.** African Cubans.

_____ 15. U.S. businesses owned many of the large plantations and mills that produced Cuba's most important crop and chief export: **a.** tobacco. **b.** bananas. **c.** soybeans. **d.** sugar.

III. **ESSAY** Choose one of the following topics. Then write your answer in paragraph form on a separate sheet of paper.

A. Explain why Puerto Ricans feared U.S. cultural imperialism as much as U.S. political and economic control.

B. What problems did Cubans have to overcome in the first two decades after independence?

Name _____ Date _____

UNIT 5 TEST: Changes in a New Century

I.   MATCHING Decide which definition in the right column best explains a term in the left column. Then write the letter of that definition in the space next to the term.

_____   1. *braceros*

_____   2. Mexican Revolution

_____   3. New Deal

_____   4. *chicanos*

_____   5. *Hispanos*

a.   Mexican workers hired to work in the United States

b.   newly arrived unskilled Mexican workers

c.   Mexican Americans who had lived in the United States for generations

d.   U.S. government programs of President Franklin D. Roosevelt

e.   struggle for freedom that followed Díaz's overthrow

II.   UNDERSTANDING TIME Choose the date in which each of the following occurred. Write it in the space to the left.

1910   1917   1931   1941   1942   1945

_____   6.   The United States enters World War II.

_____   7.   President Hoover begins to deport Mexican immigrants.

_____   8.   The Mexican Revolution begins.

_____   9.   The United States enters World War I.

_____   10.   Latino veterans begin to take advantage of the GI Bill of Rights.

_____   11.   The *bracero* program begins.

III.   MULTIPLE CHOICE Choose the answer that best completes the sentence or answers the question. Then write the letter of your choice in the space at the left.

_____   12.   To fight for better working conditions and higher wages, Mexican migrant workers in California organized: **a.** *muralistas.* **b.** *La Liga Protectiva Mexicana.* **c.** farm unions. **d.** *colonias.*

_____   13.   Mexican Americans settled in all these areas of the United States except the: **a.** Northeast. **b.** Northwest. **c.** Midwest. **d.** Southwest.

_____   14.   The *bracero* program that hired Mexican laborers to work on U.S. farms and railroads lasted for how many years? **a.** five **b.** two **c.** four **d.** twenty-two

_____   15.   Between 1910 and 1929, a flood of immigrants from Mexico arrived in the United States as a result of: **a.** the Mexican Revolution. **b.** World War II. **c.** the *bracero* program. **d.** World War I.

_____   16.   During World War II, an attempt to eliminate prejudice and discrimination against Mexican Americans and other ethnic groups in war industries resulted in: **a.** the Fair Employment Practices Committee. **b.** the repatriation program. **c.** the quota system. **d.** the zoot-suit riots.

IV. **COMPLETING THE IDEA Choose the item from the list below that best completes each of the following sentences. Then write it in the space provided.**

Great Depression	repatriated	*la huelga*
Mexican Revolution	World War II	migrant workers
barrios	Bataan death march	

18. In 1933, about 1,500 Mexican strawberry pickers in California staged _____ in an attempt to obtain higher wages.

19. During the _____, Mexicans in the United States found it hard to obtain jobs, and they were resented by U.S. citizens who were out of work.

20. During World War II, many of the Mexican Americans who served in the U.S. armed forces in the Philippines were victims of the _____.

21. During the _____, one million Mexicans were killed in the fighting.

22. Mexicans who could not prove that they were in the United States legally were _____ to Mexico during the Great Depression.

23. Mexican immigrants in the United States settled together in _____ in the cities of California and the Southwest.

24. Manuel Gonzales and "Gabby" Gabaldon were two Latino soldiers who were decorated for bravery in fighting in _____.

25. Many of the hundreds of thousands of *mojades* and *braceros* who came to the United States in the 1940s and 1950s worked as _____.

V. **ESSAY Choose one of the following topics. Then write your answer in paragraph form on a separate sheet of paper.**

A. Explain why Mexican Americans flooded into the United States during the 1920s.

B. Suppose you had been a Latino soldier serving in World War II. Write a letter to your family describing what you planned to do when you returned to the United States.

Name _____   Date _____

► CHAPTER 16 TEST: The Mexican Revolution and New Patterns
► of Immigration

**I.   MATCHING Decide which definition in the right column best explains a term in the
left column. Then write the letter of that definition in the space next to the term.**

_____ 1. migrant workers   **a.** section of a city that has large numbers of Latinos

_____ 2. Mexican Revolution   **b.** unfair treatment in work and wages

_____ 3. *tierra y libertad*   **c.** farmworkers who travel from region to region

_____ 4. *barrio*   **d.** struggle for freedom after Díaz's overthrow

_____ 5. job discrimination   **e.** Zapata's slogan

**II.   MULTIPLE CHOICE Choose the answer that best completes the sentence or answers
the question. Then write the letter of your choice in the space to the left.**

_____ 6. In 1925, the U.S. city that had the largest Mexican population was: **a.** El Paso. **b.** Santa Fe.
             c. Los Angeles. **d.** San Antonio.

_____ 7. The Mexican leader who overthrew Porfirio Díaz in 1911 was: **a.** Victoriano Huerta.
             b. Venustiano Carranza. **c.** Emiliano Zapata. **d.** Francisco Madero.

_____ 8. Under Díaz, 3,000 families owned half of Mexico's land, and half of the nation's mines and
             oil wells were owned by: **a.** Díaz. **b.** foreign investors. **c.** the United States. **d.** the Catholic
             Church.

_____ 9. The Mexican people supported the revolution because they hoped that breaking up the
             haciendas would return the land to: **a.** the villages or individual farmers. **b.** the government.
             c. the Catholic Church. **d.** U.S. businesses.

_____ 10. The Mexican peasant leader who became the hero of the revolution to poor people was:
             a. John Pershing. **b.** Venustiano Carranza. **c.** Alvaro Obregg **d.** Emiliano Zapata.

_____ 11. The death of nearly one million people and a flood of immigrants to the United States were
             part of the high price of the: **a.** U.S. seizure of Veracruz. **b.** Mexican Revolution. **c.** land
             redistribution plan. **d.** U.S. hunt for Pancho Villa.

_____ 12. Most of the Mexican migrants who streamed north into the United States were: **a.** poor
             farmers. **b.** former soldiers. **c.** miners. **d.** businesspeople.

_____ 13. The large farms in California and the Southwest, with their abundant crops, became the
             main employers of: **a.** strikebreakers. **b.** migrant workers. **c.** families in the *barrios*.
             d. meat-packing plants.

_____ 14. Mexican immigrants in the Midwest in the early 1900s were hired as workers in factories,
             steel mills, and railroads because: **a.** they were skilled workers. **b.** they were union
             members. **c.** they worked for low wages. **d.** they learned the jobs quickly.

_____ 15. One of the greatest hardships many Mexican Americans faced was: **a.** discrimination and
             segregation. **b.** lack of jobs. **c.** a ban on immigration. **d.** getting adjusted to city life.

**III. ESSAY Choose one of the following topics. Then write your answer in paragraph form
on a separate sheet of paper.**

A. If your family had lived in Mexico during the Revolution, would you have favored moving to the
United States? Explain your answer.

B. Explain the various kinds of job discrimination that Mexicans faced in the United States.

Name _____ Date _____

▶ CHAPTER 17 TEST: World War I and Latino Americans

I. **MATCHING Decide which definition in the right column best explains a term in the left column. Then write the letter of that definition in the space next to the term.**

_____ 1. *mutualistas*

_____ 2. *chicanos*

_____ 3. *colonias*

_____ 4. *Trabajadores Unidas*

_____ 5. *Hispanos*

a. communities of Mexican farm families in the United States

b. union of Mexican workers

c. newly arrived unskilled Mexican workers

d. self-help societies

e. Mexican Americans who had lived in the United States for generations

II. **MULTIPLE CHOICE Choose the answer that best completes the sentence or answers the question. Then write the letter of your choice in the space to the left.**

_____ **6.** By 1918, Mexicans and Mexican Americans were the largest group of workers in the Imperial Valley in: **a.** Arizona**. b.** New Mexico. **c.** California. **d.** Utah.

_____ **7.** The *barrios* that were established in U.S. cities were usually: **a.** Anglo communities. **b.** in poorer sections of the cities. **c.** farmworker communities. **d.** mutual aid societies.

_____ **8.** During World War I, most Mexican immigrants to the United States settled in the: **a.** Southwest. **b.** Northeast. **c.** Imperial Valley. **d.** Midwest.

_____ **9.** The state admitted to the United States in 1912 that was a center of Mexican American growing political power was: **a.** California**. b.** New Mexico. **c.** Arizona **d.** Colorado.

_____ **10.** Mexican Americans working in the factories, steel mills, and railroads of the Northeast settled in *barrios* because: **a.** they were nearest their jobs. **b.** they were used to living in cities. **c.** they could keep their customs and traditions and help one another. **d.** they wanted to return to Mexico.

_____ **11.** Immigrants from Central and Eastern Europe regarded Mexican Americans as rivals for jobs and made them: **a.** victims of racism and prejudice. **b.** take only farming jobs. **c.** settle in small towns. **d.** settle in *colonias*.

_____ **12.** By 1925, the largest population of Mexican Americans living outside the Southwest was found in: **a.** Detroit. **b.** Altoona. **c.** Cleveland. **d.** Chicago.

_____ **13.** After Puerto Ricans received the rights of U.S. citizens in 1917: **a.** none of them served in World War I. **b.** over 200,000 registered in the draft. **c.** many refused to join the army. **d.** the armed forces refused to accept Puerto Ricans.

_____ **14.** Many Mexicans came to the United States during World War I because the drafting of U.S. citizens to fight the war caused: **a.** a labor shortage. **b.** a labor surplus. **c.** stricter immigration laws. **d.** an all-volunteer army.

_____ **15.** Octaviano A. Larrazolo was a New Mexican governor who: **a.** favored the use of English only in the schools. **b.** fought in the Mexican army. **c.** was a strong supporter of Latino rights. **d.** had a new state constitution adopted.

III. **ESSAY Choose one of the following topics. Then write your answer in paragraph form on a separate sheet of paper.**

A. Explain what life was like for Mexican Americans living in the Los Angeles *barrio* in 1920.

B. Suppose you were a Mexican American worker living in a Midwest city who suffered discrimination from the groups of new European immigrants there. Write a letter to the mayor telling why you think all immigrants face common problems and should work harder to get along better.

THE LATINO EXPERIENCE IN U.S. HISTORY • © Globe Fearon

Name _____ Date _____

▶ **CHAPTER 18 TEST: From Boom to Depression**

I.   MATCHING Decide which definition in the right column best explains a term in the left column. Then write the letter of that definition in the space next to the term.

_____   **1.** New Deal

_____   **2.** *repatriados*

_____   **3.** Great Depression

_____   **4.** *la huelga*

_____   **5.** public works

a. persons who are deported to their homeland

b. the strike

c. projects to build bridges, roads, and public buildings

d. programs of President Franklin D. Roosevelt to bring the United States out of the Great Depression

e. period of high unemployment during the 1930s

II.   MULTIPLE CHOICE Choose the answer that best completes the sentence or answers the question. Then write the letter of your choice in the space to the left.

_____   **6.** Most Mexicans in the United States did not apply for citizenship because: **a.** the Immigration Act of 1924 forbade it. **b.** they planned to return home. **c.** Congress reduced Mexico's quota. **d.** they faced repatriation.

_____   **7.** The purpose of the U.S. Border Patrol, established in 1924, was to: **a.** keep Europeans out of the United States. **b.** stop Mexicans from entering the United States illegally. **c.** block all immigration from Mexico. **d.** recruit Mexicans as workers.

_____   **8.** Over 500,000 Mexicans returned to their homeland as a result of the U.S. repatriation program in: **a.** the 1930s. **b.** the 1920s. **c.** the 1940s. **d.** 1921.

_____   **9.** *La Liga Protectiva, La Orden de Hijos de America,* and The League of United Latin American Citizens were groups established to fight for: **a.** Latinos' civil rights. **b.** larger quotas for Mexican Americans. **c.** stronger *mutualistas.* **d.** repatriation.

_____   **10.** A Mexican American labor leader and fighter for civil rights in the 1930s was: **a.** Ernesto Galarza. **b.** Dennis Chávez. **c.** César Chávez. **d.** Luisa Moreno.

_____   **11.** As a result of the large influx of Mexicans in the 1920s, by 1930 the Mexican American population in the United States had reached: **a.** 500,000. **b.** 100,000. **c.** 1.2 million. **d.** 10 million.

_____   **12.** The Immigration Act of 1924 reflected Americans': **a.** fear of war. **b.** dislike of quotas. **c.** need of workers. **d.** distrust of foreigners.

_____   **13.** During the Great Depression, nearly one third of all workers in the United States were: **a.** Mexican Americans. **b.** unemployed. **c.** women. **d.** immigrants.

_____   **14.** The hard times caused by the Great Depression and high unemployment among Anglos caused President Hoover to start a program to: **a.** provide more relief for all Latinos. **b.** deport illegal Mexican immigrants. **c.** stop all immigration. **d.** repatriate all foreigners.

_____   **15.** The first successful unions for Mexican Americans were those set up by: **a.** the American Federation of Labor. **b.** farmworkers. **c.** factory workers. **d.** the New Deal.

III.   ESSAY Choose one of the following topics. Then write your answer in paragraph form on a separate sheet of paper.

A. Explain why organizing unions was so difficult for farmworkers.

B. Luisa Moreno and other Mexican American leaders protested against the repatriation policy launched by President Hoover in 1931. Write a letter like one Moreno might have sent the President, listing three important reasons why repatriation was wrong.

CHAPTER 19 TEST: Latinos and World War II

I. **MATCHING Decide which definition in the right column best explains a term in the left column. Then write the letter of that definition in the space next to the term.**

_____ 1. *braceros*

_____ 2. *mojados*

_____ 3. GI Bill of Rights

_____ 4. *pachucos*

_____ 5. Fair Employment Practices Committee

a. "wetbacks," or illegal workers hired by Texans

b. body created to end discrimination in war industries

c. Mexican laborers hired to work in the United States

d. law providing benefits for veterans of World War II

e. Mexican American youths who wore flashy clothing in the 1940s

II. **MULTIPLE CHOICE Choose the answer that best completes the sentence or answers the question. Then write the letter of your choice in the space to the left.**

_____ 6. During World War II, 17 Mexican Americans earned the highest U.S. decoration for bravery, called the: **a.** Purple Heart. **b.** Congressional Medal of Honor. **c.** Distinguished Service Cross. **d.** Silver Star.

_____ 7. As a result of the GI Bill of Rights, many Latino veterans in World War II benefited from all of the following *except*: **a.** the chance to attend West Point. **b.** the chance to go to college. **c.** the opportunity to improve their English. **d.** the opportunity to start a new business.

_____ 8. The *bracero* program was set up to provide laborers for: **a.** factories. **b.** steel mills. **c.** farms and railroads. **d.** mines.

_____ 9. Texas was excluded from taking part in the *bracero* program because: **a.** it was hostile to people of Mexican ancestry. **b.** it had no jobs. **c.** it wanted only Anglos to work on the farms. **d.** it was not willing to pay what *braceros* demanded.

_____ 10. In 1941, the U.S. government passed a law to end discrimination against Mexican Americans and other minorities in: **a.** schools. **b.** war industries. **c.** the army. **d.** elections.

_____ 11. Because they spoke Spanish, Mexican American soldiers served alongside other Spanish speakers in: **a.** North Africa. **b.** France. **c.** the Philippines. **d.** Sicily.

_____ 12. U.S. labor leaders opposed the *bracero* program because: **a.** it discriminated against Anglo workers. **b.** it encouraged too many Mexicans to come to the United States. **c.** they felt it would endanger U.S. workers' health. **d.** they felt it would lower wages for Americans.

_____ 13. *Braceros* like Juan Garza helped the U.S. war effort and endured great hardships because they: **a.** needed money to support their families in Mexico. **b.** could become U.S. citizens in a shorter time. **c.** were skilled workers. **d.** were *mojados*.

_____ 14. In Los Angeles in 1943, prejudice and discrimination against Mexican Americans led to: **a.** job layoffs. **b.** the spread of *barrios*. **c.** laws banning Spanish. **d.** the zoot-suit riots.

_____ 15. U.S. business owners asked for the *bracero* program to be extended to 1964 because: **a.** there was still a labor shortage. **b.** they believed *braceros* were good workers. **c.** they still wanted to take advantage of the *braceros'* low wages. **d.** they wanted Mexicans to have a chance to earn a good living.

III. **ESSAY Choose one of the following topics. Then write your answer in paragraph form on a separate sheet of paper.**

A. If you had been a *pachuca* or a *pachuco* in Los Angeles, what would you have done when the riots broke out in 1943?

B. Explain the advantages and disadvantages of the *bracero* program for a Mexican farmworker.

Name _____ Date _____

◆ UNIT 6 TEST: A Changing Postwar World

I. MATCHING Decide which definition in the right column best explains a term in the left column. Then write the letter of that definition in the space next to the term.

_____ **1.** *huelga*

_____ **2.** Operation Bootstrap

_____ **3.** political exiles

_____ **4.** coup

_____ **5.** mural

a. wall painting

b. sudden overthrow of a government

c. strike

d. Muñoz Marín's program for Puerto Rico

e. people who leave a country for political reasons

II. UNDERSTANDING TIME Choose the year in which each of the events listed took place. Then write the letter of the year in the space to the left.

      A. 1950   **B.** 1959   **C.** 1961   **D.** 1962   **E.** 1965   **F.** 1976

_____ **6.** Trujillo is assassinated in the Dominican Republic.

_____ **7.** Fidel Castro overthrows Batista's government.

_____ **8.** Puerto Rico becomes a commonwealth of the United States.

_____ **9.** César Chávez founds the National Farm Workers Union.

_____ **10.** The "dirty war" begins in Argentina.

_____ **11.** The Sandinistas overthrow Somoza's government in Nicaragua.

_____ **12.** The Camarioca boatlift from Cuba to the United States begins.

III. MULTIPLE CHOICE Choose the answer that best completes the sentence or answers the question. Then write the letter of your choice in the space at the left.

_____ **13.** The people who came to the United States from these nations were all fleeing revolutions or military-controlled governments *except* the: **a.** Cubans. **b.** Puerto Ricans. **c.** Dominicans. **d.** Salvadorans.

_____ **14.** The Missile Crisis, the Bay of Pigs, and the Camarioca boatlift all were related to: **a.** Puerto Rico. **b.** Colombia. **c.** Dominican Republic. **d.** Cuba.

_____ **15.** By 1980, the largest group of Latinos in the United States was Mexican Americans, and the second-largest was: **a.** Dominicans. **b.** Guatemalans. **c.** Puerto Ricans. **d.** Nicaraguans.

_____ **16.** Mexican American leaders like César Chávez, Dolores Huerta, Reies López Tijerina, and Corky Gonzales who worked to secure equal rights and greater opportunities were all part of: **a.** the Chicano movement. **b.** *La Raza Unida.* **c.** National Chicano Moratorium. **d.** *Venceremos.*

_____ **17.** By the 1970s, guerrilla warfare and harsh government repression had caused the first large group of South Americans to flee to the United States from which nation? **a.** Argentina **b.** Chile **c.** Colombia **d.** Uruguay

_____ **18.** By the 1990s, Latino writers, artists, musicians, sports figures, and entertainers had made important contributions to U.S.: **a.** computer literacy. **b.** popular culture. **c.** literacy rate. **d.** political culture.

IV. **COMPLETING THE IDEA Choose the item from the list below that best completes each of the following sentences. Then write it in the space provided.**

Bay of Pigs	*La Raza Unida*	Joaquín
nuyoricans	*El Movimiento*	*La Causa*
human rights		

19. Puerto Ricans who were born and raised on the mainland are called _____ by island Puerto Ricans.

20. _____ is the central figure in a poem by Corky Gonzalez.

21. The more radical Chicano movement led by Tijerina in New Mexico was called _____.

22. Fidel Castro drove back the U.S.-supported Cuban refugee invasion at the _____ _____.

23. _____ was the name the Mexican American farmworkers gave to their union.

24. José Angel Gutiérrez organized _____ as the first Chicano political party in Colorado, California, and the Southwest.

25. During the 1970s, military dictatorships in Central American nations increasingly violated the _____ of their people.

V. **ESSAY Choose one of the following topics. Then write your answer in paragraph form on a separate sheet of paper.**

A. Describe the conditions in one of the nations of Central America that caused large numbers of its people to flee to the United States.

B. "Castro betrayed his promise to liberate Cuba." Explain why you agree or disagree with this statement, citing evidence from the text.

▶ CHAPTER 20 TEST: The Great Migration from Puerto Rico

I.   MATCHING Decide which definition in the right column best explains a term in the left column. Then write the letter of that definition in the space next to the term.

_____   **1.** bilingual

_____   **2.** *autonomismo*

_____   **3.** commonwealth

_____   **4.** *puertorriqueños*

_____   **5.** Operation Bootstrap

a. self-governing nation associated with the United States

b. program of economic improvement for Puerto Rico

c. people of Puerto Rico

d. using two languages

e. program of self-government for Puerto Rico

II.   MULTIPLE CHOICE Choose the answer that best completes the sentence or answers the question. Then write the letter of your choice in the space to the left.

_____   **6.** The four Puerto Ricans who attacked members of the House of Representatives in 1954 strongly favored: **a.** statehood. **b.** commonwealth. **c.** independence. **d.** *autonomismo*.

_____   **7.** Governor Muñoz Marín launched Operation Bootstrap in an effort to change Puerto Rico from an agricultural society to: **a.** a socialist society. **b.** an industrial society. **c.** a creditor society. **d.** a Communist society.

_____   **8.** Before World War II, few people traveled from Puerto Rico to the United States, but after 1945, fares went down and many Puerto Ricans were able to migrate by traveling on: **a.** ships. **b.** airplanes. **c.** buses. **d.** trains.

_____   **9.** Puerto Rico's three major political parties differ mainly on the matter of: **a.** immigration to the United States. **b.** industrialization. **c.** independence and relationship to the United States. **d.** bilingualism.

_____   **10.** During the 1950s and 1960s, most Puerto Ricans who came to the United States were farmers who found jobs as: **a.** unskilled and semiskilled workers. **b.** farm laborers. **c.** professional workers. **d.** migrant workers.

_____   **11.** Puerto Rico's constitution, which went into effect in 1952, was modeled on: **a.** Mexico's 1910 laws. **b.** the U.S. Constitution. **c.** Cuba's Constitution. **d.** the Jones Act.

_____   **12.** Because more than twice as many Puerto Ricans lived here as in San Juan, this city was called "the Puerto Rican capital of the world": **a.** New York **b.** Camden, New Jersey **c.** Washington, D.C. **d.** Chicago

_____   **13.** By 1980, the two million Puerto Ricans who lived on the mainland ranked as which group in the United States? **a.** the largest Latino group **b.** the third-largest Latino group **c.** the second-largest Latino group **d.** the largest Spanish-speaking group

_____   **14.** Puerto Rico's first elected leader and head of the PPD was: **a.** Lolita Lebron. **b.** Antonio Pantoja. **c.** Pura Belpre. **d.** Muñoz Marín.

_____   **15.** Under U.S. Public Law 600, passed in 1952, Puerto Rico became: **a.** a state of the United States. **b.** a commonwealth. **c.** an independent nation separate from the United States. **d.** an independent nation with ties to Cuba.

III.   ESSAY Choose one of the following topics. Then write your answer in paragraph form on a separate sheet of paper.

A. Suppose that you were a young Puerto Rican planning on moving to the United States in the 1950s. Write a letter to the Office of the Commonwealth of Puerto Rico in New York asking for information that would help you.

B. Explain some of the changes Operation Bootstrap brought to Puerto Rico.

Name _____ Date _____

◀ CHAPTER 21 TEST: New Arrivals from the Caribbean

I. MATCHING Decide which definition in the right column best explains a term in the left column. Then write the letter of that definition in the space next to the term.

_____	1. Bay of Pigs	**a.** large commercial farms
_____	2. communes	**b.** Trujillo's "torture chambers"
_____	3. political exiles	**c.** where invasion by Cuban exiles took place
_____	4. *latifundia*	**d.** people who leave a country for political reasons
_____	5. *La Cuarenta*	**e.** farms jointly owned and worked by landless peasants

II. MULTIPLE CHOICE Choose the answer that best completes the sentence or answers the question. Then write the letter of your choice in the space to the left.

_____ 6. Rafael Trujillo ruled the Dominican Republic as a dictator for more than 30 years, from: **a.** 1930 to 1961. **b.** 1960 to 1991. **c.** 1900 to 1931. **d.** 1921 to 1952.

_____ 7. The Dominican Republic shares the island of Hispaniola with what country? **a.** Cuba **b.** Haiti **c.** Jamaica **d.** Trinidad

_____ 8. After he overthrew President Machado, Fulgencio Batista ruled Cuba as a dictator beginning in: **a.** 1961. **b.** 1959. **c.** 1922 **d.** 1952.

_____ 9. Batista ruled with the support of U.S. business interests because he: **a.** broke up the *latifundia*. **b.** was an enemy of Trujillo. **c.** protected foreign businesses. **d.** favored communism.

_____ 10. When Fidel Castro took control of Cuba, the country was: **a.** a land whose wealth was evenly distributed among its people. **b.** the most highly developed nation in Latin America. **c.** a Soviet missile base. **d.** a socialist nation.

_____ 11. Fidel Castro tried to improve Cuba's economy by turning to: **a.** state ownership of industry. **b.** blockades. **c.** private ownership. **d.** democracy.

_____ 12. Soon after Castro seized power, thousands of Cubans fled their country and moved to the United States because: **a.** Cuba suffered crop failures and famines. **b.** Castro turned Cuba into a Communist nation. **c.** the Bay of Pigs invasion failed. **d.** prices in Cuba rose sharply.

_____ 13. The United States and the Soviet Union nearly went to war in 1962 over the: **a.** Bay of Pigs invasion. **b.** Camarioca boatlift. **c.** Cuban Revolution. **d.** Cuban Missile Crisis.

_____ 14. Castro's dictatorship caused nearly 600,000 Cubans to flee their nation by 1973, nearly half of whom settled in: **a.** New York City. **b.** Miami. **c.** Jersey City. **d.** Los Angeles.

_____ 15. By the 1990s, the Dominicans were the U.S.'s: **a.** fastest-growing immigrant group. **b.** the last immigrant group from Latin America. **c.** the only Latino immigrant group that did not speak Spanish. **d.** the only immigrant group that did not settle in cities.

III. ESSAY Choose one of the following topics. Then write your answer in paragraph form on a separate sheet of paper.

Α. Explain why the 1961 Bay of Pigs invasion ended in failure.

B. Why did many Dominicans emigrate to the United States beginning in the 1960s?

Name _____ Date _____

▶ CHAPTER 22 TEST: The Struggle for Equal Rights

I.   MATCHING Decide which definition in the right column best completes a term in the left column. Then write the letter of that definition in the space next to the term.

_____ 1. *La Causa*   **a.** the push for Latino rights

_____ 2. boycott   **b.** being forced to leave a country

_____ 3. *El Movimiento*   **c.** to refuse to buy certain goods to force a change of policy

_____ 4. deportation   **d.** the United People

_____ 5. *La Raza Unida*   **e.** the farmworkers' movement

II.   MULTIPLE CHOICE Choose the answer that best completes the sentence or answers the question. Then write your choice in the space to the left.

_____ 6. César Chávez became convinced that if farmworkers were to improve their lives, they had to: **a.** join a political party. **b.** become *braceros*. **c.** reclaim lands owned by their Mexican ancestors. **d.** organize a union.

_____ 7. Chávez refused help from the AFL in organizing the farmworkers because he: **a.** believed the workers must build their own union. **b.** feared they would break the union. **c.** preached nonviolence. **d.** believed it discriminated against Mexican Americans.

_____ 8. Chávez found which group especially difficult to organize? **a.** Chicanos **b.** *aliancistas* **c.** *braceros* and illegal immigrants **d.** *La Causa* and *La Raza*

_____ 9. The black Aztec eagle and *la huelga* were symbols of the: **a.** National Farm Workers Association. **b.** Young Lords. **c.** AFL-CIO. **d.** *El Movimiento*.

_____ 10. The Mexican American leader who believed that Latinos' problems could be solved by regaining the lands in New Mexico owned by their ancestors was: **a.** Dolores Huerta. **b.** Reies López Tijerina. **c.** José Angel Gutiérrez. **d.** Corky Gonzales.

_____ 11. The Latino movement known as *La Causa* followed and was deeply influenced by: **a.** the African American Civil Rights Movement. **b.** the DiGiorgio Corporation. **c.** the AFL-CIO. **d.** the *bracero* movement.

_____ 12. By 1972, the union of farmworkers led by Chávez and Huerta was called: **a.** *El Movimiento*. **b.** *Alianza Federal de Mercedes*. **c.** *La Raza Unida*. **d.** the United Farm Workers.

_____ 13. The Mexican American activist who founded *La Cruzada Para La Justicia* to preach self-help and instill pride in Latino culture was: **a.** Dolores Huerta. **b.** Corky Gonzales. **c.** Joseph Montoya. **d.** José Angel Gutiérrez.

_____ 14. Increased respect for the Latino heritage, greater Latino political power, and more Latino opportunities for jobs and education were results of: **a.** *la huelga*. **b.** the *aliancistas*. **c.** the Chicano movement. **d.** civil disobedience.

_____ 15. By 1980, with more than 2 million Puerto Ricans and 11 million Mexican Americans in the United States, Latinos were the: **a.** largest ethnic group. **b.** the second-largest ethnic group. **c.** smallest ethnic group. **d.** fourth-largest ethnic group.

III.   ESSAY Choose one of the following topics. Then write your answer in paragraph form on a separate sheet of paper.

A. How did the conditions faced by Mexican American farmworkers in the early 1960s make them welcome Chávez and help him form a union?

B. Choose one of the outstanding Mexican American leaders in the Southwest and write a brief biography of his or her career and achievements.

CHAPTER 23 TEST: New Immigrants from Central and South America

I.   **MATCHING Decide which definition in the right column best completes a term in the left column. Then write the letter of that definition in the space next to the term.**

_____   **1.** human rights

_____   **2.** death squads

_____   **3.** social justice

_____   **4.** coup

_____   **5.** "the dirty war"

a. military thugs who murder their opponents

b. sudden overthrow of a government

c. Argentina's military government's campaign against those who opposed it

d. basic rights of people as human beings

e. Catholic Church's demand for more just societies in Latin America

II.   **MULTIPLE CHOICE Choose the answer that best completes the sentence or answers the question. Then write the letter of your choice in the space to the left.**

_____   **6.** When the Guatemalan government headed by Jacobo Arbenz Guzmán seized large foreign-owned farmlands to give to the people, the United States: **a.** supported Arbenz. **b.** backed a military coup that ousted Arbenz. **c.** invaded Guatemala. **d.** did nothing.

_____   **7.** U.S. policy in Guatemala, El Salvador, Nicaragua, and other Latin American nations was based on: **a.** opposing the spread of communism. **b.** supporting democracy. **c.** breaking up the *latifundias*. **d.** protecting human rights.

_____   **8.** In the late 1970s, Fidel Castro provided aid and encouraged rebel leaders in Central America to: **a.** overthrow their dictatorships. **b.** welcome all political exiles. **c.** set up military governments. **d.** fight the United States.

_____   **9.** In both El Salvador and Nicaragua, revolutions that overthrew military governments turned into: **a.** U.S.-controlled regimes. **b.** civil wars. **c.** priest-ruled governments. **d.** democracies.

_____   **10.** Nearly 75,000 people fled to the United States during the 1970s as a result of a military crackdown in: **a.** Guatemala. **b.** El Salvador. **c.** Argentina. **d.** Nicaragua.

_____   **11.** After World War II, the first sizable immigration to the United States began from what region? **a.** Central America **b.** Mexico **c.** North America **d.** South America

_____   **12.** By the 1980s, large South American populations were living in: **a.** the Southwest. **b.** New York and other cities. **c.** small U.S. towns. **d.** the South.

_____   **13.** The Sandinistas and the Contras fought for power in which country? **a.** El Salvador **b.** Guatemala **c.** Colombia **d.** Nicaragua

_____   **14.** Two important reasons for the arrival of growing numbers of people from South America were government repression and: **a.** airlifts by the Catholic Church. **b.** cheap airline travel. **c.** the end of U.S. quotas. **d.** famine.

_____   **15.** After the United States helped overthrow the Arbenz government in Guatemala, that nation was ruled by: **a.** Communists. **b.** military men. **c.** Fidel Castro. **d.** the United States.

III.   **ESSAY Choose one of the following topics. Then write your answer in paragraph form on a separate sheet of paper.**

A. Explain why the military governments of many Central American nations violated the human rights of their people in the 1970s.

B. During the 1980s, nearly one fourth of El Salvador's population fled, and many came to the United States. How did this migration reflect conditions in many other nations of Central America as well?

Name _____ Date _____

▶ CHAPTER 24 TEST: A Growing Voice

I. **MATCHING Decide which definition in the right column best explains a term in the left column.**

_____ 1. salsa

_____ 2. murals

_____ 3. *jíbaros*

_____ 4. bicultural

_____ 5. *nuyoricans*

    a. having roots in two cultures

    b. wall paintings

    c. music that blends the African and Spanish heritage of Caribbean Latinos

    d. second-generation mainland Puerto Ricans

    e. peasants

II. **MULTIPLE CHOICE Choose the answer that best completes the sentence or answers the question. Then write the letter of your choice in the space to the left.**

_____ 6. The United States now has become the: **a.** leading bilingual nation. **b.** fastest-growing nation. **c.** largest Latino nation. **d.** fourth-largest Spanish-speaking nation.

_____ 7. One leader of the Puerto Rican cultural revival in the United States during the 1950s and 1960s was a New York businesswoman named: **a.** Celia Vice. **b.** Linda Ronstadt. **b.** René Marqués **c.** Sandra María Esteves. **d.** Judith Ortíz-Cofer.

_____ 8. The first Latino writer to win the Pulitzer Prize for fiction was: **a.** Heberto Padilla. **b.** Oscar Hijuelos. **c.** Lourdes Casal. **d.** Antonio Martorell.

_____ 9. Chicano writers and artists were deeply inspired by: **a.** the Cuban Revolution. **b.** Caribbean cultures. **c.** *nuyoricans*. **d.** *El Movimiento*.

_____ 10. The most famous Latino publishing company is: **a.** Telemundo. **b.** *El Movimiento*. **c.** Arte Publico. **d.** *El Teatro Campesino*.

_____ 11. The first generation of Puerto Rican writers and artists in the United States made fun of: **a.** "Americanized" Puerto Ricans. **b.** *jíbaros*. **c.** the United States. **d.** island Puerto Ricans.

_____ 12. A blending of Spanish and African Caribbean cultures was found in the works of which group of artists and writers? **a.** Mexican Americans **b.** Cuban Americans **c.** Puerto Ricans **d.** Latin Americans

_____ 13. As Cuban American writers and artists began to focus on Cuban culture in the United States, they paid less attention to: **a.** their experiences as exiles. **b.** the immigration laws. **c.** U.S. politics. **d.** Chicano culture.

_____ 14. Which group of Latino writers drew inspiration from Maya and Aztec cultures? **a.** Dominicans **b.** Puerto Ricans **c.** Cuban Americans **d.** Chicanos

_____ 15. Roberto Clemente is an example of a Latino who is remembered not only for his ability as a baseball player but also for his interest in: **a.** helping other Latinos. **b.** making the highest salary as a player. **c.** becoming the first Latino baseball manager. **d.** Puerto Rican politics.

III. **ESSAY Choose one of the following topics. Then write your answer in paragraph form on a separate sheet of paper.**

    A. Choose several outstanding Latino sports figures, entertainers, writers, or artists and explain why you believe them to be superior in their fields. Cite evidence to support your answer.

    B. Compare the experiences of Cuban American writers and artists with those of Puerto Rican writers and artists in the United States. How are they similar? How are they different?

Name _____ Date _____

◆ UNIT 7 TEST: Latinos Today

I. **MATCHING Decide which definition in the right column best fits the term in the left column. Then write the letter of that definition in the space next to the term.**

_____ **1.** *La Violencia*

_____ **2.** *maquiladoras*

_____ **3.** referendum

_____ **4.** *indocumentados*

_____ **5.** coyote

    a. person who guides illegal Mexican immigrants across the border to the United States

    b. assembly plants on the Mexican side of the border of Mexico and the United States

    c. illegal immigrants

    d. unrest and internal struggles in Central American nations

    e. vote by the people on a particular issue

II. **UNDERSTANDING TIME Read the following list of events. Then number the events from 1 to 6 in the order in which they happened. There may be several events for a single year.**

_____ **6.** Violeta Chamorro defeats Daniel Ortega for president of Nicaragua.

_____ **7.** Disturbances break out in Los Angeles.

_____ **8.** Congress passes the U.S. Immigration Reform Act.

_____ **9.** Mariel Boatlift from Cuba to the United States takes place.

_____ **10.** First Latino woman is elected to the Los Angles County Board of Supervisors.

_____ **11.** Sandinistas seize control of Nicaragua.

III. **MULTIPLE CHOICE Choose the answer that best completes the sentence or answers the question. Then write the letter of your choice in the space at the left.**

_____ **12.** Many Latino immigrants in the United States today are like immigrants of the past because they: **a.** do not plan to stay in the United States for long. **b.** send money to their families back home. **c.** are highly paid professional workers. **d.** quickly give up their native language in favor of English.

_____ **13.** *La Frontera* is the 2,000-mile (3,200-kilometer) border between: **a.** the United States and Canada. **b.** Mexico and Guatemala. **c.** the United States and Mexico. **d.** Bolivia and Colombia.

_____ **14.** Only a small number of Puerto Ricans favor: **a.** complete independence from the United States. **b.** becoming a state of the United States. **c.** continuing as a commonwealth of the United States. **d.** continuing to be citizens of the United States.

_____ **15.** Cuban Americans as a group are different from other Latinos in that they: **a.** have given up the use of Spanish as the language of everyday life. **b.** live in many widely scattered cities. **c.** do almost as well economically as Anglos. **d.** are active in the established political parties.

_____ **16.** New York City is the U.S. city with the largest number of immigrants from: **a.** Cuba and Puerto Rico. **b.** Dominican Republic and Mexico. **c.** Central America and South America. **d.** Dominican Republic and Puerto Rico.

     THE LATINO EXPERIENCE IN U.S. HISTORY • © Globe Fearon

_____ 17. Although immigrants from Latin America often suffer from discrimination and prejudice in the United States, they continue to immigrate because: **a.** the United States offers freedom and jobs. **b.** the United States offers low-cost health insurance. **c.** no other country will accept them. **d.** they have traveled to the United States many times before.

IV. COMPLETING THE IDEA Choose the item from the list below that best completes each of the following sentences. Then write it in the space provided.

la migra	U.S. Census Bureau	_nuyoricans_
Mariel Boatlift	free-trade region	Immigration Reform Act
campesinos	_bodegas_	

18. The U.S. Congress passed the _____ in 1986 in an effort to end illegal immigration from Mexico.

19. In 1980, Fidel Castro allowed a large group of Cubans, including prisoners, to come to the United States in the _____.

20. Many Latin American immigrants are _____, or peasant farmers, who worked at agricultural jobs in the countryside.

21. In the 1990s, Mexico, the United States, and Canada were working to make the three nations a _____ in which goods could pass from one country to another without being subject to tariffs, or taxes on goods being exchanged.

22. _____ provides important information, such as the number of people in each Latino group, where they live, and their income and education levels.

23. Island Puerto Ricans use the term _____ to refer to second-generation mainland Puerto Ricans.

24. Undocumented aliens and illegal immigrants crossing the border from Mexico into the United States are sometimes caught by _____.

25. _____, which are found in most Latino neighborhoods, are one of the most successful types of small businesses owned by Latinos.

V. ESSAY Choose one of the following topics. Then write your answer in paragraph form on a separate sheet of paper.

A. Choose one of the Latino groups described in the text and explain the progress made by these people during the 1980s and 1990s.

B. "The United States is still the Land of Promise, as it was to immigrants in the past." Do you agree or disagree with this statement? Explain your answer.

Name _____ Date _____

▶ CHAPTER 25 TEST: Mexican Americans Today

I.   MATCHING Decide which definition in the right column best explains a term in the left column.

_____ 1. *maquiladoras*

_____ 2. *la migra*

_____ 3. free-trade region

_____ 4. *indocumentados*

_____ 5. aliens

a. citizens of another country

b. illegal immigrants

c. assembly plants in Mexico

d. U.S. border guards

e. place where goods pass from one country to another without tariffs

II.   MULTIPLE CHOICE Choose the answer that best completes the sentence or answers the question. Then write the letter of your choice in the space to the left.

_____ 6. In the 1990s, the United States, Mexico, and Canada set up the: **a.** Organization of American States. **b.** *maquiladoras* program. **c.** North American Free Trade Agreement. **d.** *Los Tigres del Norte.*

_____ 7. The Mexican American population of the United States has increased by 10 million since 1960 and now numbers: **a.** 13.3 million. **b.** 31 million. **c.** 11 million. **d.** 25 million.

_____ 8. The Texas city that is the home of the fourth-largest Latino population in the United States is: **a.** Dallas. **b.** San Antonio. **c.** El Paso. **d.** Austin.

_____ 9. Three fourths of the Latino population in Los Angeles trace their origins to: **a.** Central America. **b.** the Caribbean islands. **c.** South America. **d.** Mexico.

_____ 10. During the 1980s and 1990s, over 200,000 Mexicans migrated to which U.S. city? **a.** Newark **b.** New York **c.** Denver **d.** Jersey City

_____ 11. Many Mexican immigrants in the United States today are like those in the past because they: **a.** plan to move back to Mexico. **b.** are highly paid skilled workers. **c.** send money to their families back home. **d.** are political exiles.

_____ 12. Mexicans immigrants without the necessary papers often cross the U.S. border with the help of: **a.** a passport. **b.** a coyote. **c.** *la migra.* **d.** the *maquiladoras.*

_____ 13. The United States passed the Immigration Reform Act of 1986 in an effort to: **a.** end illegal immigration from Mexico. **b.** increase Mexican immigration. **c.** set up the Border Patrol. **d.** stop all immigration from Mexico.

_____ 14. Some Mexicans oppose the *maquiladoras* because: **a.** U.S. companies make excessive profits. **b.** women are never hired. **c.** only *indocumentados* are hired. **d.** jobs are low paying and the plants pollute the air and water.

_____ 15. The part of the border between Mexico and the United States through which most immigrants journey is called: **a.** border patrols. **b.** *La Frontera.* **c.** *la migra.* **d.** NFTA.

III.   ESSAY Choose one of the following topics. Then write your answer in paragraph form on a separate sheet of paper.

A. Suppose you and your family were entering the United States as *indocumentados* and were caught by the U.S. Border Patrol. How would you explain what you were doing to the U.S. agent?

B. How do the people of San Antonio show their close ties with Mexico?

THE LATINO EXPERIENCE IN U.S. HISTORY • © Globe Fearon

► CHAPTER 26 TEST: Puerto Ricans Today

I. **MATCHING Decide which definition in the right column best explains a term in the left column. Then write the letter of that definition in the space next to the term.**

_____ 1. *El Barrio*   **a.** popular vote of the people

_____ 2. *nuyoricans*   **b.** small house and garden on cleaned-up empty city lot

_____ 3. referendum   **c.** Puerto Rican community in New York City

_____ 4. *casita*   **d.** efforts to protect the land and water

_____ 5. environmental movement   **e.** second-generation mainland Puerto Ricans

II. **MULTIPLE CHOICE Choose the answer that best completes the sentence or answers the question. Then write the letter of your choice in the space to the left.**

_____ 6. In 1990, more than 11 percent of the total Latin population was: **a.** mainland Puerto Ricans. **b.** island Puerto Ricans. **c.** *independentistas.* **d.** *nuyoricans.*

_____ 7. The great migration from Puerto Rico in the 1950s was slowed by the: **a.** business boom in Puerto Rico. **b.** sharp decline in unskilled U.S. jobs. **c.** Immigration Act of 1986. **d.** rise in air fares.

_____ 8. Education today is an important part of the lives of mainland Puerto Ricans because: **a.** it is a way to escape poverty. **b.** they are the third generation. **c.** it helps them get unskilled jobs. **d.** they want to return to Puerto Rico with higher skills.

_____ 9. The *Atrévete* voter registration drive has helped mainland Puerto Ricans to: **a.** register their cars. **b.** obtain better medical care. **c.** increase their political power. **d.** vote on the island.

_____ 10. Puerto Ricans in the South Bronx of New York City have used one of the following to clean up vacant city lots and to fight drugs and crime: **a.** *barrios.* **b.** *casitas.* **c.** *salsa.* **d.** *plenas.*

_____ 11. The most important political issue for Puerto Ricans in the 1990s is: **a.** the use of English. **b.** the future of the New Progressive Party. **c.** the future of the Popular Democratic Party. **d.** the referendum.

_____ 12. In the November 1992 election, Victoria Munoz, the Popular Democratic Party (PPD) candidate for governor, was defeated by the New Progressive Party (PNP) candidate named: **a.** Nydia Velázquez. **b.** James Cancel. **c.** Luis Gutiérrez. **d.** Pedro Rossello.

_____ 13. The first Puerto Rican woman ever elected to the U.S. Congress is: **a.** Victoria Munoz. **b.** Miriam Colon. **c.** Nydia Velázquez. **d.** Lida Viruet.

_____ 14. The Popular Democratic Party (PPD) favors keeping the commonwealth, while the New Progressive Party (PNP) favors: **a.** a referendum. **b.** statehood. **c.** independence. **d.** merging with the United States.

_____ 15. Many people in Puerto Rico oppose the unplanned building of more factories because they: **a.** think U.S. business exploits workers. **b.** favor service industries. **c.** want to protect the environment. **d.** favor unions.

III. **ESSAY Choose one of the following topics. Then write your answer in paragraph form on a separate sheet of paper.**

A. "Second-generation Puerto Ricans live with one foot on the mainland and one foot on the island." Explain the meaning of this statement.

B. Write a *plena* or a rap song in which you warn teenagers about the violent behavior of gangs.

CHAPTER 27 TEST: Cuban Americans Today

I.   MATCHING Decide which definition in the right column best explains a term in the left column. Then write the letter of that definition in the space next to the term.

_____ 1. multinationals

_____ 2. Centro Mater

_____ 3. Mariel Boatlift

_____ 4. Refugee Act of 1980

_____ 5. embargo

a. Miami day-care center

b. U.S. law limiting the number of immigrants from any one nation

c. ban on trade with another country

d. flood of refugees fleeing Cuba in 1980

e. companies that operate in more than one nation

II.   MULTIPLE CHOICE Choose the answer that best completes the sentence or answers the question. Then write the letter of your choice in the space to the left.

_____ 6. Unlike Mexican Americans and Puerto Ricans, Cuban Americans in the United States: **a.** spread out across the nation. **b.** settle in only a few places. **c.** often return to their homeland. **d.** bring their families after they are settled here.

_____ 7. The more than one million Cuban Americans make up what part of the Latino population? **a.** one third **b.** the third-largest group **c.** the smallest group **d.** the fifth-largest group

_____ 8. The U.S. city with the second-largest Cuban American population is: **a.** Jersey City. **b.** Trenton. **c.** Union City. **d.** Miami.

_____ 9. The largest center of Cuban Americans in the United States is in: **a.** New Jersey. **b.** New York. **c.** Broward County. **d.** Dade County.

_____ 10. In 1985, Cuban Americans displayed their growing political power by electing Xavier Suárez as: **a.** mayor of Miami. **b.** governor of Florida. **c.** senator from New York. **d.** mayor of Union City.

_____ 11. The strong Latino presence in Miami has attracted immigrants and business investments from: **a.** Cuba. **b.** Canada. **c.** Latin America. **d.** Europe.

_____ 12. When 10,000 Cubans who wanted to leave their country stormed Peru's embassy in Havana in 1980, their efforts resulted in: **a.** the Mariel Boatlift. **b.** an attempt to overthrow Castro. **c.** the Refugee Act of 1980. **d.** deportation.

_____ 13. After 1991, Castro allowed Cubans to leave on flights to the United States if: **a.** they had no family in the United States. **b.** they paid the Cuban government $10,000. **c.** U.S. relatives paid $1,000 in travel and visa fees. **d.** they promised not to return to Cuba.

_____ 14. According to a survey, about 40 percent of Cuban Americans 34 years old or younger say they: **a.** would never even visit Cuba. **b.** would return to Cuba if Castro were overthrown. **c.** would never leave the United States **d.** would not return to Cuba to live.

_____ 15. The Cuban refugees of the 1980s were different from the earlier waves of Cuban exiles because they: **a.** were forced to leave Cuba. **b.** were mainly working-class people. **c.** were skilled workers and professionals. **d.** settled in and around Miami.

III.   ESSAY Choose one of the following topics. Then write your answer in paragraph form on a separate sheet of paper.

A. "Cuban Americans have achieved high levels of education and economic success." What evidence can you cite from the text to support this statement?

B. If you were a Cuban American and Cuba became a free democracy like the United States, would you and your family return to Cuba to live? Give reasons to explain your decision.

Name _____ Date _____

▶ CHAPTER 28 TEST: Central Americans and Dominicans Today

I.   MATCHING Decide which definition in the right column best explains a term in the left column. Then write the letter of that definition in the space next to the term.

_____   1. Contras

_____   2. *la Violencia*

_____   3. documentation

_____   4. *El Rescate*

_____   5. *ladinos*

a. immigration papers needed to enter the United States

b. Spanish-speaking Guatemalans

c. Nicaraguans who fought the Sandinistas

d. unrest and internal struggles in Central American nations

e. human rights group

II.   MULTIPLE CHOICE Choose the answer that best completes the sentence or that answers the question. Then write the letter of your choice in the space to the left.

_____   6. The city in which the largest number of Central Americans settled in the 1980s and 1990s was: **a.** Miami. **b.** Los Angeles. **c.** Santo Domingo. **d.** Newark.

_____   7. Immigrants from which nation are the seventh-largest immigrant group in the United States? **a.** Dominican Republic **b.** El Salvador **c.** Guatemala **d.** Honduras

_____   8. One of the most famous Central Americans in the United States is an actor-singer from Panama named: **a.** Jaime Escalante. **b.** Manuel Noriega. **c.** Ruben Blades. **d.** Violetta Chamorro.

_____   9. The nation that has the highest percentage of its population immigrating to the United States in the 1990s is: **a.** the Dominican Republic. **b.** Guatemala. **c.** Cuba. **d.** Nicaragua.

_____   10. In the case of *Phyler* v. *Doe*, the U.S. Supreme Court ruled in 1982 that: **a.** children of undocumented immigrants have no right to attend public school. **b.** children of all immigrants have a right to attend public school. **c.** undocumented aliens must pay to have their children attend public school. **d.** only native-born children may attend public school.

_____   11. Unlike immigrants from most Latin American countries, nearly three fourths of all Dominicans come from: **a.** rural farming areas. **b.** cities. **c.** suburbs. **d.** *latifundias*.

_____   12. In the Dominican Republic, the average worker receives a salary of: **a.** $40 a month. **b.** $400 a month. **c.** $40 a day. **d.** $400 a week.

_____   13. The largest group of Dominicans in the United States has settled in an area of New York City known as: **a.** Staten Island. **b.** Pico-Union. **c.** Washington Heights. **d.** Tribeca.

_____   14. The Maya of Guatemala left their country after being attacked by the: **a.** *ladinos*. **b.** Contras. **c.** guerrillas. **d.** military government.

_____   15. In 1990, after more than ten years of revolution and civil war, Nicaragua: **a.** elected a Sandinista government. **b.** signed a peace treaty. **c.** elected a non-Sandinista government. **d.** invaded El Salvador.

III.   ESSAY Choose one of the following topics. Then write your answer in paragraph form on a separate sheet of paper.

A. Explain why Los Angeles is nicknamed "the Central American capital of the United States."

B. Suppose you are a young Dominican who has lived in New York City for a dozen years and has just graduated from high school. You are returning to Santo Domingo to visit your grandparents. What will you tell them about your life in the United States?

Name _____ Date _____

► CHAPTER 29 TEST: South Americans in the United States Today

I.   **MATCHING Decide which definition in the right column best explains a term in the left column. Then write the letter of that definition in the space next to the term.**

_____ 1. *costeños*

_____ 2. inflation

_____ 3. cartels

_____ 4. *campesinos*

_____ 5. Land of Promise

a. name given the United States in early 1900s by European immigrants

b. illegal drug organizations in Colombia

c. peasant farmers

d. rapidly rising prices

e. dark-skinned Colombians of mixed African, Native American, and Spanish ancestry

II.   **MULTIPLE CHOICE Choose the answer that best completes the sentence or answers the question. Then write the letter of your choice in the space to the left.**

_____ 6. Many people left Bolivia during the early 1980s because: **a.** inflation caused living standards to fall. **b.** the Shining Path was defeated. **c.** the United States passed the Immigration Act of 1980. **d.** "the dirty war" broke out.

_____ 7. Many people from South America wish to come to the United States because it: **a.** guarantees everyone a job. **b.** has ended the quota system. **c.** offers freedom and economic opportunities. **d.** has made drugs illegal.

_____ 8. In 1992, Paraguay got a new government when General Stroessner was: **a.** defeated in the election. **b.** ousted in a coup. **c.** assassinated. **d.** kidnapped by Shining Path guerrillas.

_____ 9. The Communist group that terrorized Peru after 1980 is called the: **a.** state police. **b.** "dirty warriors." **c.** *campesinos*. **d.** Shining Path.

_____ 10. In the 1980s and 1990s, members of Colombia's government were murdered by the: **a.** Shining Path. **b.** Bogotá Brigade. **c.** drug cartel. **d.** national guard.

_____ 11. Between 1985 and 1990, the rate of immigration from the nations of South America: **a.** rose by 40 percent. **b.** leveled off. **c.** dropped. **d.** rose by 5 percent.

_____ 12. South American immigrants, along with Cuban Americans, rank at the top of Latino groups in: **a.** size of their income. **b.** literacy rate. **c.** the percentage of students who graduate from high school. **d.** the percentage of students who graduate from high school and college and in size of income.

_____ 13. Most South Americans who come to the United States settle in cities because: **a.** they have always looked for opportunities in cities. **b.** they are *campesinos*. **c.** they like to live near their jobs. **d.** they can afford city prices.

_____ 14. The largest settlement of South Americans in the United States is in which part of New York City? **a.** Manhattan **b.** Jackson Heights **c.** Queens **d.** the Bronx

_____ 15. Which South American group has established a Latino community in Chicago? **a.** Paraguayans **b.** Peruvians **c.** Colombian *costenos* **d.** Bolivians

III.   **ESSAY Choose one of the following topics. Then write your answer in paragraph form on a separate sheet of paper.**

A. In what ways did Jaime Escalante show the determination and ability displayed by many immigrants from South America?

B. Why do you think experts predict that immigration from South America will continue to rise?

Name _____ Date _____

▶ CHAPTER 30 TEST: Toward a New Century

I. MATCHING Decide which definition in the right column best explains a term in the left column. Then write the letter of that definition in the space next to the term.

_____ 1. *mercados*
_____ 2. *Hágase Contar*
_____ 3. entrepreneurs
_____ 4. Telemundo
_____ 5. Los Angeles disturbance

a. Mexican American grocery stores
b. Spanish-language cable network
c. 1992 incident in which 54 people died
d. a group that encourages Latinos to register to vote
e. people who risk money in businesses

II. MULTIPLE CHOICE Choose the answer that best completes the sentence or answers the question. Then write the letter of your choice in the space to the left.

_____ 6. By 1990, the Latino population of the United States had grown rapidly, and the ratio of Latinos to the total population was: **a.** 1 in 50. **b.** 1 in 10. **c.** 1 in 2. **d.** 1 in 5.

_____ 7. Compared to the total U.S. population, where the average age is 32, Latinos are a young people, with the average age being: **a.** 26. **b.** 18. **c.** 15. **d.** 40.

_____ 8. Latinos are concerned that so many of their young people do not graduate from high school, with the dropout rate being: **a.** 1 in 10. **b.** 1 in 100. **c.** 1 in 50 **d.** 4 in 10.

_____ 9. One result of the 1992 disturbances in Los Angeles was that: **a.** many Latinos joined unions. **b.** many Central Americans were deported. **c.** illegal immigration in the area declined. **d.** more hospitals were built.

_____ 10. Of the 36 percent of Latino children who live in poverty, most are in: **a.** two-parent families. **b.** extended families. **c.** single-parent families. **d.** foster families.

_____ 11. After the 1990 census, many election districts were redrawn to give Latino voters: **a.** less influence in elections. **b.** more votes. **c.** fewer votes. **d.** more influence in elections.

_____ 12. Proof that the Latino community of Los Angeles is doing well is shown by all of the following *except*: **a.** only 6 percent receive welfare payments. **b.** in a high percentage of families at least one member works full time. **c.** Latinos own most of the stores in the area hit by the 1992 disturbances. **d.** over 40 percent of households are headed by two parents.

_____ 13. Latinos are well represented in all of the following *except*: **a.** politics and government. **b.** the top ranks of big business. **c.** radio and television. **d.** sports and entertainment.

_____ 14. Latinos have made progress in all of the following *except*: **a.** the number of Latino representatives in the U.S. Congress. **b.** Latino positions in the President's cabinet. **c.** the number of Latino state governors **d.** the number of local elected officials.

_____ 15. All the following are shown in the story of Manuel Sotomayor *except*: **a.** a Latino must give up his or her cultural heritage to be successful in the United States **b.** education is important in the Latino experience. **c.** a Latino can be successful in the broader U.S. culture. **d.** a Latino has a responsibility to help other Latinos.

III. ESSAY Choose one of the following topics. Then write your answer in paragraph form on a separate sheet of paper.

A. What do you consider the most important achievements of Latinos in the United States? Give reasons for your answer.

B. Explain how Latinos have preserved their own cultures and also contributed to the culture of the United States.

ANSWER KEY FOR UNIT AND CHAPTER TESTS

▶ UNIT 1 TEST: Spain in the Americas

MATCHING 1. d. **2.** a. **3.** e. **4.** b. **5.** c.

UNDERSTANDING TIME *correct order:* 6, 5, 1, 2, 4, 3

MULTIPLE CHOICE 6. c. **7.** b. **8.** b. **9.** d. **10.** c. **11.** a.

COMPLETING THE IDEA 12. Las Casas **13.** missions **14.** vassals **15.** Christianity **16.** social divisions **17.** Hispaniola **18.** Menéndez **19.** Texas **20.** peonage system

ESSAY A. They forced Native Americans to accept Spanish domination, convert to Christianity, provide farm labor, abandon their traditional hunting, fishing, and gathering practices, and abandon their villages because of diseases that reduced their populations. **B.** Choice should be documented with evidence from the text.

Chapter 1: Face to Face in the Americas

MATCHING 1. c. **2.** e. **3.** b. **4.** a. **5.** d.

MULTIPLE CHOICE 6. c. **7.** b. **8.** c. **9.** d. **10.** d. **11.** c. **12.** a. **13.** b. **14.** d. **15.** a.

ESSAY A. Native Americans viewed the arrival of Columbus and his crew as a strange and unfamiliar event, one they had never imagined but perhaps one even engineered by Heaven. Native Americans provided the Spanish with food and supplies and reacted in friendly, peaceful ways until Spaniards began to use force to carry out their invasion. The Spanish regarded the islands as a new part of the world being discovered by Europeans for the first time. They viewed the land and the people living there as belonging to Spain. They believed the Native Americans should furnish the labor and supplies needed to help build new Spanish settlements. They regarded the islands as probable sources of gold and other wealth that now belonged to Spain. They also viewed it as their duty to convert the Native Americans to the Roman Catholic religion. **B.** Building on the efforts of Montesinos, las Casas, himself a former wealthy *encomendero*, became convinced that the Spanish settlers' treatment of Native Americans was harsh and unjust. By 1516,

the Spanish ruler showed his concern by naming las Casas as "Protector of the Indians." However, the continuing need for workers led las Casas to support the Spanish king's decision to send enslaved Africans to the Americas. Las Casas's campaign thus led to the introduction of African slavery and the slave trade just as large sugar plantations developed on the Caribbean islands.

Chapter 2: Struggle for an Empire

MATCHING 1. b. **2.** c. **3.** a. **4.** e. **5.** d.

MULTIPLE CHOICE 6. c. **7.** c. **8.** a. **9.** c. **10.** b. **11.** a. **12.** c. **13.** a. **14.** d. **15.** c.

ESSAY A. Possible answers: Spanish weapons, cannons, and horses; the key role of Maya, Tabascans, and other Native American vassals of the Aztec empire in supporting Cortés; Motecuhzoma's peaceful welcome of Cortés's army; the death of Motecuhzoma; the smallpox epidemic among the Aztec. **B.** Possible answers: Young Cortés's decision to forsake the study of law and go to Hispaniola in search of gold and adventure, his reward of land and gold in Cuba, his learning about gold in Yucatán and his subsequent expedition to Yucatán, the conversion of the Maya and Tabascans to Roman Catholicism, and Malintzin's stories of Aztec gold and wealth that spurred Cortés to conquer Tenochtitlán.

Chapter 3: New Ways of Life

MATCHING 1. e **2.** c **3.** a. **4.** b. **5.** d.

MULTIPLE CHOICE 6. d. **7.** c. **8.** a. **9.** d. **10.** b. **11.** a. **12.** c. **13.** b. **14.** c. **15.** a.

ESSAY A. Possible answers: From Spain, the following affected the lives of Native Americans: the Roman Catholic religion, the Spanish language and other parts of Spanish culture; crops like wheat and rye; animals like horses, cattle, pigs, sheep, and goats; diseases like measles, mumps, and smallpox. **B.** Possible answer: The *criollos'* feelings of resentment at the privileged status of *peninsulares*, their monopoly on the highest offices in church and government.

Chapter 4: Reaching Out from the Caribbean

MATCHING 1. c. **2.** a. **3.** e. **4.** d. **5.** b.

MULTIPLE CHOICE 6. d. **7.** d. **8.** b. **9.** c. **10.** b. **11.** b. **12.** c. **13.** a. **14.** c. **15.** c.

ESSAY A. In the defeat of the Armada, Spain had lost many of the vessels that it would have used in the defense of its sea lanes in the Caribbean. This left an opening for England and other European nations to move more freely in the Caribbean, 1588 was a turning point for Spain in the Americas because from then on Spain could no longer enforce its exclusive position in the region. **B.** Answers may include their difficult, dangerous life in the wilderness of Florida. Crops were difficult to grow in the sandy soil, and the settlers had to depend on supplies from Havana and other Caribbean ports. They faced the threat of attack like Drake's incursion in 1586, when St. Augustine was burned to the ground.

Chapter 5: The Spanish Borderlands
MATCHING 1. d. **2.** e. **3.** a. **4.** b. **5.** c.

MULTIPLE CHOICE 6. c. **7.** c. **8.** b. **9.** d. **10.** b. **11.** a. **12.** a. **13.** b. **14.** c. **15.** c.

ESSAY A. The pueblo people, who had never forgotten their harsh treatment by Oñate, the first Spanish governor, in the early 1600s, had lived under an uneasy truce with the Spanish in the years that followed. Tensions continued as the Spanish forced them to pay tribute and to convert to Catholicism. In 1675, several pueblos were charged with witchcraft and their leaders beaten and hanged. This action led pueblo leader Popé to plan a revolt in 1680. Popé led this uprising, which ended with the looting and burning of Santa Fe and the flight of the Spanish. For the next 13 years, the pueblo people controlled the borderlands. **B.** Possible answers: The mission system forced the Native Americans to abandon their own cultures. They had to adopt a new language, religion, and different ways of life. At the same time, they had to provide the labor to farm and build up Spain's borderlands.

▶ UNIT 2 TEST: Toward Independence

MATCHING 1. a. **2.** c. **3.** b. **4.** e. **5.** d.

UNDERSTANDING TIME 6. 1821 **7.** 1777 **8.** 1819 **9.** 1836 **10.** 1825

MULTIPLE CHOICE 11. b. **12.** b. **13.** d. **14.** c. **15.** a. **16.** b.

COMPLETING THE IDEA 17. Gálvez.

18. American Revolution. **19.** American settlers. **20.** Puerto Rico and Cuba. **21.** *patrones* **22.** *partido* **23.** missions **24.** hides and tallow. **25.** Texas.

ESSAY A. It was a vast territory that was only sparsely populated by Spanish-speaking settlers. Those settlers lived in isolated villages that were often attacked by the Apache and Comanche. These raids had discouraged settlement and trade until Spain signed agreements with the Ute and Comanche. Under Mexican rule, the large land grants created wealthy landowners who used the *partido* system to provide the labor they needed, at the same time trapping the villagers in poverty. The rift between rich and poor widened until Mexico's levy of new taxes caused a rebellion in 1835. Threatened with the loss of their power to the villagers, *ricos* supported the Mexican army that suppressed the revolt. **B.** Mexico believed that the Catholic-run missions were an obstacle to the growth of California's economy. The missions owned the best farming and ranching land. They also controlled the Native Americans who provided the labor force in this huge area.

Chapter 6: The Spanish and the American Revolution
MATCHING 1. d. **2.** a. **3.** e. **4.** b. **5.** c.

MULTIPLE CHOICE 6. b. **7.** c. **8.** c. **9.** a. **10.** b. **11.** c. **12.** a. **13.** a. **14.** a. **15.** c.

ESSAY A. Spain early on provided badly needed gunpowder, weapons, and supplies to the Patriot forces. Spain's victories gave it control of the Mississippi Valley, thus protecting Americans west of the Appalachians against British attack and keeping open the vital Mississippi waterway. Gálvez's campaigns in Florida ended the threat of a possible British attack from the Gulf coast. **B.** Possible answers: Gálvez's 1779 strategy at Baton Rouge, his campaign at Mobile and Pensacola, his grand strategy to secure the Mississippi Valley, his skillful coordination of Spain's overall policy in securing food and supply lines for his troops in Louisiana.

Chapter 7: The Road to Latin American Independence
MATCHING 1. d. **2.** b. **3.** e. **4.** c. **5.** a.

MULTIPLE CHOICE 6. b. **7.** a. **8.** d. **9.** c. **10.** b. **11.** c. **12.** c. **13.** a. **14.** b. **15.** d.

ESSAY A. Those students who say they would have supported Gutiérrez may include references to the promise made by Gutiérrez and Magee to pay their supporters $40 a month and give them free land. Native Americans living on missions and working under the *encomienda* system also might have sought their freedom by joining the rebels. Other students may say that as Native Americans they would have remained loyal to the mission fathers and the Catholic Church, which had organized their lives for so long. **B.** Possible answers: The pressure from U.S. settlers for the western land along the Mississippi Valley and the Mississippi's key role in connecting their settlements; the sparse Spanish population there; Spain's restrictive trade laws; the Spanish government's bureaucracy and inability to adapt; the French Revolution and France's takeover of Spain.

Chapter 8: Life in the Mexican Borderlands

MATCHING 1. d. 2. c. 3. b. 4. e. 5. a.

MULTIPLE CHOICE 6. a. 7. b. 8. c. 9. d. 10. a. 11. c. 12. b. 13. c. 14. b. 15. a.

ESSAY A. The vast distances and sparse population forced settlers to band together. In return for the land grant they received from the Mexican government, *patrones* who had brought parties of settlers there were responsible for governing these families and caring for their needs. They set up small towns and villages to defend their groups against attacks by Apache and Comanche, and often forged alliances with the pueblo people. **B.** Possible answers: The takeover of mission lands by government officials and their friends and the emergence of 700 huge *ranchos* with their wealthy, powerful owners by the 1830s and 1840s. The workers and servants on these ranches were Native Americans who had left the missions and now were trapped in debt under the peonage system. As the peons' lot worsened, Native Americans began raids on the ranches.

▶ UNIT 3 TEST: A Time of Upheaval

MATCHING 1. e. 2. c. 3. d. 4. b. 5. a.

UNDERSTANDING TIME 6. 2 (1845) 7. 4 or 5 (1848) 8. 1 (1836) 9. 3 (1846) 10. 4 or 5 (1848) 11. 6 (1850)

MULTIPLE CHOICE 12. b. 13. c. 14. c. 15. d. 16. a. 17 c. 18. Anglos 19. Santa Anna 20. Stephen Austin 21. New Mexico 22. Guadalupe Hidalgo 23. tax 24. bandit 25. Texas

ESSAY A. Mexican Americans resented the political and social discrimination they faced, and loss of their estates in many cases, as well as the poverty and hardships of their lives. They viewed the bandits as agents of revenge against their oppressors. **B.** After major setbacks at the Alamo and Goliad, Houston's army encountered Santa Anna's forces at the San Jacinto River. Fired by memories of the Alamo, the Anglo army struck and won a victory, killing 630 Mexican soldiers. Santa Anna was captured trying to escape and forced to sign humiliating treaties agreeing to Texas's independence, with its southern border at the Rio Grande.

Chapter 9: Revolt in Texas

MATCHING 1. e. 2. d. 3. b. 4. c. 5. a.

MULTIPLE CHOICE 6. b. 7. c. 8. d. 9. a. 10. b. 11. b. 12. c. 13. a. 14. b. 15. a.

ESSAY A. Possible answers: Ordinary *tejanos* regarded the revolt as an action undertaken by Anglos in their own interests. The *tejano* culture was very different from that of the Anglos, and *tejanos* resented the Anglos' attitude of superiority. While many resented Santa Anna's rule, they did not believe the rebellion would bring improvement in their lives, and they were uncertain about their fate in an independent Texas. **B.** Mexico banned further Anglo immigration into Texas, ended slavery, and tried to enforce trade laws restricting goods from the United States.

Chapter 10: War Between the United States and Mexico

MATCHING 1. d. 2. e. 3. a. 4. b. 5. c.

MULTIPLE CHOICE 6. c. 7. a. 8. c. 9. b. 10. a. 11. c. 12. b. 13. b. 13. a. 14. d. 15. c.

ESSAY A. The three aims were: 1) to take over California and New Mexico, 2) occupy northern Mexico, and 3) to capture Mexico City. Answers on how each aim was achieved should include key battles, military leaders on both sides, and events leading to the final Battle of Chapultepec. **B.** Possible answers: Should focus on Mexico's fear of American expansion and its hostile intent in the Slidell mission, the U.S. desire to protect Anglo settlers in California and New

Mexico, its quick annexation of Texas, and Polk's expansionist policies.

Chapter 11: Foreigners in Their Own Land

MATCHING 1. b. **2.** d. **3.** c. **4.** e. **5.** a.

MULTIPLE CHOICE 6. c. **7.** b. **8.** a. **9.** b. **10.** d. **11.** a. **12.** b. **13.** c. **14.** a. **15.** b.

ESSAY A. *Californios* succeeded in having some of their rights protected by the new state constitution. These included blocking efforts to limit their right to vote, providing for voting ballots to be printed in Spanish as well as English, and requiring that tax assessors be elected locally to prevent Anglo assessors from exploiting them. In addition, some Spanish legal practices were included in the constitution such as those dealing with water and mineral rights. **B.** Mexican Americans faced severe discrimination by Anglos. Mexican Americans kept their traditional ways of life, but sometimes learned English. Yet their lack of political power, their exclusion from Anglo society, made them feel like foreigners in their own land.

▶ UNIT 4 TEST: A Time of Growth

MATCHING 1. d. **2.** c. **3.** e. **4.** b. **5.** a.

UNDERSTANDING TIME 6. b. **7.** f. **8.** c. **9.** d. **10.** a. **11.** e.

MULTIPLE CHOICE 12. a. **13.** c. **14.** d. **15.** b. **16.** b. **17.** c.

COMPLETING THE IDEA 18. Cuban-Spanish-American War **19.** blockaded **20.** *las Gorras Blancas* **21.** *lectores* **22.** Weyler **23.** Ten Years' War **24.** protectorate **25.** guerrilla war

ESSAY A. Answers should focus on Spanish oppression and misrule, the poverty and conditions in Cuba, and the people's right to freedom and self-rule. **B.** Puerto Ricans feared that their culture, with its language and customs, would be overwhelmed by that of the United States once it took control of the island. Actually, U.S. cultural influence was more limited than had been feared. The Puerto Ricans retained their language, food preferences, dances, songs, and other aspects of their culture.

Chapter 12: Latinos in the U.S. Civil War

MATCHING 1. d. **2.** a. **3.** b. **4.** e. **5.** c.

MULTIPLE CHOICE 6. d. **7.** b. **8.** d. **9.** d. **10.** b. **11.** b. **12.** a. **13.** c. **14.** a. **15.** b.

ESSAY A. Students should make clear that the choice of sides would probably depend on their social status in New Mexico. If they were wealthy landowners, they might choose the Confederacy because they had much in common with Southern slaveholders. As other poorer Latinos there, having heard of the Union aim to end slavery, they might be sympathetic to the Union side. Or, as was the case with many New Mexicans, they might not favor either side. **B.** The choices made should reflect the reality of their situations. The women spies, for example, could readily have been found out and have been shot, while the male military figures, such as Farragut and Manuel Cháves, faced the danger of being hit by enemy fire.

Chapter 13: A Changing World

MATCHING 1. d. **2.** a. **3.** b. **4.** c. **5.** e.

MULTIPLE CHOICE 6. c. **7.** a. **8.** b. **9.** d. **10.** b. **11.** b. **12.** a. **13.** d. **14.** d. **15.** b.

ESSAY A. Answers should focus on efforts to guarantee Latinos the right to vote and to attend public schools, which were achieved, as well as efforts to secure equality, which were less successful. **B.** They read articles favoring Cuban independence and fanning support for growing Cuban nationalism.

Chapter 14: The Cuban-Spanish-American War

MATCHING 1. d. **2.** c. **3.** a. **4.** b. **5.** e.

MULTIPLE CHOICE 6. b. **7.** a. **8.** a. **9.** b. **10.** d. **11.** b. **12.** b. **13.** c. **14.** a. **15.** b.

ESSAY A. Answers should focus on the guerrilla tactics required by a rebel force vastly outnumbered by the Spanish and with few weapons or supplies. Surprise attacks on key outposts, hit-and-run assaults with Cubans striking from jungle or mountain terrain, replaced traditional battles. **B.** Because his vision of an independent Cuba saw a new nation that would surpass others because its people would be free of racial prejudice and accept all people as equals regardless of their race, wealth, or social position.

Chapter 15: Puerto Rico and Cuba Under United States Control

MATCHING 1. e. **2.** c. **3.** d. **4.** a. **5.** b.

MULTIPLE CHOICE 6. a. **7.** c. **8.** c. **9.** b. **10.** c. **11.** b. **12.** d. **13.** c. **14.** a. **15.** d.

ESSAY A. They feared that just as American business interests controlled their island's economy and appointed the governor and other key officials, Americans would also try to impose their language and culture on Puerto Ricans. These fears were never realized, though Puerto Rican politicians often played on these fears. **B.** Answers should include references to political interference by the United States through the Platt Amendment, prejudice against African Cubans, dependency on a one-crop economy, and corrupt politicians.

▶ UNIT 5 TEST: Changes in a New Century

MATCHING 1. a. **2.** e. **3.** d. **4** b. **5.** c.

UNDERSTANDING TIME 6. 1941 **7.** 1931 **8.** 1910 **9.** 1917 **10.** 1945 **11.** 1942

MULTIPLE CHOICE 12. c. **13.** b. **14.** d. **15.** a. **16.** a. **17.** b.

COMPLETING THE IDEA 18. *la huelga* **19.** Great Depression **20.** Bataan death march **21.** Mexican Revolution **22.** repatriated **23.** barrios **24.** World War II **25.** migrant workers

ESSAY A. Mexicans came to the United States fleeing the bloodshed of the Mexican Revolution and seeking jobs to earn money that they could send back to their families. They settled mainly in agricultural areas of California and the Southwest in the 1920s. **B.** Students should indicate a concern for getting jobs and establishing themselves.

Chapter 16: The Mexican Revolution and New Patterns of Immigration

MATCHING 1. c. **2.** d. **3.** e. **4.** a. **5.** b.

MULTIPLE CHOICE 6. c. **7.** d. **8.** b. **9.** a. **10.** d. **11.** b. **12.** a. **13.** b. **14.** c. **15.** a.

ESSAY A. Answers may include the following: Those who favor staying may stress people's first opportunities for freedom after 400 years of colonial rule. Those who favor emigration to the United States may focus on the lack of land reform, the continuing poverty of most Mexicans, the political instability, and the opportunities of jobs and a better life in the United States. **B.** Mexicans were forced to take the low-paying jobs Americans avoided. They did the backbreaking work as migrant farmers, were hired as low-paid, unskilled miners and factory workers, and even accepted jobs as strikebreakers. They also were excluded from joining unions and thus denied a chance to improve their working conditions.

Chapter 17: Latinos and World War I

MATCHING 1. d. **2.** c. **3.** a. **4.** b. **5.** e.

MULTIPLE CHOICE 6. c. **7.** b. **8.** a. **9.** b. **10.** c. **11.** a. **12.** d. **13.** b. **14.** a. **15.** c.

ESSAY A. It was one of the poorer neighborhoods in the city, with run-down housing and inadequate sanitation facilities, poor garbage collection, and the vast majority of families had no gas or electricity. However, it had shops and restaurants that offered Mexican products and food. The movie houses showed Spanish and Mexican films, and theaters had plays performed in Spanish. **B.** Letters should note that all immigrants suffer from inadequate housing and low-paying jobs, and the difficulties of adjusting to the new lifestyle of the United States. Instead of fighting one another, if they spoke with one voice, they would stand a better chance of improving their lives.

Chapter 18: From Boom to Depression

MATCHING 1. d. **2.** a. **3.** e. **4.** b. **5.** c.

MULTIPLE CHOICE 6. b. **7.** b. **8.** a. **9.** a. **10.** d. **11.** c. **12.** d. **13** b. **14.** b. **15.** b.

ESSAY A. The AFL and other national unions made no effort to help them organize. Mexican American farmworkers who tried to form unions were easy to replace since jobs were scarce. Mexican Americans who worked in the fields found it very hard to lose wages if they were forced to strike or walk off their jobs campaigning to establish a union. Moreover, the Wagner Act's protection did not extend to migrant workers. **B.** Letters should include the discriminatory nature of the policy in singling out Mexican Americans, the contributions they had made to the war effort at home and as members of the armed forces, and the productive role they had assumed in the labor force of the United States.

Chapter 19: Latinos and World War II
MATCHING 1. c. 2. a. 3. d. 4. e. 5. b.

MULTIPLE CHOICE 6. b. 7. a. 8. c. 9. a. 10. b. 11. c. 12. d. 13. a. 14. d. 15. c.

ESSAY A. If students say they would have taken part, they should give reasons, such as anger at military and police actions. If they say they would not have taken part, they might explain that they saw no good coming out of the disturbances for them or their friends. B. Advantages for the farmworker were that he could earn money to take home after a season of work, even though the amount was not large. The disadvantages would include low rate of pay, hard labor, poor living conditions, and having to be away from the family for long periods of time.

▶ UNIT 6 TEST: A Changing Postwar World

MATCHING 1. c. 2. d. 3. e. 4. b. 5. a.

UNDERSTANDING TIME 6. C 7. B 8. A 9. D 10. F 11. G 12. E

MULTIPLE CHOICE 13. b. 14. d. 15. c. 16. a. 17. a. 18. b.

COMPLETING THE IDEA 19. *nuyoricans* 20. Joaquín 21. *El Movimiento* 22. Bay of Pigs 23. *La Causa* 24. *La Raza Unida* 25. human rights

ESSAY A. Answers should show an understanding of the topic as discussed in the unit. Students should be factually correct in describing the conditions in the country they have chosen to discuss. B. Students who agree with the statement should focus on Castro's failures: persecution of dissent, ending of religious freedom, indoctrination/propaganda, dependence on the Soviet Union, his anti-U.S. stance, nationalization, and communism. Students who disagree with the statement should give as evidence of Castro's success increased literacy, redistribution of land, building of schools, roads, and public works.

Chapter 20: The Great Migration from Puerto Rico
MATCHING 1. d. 2. e. 3. a. 4. c. 5. b.

MULTIPLE CHOICE 6. c. 7. b. 8. b. 9. c. 10. a. 11. b. 12. a. 13 c. 14. d. 15. b.

ESSAY A. Letter might include a request for information on cities with large Puerto Rican populations, places to live, rents, cost of food and other necessities, job opportunities, and kinds of schools and their reputations. B. As industries expanded, the number of factories increased from 72 in 1952 to over 1,000 by 1970, and these new factories provided growing numbers of jobs. Public housing projects were built, and highways crisscrossed and united the people of the island. Large farms were broken up, new schools were built, and the literacy rate soared.

Chapter 21: New Arrivals from the Caribbean
MATCHING 1. c. 2. e. 3. d. 4. a. 5. b.

MULTIPLE CHOICE 6. a. 7. b. 8. d. 9. c. 10. b. 11. a. 12. b. 13. d. 14. b. 15. a.

ESSAY A. The Cuban refugee army trained by the CIA in Guatemala numbered only 1,400. The Cuban refugees were young and lacked military experience. Castro learned of the invasion plan and sent an army of 20,000 to beat back the invaders. President Kennedy refused to support the invaders with U.S. air power. B. After Trujillo's overthrow, unrest and instability continued. Many middle-class professionals and soon many others fled to the United States to escape poverty and to improve their lives.

Chapter 22: The Struggle for Equal Rights
MATCHING 1. e. 2. c. 3. a. 4. b. 5. d.

MULTIPLE CHOICE 6. d. 7. a. 8. c. 9. a. 10. b. 11. a. 12. d. 13. b. 14. c. 15. b.

ESSAY A. Farmworkers had no job security, no benefits. They moved from farm to farm and from state to state picking crops and receiving extremely low wages for long working days. Families lacked decent housing, and children frequently changed schools as the family moved, with many dropping out to go to work. B. For the leader chosen, students should summarize the person's accomplishments, importance to the Latino cause, and, if possible, personal qualities.

Chapter 23: New Immigrants from Central and South America
MATCHING 1. d. 2. a. 3. e. 4. b. 5. c.

MULTIPLE CHOICE 6. b. **7.** a. **8.** a. **9.** b. **10.** c. **11.** d. **12.** b. **13.** d. **14.** b. **15.** b.

ESSAY A. They lacked popular support and had no respect for human rights, since they were able to remain in power only by using force and murdering those who tried to oppose them. **B.** Answers should focus on the civil wars and political turmoil in those nations, the struggle between large landowners and landless peasants, the role of the Catholic Church in championing social justice, death squads, and human-rights violations.

Chapter 24: A Growing Voice
MATCHING 1. c. **2.** b. **3.** e. **4.** a. **5.** d.

MULTIPLE CHOICE 6. d. **7.** a. **8.** b. **9.** d. **10.** c. **11.** a. **12.** b. **13.** a. **14.** d. **15.** a.

ESSAY A. Answers should be based on facts to the greatest extent possible, rather than on general admiration or adulation. **B.** Cuban American artists and writers have shifted their focus away from their role as exiles. They have turned their attention more to Cuban culture in the United States while retaining a love of their Cuban heritage. Puerto Rican artists and writers in the 1950s and 1960s extolled island rural people and made fun of *nuyoricans*. Gradually, however, they celebrated both the island and mainland Puerto Rican culture.

▶ UNIT 7 TEST: Latinos Today

MATCHING 1. d. **2.** b. **3.** e. **4.** c. **5.** a.

UNDERSTANDING TIME 6. 4 (1990) **7.** 6 (1992) **8.** 3 (1986) **9.** 2 (1980) **10.** 5 (1991) **11.** 1 (1979)

MULTIPLE CHOICE 12. b. **13.** c. **14.** a. **15.** c. **16.** d. **17.** a.

COMPLETING THE IDEA 18. Immigration Reform Act. **19.** Mariel Boatlift. **20.** *campesinos*. **21.** free-trade zone. **22.** U.S. Census Bureau. **23.** *nuyoricans*. **24.** *la migra*. **25.** *bodegas*.

ESSAY A. Answers should show a thorough knowledge of the group chosen and should make clear how this group of Latinos is different from other Latinos. **B.** Students who agree may cite the fact that most Latinos are better off in the United States than they were in their homelands. Students who disagree may point out the dangers of losing one's Latino heritage, the discrimination

that many face, and the generally cold attitudes that many Latinos detect in Anglos in general.

Chapter 25: Mexican Americans Today
MATCHING: **1.** c. **2.** d. **3.** e. **4.** b. **5.** a.

MULTIPLE CHOICE 6. c. **7.** a. **8.** b. **9.** d. **10.** b. **11.** c. **12.** b. **13.** a. **14.** d. **15.** b.

ESSAY A. Answers might focus on the family's effort to improve their lives, to join relatives or friends in the United States, and the family's fear of being forced to return to Mexico after the dangerous journey. **B.** Nearly half the population traces its roots to Mexico and Mexican Americans have preserved much of their traditional *tejano* culture. *Tejano* music and musicians are heard everywhere and broadcast on radio and TV, and both Spanish and English are spoken by many San Antonians. Mexican Americans have strong political clout and have elected a Mexican American mayor as well as members of Congress.

Chapter 26: Puerto Ricans Today
MATCHING 1. c. **2.** e. **3.** a. **4.** b. **5.** d.

MULTIPLE CHOICE 6. a. **7.** b. **8.** a. **9.** c. **10.** b. **11.** a. **12.** d. **13.** c. **14.** b. **15.** c.

ESSAY A. Answers may focus on the Puerto Ricans born on the mainland whose parents were born on the island and describe their strong ties to both places. **B.** Responses will differ.

Chapter 27: Cuban Americans Today
MATCHING 1. e. **2.** a. **3.** d. **4.** b. **5.** c.

MULTIPLE CHOICE 6. b. **7.** b. **8.** c. **9.** d. **10.** a. **11.** c. **12.** a. **13.** c. **14.** b. **15.** b.

ESSAY A. Nearly 30 percent of all Cuban Americans are professionals and businesspeople. Average Cuban American family income in 1990 was $31,400, near the U.S. average for non-Latino white family income. In 1990, nearly 83 percent had graduated from high school and 24 percent had completed four or more years of college. **B.** Students who say they might return would probably list their ties to the Cuban culture as the main reason. Students who say they would not return might note the fact that they now feel as American as any other immigrant group, that they do well financially, and that they can share the Cuban heritage in the United States without returning.

Chapter 28: Central Americans and Dominicans Today

MATCHING 1. c. **2.** d. **3.** a. **4.** e. **5.** b.

MULTIPLE CHOICE 6. b. **7.** a. **8.** c. **9.** a. **10.** b. **11.** b. **12.** a. **13.** c. **14.** d. **15.** c.

ESSAY A. It is so named because it is home to more than 500,000 Central Americans, including 250,000 Salvadorans and 125,000 Guatemalans. **B.** Student may want to stress the more positive aspects of life in New York City such as the opportunity to live in a neighborhood with other Dominicans, the fact that one can earn so much more than on the island, and especially that there are freedom of speech and political freedom. If the student wishes, he or she may mention such negative sides of life in New York City as high crime and drug rates and discrimination because of one's skin color.

Chapter 29: South Americans in the United States Today

MATCHING 1. e. **2.** d. **3.** b. **4.** c. **5.** a.

MULTIPLE CHOICE 6. a. **7.** c. **8.** b. **9.** d. **10.** c. **11.** a. **12.** d. **13.** a. **14.** b. **15.** c.

ESSAY A. Like many South Americans, he showed how he valued education by going back to school to learn English. He earned an engineering degree, but decided to become a high school math teacher in one of the most difficult schools in Los Angeles. He achieved national recognition in 1982 when 18 of his Mexican American students passed the AP calculus exam. **B.** The political situation in the nations of South America is always uncertain, and economic conditions are unstable. Then the danger of drug wars in countries like Colombia and Venezuela frighten people into leaving their home countries.

Chapter 30: Toward a New Century

MATCHING 1. a. **2.** d. **3.** e. **4.** b. **5.** c.

MULTIPLE CHOICE 6. b. **7.** a. **8.** d. **9.** b. **10.** c. **11.** d. **12.** c. **13.** b. **14.** c. **15.** a.

ESSAY A. Whichever achievements students identify, they should give adequate reasons for their choices, including details about the choices themselves. **B.** Answers may focus on Latino culture in the United States in general or on a specific Latino culture. In either case, the special features and the impact of its people, food, and customs on the general U.S. culture and population should be spelled out.

Name _____ Date _____

 CHAPTER 1 Activity Sheet:
Reading a Timeline

Columbus's voyages to the Americas were important to Spain and other European powers as well. In less than 40 years after Columbus's first voyage, Europeans from Portugal, England, France, and Spain had explored lands from South America to present-day Canada. Study the timeline below and answer the questions that follow.

Exploring the Americas 1492–35

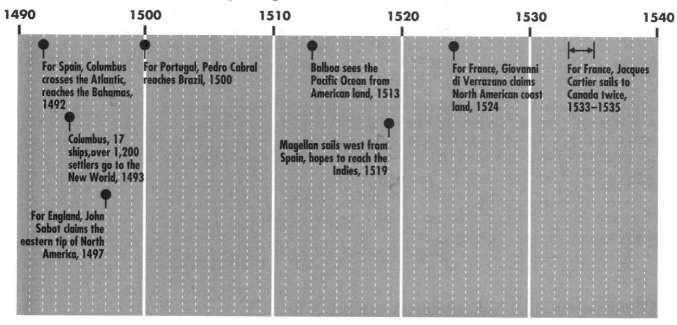

1490   1500   1510   1520   1530   1540

For Spain, Columbus crosses the Atlantic, reaches the Bahamas, 1492

Columbus, 17 ships, over 1,200 settlers go to the New World, 1493

For England, John Sabot claims the eastern tip of North America, 1497

For Portugal, Pedro Cabral reaches Brazil, 1500

Balboa sees the Pacific Ocean from American land, 1513

Magellan sails west from Spain, hopes to reach the Indies, 1519

For France, Giovanni di Verrazano claims North American coast land, 1524

For France, Jacques Cartier sails to Canada twice, 1533–1535

1. Where did Columbus land in 1492? _____

2. What happened in 1493? _____

3. **(a)** In what year was France's first voyage of discovery to the Americas? _____

   (b) Who was the leader of this trip? _____

4. **(a)** What explorer did England send to the Americas in 1497? _____

   (b) Where did he land? _____

5. In what year did Magellan set sail, hoping to reach the Indies by traveling west? _____

6. Who was the first European to see the Pacific Ocean? _____

7. Leonardo da Vinci, the great Italian artist, was born in 1452. How old was he when Magellan sailed west from Spain? _____

THE LATINO EXPERIENCE IN U.S. HISTORY • © Globe Fearon

Name _____ Date _____

CHAPTER 2 Activity Sheet:
Making Inferences

An **inference** is a conclusion or judgment reached by reasoning. We make an inference when an idea in the text is implied, not stated. We sometimes call it "reading between the lines." In the following excerpt, a messenger describes to Motecuhzoma the arrival of Cortés and his men at the Aztec capital of Tenochtitlán. Read the excerpt and answer the questions that follow it.

> "When [it] is fired, a thing like a stone ball comes out of its entrails, raining fire and shooting sparks. And the smoke that comes out of it has a foul smell, like rotten mud, which assaults the brain. If it is fired . . . at a tree, it shatters the tree into splinters—an extraordinary sight, as if someone blew the tree apart from within.
>
> Their weapons and equipment are all made of iron. They dress in iron, and they wear iron helmets on their heads; their swords are iron; their bows are iron; their shields are iron; their spears are iron.
>
> Their 'deer' carry them on their backs, and these beasts are as tall as a roof.
>
> Their bodies are covered everywhere; only their faces can be seen. They are very white, as if made of lime. They have yellow hair, though some of them have black. . . .
>
> Their dogs are huge with . . . fiery, blazing eyes . . . they are very strong and tireless and agitated. They run panting, with their tongues hanging out."
>
> When Motecuhzoma heard this, he was filled with terror. It was as if his heart grew faint, as if it shrank; he was overcome by despair.

1. From paragraph 4, what can you infer about the clothing of the Aztec?

_____

_____

_____

2. In what ways did weapons of the Spanish and the Aztec differ?

_____

_____

_____

3. What animal can we infer has not yet appeared in Mexico at the time of this description?

_____

_____

_____

4. What can you infer about the appearance of the Aztec from what the messenger finds unusual about

the Spanish? _____

_____

_____

Name _____ Date _____

 CHAPTER 3 Activity Sheet:
Understanding Graphs

A. A **bar graph** is often used to show changes over time. The bar graph below records the amounts of silver imported by Spain from 1511 to 1640. Study it and answer the questions that follow.

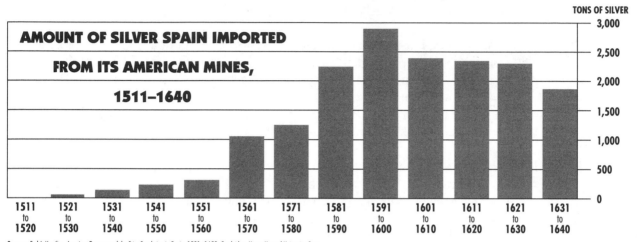

Source: Earl J. Hamilton, American Treasure and the Price Revolution in Spain, 1501–1650. Cambridge, Mass.: Harvard University Press

1. When was silver discovered in Spain's American colonies? _____

2. How much silver did Spain gain from its American mines from 1561 to 1570? _____

3. What was the peak decade between 1511 and 1640 for silver exports to Spain? _____

B. A **pictograph** uses pictures to stand for things to be related and compared. The pictographs below show the change in the Native American population of New Spain from 1519 to 1605. Study them and answer the questions that follow.

1. How many people does each picture symbol stand for? _____

2. What was the Native American population of New Spain in 1519? _____

3. What was the Native American population of New Spain in the Americas in 1605? _____

Name _____ Date _____

CHAPTER 4 Activity Sheet:
Recognizing a Point of View

A **point of view**—how a person looks and feels about something—is reflected in a person's opinions, attitudes, and judgments.

The passage below is from *Short Report on the Indies,* written in 1542 by Bartholemew de Las Casas, a Catholic priest. Read the passage and answer the questions that follow.

> God has created all these numberless people [Native Americans] to be . . . without malice [hatred] or duplicity [deceit], most obedient, most faithful . . . the most humble, most patient, most peaceful and calm, without strife [conflict] no tumults [disturbances] . . . as free from uproar, hate and desire of revenge, as any in the world.
>
> Once they have begun to learn of matters pertaining to faith, they are so eager to know them, and in fulfilling the sacraments and divine service of the Church. . . .
>
> Among these gentle [people], gifted by their Maker with the above qualities, the Spaniards entered as soon as they knew them, like wolves, tigers, and lions which had been starving for many days, and since forty years they have done nothing else; nor do they otherwise at the present day, than outrage, slay, afflict, torment, and destroy them with strange and new, and diverse [different] kinds of cruelty . . . to such extremes has this gone that, whereas there were more than three million souls, whom we saw in Hispaniola, there are today, not two hundred of the native population left.

1. What do you think Las Casas's purpose was in writing his report? _____
_____
_____

2. What was Las Casas's attitude toward the Native Americans of the Caribbean? _____
_____
_____

3. What was his opinion of the Spaniards' treatment of the people of the Caribbean? _____
_____
_____

4. According to Las Casas's observation, how have the people of the Caribbean responded to the religion of the Spaniards? _____
_____
_____

5. From this passage, what sort of person does Las Casas seem to be? _____
_____
_____

6. Name some other people you have studied who would be likely to share Las Casas's point of view.
_____
_____

Name _____ Date _____

CHAPTER 5 Activity Sheet:
Using Maps

Originally, people believed that California was an island. In 1700, a Spanish Jesuit proved that it was not. Later in the century, Spanish expeditions founded missions all along the coast. The map below shows the locations of some of the settlements set up between 1769 and 1848. Study it and answer the questions that follow.

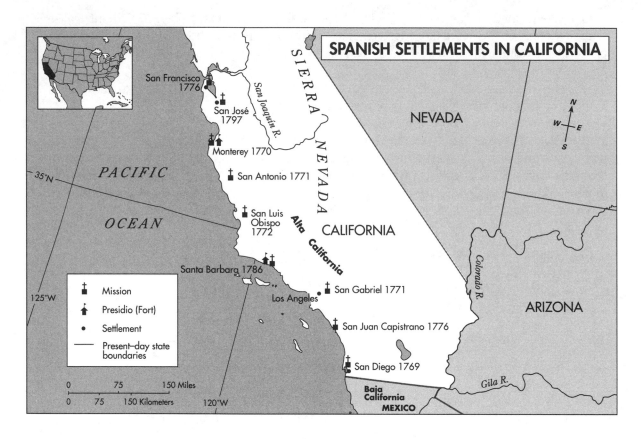

1. What was the name of the first mission? _____

2. Los Angeles (founded in 1798) was closest to which mission? _____

3. Which missions were established in 1771? _____

   _____

4. What city was founded the year that the United States declared its independence? _____

   _____

5. Name the settlements that were both presidios and missions. _____

   _____

6. Which missions became present-day cities? _____

Name _____ Date _____

CHAPTER 6 Activity Sheet:
Using a Map

    Many European countries claimed regions of the Americas in the 1600s and 1700s. In North America five nations controlled territory. Study the map below and then answer the questions.

1. The largest area of North America was claimed by which country? _____

2. Which three powers all claimed a northwestern section of North America? _____

3. What divided most of the United States from the territories claimed by Spain? _____

4. In addition to Spain, what country claimed a part of Mexico? _____

5. Which powers claimed territories that bordered on the Pacific Ocean? _____

6. In 1783, a traveler going west across the Mississippi River from the United States would enter territory controlled by what country? _____

7. If you were at the southernmost tip of present-day Florida in 1783, what country would have been in control of the land? _____

Name _____ Date _____

CHAPTER 7 Activity Sheet:
Cause and Effect

When an event or an action occurs, there generally is a reason. The reason is called a **cause** of the act. What happens as a result of the action or event is called an **effect**. Understanding the relationship between cause and effect can be helpful in analyzing the way in which things happen. Years after his triumphs in Latin America, Símon Bolívar wrote a letter recalling an important influence on his career. Read the excerpt from the letter (A) as well as a pledge made by Bolívar as a young man (B). The third selection (C) is an excerpt of a poem by José Joaquin Olmedo. It was written in celebration of Bolívar's victory over Spain.

A. I loved my wife very much.... If my wife had not died, I would not have made my second trip to Europe. It is probable that there would not have been born . . . the ideas which I acquired in my travels; in America I should not have gained the experience nor should I have made that study of the world, of men, and of affairs which has served me so well during the entire course of my political career. The death of my wife placed me at an early age in the road of politics; it caused me to follow the chariot of Mars [war] instead of the plow of Ceres [agriculture].

B. I swear before you, I swear before God of my fathers . . . by my honor and by my country, that my arm shall not rest nor my mind be at peace until I have broken the chains which bind me, by the will and power of Spain.

C. And the song of triumph
Which with a thousand echoes spreads, deafening
The deep valley and the craggy peak,
Let us proclaim Bolívar on earth
Arbiter of peace and war.

1. According to Bolívar, what caused him to make a second trip to Europe? _____

_____

_____

2. What effect did his travels have on his thinking? _____

_____

_____

3. What could he have learned or experienced during his travels that caused him to make his pledge?

_____

_____

4. Bolívar's pledge was seriously made and seriously fulfilled. What effect did his success have on José

   Joaquin Olmedo? _____

_____

_____

5. Think of an event or action that caused a change in your life. Explain the effect of that event on you.

_____

_____

THE LATINO EXPERIENCE IN U.S. HISTORY • © Globe Fearon

Name _____ Date _____

CHAPTER 8 Activity Sheet:
Building Vocabulary

Daily contact between Latino and Anglo cultures caused blending of the Spanish and English languages. Some terms were borrowed directly. Other words were changed slightly because of mispronunciation. Much of this exchange of language occurred among the cowhands as they worked together on the cattle ranches.

Mexican words adopted by cowhands:

corral   bronco
loco   sombrero
stampede (from *stampida*, meaning "crash, loud noise")

Spanish words changed by Texans:

chaps, from *chaparreras* ("leg armor")
lariat, from *la reata* ("rope")
rodeo, from *rodear* ("to round up; to surround with")
pinto, from *pinto* ("painted horse")
lasso, from *laso* ("slip knot")

The words below, taken from Chapter 8, are Spanish terms that were used to indicate certain people in the communities at that time. Choose the word that matches the description and write it on the lines provided.

santero   *patrone*
genizaros   *vaquero*
ricos   *tejano*
empresarios *mestizos*

1. Native Americans who no longer lived among their people _____

2. A cowboy _____

3. Individuals of mixed European or Native American descent _____

4. Wealthy individuals _____

5. A carver of wooden statues _____

6. A person who governed the community and cared for its people _____

7. Mexican settlers in Texas _____

8. Agents willing to recruit settlers _____

Name _____ Date _____

CHAPTER 9 Activity Sheet:
Using Primary Sources

Letters and personal journals give us the opportunity to see people from earlier times in everyday settings. The passage below is from the letters of Fanny Caldron de la Baca. She was a Scotswoman who had married a Spanish diplomat who was his country's first minister to Mexico. This excerpt describes her first impression of General Santa Anna. Read it and then answer the questions that follow.

> In a little while entered the General Santa Anna himself, a gentlemanly, good-looking, quietly dressed, rather sad-looking person, with one leg, apparently a good deal of an invalid, and to us decidedly the most interesting figure in the group. He has . . . fine dark eyes, soft and penetrating, and an interesting expression of face. Knowing nothing of his history, one would have said a philosopher, living in dignified retirement . . . who, if he were ever persuaded to emerge from his retreat, would only do so to benefit his country. . . . It was only now and then that the expression of his eye was startling, especially when he spoke of his leg, which is cut off below the knee. He speaks of it frequently . . . and when he gives an account of his wound, and refers to the French on that day, he appears to be bitter . . . He made himself very agreeable, spoke a great deal of the United States, and of the persons he had known there, and in his manners was altogether a more refined hero than I had expected to see. To judge from the past, he will not long remain in this present state of inaction. . . .

1. What is Fanny de la Barca's first impression of Santa Anna's appearance? _____
_____
_____

2. **a.** According to de la Barca, how does Santa Anna feel about the French? **b.** Why does he feel this
way? _____
_____
_____

3. How was Santa Anna different from what de la Barca had expected? _____
_____
_____

4. What prediction does de la Barca make about Santa Anna? _____
_____
_____

5. This letter was written in 1839. Was de la Barca right about the General's upcoming activities?
_____
_____

6. From her account, do you think de la Barca's impression of Santa Anna was generally favorable or unfavorable? Explain. _____
_____
_____

Name _____ Date _____

CHAPTER 10 Activity Sheet:
Using Maps to Understand History

As a result of war with Mexico, the United States added 1,193,050 square miles (309,130,360 hectares) to its territory (an area five times the size of France). Study the map below and answer the questions that follow.

1. What states were once Mexican territory? _____

2. Which territory was obtained from Great Britain in 1846? _____

3. The present state of Colorado is formed from how many previous territories? _____

4. To which country did the present state of Florida once belong? _____

5. The first passenger steamboat was introduced in 1803, in France. What other event was in the French news that year? _____

6. Which three territories were added to the United States within a three-year span? _____

    _____

7. Electric lighting was introduced in 1878. That was 30 years after which event depicted on the map?

    _____

8. What are the names of the present-day states that were formed from the territory annexed in 1845?

    _____

◢ CHAPTER 11 Activity Sheet:
Compare and Contrast

Mexican representatives wanted certain terms included in the Treaty of Guadalupe Hidalgo. They insisted on protection for the Mexicans who inhabited the territories claimed by the United States. Their concerns were addressed in Article VIII of the treaty, an excerpt (A) from which is printed below. Also printed is a paragraph (B) written by Juan Nepomunceno Cortina, the notorious "social bandit." Read both passages and answer the questions that follow.

A. Mexicans now established in territories previously belonging to Mexico, and which remain for the future within the limits of the U.S., as defined by the present treaty, shall be free to continue where they now reside . . . retaining the property which they possess in the said territories . . . without their being subjected, on this account, to any contribution, tax or charge whatever. Those who shall prefer to remain in the said territories, may either retain the title and rights of Mexican citizens, or acquire those of citizens of the U.S. . . . In the said territories, property of every kind, now belonging to Mexicans, not established there, shall be inviolably [safe from violation] respected. The present owners, the heirs of these, and all Mexicans who may hereafter acquire said property by contract, shall enjoy with respect to it, guarantees equally ample as if the same belonged to citizens of the U.S.

B. Mexicans! Is there no remedy for you? Inviolable [holy] laws, yet useless, serve, it is true, certain judges and hypocritical [deceiving] authorities, cemented in evil and injustice, to do whatever suits them, and to satisfy their vile avarice [greed] at the cost of your patience and suffering; rising in their frenzy, even to the taking of life. . . .

1. How does the tone of Article VIII compare to the tone of Cortina's paragraph?

_____

2. How, according to Article VIII, were the Mexicans to be treated after the war?

_____

3. Compare the treatment required by the treaty with how, according to Cortina, the Mexicans were treated.

_____

4. If what Cortina says is true, can you understand why he felt the way he did? Explain.

_____

5. His words were obviously meant to provoke an angry response from his people. Do you think this kind of attitude helps to solve differences? _____

6. What usually happens when hostility and anger increase?

_____

_____

Name _____ Date _____

CHAPTER 12 Activity Sheet:
Comparing Points of View

Slavery was a major issue in the 1800s. The Civil War in the United States was fought by two sections of the country that held opposing views, and throughout the world people debated the issue. Below are three viewpoints—from an enslaved African American woman, a white college professor, and a Cuban patriot. Read them and answer the questions that follow.

I can testify, from my own experience and observation that slavery is a curse to the whites as well as to the blacks. It makes the white fathers cruel; the sons violent; it contaminates [infects] the daughters and makes the wives wretched [unhappy]. And as for the colored race, it needs an abler pen than mine to describe the extremity [extent] of their sufferings, the depth of their degradation [shame].

Harriet Jacobs, an enslaved African American

We have no doubt but that [slaves] form the happiest portion of our society. A merrier being does not exist on the face of the globe than the Negro slave of the United States. . . . Why, then, since the slave is happy, and happiness is the great object of all animated [living] creation, should we endeavor [try] to disturb his contentment by infusing [putting] into his mind a vain and indefinite desire for liberty. . . .

Thomas R. Dew, college professor

Affinity [closeness] of character is more powerful than affinity of color. . . . Negroes are too weary of slavery to voluntarily enter the slavery of color. . . . Conceited and self-seeking men will go to one side, and generous and unselfish men will go to the other, regardless of their color. True men, black or white, will treat each other with loyalty and tenderness for the sake of merit alone.

José Martí, after slavery was abolished in Cuba

1. From Harriet Jacobs's point of view, how does slavery affect both whites and African Americans?

   _____

2. Compare Thomas Dew's and Harriet Jacobs's views on slavery's impact on African Americans.

   _____

3. According to Dew, what should be done about slavery? _____

   _____

4. What is the meaning of Martí's expression, "the slavery of color"? _____

   _____

5. Martí recognizes important differences among people. What are they? _____

   _____

6. Why do you suppose Dew's and Jacobs's points of view are so different? _____

   _____

7. Imagine that Martí had the opportunity to meet Dew. What do you suppose he would have said to him? _____

   _____

Name _____ Date _____

 CHAPTER 13 Activity Sheet:
Interpreting a Map of Mexico

For many years, Mexico's economy was based mainly on agriculture and mining. The discovery of oil and the development of large-scale industry led to economic expansion. Study the map of Mexican industry and natural resources below and answer the questions that follow.

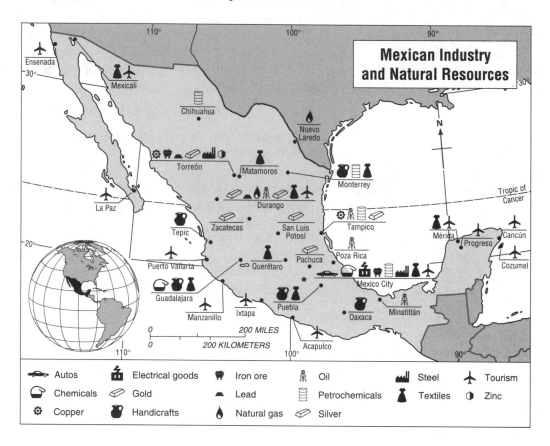

1. What minerals can be found in Mexico's mines? _____

2. What cities are major tourist centers? _____

3. If you went to Matamoros, what could you expect to purchase? _____

4. Name four of the important industries of Mexico City. _____

5. If you wanted to work for a company that manufactured electrical goods, which city would you go to?

   _____

6. If someone wanted a job in the steel industry, where should he or she go? _____

7. What do Tepic and Oaxaca have in common? _____

8. A chemical engineer is interested in a position. Where should he or she go for a job? _____

   _____

THE LATINO EXPERIENCE IN U.S. HISTORY • © Globe Fearon

Name _____ Date _____

▼ CHAPTER 14 Activity Sheet: Using Persuasion

Persuasion requires careful use of language. It is, of course, important to make a good case for your position—without using exaggeration or causing resentment. It is also important to be sensitive to the other person's point of view so as not to appear concerned only with your own. When José Martí was recruiting people for the revolutionary cause, he wrote to General Maximo Gomez to convince him to take command of the Army of Cuban Liberation. Read the excerpt below taken from the letter and answer the questions that follow.

> Great times require great sacrifices. And I am confidently asking you to leave in the hands of your growing children and your abandoned companion the fortune you are building for them with hard work, at the risk of death, to help Cuba in its freedom. I am asking you to exchange the pride in your well-being and the glorious peace of your repose [rest] for the hazards of revolution.... And I have no doubt, Major General, that the Cuban Revolutionary Party—today all that remains of the revolution in which you bled and were victorious—will obtain your services in whatever branch it offers you, for the purpose of commanding, with the example of your self-sacrifice and recognized skill, the republican war that the Party is under obligation to prepare...for the freedom and well-being of all its inhabitants...I will have no greater pride than the company and advice of a man who has never tired of noble misfortune, and day after day for ten years has been facing death to defend man's redemption [rescue] in the freedom of our country.

1. What does Martí state to persuade General Gomez that the cause is an important one?

   _____

   _____

2. What is Martí's opinion of Gomez's abilities? _____

   _____

   _____

3. In the letter, Martí shows that he is aware that his friend may have personal reasons not to serve.

   What does he say that demonstrates this? _____

   _____

   _____

4. What do you suppose was General Gomez's reaction to the letter? _____

   _____

   _____

5. If you received this letter, would you find it persuasive? _____

   _____

   _____

6. For what else besides his military skills does Martí value Gomez? _____

   _____

   _____

CHAPTER 15 Activity Sheet:
Reading Tables

The table below provides different kinds of information about Cuba and Puerto Rico. You can quickly compare facts about each island. Read the table and answer the questions that follow.

COMPARING CUBA AND PUERTO RICO

	CUBA	PUERTO RICO
Population	10,587,000	3,286,000
Geographic Area	44,218 square miles (114,500 sq. km.)	3,435 square miles (8,900 sq. km.)
Type of Government	Communist state	Commonwealth of the United States
Gross National Income	$26.9 billion	$14.1 billion
Per Capita Income	$1,590	$4,301
Literacy Rate	96%	92%
Urban Population	70%	66.8%
Monetary Unit	Peso	U.S. Dollar
Major Languages	Spanish	Spanish, English
Major Ethnic Groups	Spanish, African	Hispanic

1. Which island has the larger population?

   _____

2. On which island does a larger percentage of the population live in cities?

   _____

3. On which island would you pay for a jacket in dollars?

   _____

4. On which island does a larger percentage of the population read and write?

   _____

5. How do the governments of Cuba and Puerto Rico differ?

   _____

6. Imagine that you are sailing around both islands. Which trip takes longer?

   _____

7. On which island would you more likely need a Spanish-English dictionary?

   _____

8. Which island produces the most goods?

   _____

9. How does average income in Cuba differ from that in Puerto Rico?

   _____

Name _____ Date _____

▌ CHAPTER 16 Activity Sheet:
Identifying Values

Values are the principles, beliefs, and goals that are most important to individuals or groups. Values help people make the decisions in their lives that are right for them. In a letter to Venustiano Carranza, Emiliano Zapata reveals his personal values. Read the excerpt from the letter below and answer the questions that follow.

> As the citizen I am, as a man with a right to think and speak aloud, as a peasant fully aware of the needs of the humble people, as a revolutionary and a leader of great numbers . . . I address myself to you Citizen Carranza. . . . From the time your mind first generated the idea of revolution . . . and you conceived the idea of naming yourself Chief . . . you turned the struggle to your own advantage and that of your friends who helped you rise and then shared the booty—riches, honors, businesses, banquets, sumptuous [lavish] feasts. . . .
>
> It never occurred to you that the Revolution was fought for the benefit of the great masses, for the legions of the oppressed whom you motivated by your harangues [long speeches]. It was a magnificent pretext [trick] and a brilliant recourse [way] for you to oppress and deceive. . . .
>
> In the agrarian [land for farming] matter you have given or rented our haciendas to your favorites. The old landholdings . . . have been taken over by new landlords . . . and the people mocked in their hopes.

1. According to Zapata, what rights does he have as a citizen? _____
_____

2. According to Zapata, for whose sake is the revolution being fought? _____
_____

3. In Zapata's opinion, what is important to Carranza and his friends? _____
_____

4. According to this letter, do Zapata and Carranza's values seem to differ? Explain. _____
_____

5. What do you suppose Zapata wanted to do with the lands given away by Carranza? _____
_____

6. Why does Zapata believe that Carranza deceived the people? _____
_____

7. According to Zapata, who would benefit most if Carranza had his way? _____
_____

8. From the qualities and values revealed in this letter, can you understand why Zapata became an important leader? Explain. _____
_____

Name _____ Date _____

CHAPTER 17 Activity Sheet:
Drawing Conclusions

We draw conclusions about issues from the evidence we have before us. To arrive at the correct conclusion, we must pay close attention to all the facts at hand. If, however, we only see those things we want to see, it is likely that we will reach a wrong conclusion.

Many Mexicans came to the United States during World War I to work as unskilled laborers on farms and railroads. These jobs became available as Anglos entered the armed services or went to work in the factories that made military equipment. The Mexicans, desperate for jobs, were not in a position to control their working conditions. One of the selections below (A) is from an account by an immigrant worker. Passage (B) is from a magazine article written at the time. The third paragraph (C) is from a Texas farmer who employed Mexican laborers.

A. Like all the others, I often went to work without knowing how much I was going to be paid. I was never hired by a rancher, but by a contractor or a straw boss who picked up crews in town and handled payroll. The important questions that were in my mind—the wages per hour or per box, whether the beds would have mattresses and blankets, the price of meals, how often we would be paid—were never discussed, much less answered, beforehand. Once we were in camp, owing the employer for the ride to the job, having no means to get back to town except by walking and no money for the next meal, arguments over working conditions were settled in favor of the boss.

B. Working conditions among these laborers have been intolerable for many years. Wages by the hour were 10 cents and less. Piece work [work paid for at a fixed price per part] was common; the price for picking a crate of berries, 19 to 30 cents, depending on the variety, and this seldom netted the picker more than 90 cents a day. Hours were long; ten hours were standard, twelve were more often the rule.

C. I prefer Mexican labor to other classes of labor. . . . It is more [grateful] and you get more for your money. . . . The Mexicans don't live on hardly anything—tortillas and beans and a little meat—you can put 30 of them in a house, and they cook out over an open fire. The whites want a kerosene stove, and longer picking sacks. . . .

1. What conclusions can you draw from the Mexican worker's account of his experiences?

_____

2. The magazine writer seems to have researched his information. What is his conclusion?

_____

3. What conclusion does the farmer draw about Mexican laborers? _____

_____

4. Why do you think that the farmer feels the way he does? _____

_____

5. Why do you think that the Mexican workers did not complain to their employers? _____

_____

6. If you had wanted information about working conditions at the time, how would you have gone about it? _____

_____

THE LATINO EXPERIENCE IN U.S. HISTORY • © Globe Fearon

Name _____   Date _____

CHAPTER 18 Activity Sheet:
Making Decisions

Frida Kahlo (1910–1954) is a Mexican artist whose paintings hang in museums throughout the United States. She began to paint when she was in her teens. At the time, she was confined to her bed as the result of a serious accident. Her paintings illustrate the major dramas of her life. She painted her ongoing struggle with severe physical pain and her stormy relationship with Diego Rivera, the Mexican artist whom she married. Kahlo was eager to know what Rivera thought of her early work. Rivera's comments would affect her decision concerning her life's work. In the excerpt below from a biography of Kahlo, she remembers the time she first went to see Rivera with her work. Read the excerpt and answer the questions that follow.

As soon as they gave me permission to walk. . . . I went, carrying my paintings, to see Diego Rivera, who at that time was painting the frescoes [murals] in the . . . Ministry of Education. . . . I was bold enough to call him so that he would come down from the scaffolding to see my paintings . . . . I said, "Diego, come down." And just the way he is, so humble, so amiable [good natured], he came down. "Look . . . I have come to show you my painting. If you are interested in it, tell me so, if not, likewise, so that I will go to work at something else to help my parents." . . . Then he said to me: "Look, in the first place, I am very interested in your painting. . . . Go home, paint a painting, and next Sunday I will come and see it and tell you what I think." This he did and he said: "You have talent."

1. What was Kahlo's opinion of Rivera? _____

_____

_____

2. Why does Kahlo describe herself as "bold"? _____

_____

_____

3. What would Kahlo have decided to do if Rivera had thought little of her talent?_____

_____

_____

4. What was Rivera's initial reaction to Kahlo? _____

_____

_____

5. What did Rivera finally tell Kahlo? _____

_____

6. From this excerpt, what sort of person does Kahlo seem to be? _____

_____

_____

Name _____ Date _____

 CHAPTER 19 Activity Sheet:
Developing Library Skills

Newspaper accounts are valuable in that they offer a fresh look at what happened at the time. On April 29, 1942, during World War II, U.S. President Franklin Delano Roosevelt met with Mexican President Manuel Avila Chamacho. The next day, the *New York Times* reported the occasion. Read the excerpt of President Chamacho's speech below and answer the questions that follow.

"All the News That's Fit to Print."

The New York Times

 LATE CITY EDITION

NEW YORK, WEDNESDAY, APRIL 30, 1942

ROOSEVELT, ON TOUR, VISITS MEXICAN PRESIDENT; THEY PLEDGE FIGHT FOR 'GOOD NEIGHBOR WORLD'...

AVILA CAMACHO'S ADDRESS

Mr. President:

...Your visit to Mexico is proof of the progress attained by our two peoples in their desire to know each other; to understand each other... Mexico has not altered...her basic policy in order to find herself at the side of those nations which are fighting for the civilization of the world and for the good of humanity. What are the causes of our firm and sincere cordiality?... We both place our hope in the soundness of principles and in the perfectibility of people...

Mexico will never forget your participation in the structures of that new American policy which...we could proclaim as ours. Good neighbors. Good friends. That is what we have always wished to be for all the peoples of the world...

In order to bring about such a living together, we must destroy the machinery of barbarism constructed by the dictators: Such a campaign is not won alone in the trenches of the enemy. It is also won at home through greater unity, through more work, through greater production and through the benefit of pure democracy in which our brothers, our comrades and even our enemies may discover a principle capable of giving to their lives a better content. The difficulties with which we will be confronted will be very great. I recognize it. However, the energies of the people who are fighting against Nazi-facism and the honesty of the statesmen who direct them are (guarantees) that the faith will not be destroyed.

In order to contribute to the work of the post-war period the U.S. and Mexico are placed in a situation of undeniable possibilities. Geography has made of us a natural bridge...between the cultures of the

continent. If there is any place where the idea of good neighborhood may be proved effectively, it is right here... These interviews permit us to consider at close range our problems and try to solve them with the best and clearest understanding...

You have been witness to the enthusiasm with which my fellow countrymen have assumed the burden assigned to them... Our workmen, every day in greater numbers, are going to the fields of the U.S. to lend their assistance in tasks which for the time being have had to be abonadoned by farmers who have been drafted. This assistance...is a demonstratoin of the strong will which animates us...

I repeat to you, Mr. President...the desire that the relations between Mexico and the United States of America may develop along the channels of mutual esteem and unceasing devotion to liberty.

---

1. For President Chamacho, what is significant about President Roosevelt's visit to Mexico?

   _____

2. According to Chamacho, why is Mexico in a good geographic position?

   _____

3. According to Chamacho, how were Mexican workmen assisting the United States during wartime?

   _____

4. President Chamacho believes that Mexico and the United States have common goals. What would you
   say they are? _____

5. Why is it important for Mexico and the United States to have a good-neighbor policy?

   _____

THE LATINO EXPERIENCE IN U.S. HISTORY • © Globe Fearon

Name _____ Date _____

 CHAPTER 20 Activity Sheet:
Analyzing Statistics

By 1980, the number of people who had emigrated from Puerto Rico to the United States was 2,013,945. According to census data gathered in that year, statistics showed the information below. Study the data and answer the questions that follow.

——— STATISTICAL PROFILE OF PUERTO RICANS ———

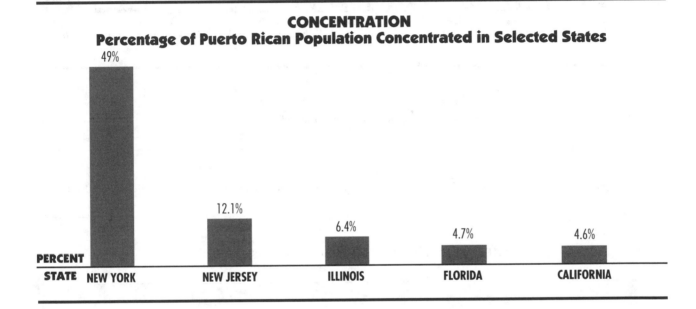

CONCENTRATION
Percentage of Puerto Rican Population Concentrated in Selected States

| PERCENT | 49% | 12.1% | 6.4% | 4.7% | 4.6% |
| STATE | NEW YORK | NEW JERSEY | ILLINOIS | FLORIDA | CALIFORNIA |

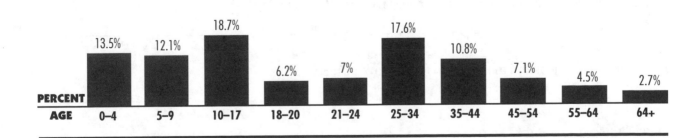

AGE OF PUERTO RICAN POPULATION
Age Distribution

| PERCENT | 13.5% | 12.1% | 18.7% | 6.2% | 7% | 17.6% | 10.8% | 7.1% | 4.5% | 2.7% |
| AGE | 0–4 | 5–9 | 10–17 | 18–20 | 21–24 | 25–34 | 35–44 | 45–54 | 55–64 | 64+ |

EMPLOYMENT IN PUERTO RICAN POPULATION

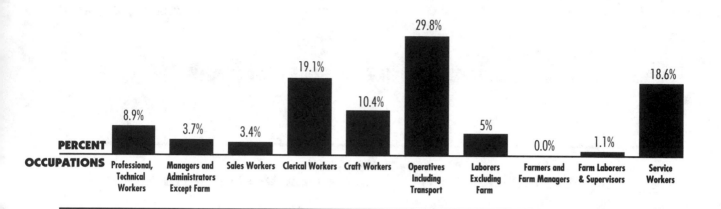

PERCENT OCCUPATIONS

Professional, Technical Workers	Managers and Administrators Except Farm	Sales Workers	Clerical Workers	Craft Workers	Operatives Including Transport	Laborers Excluding Farm	Farmers and Farm Managers	Farm Laborers & Supervisors	Service Workers
8.9%	3.7%	3.4%	19.1%	10.4%	29.8%	5%	0.0%	1.1%	18.6%

1. In which state did the highest percentage of Puerto Ricans settle?

_____

2. What percentage of Puerto Ricans in the United States were in professional and technical positions?

_____

3. What percentage of Puerto Ricans in the United States were 4 years old and younger?

_____

4. What was the total percentage of Puerto Rican people in the United States who were between 18 and 24 years old?

_____

5. What was the total percentage of the people who were over 45 years old?

_____

6. Service workers made up what percentage of Puerto Rican employees?

_____

7. What kinds of jobs did most Puerto Ricans have in 1980?

_____

8. The highest percentage of Puerto Ricans in the United States were what age in 1980?

_____

Name _____ Date _____

 **CHAPTER 21 Activity Sheet:
Discovering Cultural Diversity in Food**

Throughout the United States, many tasty dishes of Latin American origin can be found. The menu below comes from a restaurant owned by people from the Dominican Republic. Read the menu and answer the questions, using Spanish terms. Some questions will require you to look in more than one category.

SOPA • SOUP

sopa de pollo
chicken soup . . . .
sopa de pescado
fish soup . . . .

AVES • POULTRY

pollo frito
fried chicken . . . .
arroz con pollo
chicken with rice . . . .

CARNES DE RES • BEEF

carne con vegetales
meat with vegetables . . . .
bistec en salsa
steak in sauce . . . .

PESCADO • FISH

pescado con coco
fish in coconut sauce . . . .
pescado frito
fried fish . . . .

MARISCOS • SEAFOOD

arroz con langosta
rice with lobster . . . .
ensalada de camarones
whole shrimp salad . . . .

BEBIDAS • BEVERAGES

cafe con leche
coffee with milk . . . .
gaseosas
soda . . . .
jugo de naranja
orange juice . . . .
limonada
lemonade . . . .
batido de mango
mango shake . . . .

ACOMPANAMIENTOS
SIDE ORDERS

arroz y habichuelas
rice and beans . . . .
papas fritas
fried potatoes . . . .

Comida Hispana
RESTAURANT

**The Best
Spanish Food**

---

1. You would like some soup, and you are not in the mood for chicken. What will you ask for? (in Spanish) _____

2. If you want something tart to drink, what will you order? _____

3. If the chef agrees to cook you lobster in coconut sauce, what will the dish be called? _____

_____

4. Your dinner companion would like you to order rice and fish. What do you ask the waiter for?

_____

5. You are very fond of chicken salad. What will it be called in this restaurant? _____

6. For a side order, your friend wants some fried beans. What would be the name of that dish?

_____

7. Someone at your table wants rice and steak. What will that be called? _____

Name _____ Date _____

CHAPTER 22 Activity Sheet:
Reading a News Story

The main job of newspaper reporters is to give the facts. Most often, they answer the questions **Who, What, When, Where, Why,** and **How** something happened. When they report the death of an important person, they also include the accomplishments of that person. Read the excerpt below from the account of the death of union leader César Chávez that appeared in the *Los Angeles Times* on April 24, 1993. Then answer the questions that follow.

César Chávez, who organized the United Farm Workers union, staged a massive grape boycott in the late 1960s to dramatize the plight [condition] of America's poor farmers, and later became a Gandhi-like leader to urban Mexican Americans, was found dead Friday in San Luis, Ariz., police said. He was 66.

Authorities in San Luis, a small farming town on the Mexican border about 25 miles south of Chávez's native Yuma, said the legendary farm workers' leader apparently died in his sleep at the home of a family friend.

"He was our Gandhi," said Democratic state Sen. Art Torres, a prominent Chicano politican from Los Angeles' Eastside. . . .

A dedicated advocate of nonviolence, Chávez galvanized [stimulated] public support on behalf of farm workers, many of them illegal immigrants who averaged as little as $1,350 a year in the farm industry that at the time grossed $4 billion annually. . . .

Chávez's greatest achievement was the 1968 boycott of California grapes. Beginning in the spring, more than 200 union supporters, many of them earning $5 a week for their help, farmed out across the United States and Canada to urge consumers not to buy grapes. . . . By August, California growers estimated that the boycot had cost them about 20 percent of their revenue.

U.S. Senator Edward Kennedy said Chávez "was one of the greatest pioneers for civil rights and human rights of our century."

1. Where did Chávez die?

   _____

   _____

2. To whom did California State Senator Art Torres compare Chávez?

   _____

   _____

3. At the time that Chávez organized the farmworkers, what was their average annual wage?

   _____

   _____

4. According to this article, what was Chávez's greatest achievement?

   _____

   _____

5. Why did U.S. Senator Edward Kennedy praise Chávez?

   _____

   _____

Name _____ Date _____

 CHAPTER 23 Activity Sheet:
Identifying Trends

A general course or tendency that develops over time is called a **trend**. By looking at charts, graphs, and statistics, we can often predict the trend that is developing. The line graph below compares population growth in Northern America and Latin America (the figures are in millions); the table provides population figures for some Latin American countries (the figures are in thousands). Examine them and answer the questions that follow.

POPULATION TRENDS IN CENTRAL AMERICA

Country	year 1930	year 1985	year 2000
Costa Rica	499	2,600	3,596
El Salvador	1,443	5,552	8,708
Guatemala	1,771	7,963	12,222
Honduras	948	4,372	6,978
Mexico	16,589	78,996	109,180
Nicaragua	742	3,272	5,261
Panama	502	2,180	2,893

COMPARISON OF POPULATION TRENDS IN LATIN AMERICA AND NORTHERN AMERICA

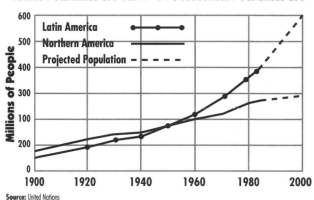

Source: United Nations

1. By the year 2000, about how many more millions of people will be in Latin American countries than will be living in Northern America (Canada and the United States)?

   _____

2. In about what year were the populations of Latin America and Northern America equal?

   _____

3. According to the graph, for how many years did Latin America have a smaller population than North America?

   _____

4. According to the table, which country will most likely have the largest population in the year 2025?

   _____

5. Costa Rico had the smallest population in 1930. Which country will most likely have the smallest population in 2025?

   _____

6. Large population increases can have significant social and economic impacts on a society. Explain.

   _____

Name _____ Date _____

CHAPTER 24 Activity Sheet:
Using Reference Materials

The reference section of a library contains shelves of books that you can use to look up thousands of facts. There are many kinds of encyclopedias, dictionaries, and atlases (books of maps), as well as volumes of information on specific subjects. Suppose, for instance, that you were interested in finding out about an important person in the movies. You would look up the person in your library's copy of *Contemporary Theatre, Film, and Television.*

Printed below is part of an entry from that book about Miriam Colon, the founder of the Puerto Rican Traveling Theatre Company. This group, with Colon as its guiding force, has produced works by many important Latino playwrights. In 1992, the group celebrated its 25th anniversary with a staging of *The Ox Cart* by René Marques. Read the entry and answer the questions that follow.

COLON, Miriam 1945—

PERSONAL: Born in 1945, in Ponce, Puerto Rico; married George P. Edgar, 1966.

EDUCATION: Attended University of Puerto Rico; trained for the stage at the Erwin Piscator Dramatic Workshop and Technical Institute and with Lee Strasberg at the Actors Studio. Also studied with Marcos Colon, Leopoldo Lavandero, and Ludwig Schajowicz.

VOCATION: Actress, director, and producer.

PRINCIPAL STAGE WORK: Producer *Crossroads,* 1969; producer/director *The Golden Streets,* 1970; producer *Puerto Rican Short Stories,* 1971

PRINCIPAL FILM APPEARANCES: One-Eyed Jacks, 1961. . . The Possession of Joel Delaney, 1972. . . .

PRINCIPAL TELEVISION APPEARANCES: Dick Van Dyke Show . . . Ben Casey . . . Gunsmoke . . . Bonanza

RELATED CAREER: founder, artistic director, Puerto Rican Traveling Theater, New York City, 1966.

1. Where was Miriam Colon born? _____

2. What school did she attend? _____

3. What was the name of the play she produced in 1969? _____

4. In 1961, Miriam Colon appeared in a movie. What was the name of that movie?

_____

5. When did Miriam Colon organize the Puerto Rican Traveling Theater? _____

6. Name a television show in which Miriam Colon appeared. _____

THE LATINO EXPERIENCE IN U.S. HISTORY • © Globe Fearon

Name _____ Date _____

 CHAPTER 25 Activity Sheet:
Understanding Poetry

Some people find that they can express their most personal feelings in a poem. The poem, "i yearn," was written by Ricardo Sanchez, a young Mexican American. Read an excerpt from the poem below and answer the questions that follow.

i yearn this morning
what i've yearned
since i left
          almost a year ago . . .
it is hollow
this
being away from everyday life
of the barrios
of my homeland . . .
i yearn to hear spanish
spoken in caló—
that special way
chicanos roll their
          tongues
to form words which dart or glide;

i yearn for foods that have character
and strength—the kind
that assail yet caress
you with the zest of life;
more than anything,
i yearn, my people,
for the warmth of you
greeting me with "¿qué tal,
hermano?" [how goes it, brother?]
and the knowing that you
          mean it
when you tell me that you love
the fact that we exist . . .

1. What does Sanchez mean by "it is hollow"? _____

_____

2. What is he saying about the Spanish language when he writes "words which dart or glide"?

_____

3. What does he miss most about his people? _____

_____

4. According to the poem, Sanchez left home almost a year ago. Do you think he will feel differently in

time? Explain. _____

_____

5. What makes it difficult to move from one's homeland? _____

_____

6. Why do you think Sanchez chose a poem as the form in which to express his feelings?

_____

_____

Name _____ Date _____

 CHAPTER 26 Activity Sheet:
Exploring Cultural Heritage

Aurora Levins Morales, the daughter of a Jewish American father and a Puerto Rican mother, lives in California. "Ending Poem" is from a book called *Getting Home Alive.* You will see in the poem how she examines the Puerto Rican and mainstream U.S. cultures, as well as the Jewish, African, and European influences that make up the Morales family. Read the excerpt of the poem below and answer the questions that follow.

I am what I am.
A child of the Americas.
A light-skinned mestiza of the Caribbean.
   A child of many diaspora, born into this continent
      at a crossroads.
   I am Puerto Rican. I am U.S. American.
I am New York Manhattan and the Bronx.
A mountain-born, country-bred, homegrown jibara child,
up from the shtetl, a California Puerto Rican Jew.
A product of the New York ghettoes I have never known.
I am an immigrant
and the daughter and granddaughter of immigrants. . . .
I come from the dirt where the cane was grown.
My people didn't go to dinner parties. They weren't invited.
I am caribeña island grown.
Spanish is in my flesh, ripples from my tongue, lodges in
   my hips,
   the language of garlic and mangoes. . . .
I am not African.
Africa waters the roots of my tree, but I cannot return.
I am not Taína
I am a late leaf of that ancient tree,

and my roots reach into the soil of two
   Americas.
Taína is in me, but there is no way back.
   I am not European, though I have dreamt of
      those cities.
   . . . .
Europe lives in me but I have no home there.
The table has a cloth woven by one, dyed by
   another,
embroidered by another still.
I am a child of many mothers.
They have kept it all going
All the civilizations erected on their backs.
All the dinner parties given with their labor.
We are new.
They gave us life, kept us going,
brought us to where we are.
Born at a crossroads.
Come, lay that dishcloth down. Eat, dear, eat.
History made us.
We will not eat ourselves up inside anymore.
And we are whole.

1. What does Morales mean by "We are new"? _____

   _____

   _____

2. Explain the line, *And we are whole.* _____

   _____

3. If you were to write a poem similar to Morales's, how would you describe yourself?

   _____

   _____

   _____

   _____

   _____

Name _____ Date _____

CHAPTER 27 Activity Sheet:
Main Idea and Supporting Details

Read the material below. Then complete the statement of the main idea and supply details that support the main idea in the space provided.

For the past several decades, there has been a strong Latin American influence on music in the United States. By the mid–1800s, U.S. music already had a Latin flavor, the contribution of the Mexicans who lived in California and Texas when these states entered the Union. By the end of the century, a Cuban dance, the *habanera*, became popular in the United States. It strongly influenced the Argentine tango, which became a countrywide dance craze in the United States. By the 1930s, a rhythmic African Cuban dance music called the rumba swept through the nation. Soon, other forms of Latin music could be heard on U.S. radios and in dance halls—the mambo, the samba, the cha-cha-cha, and the merengue.

One form of Latin music that has recently hit the U.S. music scene is salsa. Salsa as a musical form began in Cuba. The name *salsa* was given to this music when it was brought to Puerto Rico. Salsa mixes African melodies and rhythmic drumming styles with instruments and singing styles from Spain. Later, brass band and dance music popular in Europe in the 19th century and jazz from the 20th century added to the mix. Although it has come to be known as the national dance music of Puerto Rico, it is popular throughout the Caribbean. Salsa has been called the rhythm of the tropics.

Like other forms of Latin music, salsa has influenced jazz and rock. These influences continue into the 1990s. Pop artists David Byrne, Gloria Estefan, and Peter Gabriel have used the complex rhythms of salsa in their arrangements. Today, the rhythms of salsa can be heard everywhere—from the latest rap record to movie soundtracks to TV commercials.

1. Main idea: Salsa is a form of popular music that

_____

_____

_____

_____

_____

_____

_____

_____

2. Supporting details:

_____

_____

_____

_____

_____

_____

_____

_____

Name _____ Date _____

 CHAPTER 28 Activity Sheet:
Languages in the United States

According to the 1990 census, 31,845,000 people—or 14 percent of U.S. residents 5 years old and over—speak a language other than English at home. This is an increase of almost 38 percent over the 1980 total of 23,060,000. This jump is due largely to the immigration of Latino people. More than half of all people whose first language is not English speak Spanish. Study the table below that gives census information about speakers of some languages. Then answer the questions that follow.

Language Used at Home	Total Speakers	
	1990	**1980**
Spanish	17,339,000	11,549,000
Chinese	1,249,000	632,000
Italian	1,309,000	1,633,000
Polish	723,000	826,000
Korean	626,000	276,000
Vietnamese	507,000	203,000
Japanese	428,000	342,000

1. How many more Spanish speakers were there in 1990 than in 1980? _____

2. a. How many people were speaking Vietnamese at home in 1980? _____

   b. How many in 1990? _____

3. What language was spoken at home by 1,309,000 people in 1990? _____

4. Which languages had fewer speakers in 1990 than in 1980? _____

   _____

5. Which languages doubled the number of their speakers between 1980 and 1990?

   _____

   _____

6. Review the facts presented in this activity sheet. Do you think people living in the United States should be fluent in at least two languages? Why or Why not? _____

   _____

   _____

   _____

   _____

   _____

   _____

THE LATINO EXPERIENCE IN U.S. HISTORY • © Globe Fearon

Name _____ Date _____

CHAPTER 29 Activity Sheet:
Summarizing

Sometimes, because of the demands of time or convenience or space, we are asked to summarize material. Gabriel Garcia Marquez is a writer from Colombia who is admired and widely read in the United States. The selection below is an excerpt from a speech he delivered when he accepted the Nobel Prize for Literature in 1983. Read the excerpt and answer the questions that follow.

Latin America neither wants, nor has any reason, to be a puppet without a will of its own.

Why do the Western nations respect our originality in literature but mistrust our originality in our attempts at social change? Why do they think the social justice sought by progressive [open-minded] Europeans is not also the goal of Latin Americans? Why don't they understand that since the conditions are different, the methods must also be different?

The most prosperous countries of the world have succeeded in accumulating powers of destruction great enough, a hundred times over, to destroy not only all the human beings that have existed to this day but also the totality of all living beings that have ever drawn breath on this planet of misfortune.... Faced with this awesome reality, we the inventors of tales, who will believe anything, feel entitled to believe that it is not yet too late for people to try to create a perfect world. A world where no one will be able to decide for others how they die, where love will prove true and happiness be possible, and where the races condemned to one hundred years of solitude will have, at last and forever, a second opportunity on earth.

1. According to Garcia Marquez, what is the attitude of the West toward Latin America?

_____

_____

_____

2. What does Garcia Marquez see as the main cause of Latin America's suffering? _____

_____

_____

_____

3. What is Garcia Marquez's dream for the future? _____

_____

_____

_____

4. a. What other people might agree with Garcia Marquez? _____

_____

_____

b. Who might disagree? _____

_____

_____

Name _____ Date _____

 CHAPTER 30 Activity Sheet:
Predicting Trends

The Latino population is the fastest-growing cultural group in the United States. In 1980, the total U.S. population was 226,546,000 and the Latino population was 14,609,000. This was about 6.4 percent of the total population. In 1990, while the total population of the United States had increased to 248,710,000, the Latino population jumped to 22,354,000, or 9 percent of the total population. Social scientists predict that the Latino population will grow to over 50 million by the year 2020. Use these facts, information from the text, and the chart below to answer the questions.

◆◆◆ STATES WITH THE LARGEST LATINO POPULATIONS ◆◆◆				
State	Latino Population	Rank	Percentage in State	Percentage of U.S. Latinos
California	7,687,938	1	25.8	34.4
Texas	4,339,905	2	25.5	19.4
New York	2,214,026	3	12.3	9.9
Florida	1,574,143	4	12.2	7.0
Illinois	904,446	5	7.9	4.0
New Jersey	739,861	6	9.6	3.3
Arizona	688,338	7	18.8	3.1
New Mexico	579,224	8	38.2	2.6
Colorado	424,302	9	12.9	1.9

Sources: United States Decennial Census, 1990. United States Bureau of the Census, 1991.
U.S. Immigration and Naturalization Service, 1991.

1. Which state has the largest number of Latinos? _____

2. a. In which state do Latinos make up the greatest percentage of the population? _____

b. What effect do you think this has on the state as a whole? _____

_____

3. What historical reasons are there for the high percentages of Latinos in California, Texas, New Mexico, and Florida? _____

_____

4. If the social scientists' prediction about the growth of the Latino population is correct,

a. about how many Latinos will there be in the United States in the year 2000? _____

b. in which states will Latinos have the most influence in the year 2020? _____

5. How do you predict that the United States will change if the Latino population grows as expected?

_____

_____

THE LATINO EXPERIENCE IN U.S. HISTORY • © Globe Fearon

ANSWER KEY FOR ACTIVITY SHEETS

▶ UNIT 1 ACTIVITY SHEETS

Chapter 1: Reading a Timeline

1. Bahamas
2. Columbus brings 17 ships, over 1200 settlers
3. **a.** 1524 **b.** Giovanni de Verrazano
4. **a.** John Cabot **b.** eastern tip of North America
5. 1519
6. Balboa
7. 48 years old

Chapter 2: Making Inferences

1. clothing doesn't cover as much of their body
2. The Spanish had guns and iron weapons
3. horses
4. The Aztec have darker skin, wear less clothing, and do not use iron materials, or guns.

Chapter 3: Understanding Graphs

A) 1. 1521
   2. 1000 tons
   3. 1591-1600
B) 1. 1 million
   2. 25 million
   3. 1 million

Chapter 4: Recognizing a Point of View

1. To raise support for the Native Americans, and try to force the Spanish Crown to stop the cruel treatment.
2. He was sympathetic.
3. He felt it was extremely cruel.
4. They are faithful and eager to learn.
5. Answers may include religious, kind, sympathetic, or angry.
6. Answer may include any individual sympathetic to the Native Americans.

Chapter 5: Using Maps

1. San Diego
2. San Gabriel
3. San Gabriel, San Antonio
4. San Juan Capistrano, San Francisco
5. Monterey, Santa Barbara
6. San Diego, Santa Barbara, San Jose and San Francisco

▶ UNIT 2 ACTIVITY SHEETS

Chapter 6: Using a Map

1. Spain
2. Great Britain, Russia and Spain
3. Mississippi River
4. British
5. Spain, Great Britain, and Russia
6. Spain
7. Spain

Chapter 7: Cause and Effect

1. make a second trip to Europe
2. gave him experience, and allowed him the study of "the world, of men, and of affairs," which aided him throughout his life
3. revolution
4. inspired him
5. Responses will differ.

Chapter 8: Building a Vocabulary

1. vaquero
2. mestizo
3. riches
4. santero
5. patrone
6. tejano
7. empresarios

▶ UNIT 3 ACTIVITY SHEETS

Chapter 9: Using Primary Sources

1. Answer may include any of the following: gentlemanly, good looking, well dressed, one leg, soft, dark eyes and sad expression.
2. **a.** bitter **b.** He lost his leg fighting them.
3. more refined
4. he will not long be inactive
5. No
6. Her description is favorable, since the words she uses to describe him are positive (gentlemanly, well dressed, refined).

Chapter 10: Using Maps to Understand History

1. Texas, New Mexico, Arizona, Nevada, California, Utah, western Colorado
2. Oregon Country
3. 3
4. Spain
5. Louisiana Purchase
6. Texas Annexation (1845), Oregon Country (1846), Mexican Cession (1848)
7. Mexican Cession
8. Texas, New Mexico, Colorado

Chapter 11: Compare and Contrast

1. The tone in the first paragraph is straightforward and not emotional, where the second paragraph is angry, and emotional.
2. as citizens of the United States
3. According to Cortina, Mexicans were treated badly, which is in opposition to the mandates in the treaty
4. Responses may differ.
5. Responses may differ.
6. violence, war

▶ UNIT 4 ACTIVITY SHEETS

Chapter 12: Comparing Points of View

1. makes the white slave-owning family unhappy (violent, cruel, wretched), and forces the African slaves to endure extreme suffering and degradation
2. Dew says slaves are the happiest portion of society, where Jacobs says they endure extreme suffering, degradation and cruelty.
3. nothing
4. Being trapped in the cycle of judging a person by color
5. conceited and self-serving people vs. generous and unselfish
6. their background: Jacobs was enslaved, Dew is free college professor
7. Answers may include references to judging a person on character rather than skin tone, and the evil essence of slavery.

Chapter 13: Interpreting a Map of Mexico

1. copper, gold, iron ore, lead, natural gas, oil, petrochemicals, silver, steel, zinc
2. Ensenada, Mexicali, La Paz, Durango, Mexico City, Puerto Vallarta, Manzanillo, Acapulco, Cozumel, Cancun, Progreso, Merida
3. textiles
4. automobiles, chemicals, electrical goods, iron ore, petrochemicals, steel, textiles, tourism
5. Mexico City
6. Torreon or Mexico City
7. both produce handicrafts

Chapter 14: Using Persuasion

1. the cause is the same one he "bled for" earlier in life
2. holds his abilities in high esteem
3. mentions Gomez's family and his hard work to support them
4. Responses may differ.
5. Responses may differ.
6. leadership, self-sacrifice, skill

Chapter 15: Reading Tables

1. Cuba
2. Cuba
3. Puerto Rico
4. Cuba
5. Cuba is Communist, Puerto Rico is democratic
6. Cuba
7. Cuba
8. Cuba
9. Cuba
10. per capita income in Puerto Rico is higher than in Cuba

▶ UNIT 5 ACTIVITY SHEETS

Chapter 16: Identifying Values

1. the right to think and speak aloud
2. the ordinary people
3. the riches, honors, businesses, feasts, and banquets
4. Zapata is working for the benefit of the people, while Carranza is working for his personal benefit.
5. Distribute them among the peasants.

6. made them believe that the revolution would help them
7. Carranza and his friends
8. Responses may differ.

Chapter 17: Drawing Conclusions

1. not a very secure job, low wages, bad working conditions
2. working conditions were intolerable and unfair
3. Mexican labor is better
4. cheaper and easier to satisfy
5. desperate for jobs
6. Answers may include asking the Mexican workers or the straw bosses.

Chapter 18: Making Decisions

1. humble, amiable
2. she was a young girl and she called Rivera down from his work to see her painting
3. work at something else to help her parents
4. he was interested in seeing her work
5. that she had talent
6. good natured and kind

Chapter 19: Developing Library Skills

1. it is proof of the progress attained by Mexico and the U.S. in their desire to know and understand each other
2. it has made a natural bridge between the U.S. and Mexico
3. took jobs abandoned by drafted farmers
4. desire to understand each other and devotion to liberty
5. to keep peace and have assistance when needed for both countries

▶ UNIT 6 ACTIVITY SHEETS

Chapter 20: Analyzing Statistics

1. New York
2. 8.9%
3. 13.5%
4. 13.2%
5. 14.3%
6. 18.6%
7. Operatives Including Transport
8. age 10-17

Chapter 21: Discovering Cultural Diversity in Food

1. *sopa de pescado*
2. *limonada*
3. *langosta con coco*
4. *arroz con pescado*
5. *ensalada de pollo*
6. *habichuelas fritas*
7. *arroz con bistec*

Chapter 22: Finding Relevant Facts

1. at home in San Luis
2. Gandhi
3. $1,350
4. the 1968 boycott of California grapes
5. said he "was one of the greatest pioneers for civil rights and human rights of our century"

Chapter 23: Identifying Trends

1. 3 million
2. between 1950–1955
3. about 45 years
4. Mexico
5. Panama
6. not enough resources to maintain booming population

Chapter 24: Using Reference Materials

1. Colon was born in Ponce, Puerto Rico.
2. She attended the University of Puerto Rico and studied at the Erwin Piscator Dramatic Workshop and Technical Institute and the Actors Studio.
3. She produced *Crossroads*.
4. Colon appeared in *One-Eyed Jacks*.
5. She organized the Puerto Rican Traveling Theater in 1966.
6. Any of the following: *Dick Van Dyke Show, Ben Casey, Gunsmoke, Bonanza*

▶ UNIT 7 ACTIVITY SHEETS

Chapter 25: Understanding Poetry

1. what he yearns for is not being fulfilled
2. it flows
3. their warmth
4. Responses may differ.
5. Responses may differ.

6. Answers may include differences in culture, leaving the family, going to an unfamiliar place
7. Responses may differ.

Chapter 26: Exploring Cultural Heritage

1. Answers may include references to the fact that we are new and different, a combination of our diverse heritage
2. Responses may differ, but may include the following: Morales is alluding to the fact that she is not part Jewish, and part Latino, but rather she is a whole
3. Responses may differ.

Chapter 27: Main Idea and Supporting Details

1. mixed African melodies and rhythmic drumming styles with instruments and singing styles from Spain
2. influence jazz and rock

Chapter 28: Languages in the United States

1. about 6,000
2. a. 203,000 **b.** 507,000
3. Italian
4. Italian and Polish

5. Chinese, Korean, Vietnamese
6. Responses may differ. Students should take into account the growing numbers of ethnic groups and the languages brought with them.

Chapter 29: Summarizing

1. The West accepts their originality in literature, but not in social change
2. age-old inequalities
3. love, happiness, second opportunity for the races hindered by prejudice
4. a. almost any other minority group
b. Europeans

Chapter 30: Predicting Trends

1. California
2. a. New Mexico **b.** more predominant Latino culture
3. Students' answers may vary but should make references to location of Spanish settlers, and the immigration from Mexico, Latin America, Cuba, and Puerto Rico.
4. a. 30 million **b.** Answers may vary, but should include any states with a high percentage of Latinos
5. Latino culture, such as language, food, and traditions, will become a more prominent aspect of American life.

DIRECTORY OF COMMUNITY RESOURCES, BOOKS, AND AUDIOVISUAL MATERIALS

COMMUNITY RESOURCES

Afro-Hispanic Institute
3306 Ross Place NW
Washington, DC 20008

Artes del Valle
P.O. Box 627
Center, CO 81125

ASPIRA Association
1112 16th St. NW, Ste. 340
Washington, DC 20036

Association for Puerto
Rican-Hispanic Culture
c/o Peter Bloch
83 Park Terrace, W.
New York, NY 10034

Caribbean/Central American Action
1211 Connecticut Ave. NW,
Ste. 510 Washington, DC 20036

Caribbean Cultural Center
408 W. 58th St.
New York, NY 10019

Casa Aztlan
1831 South Racine Avenue
Chicago, IL 60608

Casa de Unidad
1920 Scotten
Detroit, MI 48209

Casa El Salvador
1837 West Ohio
Chicago, IL 60622

Center for Cuban Studies
124 West 23rd St.
New York, NY 10011

Central America Resource Center
P.O. Box 2327
Austin, TX 78768

Centro de la Comunidad Unida
1028 South 9th Street
Milwaukee, Wisconsin 53204

Centro Cultural Chicano
1704 Dupont Ave. N.
Minneapolis, MN 55411

Chicano Awareness Center

4825 S. 24th St.
Omaha, NE 68107

Club Hispanoamericano de
Tidewater
507 Earl St.
Norfolk, VA 23503

Conference on Latin American
History
c/o L. Ray Sadler
New Mexico State University
Dept. of History
P.O. Box 3–H
Las Cruces, NM 88003

Coronado National Memorial
Rural Rt. 2, Box 126
Hereford, AZ 85615

El Centro
1333 South 27th St.
Kansas City, KS 66106

El Museo del Barrio
1230 5th Ave.
New York, NY 10029

El Paso Museum of Art
1211 Montana Avenue
El Paso, TX 79902

Flor de Caña
7 Elmer Street
Cambridge, MA 02138

Fondo de Sol
2112 R. St. NW
Washington, D.C. 20008

Cuban Museum of Arts and
Culture
1300 SW 12th Ave.
Coral Gables, FL 33129

Guadalupe Center
2641 Belleview
Kansas City, MO 64108

Guatemala Solidarity Committee
147 NW 80th St.
Seattle, WA 98117

International Museum of Cultures
7500 W. Camp Wisdom Road
Dallas, TX 75236

Mexican American Cultural
Heritage Center
Thomas Edison Jr. High School
2940 Singleton Blvd.
Dallas, TX 75121

Mexican American Legal Defense
and Educational Fund
634 S. Spring St., 12th floor
Los Angeles, CA 90014

Mexican Museum
Fort Mason, Bldg. D.
Laguna and Marina Blvd.
San Francisco, CA 94123

Minority Arts Resource Council
1421 West Girard Ave.
Philadelphia, PA 19130

Museum of New Mexico
113 Lincoln Ave.
P.O. Box 2087
Santa Fe, NM 87504

National Congress for Puerto Rican
Rights
160 West Lippincott St.
Philadelphia, PA 19133

Puerto Rican, Latin American
Cultural Center (PR/LACC)
University of Connecticut
267 Glenbrook Rd.
U–188
Storrs, CT 06269

Puerto Rican Traveling Theater
304 West 47th Street
New York, NY 10036

San Antonio Museum of Art
200 West Jones Avenue
San Antonio, TX 78215

Santa Barbara Historic Society
136 East De la Guerra Street
Santa Barbara, CA 93101

Spanish Museum and Library
Broadway and 155th Street
New York, NY 10039

BOOKS

Aaseng, N. *Jose Canseco: Baseball's 40-40 Man.* Lerner Publications, 1989.

Alarcón, Francisco X. *Snake Poems: An Aztec Invocation.* Chronicle Books, 1992.

Anaya, R. *Heart of Aztlan.* University of New Mexico, 1979.

Baca, J. *Black Mesa Poems.* New Directions, 1989.

Catalano, J. *Mexican Americans.* Chelsea House, 1987.

Clark, A. *Secret of the Andes.* Viking Press, 1980.

Coleman, Alexander. *A Fountain, A House of Stone.* Farrar, Straus, Giroux, 1991.

Conover, T. *Coyotes: A Journey Through the Secret World of America's Illegal Aliens.* Random House, 1987.

Dwyer, Carlota Cárdenas de. *Chicano Voices.* Houghton Mifflin Co., 1975.

Empringham, Toni. *Fiesta in Aztlan: Anthology of Chicano Poetry.* Capra Press, 1982.

Espada, Martín. *Trumpets from the Islands of their Eviction.* Bilingual Press, 1987.

Exploring Latin America. Globe Book Company, 1988.

Faderman, Lillian and Salinas, Luis Omar. *From the Barrio: A Chicano Anthology.* Canfield Press, 1973.

Foner, Philip S. *José Martí: Major Poems.* Holmes and Meier Publishers, Inc., 1982.

Freedom Fighters. Fearon/Janus/Quercus, 1994.

Galarza, E. *Barrio Boy.* University of Notre Dame Press, 1965.

Gallenkamp, C. *Maya: The Riddle and Rediscovery of a Lost Civilization.* Viking Press, 1985.

González, Ray. *After Aztlan: Latino Poets of the Nineties.* David R. Godine, 1992.

Hispanic America to 1776. Globe Book Company, 1993.

Hispanic Biographies. Globe Book Company, 1989.

Hispanics in U.S. History. Globe Book Comapny, 1989.

Latino Caribbean Literature. Globe Book Company, 1994.

Latino Poetry. Globe Book Company, 1994.

Laviera, Tato. *AmeRícan.* Arte Publico Press, 1981.

Goodwin, David. *César Chávez: Hope for the People.* Ballantine Books.

Lewis, O. *Children of Sanchez: An Autobiography of a Mexican Family.* Random House, 1961.

Mexican American Literature. Globe Book Company, 1993.

Mohr, N. *Nilda.* Arte Publico Press, 1986.

Mohr, N. *El Bronx Remembered.* Arte Publico Press, 1986.

Morales, Aurora Levins and Rosario. *Getting Home Alive.* Firebrand Books, 1986.

O'Connor, J. *Story of Roberto Clemente.* Dell, 1991.

Regional Studies: Latin America. Globe Book Company, 1993.

Shulman, Irving. *West Side Story.* Pocket Books, 1961.

Tapestry. Globe Book Company, 1993.

Thomas, P. *Down These Mean Streets.* Random House, 1967.

Trevino, E. *I, Juan De Pareja.* Farrar, Strauss & Giroux, 1965.

Trueblood, Alan S. *A Sor Juana Anthology.* Harvard University Press, 1988.

Vigil, Evangelina. *Women of her Word: Hispanic Women Write.* Arte Publico Press, 1983.

Walker, P. *Pride of Puerto Rico: The Life of Roberto Clemente.* Harcourt Brace Jovanovich, 1988.

AUDIOVISUAL MATERIALS

Afro-Caribbean Festival. New Jersey Network. 90 minutes.

Against Wind and Tide: A Cuban Odyssey. Filmakers Library, Inc. 55 minutes.

Age of Discovery: Spanish and Portuguese Explorations (Revised). IJHC. 12 minutes.

All Our Lives. Cinema Guild. 54 minutes.

America's First City: Teotihuacan. Films, Inc. 17 minutes.

And Justice for Some. Downtown Community TV Center. 7 minutes.

Ano Nuevo. Cinema Guild. 55 minutes.

Aqui Se Habla Espanol. New Jersey Network. 60 minutes.

Argentina. Journal Films Inc. 16 minutes.

Battle of Vieques, The. Cinema Guild. 40 minutes.

Becoming American. New Day Films. 59 minutes.

Beyond Black and White. Motivational Media. 28 minutes.

Caudillo: The History of the Spanish Civil War. Films for the Humanities. 111 minutes.

Central America: History and Heritage. Phoenix/BFA Films. 21 minutes.

Chicano. Phoenix/BFA Films. 23 minutes.

Chicanos in Transition. Centre Productions, Inc. 30 minutes.

Chicanos Unidos. National Municipal League, Inc. 30 minutes.

The Closing Door. Cinema Guild. 59 minutes.

Crossfire El Salvador. PBS Video. 58 minutes.

Cuba: In the Shadow of Doubt. Filmakers Library, Inc. 58 minutes.

Cuba: Refugees and the Economy. Journal Films, Inc. 30 minutes.

Cuba: The Castro Generation. CRM/McGraw-Hill Films. 49 minutes.

Dominican Republic, Cradle of the Americas. Museum of Modern Art of Latin America

Drop Out Now, Pay Later. Handel Film Corporations. 24 minutes.

El Dialogo. Downtown Community TV Center. 57 minutes.

Enough Tears of Crying. Women Make Movies. 28 minutes.

Equal Opportunity. Barr Films. 22 minutes.

The Feathered Serpent. Lionel Television Productions. 36 minutes.

Francisco Franco. HC. 26 minutes.

Freedom or Survival. New Jersey Network. 30 minutes.

From Dreams to Reality—A Tribute to Minority Inventors. National AudioVisual Center. 28 minutes.

Fronteras. San Diego S.V. 30 minutes.

Ghost Dances. Home Vision. 40 minutes.

Hispanic America. Dallas County Community College District. 28 minutes.

Hispanic Americans. Dallas County Community College District. 28 minutes.

Juan Felix Sanchez. University of California at Berkeley. 27 minutes.

Juan Peron. King Features Entertainment. 14 minutes.

La Conquista (The Conquest). Video Knowledge, Inc. 60 minutes.

La Querencia—A Homeland Facing Change. Self Reliance Foundation. 30 minutes.

Lemon Grove Incident, The. San Diego State University. 60 minutes.

Living in America: A Hundred Years of Ybor City. Filmakers Library, Inc. 53 minutes.

Machito: A Latin Jazz Legacy. American Federation of Arts. 58 minutes.

▶ TEACHING STRATEGIES FOR ESL/LEP STUDENTS

Although the thought of teaching social studies in a language-diverse classroom may seem overwhelming at first, it is comforting to realize that techniques for teaching ESL/LEP students are simply good teaching techniques that are directed toward students' special needs. (The ESL/LEP population includes students for whom English is a second language as well as native English speakers with limited proficiency.) With an awareness of those needs and what works for students, teachers can easily adapt their instructional styles to language-diverse classrooms.

LESSON PLANS

Students with survival skills in English are ready to learn in that language. They can learn the concepts in the content areas as they develop scholastic and communicative language skills. To help them succeed, it is important to develop content-driven, activity-based lessons at the appropriate grade level and appropriate stage of language-skills development. Lesson plans created with the following components, developed in sheltered English classrooms, meet the needs of ESL/LEP students and lead to their success:

1. **Lesson Theme/Topic**—organizes the thinking needed to learn concepts.
2. **Key Concepts**—focus the learning process on the main reason for studying the particular theme or topic. Concepts also organize the learning process.
3. **Essential Vocabulary**—consists of the terms that are required to learn the key concepts of the lesson. Learning the vocabulary can begin to build the background necessary for understanding the material. A vocabulary activity can also be incorporated into the next section.
4. **Set**—reveals if students have the background knowledge required for the lesson. If not, the teacher builds this background knowledge. This phase requires interaction between the teacher and the class.
5. **Input**—includes all the activities the teacher does with students either in groups or as a class to provide the facts they need to start the learning process. Activities may result from the text, realia, audiovisual materials, and so on.
6. **Guided Practice**—creates interaction among groups of students and the text, the targeted vocabulary, one another, and the teacher to practice their growing knowledge of the concepts of the lesson. At this point, the teacher must monitor student progress and adjust the lesson accordingly.
7. **Follow-Up Activities**—include independent activities in which students practice the skills they have developed throughout the lesson. These provide an opportunity for the teacher to do formative evaluation, to ascertain if the students are ready for their final evaluation, and if they meet the objectives of the lesson. Writing exercises promote word and concept retention.
8. **Evaluation**—sets up demonstrations of mastery of the concepts. Evaluation activities need not be dependent on language. They may include such activities as making a collage and role playing. However, they can be language-based such as developing semantic maps or outlines or using previously developed semantic maps or outlines to write essays. The method of evaluation should match the stage of language development of the students and must hold them accountable for the academic concepts to be learned.

Among effective strategies to consider when developing and presenting lessons for ESL/LEP students are the following:

- **Modeling**—visual or auditory examples used to explain what is expected
- **Contextual Clues**—use of realia, pantomime, gestures, and connection of the familiar with the unknown; act out meaning when possible.
- **Built-in Redundancy**—repetition, paraphrasing, restatement, and use of synonyms
- **Age Appropriateness**—tasks reasonably difficult for the age of the students
- **Humor**—spontaneous and planned humor to lower anxiety level and increase chances for success
- **Equal Status Activities**—two-way cooperative interactions between and among learners such as peer tutoring, inclusion of student interests and experiences, and crosscultural activities
- **Cooperative/Collaborative Activities**—structured techniques with positive interdependence and individual accountability

Experienced social studies teachers working with ESL/LEP students have some suggestions that may be helpful to first-time teachers of language-diverse students. They recommend that students have a good dictionary. Often these teachers plan simple questions to get students involved. ESL/LEP teachers provide basic word lists to be learned and memorized for automatic recognition and mark the key words in each lesson. They provide an outline of the main ideas and simplify English to increase students' comprehension. ESL/LEP teachers involve students in meaningful interaction. The focus is on meaning rather than on form.

Teachers might consider these additional activities as they implement the ESL/LEP strategies:

- Summarize a paragraph or two, perhaps in the primary language. Then, have students translate to English, using a dictionary.
- Paraphrase a paragraph or primary source.
- In small groups, have students role play dialogues or events in history with a student who is more proficient in English.
- Have students make illustrated timelines.
- Have students create visual displays—collages, posters, bulletin board displays, and so forth.
- Write down each of the people, places, or events in a particular era of history on a series of cards. In small groups, have students make connections among the cards or arrange them in chronological order.
- Write out each sentence of a three-to-five sentence paragraph on separate index cards. In small groups, have ESL/LEP students arrange sentences in the order that makes the most sense. Ask them to explain why.
- Whenever possible, relate incidents in history or characters in history to student experiences in their primary languages or cultures. For example, after studying the American Revolution, discuss the significance of the Fourth of July. Ask students: How is Independence Day celebrated in your community or culture?
- Have students listen to a taped version of a paragraph, speech, or primary source. Ask them to write words they are not familiar with. Explain new vocabulary and replay the tape until students understand.
- Reproduce a "cloze" version of a paragraph—with fill-ins every fifth word.
- Ask students to choose the sentence that explains the main idea of a paragraph or choose one or two sentences that support the main idea.
- Create picture cards for vocabulary terms.

- Practice tenses by making predictions. For example: What do you think the U.S. government will do about the rebellion in Texas?
- In small groups, have students play 20 Questions or Who Am I.

Developing lessons using the lesson plan format explained above and implementing the strategies and techniques presented here will help students focus on the essential material in a lesson and also help teachers keep track of what students are learning. Focusing on the essentials enables both teacher and student to work on developing content-area concepts and specific language skills that help students succeed.

USING *THE LATINO EXPERIENCE IN U.S. HISTORY* WITH ESL/LEP STUDENTS

These ESL/LEP activity sheets take into account that while ESL/LEP students may have trouble communicating their thoughts in English, they are capable of thinking at the same levels as other students. Speaking another language takes practice, so these activity sheets are meant to be used in small interactive groups. Vocabulary should be done ahead of reading, if possible, since students read better when key words have been identified previously.

• Using the Unit 1 Overview

The Cooperative Learning Activity in the unit overview, p. 20, is a good source of suggestions for use with ESL/LEP students on the overall content of the unit. The activity can readily be applied and adapted to the needs of your students.

• Using the Unit 1 Big Picture Activity Sheet

If possible, work on this vocabulary list before the students read the chapter. In this way, students will have a preconception of a word before they actually encounter it in the text. Allow them to define the words in any way that makes sense to them.

CHAPTER 1 Face to Face in the Americas (pp. 10–21)

Setting the Stage. Refer students to the opening picture. Read aloud the first line of the caption: The first meeting of two worlds. Ask: Based on the picture, what "two worlds" meet in this chapter? *(Europe/Americas; Native American/European)*

1 A Meeting in the Caribbean (pp. 11–13)

Writing a Letter. Read aloud the last paragraph in this section (pp. 12–13.) Then challenge students to use their historic imaginations to write the letter mentioned in the paragraph.

2 Resistance and Conquest (pp. 13–15)

Spanish to English. Write the following Spanish terms on the chalkboard: *hidalgos, presidio, conquistador, adelantados*. Have students write definitions for each term in English.

3 Experiment in Empire Building (pp. 15–17)

Comparing Pictures and Words. Deliver a dramatic reading of Montesino's sermon on p. 17. Then have students look at the picture on p. 21. Ask: Does this picture tend to prove or disprove Montesino's charges? Explain.

4 Out of Africa (pp. 17–19)

Exploring Language. Write the phrase Turning Point in History on the chalkboard. With the class, explore the meaning of the phrase. *(an event that recharts the course of history)* Then have students complete the following sentence: The arrival of Africans in the Americas was a turning point in history because _____.

• Using the ESL/LEP Activity Sheet

If possible, work on the vocabulary list on the activity sheet before students read the chapter. In this way, students will have a preconception of the words before they meet them in the text. Allow them to define the words in any way that makes sense to them.

CHAPTER 2 Struggle for Empire (pp. 22–33)

Setting the Stage. Have students look at the Snapshot of the Times on p. 24. Ask: How long did it take for Cortés to defeat the Aztec? *(about 2 years)* Then have students skim through pictures in this chapter looking for any clues that might explain such a swift victory.

1 Seeking Adventure and Gold (pp. 23–25)

Designing Storyboards. Storyboards depict a series of events in the form of illustrations, much like a comic strip. Have students design storyboards for this section. You might repeat this activity for the remaining sections.

2 Marching to Tenochtitlán (pp. 25–29)

Writing Diary Entries. Divide the class into cooperative learning groups. Ask half the groups to write diary entries about the march to Tenochtitlán from the Spanish point of view. Ask the others to write entries from the Aztec point of view. Have groups exchange entries.

3 Toppling an Empire (pp. 29–31)

Writing Poetry. Read aloud the poem on p. 33. Assign pairs of students to write rhymed or unrhymed poems about the Aztec defeat. Encourage them to illustrate the poems.

• Using the ESL/LEP Activity Sheet

The history of the Americas begins with a desire for *more*—more wealth, more power, more land. Using the word *gold* as a metaphor permits students to approach this concept in a simple way. It may be useful to continue to apply this metaphor in later chapters, where some of the more painful episodes in the conquest of the Americas are detailed.

CHAPTER 3 New Ways of Life (pp. 34–45)

Setting the Stage. Refer students to the pictures on pp. 34 and 35. Ask them to identify the roles (jobs) of Native Americans. *(laborers, traders, entertainers, etc.)* Then ask students to complete the following sentence: Native Americans contributed to the growth of Mexico through _____.

1 Extending Spain's Reach (pp. 35–37)

Writing a Balance Sheet. Read aloud the Critical Thinking question on p. 37. Have students work up a balance sheet on the positive and negative deeds of the conquistadors. Ask: What is your opinion of the conquistadors? Why?

2 New Religious Voices (pp. 37–38)

Illustrating an Idea. Review some of the features of the mission system. Then challenge students to draw a poster showing how a mission might have looked or operated. If possible, arrange to have library references available.

3 The Columbian Exchange (pp. 38–40)

Organizing Information. Have students work in groups to list some of the items involved in the Columbian Exchange under each of the following heads: Africa, Europe, Americas. Encourage students to illustrate each item.

4 A Center of Spanish Culture (pp. 40–43)

Illustrated Timeline. Have students design an illustrated timeline for the following events: 1535— King takes control of New Spain; 1537—First printing press set up; 1542—*Encomienda* system ends; 1544— Silver discovered; 1551—University of Mexico founded; 1566—Silver fair held at Veracruz.

• Using the ESL/LEP Activity Sheet

The drawing of pictures of the cruel and violent events of this chapter may help to develop an understanding of the events and of the concept of persecution. Depending on the class, you may wish to draw

parallels between the conquest and the story of the Trojan horse in Greek mythology.

CHAPTER 4: Reaching Out from the Caribbean (pp. 46–53)

Setting the Stage. Refer students to the map on p. 53. Ask: If you were a military advisor to the rulers of Spain, what strategic reasons would you give for holding on to islands in the Caribbean?

1 La Florida (pp. 47–48)

Past and Present. Tell students to imagine that it is the year 2000. Have them design a poster for the 435th birthday of St. Augustine.

2 Outposts of Empire (pp. 48–51)

Presenting Ideas. Assign groups of students to prepare mock TV broadcasts of the following: the attack on San Juan, the attack on St. Augustine, and the completion of Castillo de San Marcos. Call on volunteers to deliver the news reports aloud.

• Using the ESL/LEP Activity Sheet

This activity sheet helps students gain an understanding of why people came to the Americas. Depending on the class, you might use the words on the activity sheet as a springboard to a discussion of racial prejudice and colonialism.

CHAPTER 5 The Spanish Borderlands (pp. 54–65)

Setting the Stage. Refer students to the Snapshot of the Times on p. 56. On a sheet of notebook paper, have students copy down each of the people or places mentioned in the list of events. As students read the chapter, have them write a brief identification next to each item.

1 The Kingdom of New Mexico (pp. 55–58)

In Your Own Words. Divide the class into seven groups. Assign one group the section opener and the other groups one of the subsections. Challenge students to summarize the material in each passage in a short oral report.

2 Across the Rio Grande (pp. 58–61)

Spanish to English. Write the following Spanish terms on the chalkboard: *mustangs, ranchos, vaqueros, mestizo, peninsulare, corral, lazo, bronco,* and *entrada.* Using context clues, the glossary, or a dictionary, have students write definitions of each word in English.

3 Along the Pacific Coast (pp. 61–63)

Who Am I? Ask several volunteers to write identification questions for figures mentioned in the section. Each question should end with the phrase: Who Am I? For example: I was the priest who helped lead the way into Alta California. Who Am I? *(Fray Serra)* Challenge the rest of the class to guess the name.

• Using the ESL/LEP Activity Sheet

Designing postcards and stamps helps students focus on an event and re-create it on a more personal level. The worksheet can be used to explore the "niceties" (i.e., the social requirements) of writing a postcard. As for the stamps, you might have the students explain why they chose a particular design. Since not all students may be able to draw a stamp, you might team up students. An alternative is to show students how to "block" spaces and label them (mountains go here, for example) so that the drawing requirements are kept to a minimum.

• • • • • • • • • • • • • • • • • • •

• Using the Unit 2 Overview

The Cooperative Learning Activity in the unit overview, p. 32, suggests techniques especially useful for teaching ESL/LEP students the overall content of the unit. The activity can readily be applied and adapted to the needs of your students.

• Using the Unit 2 Big Picture Activity Sheet

Knowing these words ahead of time may help students in their reading. The students' answers may vary, depending on what they think is important about a word.

CHAPTER 6 The Spanish and the American Revolution (pp. 74–83)

Setting the Stage. Refer students to the picture on p. 74 and the Snapshot of the Times on p. 75. Ask: What guesses can you make about how the Spanish helped the United States gain its independence?

1 Supplying the Patriot Side (pp. 75–77)

Position Statement. Challenge students to summarize Gálvez's views on the American Revolution by completing the following position statement: I, Bernardo de Gálvez feel that Spain should *help/not help* the Patriots because _____.

2 Joining the Fight (pp. 77–80)

Illustrating Ideas. Assign groups of students to design a postage stamp or coin to commemorate the contributions of Bernardo de Gálvez to the American Revolution.

3 The First Cattle Drives (pp. 80–81)

Pictorial Map. Using an opaque projector, have groups of students trace the map on p. 78 onto posterboard. Assign them to draw pictures on the map illustrating some of the events or ideas in this section. For example, they might draw *vaqueros* and cattle along the trail or a mission at Nacogdoches.

• Using the ESL/LEP Activity Sheet

This exercise can increase student understanding of an individual in the borderlands region and the kind of life that person led. Class discussion after students read their letters should focus on heightening this understanding.

CHAPTER 7 The Road to Latin American Independence (pp. 84–93)

Setting the Stage. Tell students that pictures often represent a point of view, or opinion, of a person or an event. Refer them to the picture on p. 84. Ask: What is the artist's point of view of Mexican independence? How can you tell?

1 Challenges in the North (pp. 85–87)

Cause and Effect. Write the following headline on the chalkboard: The U.S. Wins All Spanish Lands East of the Mississippi. Divide the class into seven groups and assign each group one of the subsections. Tell students to look for causes of this 1819 news-making event. Have students share their findings.

2 Independence for Mexico (pp. 88–89)

Illustrating History. Assign students to prepare an illustrated children's book entitled *The Mexican Revolution*. Each page in the book should show one event along with one or two sentences identifying the event. If possible, borrow some children's books as models. If the students have difficulty drawing the events, they may block out the elements of a drawing and provide word descriptions of what they are trying to depict.

3 Changes in Spanish America (pp. 89–91)

Writing Questions. Have students work in small groups and write Who, What, or Where questions on index cards. (Models appear in the Chapter 7 Close Up.) Allow a member from each group to challenge other groups to answer his or her questions quickly.

• Using the ESL/LEP Activity Sheet

This activity sheet should make students think about what it really means to wage a war for independence, especially for those who are economically disadvantaged. This might lead to a discussion of why freedom fighters would use guerrilla tactics in their struggle, a topic that can be taken up again in appropriate later chapters.

CHAPTER 8 Life in the Mexican Borderlands (pp. 94–103)

Setting the Stage. Have students brainstorm a list of adjectives or characteristics of the town pictured on p. 94. Record responses on the chalkboard. Next, tell students to imagine they lived in Mesilla. Challenge them to write a letter to a friend in Spain that vividly depicts the town.

1 Life in New Mexico (pp. 95–98)

Mock Interview. Divide the class into small groups. Have some of the students take the parts of the various social groups mentioned in the section. Tell other students to write interview questions to ask these people about daily life in New Mexico. Allow time for "reporters" to share their interviews.

2 Life in Mexican California (pp. 98–99)

Translating into English. Assign students to paraphrase the main points in this section in their primary language. Then have them translate these points into English, using a dictionary if necessary.

3 Changing Ways in Texas (pp. 100–101)

Oral History. Have students imagine that it is the late 1800s. An aged *tejano* is telling a grandchild about life in Texas in the 1820s. Ask: What would you tell the child? *(Students may use foreign words, but they must translate them for the English-speaking grandchild.)*

• Using the ESL/LEP Activity Sheet

Tell students that the words on this activity sheet are used frequently in later lessons, so they should make an effort to define them accurately and to remember their meanings.

• • • • • • • • • • • • • • • • • • •

• Using the Unit 3 Overview

The Cooperative Learning Activity in the unit overview, p. 40, suggests techniques especially useful for teaching ESL/LEP students the overall content of the unit. The activity can readily be applied and adapted to the needs of your students.

• Using the Unit 3 Big Picture Activity Sheet

Because so much of Latin American history is full of revolutions, government overthrows, and U.S. intervention, it is good for students to know the words involved in such developments. It may be necessary to review the differences between local and centralized control before beginning the activity sheet. Answers can be used as a springboard for a debate about forms of government.

CHAPTER 9 Revolt in Texas (pp. 112–121)

Setting the Stage. Read aloud the opening story on pp. 112–113. Encourage students to stop you whenever they do not know the meaning of a word. Working individually or in small groups, have students write a short report summarizing the findings of the survey team.

1 A Time of Unrest (pp. 113–114)

Vocabulary. Assign students to write a definition of the terms *federalism* and *centralism*. Then have them complete the following sentences: "*Federalists* in Texas wanted _____." "*Centralists* in Texas wanted _____."

2 Alarms in Texas (pp. 114–117)

Who Am I? Write the following incomplete sentence on the chalkboard: I believe that _____. Who Am I? On index cards, have students complete this sentence for each of the figures mentioned in the section. Have students pair off several times to use their cards in games of Who Am I?

3 Texas Gains Independence (pp. 117–119)

Writing Headlines. Challenge students to list major events described in this section in the form of newspaper headlines. They may phrase the headlines in their primary language but they should write an English translation below.

• Using the ESL/Activity Sheet

The activity sheet provides an opportunity to crystallize information from the chapter on a topic that is of continuing importance, not only with respect to Texas but also in terms of California and New Mexico.

CHAPTER 10 War Between the United States and Mexico (pp. 122–131)

Setting the Stage. Refer students to the section titles. Point out that *background* is a clue word for *causes*, while *aftermath* is a clue word for *effects*. To help students take note of the causes and effects of the war, have them draw up a chart with one column headed Causes, and the other headed Effects. After they finish reading the chapter, have students summarize this data.

1 Background to War (pp. 123–125)

Identifying Issues. Working in cooperative learning groups, have students write one or two sentences stating the issue discussed in each subsection. Go over these issues with the class as a whole and have students record them on their cause-and-effect chart.

2 Mexico and the United States at War (pp. 126–128)

News Bulletins. Divide the class into six groups. Assign each group one of the subsections, including the opening paragraphs. Challenge students to prepare a short news bulletin on the major event described. Bulletins should begin: Flash! We have just received news that _____.

3 Aftermath of the War (pp. 128–129)

Identifying Effects. Read aloud the section, sentence by sentence. Challenge students to identify any sentence that states an effect of the war. Call for a class consensus. Whenever students agree upon an effect, have them record it on the cause-and-effect sheet referred to above.

• Using the ESL/LEP Activity Sheet

This activity sheet reinforces the main events of the War Between the United States and Mexico, which are given in chronological order.

CHAPTER 11 Foreigners in Their Own Land (pp. 132–141)

Setting the Stage. Read aloud the chapter title. Ask: What does this title tell you about the treatment of Mexicans who lived in lands taken over by the United States?

1 Living Under a New Flag (pp. 133–135)

Vocabulary. Write the term *discrimination* on the chalkboard. Then read aloud the following definition: unjust treatment of a group based upon national origin, race, religion, or sex. Challenge students to write down examples of discrimination against *californios* mentioned in the section.

2 Land Claims and Courts (pp. 135–137)

Illustrating an Issue. Explain that political cartoons present issues in visual form. The cartoonist's "tools" include symbols, labels, and exaggerated features. Have students draw a political cartoon on the land grant issue from the *californios'* point of view. If they cannot draw the cartoon, have them provide a description of it.

3 Looking for Justice (pp. 137–139)

Composing a *Corrido*. Tell students that Texas *vaqueros* composed many *corridos,* or ballads, about social bandits such as Cortina. Have students work in groups to write their own *corrido* about Cortina or other social bandits. Distribute copies to the class. If they wish, they might write the *corrido* in their primary language, with English translations provided.

• Using the ESL/LEP Activity Sheet

The politics of the Latino struggle for influence and acceptance will figure heavily in the remaining chapters of the textbook. The words on the activity sheet relate directly to this struggle and should be thoroughly understood by the students. To ensure an understanding of the words, you may wish to play charades or other games involving these words.

• • • • • • • • • • • • • • • • • • • •

• Using the Unit 4 Overview

The Cooperative Learning Activity in the unit overview, p. 48, suggests techniques especially useful for teaching ESL/LEP students the overall content of the unit. The activity can readily be applied and adapted to the needs of your students.

• Using the Unit 4 Big Picture Activity Sheet

Students will understand the events in the next few chapters if they have a grasp of the overall content and an acquaintance with the key words involved. Have students define the words in whatever language they are comfortable with.

CHAPTER 12 Latinos in the U.S. Civil War (pp. 150–159)

Setting the Stage. Read aloud the chapter-opening story on pp. 150–151. Encourage students to ask the meaning of unfamiliar words. Brainstorm reasons Latinos like Velázquez might have fought in the Civil

War. Record responses and have students evaluate them at the end of the chapter.

1 The Civil War in the U.S. Southwest (pp. 151–154)

Mapping the War. Have students use an atlas and opaque projector to trace an outline map of the United States on posterboard. Assign students to use the atlas to locate and label geographic places named in the section. Encourage them to illustrate or write a description next to each entry. Continue this activity in Section 2.

2 Fighters for Two Flags (pp. 154–157)

Biographical Dictionary. With the class, list the names of Latinos involved in the Civil War. Place these names in alphabetical order. Then have groups of students write an entry on each person. Encourage groups to revise and correct each other's entries.

• Using the ESL/LEP Activity Sheet

Have students work in groups and allow them to use whatever language they are comfortable with to define these words.

CHAPTER 13 A Changing World (pp. 160–171)

Setting the Stage. Refer students to the Snapshot of the Times on p. 162. Assign them to plot these events along a horizontal time line, leaving space for illustrations or descriptions of each event. As students come across each item in the chapter, have them add pictures or words to the time line.

1 New Spanish Immigration (pp. 161–162)

Checking the Facts. Working in pairs, have half the class write true statements about Spanish immigration on index cards. Have the other half write incorrect statements. Use these cards for a verbal true-false quiz. Call on students who wrote each question to indicate the answer. Correct all incorrect statements.

2 Newcomers from Puerto Rico and Cuba (pp. 162–166)

Dramatization. Read aloud the eyewitness description of a *lector* on pp. 165–166. Then divide the class into groups. Challenge each group to write an editorial on conditions in the cigar factories. Have each group select a *lector* to do a dramatic reading for the class.

3 New Mexico (pp. 166–169)

Creative Writing. Tell students to imagine they are *nuevomexicanos* in 1912. Challenge them to write a poem celebrating statehood. Verses can be in students' primary language, with an English translation appearing below.

• Using the ESL/LEP Activity Sheet

This activity sheet can be used to explore the whole question of literacy as one of the most important tools a person can have. You can have students select something to read aloud to the class, giving them time to practice. The activity sheet can also be used to explore the politics of reading and literacy, with governments keeping people illiterate so that they would not have access to ideas and information the governments would not wish them to have.

CHAPTER 14 The Cuban-Spanish-American War (pp. 172–183)

Setting the Stage. Refer students to the Snapshot of the Times on p. 178. Ask: What do you think was outcome of the Cuban-Spanish-American War? How did you reach your answer?

1 Background to Revolution (pp. 173–174)

Illustrating an Idea. With the class, list causes of the Cuban revolution on the chalkboard. Assign groups of students to draw a poster illustrating each cause. Arrange these posters in a display called "Seeds of Revolution."

2 The War of 1895 (pp. 174–178)

Creative Writing. With the class, devise an opening line to a poem that a Cuban child might have written on José Martí. Write this line on a sheet of paper. Then pass it around to groups of students, challenging each group to add a verse or two. Read the completed poem aloud.

3 Uncertain Victory (pp. 179–181)

Forming Speculations. Read aloud the last paragraph of this section on p. 181. Ask: What do you think José Martí would have thought about the outcome of the war? Why?

• Using the ESL LEP Activity Sheet

For this activity sheet, students will work on gaining contextual clues from the sentence, which will help their reading. They will then use the text as a reference as they look up answers and information.

CHAPTER 15 Puerto Rico and Cuba Under United States Control (pp. 184–193)

Setting the Stage. Refer students to the picture on p. 184. Ask: How does this picture relate to the subject of this chapter?

1 The United States and Puerto Rico (pp. 185–188)

Vocabulary. With students, compose a definition for each of the following terms on the chalkboard: autonomy, home rule, *jíbaros,* and cultural imperialism. Working in pairs, challenge students to use each of these terms in a short speech a Puerto Rican patriot might have given in favor of independence.

2 The Republic of Cuba (pp. 188–191)

Identifying Supporting Evidence. Read aloud the following statement from the text: "The United States had no intention of giving up its investments in Cuban sugar." Working in small groups, have students write down sentences from the section that support this statement.

• Using the ESL/LEP Activity Sheet

One function of an activity sheet like this is to help students recognize English letter patterns. The activity sheet can be used simply as a puzzle to be solved or as a springboard into other activities. For example, once the words are circled, students could define them. You could turn the activity sheet into a game by dividing the class into mixed-ability groups. The first group to find a word would get a point, and the first group to define the word would also get a point.

• Using the Unit 5 Overview

The Cooperative Learning Activity in the unit overview, p. 58, suggests techniques especially useful for teaching ESL/LEP students the overall content of the unit. The activity can readily be applied and adapted to the needs of your students.

• Using the Unit 5 Big Picture Activity Sheet

Have students define these key words of the unit before they read the unit so that they have some preconception of the content of the unit. They may define the words in any way that makes sense to them.

CHAPTER 16 The Mexican Revolution and New Patterns of Immigration (pp. 202–211)

Setting the Stage Read aloud the question under Thinking About History. Then refer students to the Snapshot of the Times on p. 207. Ask: What item on this list of events helps you to answer this question?

1 Background to Revolution (p. 203)

Organizing Information. Assign students to draw a two-column chart entitled "The Two Sides of Díaz." Tell them to label one column "The Reformer" and the other column "The Dictator." Have students organize actions taken by Díaz under the correct column.

2 A Long Struggle (pp. 204–206)

Designing Story Boards. Have students illustrate the Mexican Revolution in the form of story boards. (Story boards consist of frames much like those in a comic strip.) Assign each subsection to a group of students. But encourage them to consult with each other on the "flow of action."

3 North from Mexico (pp. 206–209)

Writing a Letter. Assign students to imagine they have just fled Mexico for the United States. The year is 1915. Challenge students to describe their experiences in a letter to a friend still in Mexico.

• Using the ESL/LEP Activity Sheet

Since this assignment is all writing, you could balance it out by asking students to read their letters out loud. Listeners may supply feedback, commenting on whether the letters accomplished their purpose. Another possibility is to have a student read the letter as if it were intended for him or her and to react verbally to the message. Still another possibility is to have students exchange letters and write replies to them.

CHAPTER 17 Latinos and World War I (pp. 212–223)

Setting the Stage. Write the following items on the chalkboard: Time, Place, Key Actors, Meaning of the Story. Have students take notes on each of these items as you read aloud the chapter-opening story. Tell students to stop you whenever they want anything repeated or spelled. Focus discussion on the meaning of the story for the students.

1 Going to War (pp. 213–214)

Writing a Paragraph. Assign students to write a paragraph on Latino service in the war. To help students get started, write the following topic sentence on the chalkboard: "Both Puerto Rican and Mexican American soldiers served the nation in World War I."

2 Growing Immigration (pp. 214–219)

Spanish to English. Write the following terms on the chalkboard: *colonias, barrios, chicanos, mutualistas, Hispanos.* Have students write a definition in English of each of these terms. Then ask them to use these terms in sentences describing Mexican immigration from 1910 to 1920.

3 Moving North (pp. 219–221)

Presenting Ideas Orally. Have students work in cooperative learning groups to prepare mock radio reports entitled "Mexican Americans on the Move." If possible, provide a tape recorder so students can "edit" their broadcasts. Help with English pronunciations as necessary.

• Using the ESL/LEP Activity Sheet

These words on the activity sheet are important to the chapter, and many are the key to understanding the slow political changes involving Latinos that have taken place in the course of the 20th century.

CHAPTER 18 From Boom to Depression (pp. 224–235)

Setting the Stage. Assign students to look up the economic meaning of *boom* and *depression* in a dictionary. Call on students to share their findings. Challenge them to use these definitions to write a new chapter title.

1 Boom Times of the 1920s (pp. 225–227)

Illustrating Ideas. Have students select one of the organizations mentioned in this section. Assign them to design posters informing Latinos of the program's main goals. Encourage students to create bilingual posters, with phrases in Spanish and English.

2 Hard Times and the New Deal (pp. 227–230)

Illustrating History. Review the "shouting walls" described in the Focus On feature for Chapter 16. Using sheets of posterboard, have students design murals showing hardships suffered by Latinos in the Great Depression.

3 Organizing for Strength (pp. 230–233)

Creative Writing. Challenge groups of students to write a *corrido,* or ballad, about one of the strikes

mentioned in this chapter. Lyrics can be in students' primary language. But English translations should be written below the verses.

• Using the ESL/LEP Activity Sheet

The *mutualistas* and unions represented two ways the Latino newcomers could gain some social control and political clout, even in the face of prejudice and adversity. Point out how *mutualistas* and unions were one step in legitimizing a group that was considered "foreign." Also make clear that they were a springboard to show what one disenfranchised group was capable of doing through organized community effort.

CHAPTER 19 Latinos and World War II (pp. 236–247)

Setting the Stage. Have students look at the pictures in this chapter. Ask: What do these pictures tell you about experiences of Latinos during the World War II era?

1 Latinos in the Armed Forces (pp. 237–239)

Illustrated Biographies. Using only pictures or symbols, assign students to illustrate the feats of one of the following: Félix Longoria, Adolfo Garduno, Santa Fe Battalion, Manuel S. Gonzales, Guy Gabaldón, or José P. Martínez. Challenge the class to guess the identity of each figure or group depicted.

2 The Home Front (pp. 239–242)

Creative Writing. Have students rewrite the story of Juan Garza as he might have told it himself. Encourage Spanish-speaking students to contribute to the dialogue, offering phrases that Garza might have used to describe his experiences. (English translations should appear in parentheses.)

3 Facing Prejudice (pp. 242–245)

Illustrating an Idea. Read aloud the Focus On feature on p. 246. Then assign students to create a poster for the opening of the 1978 production of *Zoot Suit.* Remind students to refer to Section 3 for descriptions of clothing worn by *pachucos* and *pachucas.*

• Using the ESL/LEP Activity Sheet

Students can use this chapter to explore different wartime experiences. For those with greater language proficiency, the chart can be used as a basis for a compare/contrast essay. To facilitate speaking skills, students can assume roles and talk about "their" experiences.

• Using the Unit 6 Overview

The Cooperative Learning Activity in the unit overview, p. 68, suggests techniques especially useful for teaching ESL/LEP students the overall content of the unit. The activity can readily be applied and adapted to the needs of your students.

• Using the Unit 6 Big Picture Activity Sheet

Understanding these words will lay the groundwork for an understanding of the social context of the next few chapters. Have the students work in groups to talk about the meaning of these words. You may want to ask for modern-day examples for some of the terms.

CHAPTER 20 The Great Migration from Puerto Rico (pp. 256–267)

Setting the Stage. Read aloud the definition of *migration:* "movement from one place to another." Then refer students to the table on p. 262. Ask: How do the figures help explain the choice of title for this chapter? *(Focus on the huge increase in first-generation Puerto Ricans on the mainland.)*

1 A New Form of Government (pp. 257–260)

Comparing Points of View. Assign students to write short dialogues in which members of the PPD, PIP, and PNP explain their positions on the political status of Puerto Rico.

2 Meeting New Challenges (pp. 260–262)

Creative Writing. Challenge students to write a short story about the experiences of a Puerto Rican teenager who moves to the mainland in the 1950s. Encourage students to include some Spanish expression or words. (Translations should appear in parentheses.)

3 Lending a Helping Hand (pp. 262–265)

Using Historical Imagination. Read aloud the story of Pura Belpré on pp. 264–265. Then ask students to use their historical imagination to suggest how Belpre might have answered the question at the start of the section: "How can a poor community help itself?"

• Using the ESL/LEP Activity Sheet

This activity sheet will give students a chance to practice their personal vocabularies

CHAPTER 21 New Arrivals from the Caribbean (pp. 268–281)

Setting the Stage. Assign the chapter-opening story on pp. 268-269. Then ask teams of students to prepare news bulletins on events in the Caribbean on New Year's Eve 1959. Students can deliver bulletins in their primary language followed by a translation in English.

1 Upheaval in Cuba (pp. 269–273)

Time Capsules. Assign cooperative learning groups one of the three pivotal years covered in this section: 1959, 1960, 1961. Have each group create a time capsule that captures the spirit of the era. Items for the capsule can include illustrations of major events, poems, biographies, monthly calendars, and so on. Have students share their creations with the class.

2 A Growing Cuban Presence (pp. 273–277)

Defining Freedom. Read aloud the story of Miguel Seco on pp. 275–276. Ask: What freedoms were denied to Miguel in Cuba? Next, challenge students to write a definition of freedom as Miguel might define it.

3 Turmoil in the Dominican Republic (pp. 277–279)

Developing Empathy. Request volunteers who have moved to a strange country or neighborhood to share their experiences. Include these students in each of several cooperative learning groups. Challenge them to write a short story about some of Daysi Parris's hopes and fears as she traveled aboard a plane to the United States.

• Using the ESL/LEP Activity Sheet

A possible approach is to look at different types of newspaper coverage, from obituaries to supermarket tabloid stories. Encourage a variety of responses, from an interview with Castro to a sympathetic obituary about Trujillo. Encourage some students to write the same story but from different viewpoints. Have the stories read aloud.

CHAPTER 22 The Struggle for Equal Rights (pp. 282–295)

Setting the Stage. Write the phrase *Sal Si Puedes* on the chalkboard. If you have any Spanish-speaking students, have them translate it. ("Get Out If You Can.") Next, read aloud the chapter-opening story. Then have students look at the pictures in the chapter.

Ask: How did Latinos attempt to "get out" of the tough conditions that faced them?

1 La Causa (pp. 283–287)

Illustrating Goals. With the class, list the goals of La Causa on the chalkboard. Then assign groups of students to illustrate each of these goals in the form of a poster. Encourage them to use Spanish words. Arrange these posters in a display called "The Justice of Our Cause."

2 A Time for Action (pp. 287–293)

Living Time Line. With the class, arrange major events in this section in a horizontal time line. Then assign groups of students to create an acto for each of these events. Spanish dialogue can be included. But a narrator should jump in to translate into English. Present the actos in chronological order to correspond with the time line.

• Using the ESL/LEP Activity Sheet

Discuss the idea that people can bring about social and political change in many ways. One way is through activism, which means taking definite action to effect change. Activism need not be violent. Ask students to find examples of activism that are pertinent to their lives from newspapers .

CHAPTER 23 New Immigrants from Central and South America (pp. 296–303)

Setting the Stage. Read aloud the question in Thinking About the Chapter. Then refer students to the Snapshot of the Times on p. 301. Ask: Based on this list, how would you answer the chapter-opening question?

1 Struggle for Democracy in Central America (pp. 297–299)

Dramatization. Divide the class into three groups. Ask each group to devise a skit in which recent immigrants explain the state of affairs in one of the following nations: Guatemala, El Salvador, Nicaragua. Encourage students to use as many of the boldfaced vocabulary terms in their skits as possible.

2 New Voices from South America (pp. 299–301)

Writing Diary Entries. Challenge students to retell the stories of Rodolfo and Monica Singer in the form of diary entries. Entries should include mention of the "dirty war" and the tough decision to stay in the United States.

• Using the ESL/LEP Activity Sheet

The actual events of the chapter may be hard for the students to remember. But the gist is that people fled from the violence in their homelands. Make students aware of the subtext of this chapter, which is the changing perception of the United States, from oppressor to place of refuge

CHAPTER 24 A Growing Voice (pp. 304–319)

Setting the Stage. Open the chapter by reading aloud the story of Antonio Martorell on pp. 304–305. Encourage students to ask the meaning of any unfamiliar words. Then challenge them to complete the following sentence: "I, Antonio Martorell, have contributed to U.S. culture by _____."

1 New Cultural Perspectives (pp. 305–315)

Biographical Dictionary. As a class project, have students compile an alphabetical list of the various Latino artists, writers, and performers mentioned in this chapter. For each person, have students design a profile page to be included in a biographical dictionary. Bind these pages together and contribute the resulting reference book to the school or community library.

2 Reshaping Popular Culture (pp. 315–317)

Illustrating Ideas. Read aloud the biography of Roberto Clemente on p. 317 Challenge students to design the commemorative postage stamp mentioned in the biography.

• Using the ESL/LEP Activity Sheet

Since the chapter deals with various forms of art, you might use the activity as a springboard into a discussion of what art means to a people. If library resources are available, students might find additional people to write about and discuss how their art enriched the people.

• Using the Unit 7 Overview

The Cooperative Learning Activity in the unit overview, p. 80, suggests techniques especially useful for teaching ESL/LEP students the overall content of the unit. The activity can readily be applied and adapted to the needs of your students.

• Using the Unit 7 Big Picture Activity Sheet

The terms on this activity sheet relate to some of the key ideas of the next few chapters. Have students define them as best they can and then have a class discussion of what they mean.

CHAPTER 25 Mexican Americans Today (pp. 328–337)

Setting the Stage. To organize reading, tell students to prepare a two-column chart entitled "Toward a New Century." Have students label one column "Triumphs" and the other "Challenges." Review each subsection in the chapter by asking students to identify any items that should appear on the chart.

1 A Tale of Three Cities (pp. 329–332)

Summarizing Information. Have students work in pairs to summarize the profiles of the three cities presented in this section. Summaries can be written first in the primary language and then translated into English.

2 The Lure of *El Norte* (pp. 332–335)

Pictorial Map. Using an atlas and an opaque projector, have students trace an outline map of the United States and Mexico on posterboard. Challenge them to illustrate the map with pictures showing how the two nations are linked. Students might draw pictures of *maquiladoras*. They may also include symbols for cities mentioned in Section 1 or the trolley cars discussed in the Focus On feature.

• Using the ESL/LEP Activity Sheet

This activity sheet will give students a chance to become familiar with important new terms.

CHAPTER 26 Puerto Ricans Today (pp. 338–347)

Setting the Stage. Refer students to the photo of New York's Puerto Rican day parade on page 338. Ask: What evidence of Puerto Rican pride can you identify in the photo?

1 On the Mainland (pp. 339–342)

Writing *Plenas*. Divide the class into small groups. Challenge them to write a *plena* about some issue concerning the Puerto Rican community on the mainland today. Lyrics can be written in Spanish with an English translation below.

2 Ties to the Home Island (pp. 343–345)

Writing a Letter. With the class, identify some of the issues facing Puerto Ricans today. Then tell students to imagine they are young Puerto Rican adults like Lida Viruet or James Cancel. Challenge them to write letters to the legislature in San Juan about the issue that most concerns them.

• Using the ESL/LEP Activity Sheet

This assignment can be modified to write a poem or design a poster. If possible, bring to class a protest song and encourage the students to write one. Even if the songs are not in English, students may explain the words to the class.

CHAPTER 27 Cuban Americans Today (pp. 348–357)

Setting the Stage. Read aloud the chapter-opening story on pp. 348-349. Encourage students to ask the meaning of any unfamiliar words. Then call on volunteers to paraphrase the problems facing many Cuban refugees in Miami. Ask: How did Centro Mater provide a solution to some of these problems?

1 New Waves of Refugees (pp. 349–351)

Illustrated Chronology. Using information in Chapter 21 and this section, have students summarize the major waves of Cuban migration in an illustrated chronology. Items might include: 1959–1962—Fleeing Revolution; 1965—Camarioca Boatlift; 1965–1973—Cuban-Miami Airlift; 1980—Mariel Boatlift; 1991—Flight 8506.

2 A Strong Cuban American Presence (pp. 352–355)

Illustrating an Idea. Challenge students to design a poster entitled: "Miami: Gateway of Latin America." Encourage them to include pictures or symbols showing the role of Cubans in building the "gateway."

• Using the ESL/LEP Activity Sheet

The purpose of this activity sheet is to have students identify the various elements of the community in which they live. If students do not have a sense of belonging to a community, then the assignment may help give them a sense of what such belonging is like. One way to approach this is to have the class identify itself as a community and to design a fair that would encompass the various elements making up the class.

CHAPTER 28 Central Americans and Dominicans Today (pp. 358–367)

Setting the Stage. Refer students to the Snapshot of the Times on p. 360. Ask: Which items explain why thousands of Central Americans and Dominicans migrated to the United States in the 1980s?

1 Leaving Central America (pp. 359–360)

Using Historical Imagination. Working in cooperative learning groups, have students describe the flight of a Mayan family from Guatemala to Los Angeles. Students should try to weave the following terms into the story: *ladinos,* death squads, Sanctuary Movement.

2 A Growing Central American Presence (pp. 360–362)

Identifying Topics. Have students, working in groups, write a sentence identifying the main topic, or subject, of each subsection in this section. Below each sentence have students list two things that they learned about this topic.

3 Dominicans in the United States (pp. 362–365)

Turning Words into Pictures. Using information in this chapter, assign students to draw a street scene entitled "Quisqueya Heights." Encourage them to use Spanish signs on the windows of shops and stores. Students can even add dialogue from some of the passersby.

• Using the ESL/LEP Activity Sheet

This activity sheet gives students practice in creating a board game. Students must articulate a goal and the steps in achieving that goal. In achieving the goal, they must consider the welfare of the community. That is why, after one student has attained the goal, he or she must re-enter the game as an advocate. If resources are scarce, consider using numbers on squares that students draw from a bag. For the board itself, brown paper bags may be used. Once students have worked in small groups, consider having the whole class create a simulation game for refugees.

CHAPTER 29 South Americans in the United States Today (pp. 368–375)

Setting the Stage. Have students locate Paraguay on the map of Latin America on p. 396. Working in pairs, have them write a description of Paraguay's geographic location. Then read aloud the chapter-opening story on pp. 368-369. Ask: What can you learn about Paraguay from the story of Florencia Florentin Rivarola?

1 The Lure of Freedom (pp. 369–371)

Organizing Information. On a sheet of paper, have students list each South American nation mentioned in this chapter. Next to each nation, tell students to write causes of immigration to the United States. When students are done, ask: What were the two most common causes for people coming to this country in the 1980s?

2 Building New Lives (pp. 371–373)

Writing a News Article. Review the skills lesson on p. 375. Then ask students to write a news article on South Americans in the United States today. To get students started, write the following headline on the chalkboard: "South Americans—The Nation's Newest Success Story."

• Using the ESL/LEP Activity Sheet

If your students are comfortable, have them talk about changes in their own lives as they switched homes. Or use the sheet to explore how different options exist for different classes of people and how education creates options for people.

CHAPTER 30 Toward a New Century (pp. 376–391)

Setting the Stage. Brainstorm with the class all the examples of Latino culture that they can identify in the United States today. Encourage students to think of foods, music, clothing styles, famous people of Latino ancestry, and so on. List these items on the chalkboard. Modify and add to the list as students work their way through the chapter.

1 Latinos in the 1990s (pp. 377–381)

Interpreting Statistics. Refer students to the statistical profile of Latinos on pages 378–379. To help them unlock the story in each table, chart, or graph, write the following incomplete sentence on the chalkboard. "These figures tell me that ____." Working in groups, have students complete this sentence for each item on the page.

2 The Growing Reach of Latino Culture (pp. 381–389)

Preparing a Festival. After completing this section, meet with members of the class to prepare a Latino festival. Encourage students to draw posters and to bring in examples of Latino culture such as music, food items, clothing, and so on.

• Using the ESL/LEP Activity Sheet

Have students review their interview questions to see if they are relevant and open-ended enough to start a discussion. Then have them assume different personalities so that they can interview one another. The questions about the textbook ask the student to reflect on his or her own learning. If used as focusing questions for a discussion, students can share with you and with one another what they found valuable in the class and the book.

Name _____ Date _____

◥ THE BIG PICTURE 1 ESL/LEP Activity Sheet: Spain in the Americas

Below are some important words that you will need to know. Define them in your own words so that you understand what they mean. Use your own knowledge, a friend, or a dictionary. Draw pictures if that helps you explain what a word means.

culture _____

_____

migration _____

_____

Aztec _____

_____

Africa _____

_____

slavery _____

_____

Spain _____

_____

colonies _____

_____

Christianity _____

_____

England _____

_____

France _____

_____

the Americas _____

_____

Name _____ Date _____

 CHAPTER 1 ESL/LEP Activity Sheet:
Face to Face in the Americas

Draw a picture or use words to define these things.

GOLD	WHITE GOLD	BLACK GOLD

Why are these important to U.S. history? See if you can fill the block with reasons, ideas, or pictures.

GOLD	WHITE GOLD	BLACK GOLD

II. Pretend you are a ship's captain. Design a poster that invites people to come sailing with you. You could invite people to sail with you to the Indies. Or you could make your adventure more modern and take a trip to another planet. Be sure to include reasons to make people want to sail with you.

CHAPTER 2 ESL/LEP Activity Sheet:
Struggle for an Empire

Use pictures or words to describe how Cortés conquered the Aztec.

Cortés leads a voyage to the Yucatán and tells the Maya to give up their gods.	Cortés decides to march west to the Aztec city of Tenochtitlán
The Emperor Motecuhzoma thinks that Cortés is Quetzalcoatl, a god, and welcomes him.	After a while, the Aztec realize that the Spanish are men, not gods. The Aztec become angry.
Cortés takes Motecuhzoma hostage (prisoner), then goes to meet Velázquez at Veracruz.	While Cortés is gone, the Spanish kill Aztec nobles.
When Cortés comes back, the Aztec attack his men. Cortés escapes and attacks the city.	Cuauhtémoc, the Aztec ruler, surrenders to Cortés. He hopes this will save his people.

CHAPTER 3 ESL/LEP Activity Sheet:
New Ways of Life

I. People came to the Americas for many reasons. Look at the list of people below. First, draw a picture of that person. Then explain what each person does and give a reason why he or she came to the Americas.

Name and picture of person	What does he or she do?	Why did he or she come to the Americas?
conquistador		
soldier		
friar		
enslaved person		
merchant		
viceroy		

II. It is important to know and understand the words below. Define them in the best way you can. Then check your definitions in a dictionary.

criollo _____

_____

peninsulares _____

_____

mestizos _____

_____

Name _____ Date _____

CHAPTER 4 ESL/LEP Activity Sheet:
Reaching Out from the Caribbean

You are traveling with Ponce de León. Design a postcard that shows something from your trip. It could be a picture from La Florida. (Remember, La Florida included almost all the east coast of the United States, from Florida to Delaware!) Or it could be pictures of animals you saw, or people you met.

Use the space below to design the front of your postcard to someone.

Greetings from _____

Now that you have designed your postcard, write a message to someone on the back. Include the date.

Date:

Dear _____,

To: _____

_____

_____

_____

If you have time, design the first stamp from the Americas.

Name _____   Date _____

 CHAPTER 5 ESL/LEP Activity Sheet:
The Spanish Borderlands

   Choose someone from the chapter. Pretend that you are that person. Write a letter to a friend or family member who lives in your hometown. You can write about the weather, about people you have met, the food you ate, or about the lands you have seen. Try to include the reasons why you are in the Spanish Borderlands. (Of course, you do not have to be Spanish to be in the Borderlands.)

_____ , _____

_____

_____

_____

_____

_____

_____

_____

_____

_____

_____

_____

_____

_____

_____

                                    _____

Name _____ Date _____

▼ THE BIG PICTURE 2 ESL/LEP Activity Sheet: Toward Independence

As you read this chapter, you may come across some new terms and people. You need to know these words so you can understand the next few chapters. Take some time now to define these terms in your own words. You may get help from a friend or a dictionary, but remember to write your own definition. Draw pictures if that helps you explain what a term means.

indentured servants _____

_____

independence_____

_____

Monroe Doctrine_____

_____

revolution_____

_____

emancipation_____

_____

manufacturing_____

_____

New Orleans_____

_____

legislature_____

_____

U.S. Constitution_____

_____

treaty_____

_____

Father Miguel Hidalgo_____

_____

THE LATINO EXPERIENCE IN U.S. HISTORY • © Globe Fearon

Name _____ Date _____

CHAPTER 6 ESL/LEP Activity Sheet:
The Spanish and the American Revolution

Work with a partner to make a list of things that armies need. Many examples are found in the chapter, and you can use information from your own knowledge. When you are finished, figure out how the Patriots could get all the supplies they needed. (You do not have to fill in all the blocks.)

Item	How could the Patriots get this item?

In your own words, explain how Spain helped the Patriots in the American Revolution.

_____

_____

_____

_____

_____

_____

_____

_____

_____

_____

◢ CHAPTER 7 ESL/LEP Activity Sheet:
The Road to Latin American Independence

WHO WOULD SAY. . . .

Below is a list of quotes. They are not real, but they could be. Look through the chapter and figure out who could have said words like these.

1) "Let's go, men! Through the Andes and on to victory!"

   Spoken by _____

   _____

2) "Men and women of Dolores! It is time to take back our land! We will rule our own country!"

   Spoken by _____

   _____

3) "To my Spanish American brothers and sisters: It is the right of all men and women to live freely. Personal freedom is more important than anything else. We need to claim that freedom!"

   Spoken by _____

   _____

4) "We can make Florida strong! We just need to work hard!"

   Spoken by _____

   _____

5) "People of California! Join me in the revolution against Spain! If you don't join me, I'll burn your town!"

   Spoken by _____

   _____

6) "Slaves of Haiti! Unite and fight!"

   Spoken by _____

   _____

7) "My dear Mexican sisters, soon I will be out of prison and we will continue to fight for Mexico's freedom."

   Spoken by _____

   _____

8) "As governor of Louisiana, I do not wish to fight with my English-speaking neighbors. Therefore, I offer you free land!"

   Spoken by _____

   _____

CHAPTER 8 ESL/LEP Activity Sheet:
Life in the Mexican Borderlands

I. Work with a partner to define these words.

nuevomexicanos _____

patrón _____

santero _____

españoles _____

vaquero _____

genízaros _____

ricos _____

partido system _____

ranchos _____

tejano _____

empresario _____

II. Now it is your turn to show what you know. Fill in the chart below with information, memories, ideas—anything you know about New Mexico, Texas, and California.

California	New Mexico	Texas

Name _____ Date _____ · © Globe Fearon

THE BIG PICTURE 3 ESL/LEP Activity Sheet: A Time of Upheaval

I. Different people have different ideas about what kind of government is best and about what government should do for its citizens. Look at the list of people below and think about what is important to them. Work with a partner to explain what each person below does. Then decide what kind of government the person would like to have.

Type of person	What did the person do?	What kind of government would the person like?
cotton farmer		
trapper		
military general		
gaucho		
enslaved person		
university student		
priest		

II. Define these terms.

nationalism _____

_____

caudillo _____

_____

Gadsden Purchase _____

_____

CHAPTER 9 ESL/LEP Activity Sheet:
Revolt in Texas

How are the two cultures of Texas similar? How are they different? Using information from the chapter and from your own experience, compare the *tejano* and Anglo cultures of Texas. Then complete the chart.

	Tejano	Anglo
Language		
Foods		
Religion		
Government		
Attitude		

Can you think of other ways that the cultures are different? Can you think of other things that are similar about these two groups?

_____

_____

_____

_____

_____

_____

_____

_____

_____

Name _____ Date _____

 CHAPTER 10 ESL/LEP Activity Sheet:
War Between the United States and Mexico

Use the words in the word bank to complete the sentences below.

Word Bank

Battle of San Pascual	General Zachary Taylor	John Slidell
el desierto muerto	Rio Grande	Guadalupe Hidalgo
General Mariano Arista	Texas	*los niños héroe*s

1. In 1837, the United States recognized _____ as an independent nation. This did not make Mexico happy.

2. Mexico and Texas argued whether the southern border of Texas lay along the Nueces River or along the _____.

3. Texas and Mexico sent war parties across an area where the Comanche hunted, called _____ _____, to attack one another.

4. U.S. President Polk sent _____ to Mexico to help work out an agreement between Mexico and the United States.

5. _____ took several thousand U.S. soldiers to the Rio Grande where they began to build a fort.

6. _____, the Mexican general, told the U.S. soldiers not to build the fort on Mexican soil.

7. The _____ was a victory for the *californios*, who trapped U.S. soldiers on the night of December 6, 1846.

8. The boy heroes, _____, were young cadets who were killed at Chapultepec when it was attacked by U.S. troops.

9. In 1848, officials of Mexico and the United States met at the village of _____ to sign a peace treaty. Mexico lost almost half its land.

Name _____ Date _____

▼ CHAPTER 11 ESL/LEP Activity Sheet: Foreigners in Their Own Land

I. Work with a partner to define these words. Then give some examples that explain each word. You can use historical examples or modern-day examples.

influence _____

_____

power _____

_____

delegate _____

_____

minority _____

_____

discrimination _____

_____

social bandit _____

_____

II. What does becoming "Americanized" mean for you?

_____

_____

_____

_____

_____

_____

_____

BIG PICTURE 4 ESL/LEP Activity Sheet:
A Time of Growth

Fill each square with pictures, words, or sentences that describe or explain each event.

Civil War	Reconstruction
Industry	Immigration
Expansionism	Economic growth
Dictatorship	Intervention

Name _____ Date _____

▌ CHAPTER 12 ESL/LEP Activity Sheet:
Latinos in the U.S. Civil War

Define these words:

Union _____

_____

Confederate _____

_____

secede _____

_____

truce _____

_____

spy _____

_____

You are a newspaper reporter. Choose one of the people discussed in the chapter to interview. Think of at least three questions to ask that person.

Person to interview: _____

Questions to ask: _____

_____

_____

_____

_____

_____

_____

_____

Name _____ Date _____

CHAPTER 13 ESL/LEP Activity Sheet:
A Changing World

What was a *lectore*? _____

Think about reading and how important it is to be able to read. See if you can list five reasons why reading is important for you.

1. _____

_____

2. _____

_____

3. _____

_____

4. _____

_____

5. _____

_____

Now list another five reasons why a *lectore* was important for the cigar makers.

1. _____

_____

2. _____

_____

3. _____

_____

4. _____

_____

5. _____

_____

Draw a picture of a *lectore* in a cigar factory.

▼ CHAPTER 14 ESL/LEP Activity Sheet:
The Cuban-Spanish-American War

Each of the following sentences contains information about Cuba, Spain, or the United States. Fill in each blank with the name of the country that is being described. Some sentences contain two blanks. That means that two different names should be used. Look for clues in the information in the sentence.

1. The people of _____ felt that _____ took a lot and did not give much in return.

2. José Martí was an exile from _____. He called _____ materialistic even though it was a democracy.

3. _____ sent "the butcher" to _____.

4. A ship from _____ exploded in the harbor of Havana.

5. The "ever faithful isle" is _____.

6. Weyler forced a reconcentration (*reconcentración*) in _____.

7. The military leaders of _____ decided to wage guerrilla war with _____.

8. When _____ signed a peace treaty with _____, _____ was given Puerto Rico, the Philippines, Guam and Wake.

9. _____'s climate and soil were perfect for growing sugar, tobacco, and coffee.

10. _____ helped Cuba gain its independence from _____.

11. After Spain granted _____ its independence, _____ set up a military government in Cuba.

Now arrange the sentences in chronological order.

_____

_____

_____

_____

_____

_____

_____

_____

_____

_____

Name _____ Date _____

CHAPTER 15 ESL/LEP Activity Sheet:
Puerto Rico and Cuba Under United States Control

Find these words in the puzzle below. Words may be written horizontally, vertically, backwards, or diagonally. Then, write in the blank next to each word the number of the page where each term is described.

____ autonomy
____ Cuba
____ cultural imperialism
____ Foraker Act
____ home rule
____ *jíbaros*
____ Jones Act
____ King Sugar
____ Morales
____ Platt Amendment
____ protectorate
____ Puerto Rico
____ Rivera
____ yellow jack

```
C A P I R A B L Y Z A A S O R A B I J
C U T X A Q I D A R U E M L O N R E A
P L L E I U N O E J T O N E M J U P C
R Q J T N A L V I P O P I H T A I L K
O N A M U N I E S S N Q U I L L T A G
T A G E R R Z E R O O G F V O T E T R
E F L I H O A M I N M O R A L E S T I
C K C A J W O L L E Y F A N D U L A S
T W I R L L X O I M O H I H Q U A M N
O G Y L O P O N O M L V S E N D Z E Q
R E X A T C I S Y G P J E T H P Y N J
A T R E U V E W I N S E T W I E Q D O
T B O B U L X J H O M E R U L E A M E
E J A C A S T E X A S Q U I E T X E N
L F O R A K E R A C T O W N A M E N D
E T O A W O L L E H R A G T O L N T M
Z M O F R I E N D R A G U S G N I K E
Y O J O N E S A C T M I N G Y L N S X
Q U Y E X O C I R O T R E U P A R O M
```

Name _____ Date _____

▼ **THE BIG PICTURE 5 ESL/LEP Activity Sheet:**
Changes in a New Century

Fill in each square with pictures, words, or sentences that describe or explain each event.

Prosperity	Progressivism
World War I	Isolationism
The Great Depression	The New Deal
World War II	Pan-American Union

▼ CHAPTER 16 ESL/LEP Activity Sheet: The Mexican Revolution and New Patterns of Immigration

Review some of the events described in the chapter. Pick one that interests you. You will be writing a letter about the event as if you were a part of it. Some possibilities are:

- You want to join the Mexican Revolution. Whom will you fight for? Why is it important for you to fight?
- You decide to go to the United States. Why? Where will you go?

Now plan your letter. What event will you write about? _____

Think about how you were changed by the event. What happened to you? _____

_____

Who will read your letter? _____

What will that person want to know about your experiences? _____

_____

Write your letter here:

Date _____

Dear _____,

_____

_____

_____

_____

_____

_____

_____

_____

_____

Sincerely,

_____

▼ CHAPTER 17 ESL/LEP Activity Sheet:
Latinos and World War I

I. Define these words:

Foraker Act _____

Jones Act _____

Congressional Medal of Honor _____

skilled labor _____

unskilled jobs _____

colonias _____

barrios _____

mutualista _____

labor union _____

strike _____

segregation _____

migrant worker _____

II. Imagine that it is the 1920s and you have just arrived in the United States or you have moved to a new part of the country. Write a short note to a friend. Include information about the weather, your new job (if you have one), and people you have met. Try to use some of the words you just defined.

_____

_____

_____

_____

_____

_____

_____

_____

_____

_____

CHAPTER 18 ESL/LEP Activity Sheet:
From Boom to Depression

I. Look at your vocabulary list from the last Activity Sheet. You explained *mutualista* and union. Now use your own words to explain how these organizations helped Latino groups in the United States.

mutualista _____

_____

_____

_____

union _____

_____

_____

_____

II. In the 1930s, many labor leaders were called Communists. In small groups research and discuss what communism is. You may wish to use the library or other reference books to find the information. Then answer the following questions:

What is communism? _____

_____

_____

_____

Why do you think labor leaders were accused of being Communists? _____

_____

_____

_____

▼ CHAPTER 19 ESL/LEP Activity Sheet:
Latinos and World War II

I. Compare the experiences of Latinos who worked for the war effort at home and abroad:

Abroad	At Home

II. Define:

GI Bill of Rights _____

_____

_____

Fair Employment Practices Committee _____

_____

_____

III. Read about pachucas, pachucos, and zoot suits. Do you wear clothes that show your personality or tell something about you? Think about jewelry, hats, and maybe even glasses. What do you wear that is special and what does it mean?

_____

_____

_____

_____

_____

Name _____ Date _____

I. Define these words any way you wish, with pictures, words from other languages, or complete sentences in English.

superpowers _____

Cold War _____

communism _____

McCarthyism _____

suburbs _____

Chicano _____

The Great Society _____

segregation _____

Martin Luther King, Jr. _____

Fidel Castro _____

civil rights _____

nonviolent protest _____

César Chávez _____

II. Choose one of the Latin American countries mentioned in this chapter. Look up the country in the index and read what previous chapters said about it. Then write a story, draw a comic strip, create an illustrated timeline, or prepare a report about the history of the country.

_____

_____

_____

_____

_____

_____

_____

_____

_____

Name_____ Date _____

CHAPTER 20 ESL/LEP Activity Sheet:
The Great Migration from Puerto Rico

Below is the front of a postcard. You have recently moved from Puerto Rico to the United States. Draw a picture of where you have moved to.

Here is the back of that postcard. Write a letter to a friend in Puerto Rico describing your new home.

Address:

_____

_____

_____

Name _____ Date _____

▼ CHAPTER 21 ESL/LEP Activity Sheet:
New Arrivals from the Caribbean

I. Word Bank

autonomy _____

poverty line _____

mainland _____

underground _____

corruption _____

vision _____

II. Write a newspaper article about one of the events or people described in the chapter.

First, choose your subject. _____ on page ____

Next, decide on a headline. _____

What are some important facts that you will include in the article? Make a list of names, dates, and events to include. See if you can use some words from the Word Bank.

_____

_____

_____

_____

_____

_____

_____

_____

_____

_____

Now write your article.

Name _____ Date _____

▼ CHAPTER 22 ESL/LEP Activity Sheet:
The Struggle for Equal Rights

I. What were some of the methods Mexican Americans used to gain equal rights? Make a list.

_____

_____

_____

_____

_____

_____

_____

_____

_____

II. Chapter 22 is all about **activism**. After reading the chapter, what do you think *activism* means? Can you name other groups who have used activism?

_____

_____

_____

_____

_____

_____

_____

_____

_____

CHAPTER 23 ESL/LEP Activity Sheet:
New Immigrants from Central and South America

This chapter discusses human rights. List as many examples as you can of human rights.

_____

_____

_____

_____

_____

_____

Now describe some examples of human rights violations discussed in the chapter.

_____

_____

_____

_____

_____

_____

How would life in the United States be different for people arriving from South and Central America?

_____

_____

_____

_____

_____

_____

CHAPTER 24 ESL/LEP Activity Sheet:
A Growing Voice

Design a stamp that commemorates the work of one of the people discussed in the chapter.

Now write a biography of that person. Include some examples of contributions to his or her culture and the world.

_____

_____

_____

_____

_____

_____

_____

_____

_____

_____

_____

_____

Name _____ Date _____

▌ THE BIG PICTURE 7 ESL/LEP Activity Sheet: Latinos Today

Define these words. Some of them are from *The Big Picture* and some are from later chapters in the book. Use your own words.

conservative _____

_____

amnesty _____

_____

recession _____

_____

strong-arm tactics _____

_____

refugee _____

_____

alien _____

_____

North American Free Trade Agreement (NAFTA) _____

_____

maquiladoras _____

_____

ladinos _____

_____

embargo _____

_____

inflation _____

_____

campesinos _____

_____

demographics _____

_____

Name _____ Date _____

▼ CHAPTER 25 ESL/LEP Activity Sheet:
Mexican Americans Today

Practice your research techniques! Imagine that you are a reporter. You have been asked to write about Mexico and the United States. Your editor wants you to choose the subject. Check the Table of Contents of *The Latino Experience in U.S. History.* What chapters are about Mexico? Review those chapters to learn more about Mexico's relationship with the United States. Or you might focus on the cultural identity of Mexican Americans.

When you finish looking up information, decide what you will write about. Will your topic be important Mexican and Mexican American Women? Or how Mexican and Mexican American workers gained power? Perhaps you just want to write about the historical relationship between the United States and Mexico. Write your subject here:

_____

_____

Now write down the ideas that are important for your topic. Again check the chapters for more ideas. Do not worry about neatness or complete sentences—just note your ideas on paper! Write your ideas here:

_____

_____

_____

_____

_____

The final step is writing. Writing is easier if you have a **topic sentence**. A topic sentence presents the main ideas you want to communicate. After you write your topic sentence, use the ideas from the chapters to support what you want to say. Write your topic sentence here:

_____

_____

Now, finish writing your article on a separate sheet of paper.

Finally, choose a title for your article. Make it interesting so that readers will want to discover what you have to say. Write the title of your article here:

_____

_____

CHAPTER 26 ESL/LEP Activity Sheet: Puerto Ricans Today

Brainstorm with a partner about an issue that concerns your community.

_____

_____

_____

_____

_____

_____

Write a song or a poem about this issue. If you speak a language other than English, see if you can mix the two languages together.

_____

_____

_____

_____

_____

_____

_____

_____

_____

_____

If you wish, tape your song or poem or present it live to your class. You might want to teach your classmates any words that they may not know.

▮ CHAPTER 27 ESL/LEP ACTIVITY SHEET:
Cuban Americans Today

Imagine that you are a Cuban American. Plan a *Calle Ocho* festival for the Cuban American community. Or, plan a festival or fair similar to the *Calle Ocho* festival for your own community or school.

What type of festival are you planning? _____

What groups will be represented? _____

What foods will be served? _____

What music will be played? _____

What crafts will be sold? _____

Now draw a map for your fair. Decide where the booths, stages, and restaurants go. Label each location with the item to be sold or the entertainment to be provided.

Name _____   Date _____

 CHAPTER 28 ESL/LEP Activity Sheet:
Central Americans and Dominicans Today

You are going to create a **simulation game!** A simulation game takes a skill from real life that people need to practice and turns it into a game. For example, pilots practice on **flight simulators** until they understand how to fly an airplane. In this way, no one gets hurt if they crash! Your game will be designed to help new immigrants learn skills that they will need to live successfully in the United States.

Work with a small group. Decide on the goal for your game. Is it getting a driver's license, an "A" in math, or a job? After you decide on a goal, list all the steps necessary to achieve that goal. Think of at least five steps, but don't have too many! Write the steps on a separate piece of paper.

Now, for every step, list something that will slow down reaching the goal and something that will speed it up. For example, suppose that the goal is getting an "A" in math. Losing the textbook would slow a student down and studying would speed up earning an "A." Use the same paper for your list.

Gather materials. You will need paper to use as a board and index cards to write instructions on. How will you move? With dice? Will you draw numbers out of a bag? For example, your goal is to get an "A" in math. Here is the game board.

Start (roll dice)		Pick up Slow Down card		Pick up Speed Up card		Miss class. Lose turn.	

The game is over when everyone finishes. That way everybody wins. When someone achieves the goal, he or she must then help others achieve it, too. So you will need to make a set of "instructor's cards" that early finishers can use to help other players. For example:

Here are some examples of the playing cards:

SLOW DOWN CARD Lose book	SPEED UP CARD Study hard!	INSTRUCTOR'S CARD Your student gets 100 percent on a pop quiz. Move student to head of the class.
SLOW DOWN CARD Go back one space	SPEED UP CARD Move ahead 3!	INSTRUCTOR'S CARD Help a student study. Move student ahead 2 space.

Name_____ Date_____

 CHAPTER 29 ESL/LEP Activity Sheet:
South Americans in the United States Today

I. Fill in the chart with information from the chapter.

	How (s)he felt	Language	Government
Florencia Rivarola in Paraguay			
Florencia Rivarola in Miami			
Florencia Rivarola visiting Paraguay			
Jaime Escalante in Bolivia			
Jaime Escalante in California			

II. Choose someone discussed in this chapter to honor. Whom do you choose?

_____

Why?

_____

_____

_____

Design a medal or an award for your honoree here.

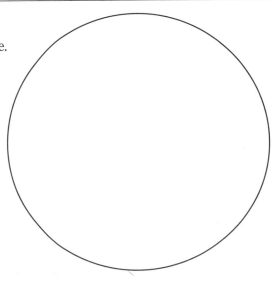

CHAPTER 30 ESL/LEP Activity Sheet:
Toward a New Century

I. Choose a person in the chapter to interview. Why did you choose that person? What would you ask that person?

_____

_____

II. It is now time to think back over the book. What things or ideas made a big impression on you?

_____

_____

What did you like learning about?

_____

_____

What did you not like?

_____

_____

What would you like to learn more about?

_____

_____

What would you add to this book?

_____

_____

If the teacher asked your advice on how to use this book with another class, what would you say?

_____

_____

ANSWERS TO THE ESL/LEP ACTIVITY SHEETS

▶ UNIT 1 BIG PICTURE

culture—a way of living for a group of people. *migration*—movement of a group from one place to another. *Aztec*—a Native American empire in central America. *Africa*—a continent south of Europe and west and south of Asia. *slavery*—the ownership by one group of people of other people. *Spain*—a European country on the Iberian peninsula. *colonies*—territories owned and controlled by an outside power. *Christianity*—one of the world's leading religions. *England*—an island country off the northwest coast of Europe. *France*—a country in Western Europe. *the Americas*—North and South America.

Chapter 1

gold—a valuable metal. It was the desire for gold/treasure that spurred the colonization of the Americas.
black gold—slaves from Africa, used to run the sugar mills. *white gold*—sugar. Refining sugar in sugar mills became an important industry in the Americas.

Chapter 2

Judge the word or poster on how it reflects an understanding of the content rather than the precision of the language or art.

Chapter 3

conquistador—a Spanish explorer of the Americas who conquered the inhabitants and gained wealth for Spain. *soldier*—a man who is in an army. *friar*—priest who came to convert Native Americans. *enslaved person*—someone brought to the New World to work the land. *merchant*—a person who trades in goods. *viceroy*—a representative of the royal family in the Americas. *criollos*—people of Spanish heritage born in the Americas. *peninsulares*—people born in Spain who settled in the Americas. *mestizos*—people of mixed Native American and Spanish ancestry.

Chapter 4

Judge the students' efforts on their understanding of the content rather than the quality of their drawing or writing.

Chapter 5

Ideally, the students' efforts should reflect ability to personalize the required content.

▶ UNIT 2 BIG PICTURE

indentured servants—people who contracted to work without pay for a period of years in return for passage to the Americas. *independence*—freedom to make one's own laws, rules, and decisions. *Monroe Doctrine*—1823 U.S. policy not to get involved in European affairs as long as European countries stayed out of the Americas. *revolution*—a radical change or overthrow of a government. *emancipation*—the freeing of people from slavery. *manufacturing*—the making of goods, often on a large scale in a factory. *New Orleans*—a Spanish port city at the mouth of the Mississippi taken by France (1800) and bought by the United States (1803). *legislature*—a body of people who make the laws. *U.S. Constitution*—the plan of government for the United States. *treaty*—an agreement between two or more countries. *Father Miguel Hidalgo*—Mexican priest who began Mexico's struggle for independence from Spain.

Chapter 6

Possible items: gunpowder, guns, blankets, medicine, food, shovels, horses, wagons, axes, paper. Possible sources: trade, raid/steal, buy, beg, borrow, bring/make your own. Spain gave supplies to the American rebels and also fought the British.

Chapter 7

1. Simón Bolívar 2. Father Miguel Hidalgo 3. Juan Bautista Vizcardo y Guzmán 4. Vicente Manuel de Zéspedes 5. Hipólito Bouchard 6. Toussaint L'Ouverture 7. Leona Vicario 8. Esteban Miró

Chapter 8

I. *nuevomexicanos*—Spanish-speaking settlers in New Mexico. *patrone*—a person who got people to settle down in a town and then took care of the town and its people. *santero*—a carver of saints. *españoles*—Spaniards. *vaquero*—cowboy. *genízaros*—Native Americans not attached to a tribe or nation. *ricos*—wealthy people. *partido sys-*

tem—a system of labor in which a person takes care of another person's sheep and receives some of the lambs in return. *ranchos*—large farms. *tejanos*—Mexican settlers in Texas. *empresario*—an agent who got people to settle in Texas. **II.** Responses will differ.

▶ UNIT 3 BIG PICTURE

I. *cotton farmer*—farmer who raises cotton; a government that would permit slavery and promote textile mills, perhaps limiting fabric imports; strong central government. *trapper*—person who catches animals for their furs; would not want land to be given to homesteaders so would not want much regulation; would favor local, informal control. *military general*—commander in the army; would like a strong central (military) government; *gaucho*—Argentine cowboy; would not want much control by a central government, so would favor local control. *enslaved person*—a person owned by another; would probably favor centralized government that might be free of local tyrannies. *university student*—a scholar; answers will vary: since generally, universities are the homes of intellectuals and often the beds of rebellion, a student would want a democracy (elected officials) and a policy of land reform and liberty for all. *priest*—a religious leader, a clergyman; would want a strong centralized government and no separation of church and state. **II.** *nationalism*—feeling of pride in and devotion to one's country. *caudillo*—military dictator. *Gadsden Purchase*—1853 U.S. purchase from Mexico of parts of New Mexico and Arizona.

Chapter 9
Answers should make clear that *tejanos* were Texans who spoke Spanish, ate Mexican food, were Catholic, and were loyal to Mexican law. Anglos in Texas spoke English, ate "salted meat and cornbread," were Protestant, and favored the government of the United States.

Chapter 10
1. Texas 2. Rio Grande 3. *el desierto muerto* 4. John Slidell 5. General Zachary Taylor 6. General Mariano Arista 7. Battle of San Pascual 8. los niños héroes 9. Guadalupe Hidalgo

Chapter 11
influence—with the ability or money to affect people, policies, or government. *power*—strength, influence. *delegate*—representative, a person who is entrusted to represent others at an official function. *minority*—a group of people often seen as different from the larger part of society because of language, skin color, or religion. *discrimination*—the treatment, by laws or attitudes, of certain groups of people that keeps them from being treated as equal. *social bandit*—an outlaw who acts on behalf of an oppressed group.

▶ UNIT 4 BIG PICTURE

I. *Civil War*—the 1861–1865 war between the North and the South. *Reconstruction*—the period after the Civil War when the South was punished economically and former enslaved African Americans were made U.S. citizens. *Industry*—large-scale business activity that grew after the Civil War. *Immigration*—entrance of people from other countries, especially in the period of the late 1800s and early 1900s. *Expansionism*—U.S. desire to acquire additional land, especially as far west as the Pacific. *Economic Growth*—expansion of industry and parts of the economy. *Dictatorship*—control of a country by one person who maintains rule through force. *Intervention*—although the word is not mentioned in the chapter, the idea should be understood by students as one that was applied to U.S. relations with some Latin American countries in the later 1800s and early 1900s. **II.** Responses will differ.

Chapter 12
Union—the United States or North in the Civil War. *Confederate*—the Confederate States of America, or the South, in the Civil War. *secede*—to break away from a country. *truce*—an agreement to agree not to fight. *spy*—a person who secretly works to get information about an enemy. Interview questions should be searching and be phrased so that they elicit more than single-word answers.

Chapter 13
Reasons for the ability to read might include need to read street signs and other public signs; need to read forms for jobs and school; read for pleasure;

read for advancement on jobs; read to keep up with the news. A *lectore* was important because: many workers could not themselves read; work was made more interesting while being read to; need for news about revolutionary activity; interest in literary works; gave sense of community to workers.

Chapter 14

1. Cuba, Spain 2. Cuba, United States 3. Spain, Cuba 4. the United States 5. Cuba 6. Cuba 7. Cuba, Spain 8. Spain, the United States, the United States 9. Cuba 10. The United States, Spain 11. Cuba, the United States Order: 9,5,1,2,7,3,6,4,10, 8,11 (Since some questions, such as 1,5,9, and 7, are general information and therefore not particularly easy to place in chronological order, students may have a different solution to the chronology question.

Chapter 15

Page numbers: autonomy, 187; Cuba, 186; cultural imperialism, 187; Foraker Act, 186; home rule, 186; jíbaros, 187; Jones Act, 186; King Sugar, 190; Morales, 190; Platt Amendment, 189; protectorate, 189; Puerto Rico, 185; Rivera, 186; yellow jack, 188

▶ UNIT 5 BIG PICTURE

Prosperity—wealth. *Progressivism*—social reform. *World War I*—war in Europe, 1914–1918. *Isolationism*—U.S. policy not to get involved in the affairs of European nations. *Great Depression*—period of great unemployment 1929–1940s. *The New Deal*—President Franklin Delano Roosevelt's program to help end the Great Depression. *World War II*—multinational war, 1939–1945. *Pan-American Union*—Organization of the countries of North, Central, and South America formed in 1889.

Chapter 16

There are no correct answers to this worksheet. Students may write, for example, a goodby note to their mothers or a critical letter about life in the United States.

Chapter 17

I. *Foraker Act*—Puerto Rico would remain under the control of the U.S. government. *Jones Act*—1917 U.S. law granting U.S. citizenship to Puerto Ricans who wanted it. *Congressional Medal of Honor*—highest U.S. military honor. *skilled labor*—work that requires some training. *colonias*—areas where Mexican and Mexican American agricultural workers settled. *barrios*—sections of a city where Mexican and Mexican Americans settle. *mutualista*—a society or group meant to help Mexican and Mexican Americans in the United States. *labor union*—organization of workers to improve working conditions and wages. *strike*—refusal of workers to work until their demands are met. *segregation*—separation of people because of skin color, race, religion, or sex. *migrant worker*—worker who travels from region to region doing seasonal agricultural work. **II.** In the note, students should use events in the chapter or articulate their own experiences.

Chapter 18

I. The discussion of *mutualistas* and unions should show students' understanding that workers and immigrants used whatever resources they could to gain some social control and political clout through community effort. **II.** Communism is a form of government in which the government owns and controls all economic enterprises. Since most people feared communism, calling labor leaders Communists was a way that industrialists could discredit unions.

Chapter 19

I. Possible answers: *Abroad*—danger, not much food, exhaustion, marching, mostly men, weapons, not as much discrimination, meeting people from different places. *At home*—new jobs, war factories, availability of skilled jobs, more money, mostly women and children, importation of *braceros*. **II.** *GI Bill of Rights*—a law that grants soldiers returning to civilian life benefits such as education and job training. *Fair Employment Practices Committee*—set up to make sure companies with federal contracts did not discriminate against particular groups of people. **III.** *pachucas*—Mexican American women who socialized with zoot-suiters. *pachucos*—Mexican American men who wore zoot suits. *zoot suits*—suits with oversized jackets, wide lapels, and padded shoulders and baggy, narrow-waisted pants.

► UNIT 6 BIG PICTURE

I. *superpow*ers—United States and the former Soviet Union. *Cold War*—the extreme distrust and competition between the United States and the Soviet Union from the end of World War II to 1991. *communism*—system of dictatorial single-party government and state-owned industries. *McCarthyism*—the practice of charging people with political disloyalty on the basis of little or no evidence. *suburbs*—residential areas on the outskirts of cities. *Chicano*—Mexican American person who takes pride in his or her cultural heritage. *The Great Society*—laws and programs devised by President Lyndon B. Johnson in the attempt to create a more just and equitable society. *segregation*—separation of people by race or religion. *Martin Luther King, Jr.*—African American minister who was one of the leaders of the Civil Rights Movement in the 1960s. *Fidel Castro*—Cuban Communist leader. *civil rights*—the right of all persons to be treated equally under the law. *nonviolent protest*—the use of peaceful means to gain attention for a cause, such as sit-ins, marches, and boycotts. *César Chávez*—organizer of Mexican American migrant workers' union. **II.** Students' efforts show evidence of use of and understanding of data relating to the country chosen.

Chapter 20
The postcard should show evidence of increasing ease with use of English and ability to use personal experience in the writing.

Chapter 21
autonomy—self-government. *poverty line*—officially defined level of income below which a family cannot meet its basic needs. *mainland*—for Puerto Ricans, the continental United States. *underground*—secret antigovernment movements. *corruption*—dishonesty on the part of government officials. *political exile*—person who leaves his or her country for political reasons.

Chapter 22
I. Some possible answers: registering to vote, forming a union, relying on themselves, not government or agencies, to make changes, helping one another with food and money, strikes, boycotts, civil disobedience, working in national poli-

tics. **II.** Activism means actively trying to change the political status quo through action. Students might include *La Causa* and *El Teatro Campesino*.

Chapter 23
Examples of human rights—habeas corpus, the right to a fair trial, arrest only with reason, freedom to speak against the government without fear of arrest or punishment, not having your possessions taken by government agencies without due cause. *Violations mentioned in the chapter*: killing of Rutilio Grande and Oscar Romero (El Salvador), "the dirty war" (Argentina), death squads (Guatemala). *Examples of U.S. life*—may range from "speaking English" to "not being shot at" and "backward seasons" (since summer in South America is in December).

Chapter 24
Biographies should show a sense of organization of facts and correct use of as many terms learned in the chapter as possible.

► UNIT 7 BIG PICTURE

conservative—one who desires as little change as possible. *amnesty*—freeing of a political prisoner. *recession*—an economic downturn. *strong-arm tactics*—using force or threatening to use force to achieve one's goals. *refugee*—person who leaves one's homeland to escape persecution and violence. *alien*—person who lives in a country but is not a citizen of it. *North American Free Trade Agreement (NAFTA)*—an agreement between Canada, United States, and Mexico to trade without imposing tariffs. *maquiladoras*—assembly plants in Mexico. *ladinos*—wealthy Guatemalan landowners. *embargo*—ban on trade with a country. *inflation*—rapidly rising prices. *campesinos*—peasant farmers. *demographics*—the nature of a population.

Chapter 25
Key chapters for research are 8,11,19, 19, and 22. Students should be able also to use outside research materials such as encyclopedias. Evaluate the assignment on the extent of the research, the ability to organize it, and the use of English in the article.

Chapter 26

Possible topics: drugs, elections, hopelessness, living in a country with a strange language, taxes, growing up, falling in love.

Chapter 27

Evaluate the activity sheet on the extent to which the answers show understanding of the content of the chapter.

Chapter 28

There are no definite "answers" to this activity. Since this is a group activity, its success depends on the ability of each student to understand the rules and activity and to cooperate to make it a success.

Chapter 29

I. Florence Rivarola was poor, uneducated, and spoke Guarani in Paraguay. She learned Spanish there. The move to the United States was hard, but she learned to stand up for herself. She learned to live without fear. She learned English. Returning to Paraguay, she saw how hard it was for people there, how many people lived in fear and poverty. Now she speaks three languages. Jaime Escalante in Bolivia spoke Spanish and taught high school. Things were unstable and he was afraid. In the United States he had nothing but he worked hard and was sure of succeeding. **II.** Answers should reflect an appreciation of the person honored and the reason why he or she is chosen.

Chapter 30

In this open-ended activity sheet, students should be able to take a long backward look at the textbook as a whole and express definite opinions about it. Progress in their use of English should be noted.

THE WRITING PROCESS AND SOCIAL STUDIES

Writing is a skill that students need for success in virtually every academic subject as well as for success in the world beyond the classroom. Some people say that teaching writing is important, but that this task is the responsibility of language arts teachers. However, students must learn that the skills of writing apply to every discipline. By using techniques of the writing process in social studies classes, by requiring students to express themselves well on paper, and by holding them to the conventions of standard English usage, social studies teachers greatly add to students' overall proficiency. So the real question is "What can a social studies teacher do to develop writing skills in the classroom?"

Today, teachers know that writing is a complex process that involves the application of a wide range of thinking skills and language abilities. Teachers recognize that the process involves a series of steps. Writers practice very different skills and undertake very different activities at each of these steps. By understanding the steps of the writing process and employing them in teaching, teachers can focus on the techniques and tools students need, the knowledge they must develop, and the choices they must learn to make at each step to become effective writers.

The first step of the writing process is called, **prewriting**. This is the discovery stage. Student-writers get warmed up, choose ideas, gather details, and sort through information. Students address issues of audience, voice, and purpose. Prewriting is a rich, productive stage that generates a flow of material and ideas for writing and focuses the writer's attention on the topic.

The goal of prewriting is for students to develop the content and to explore the possibilities so fully in their minds that papers will virtually write themselves. To facilitate prewriting, students can practice many techniques. The following strategies help writers get words on paper: journals, logs, reading logs, brainstorming, clustering, mapping, charts, oral activities, outlining, taking notes. Several of these techniques are employed in the Writing Workshops.

Writers need to get their ideas recorded in some sort of tentative, first-draft shape as easily and quickly as possible. This occurs in the **writing/drafting** phase of the writing process. After students have identified their ideas, they are ready to make choices as to what and how they will write. Students must be familiar with the options available to them to achieve their goal. At this stage, writers turn their prewriting ideas into coherent, organized writing.

At this stage students should try to get ideas down quickly, with a minimum of worry, expecting that changes can be made later. Choices resulting from audience, voice, purpose, and form are made at this time. Students consider diction, sentence structure, and connections in order to write what they want to communicate. The guidelines offered in the Writing Workshops help student-writers with problems of organization, diction, and form while keeping them focused on audience, voice, and purpose.

After students have generated the first draft, they are ready to move to the next phase of the writing process, **revising.** Effective revision almost always

WHY WRITE IN SOCIAL STUDIES?

WHAT IS THE WRITING PROCESS?

involves the positive, informed response of outside readers and rethinking and revising by the writers themselves. Writers look for places to improve content and sense, word choices, and sentence style. Peer response, while it can be utilized at any stage of the writing process, is especially effective during revision because it allows writers to receive feedback about the first draft. When students know their peers will listen to, read, and respond to their writing, they care about their work because they care about what their audience thinks. In every Writing Workshop, students are asked to respond to another's writing as they "Talk It Over." Armed with suggestions from partners, students are given the opportunity to "Make the Changes" that will improve their papers.

Editing is an important part of this stage. While formal correctness is not the only objective in writing, it is important because errors can impede communication. Therefore, after papers have been revised, students act as editors to edit and proofread. Proofreading is the job of cleaning up the manuscript, or eliminating surface errors. Students need to understand that proofreading is not revision but simply correcting errors in spelling, usage, and mechanics so their audience can easily understand their writing. At the editing stage, peer response can again be a valuable tool. The editing phase in the Writing Workshops gives students the opportunity to help one another eliminate surface mistakes. Fewer mistakes make a teacher's job less tedious.

A final step in the writing process is **postwriting**. This step gives credibility and value to the act of writing. Postwriting includes **evaluating** and **publishing** student work. This step goes beyond simply grading. Putting student work on display benefits the classroom because students work harder and learn from others' points of views. Publishing can range from simply posting work on the bulletin board to entering it in a national competition where money and nationwide recognition are the reward. The goal of honoring student writing is to help students realize that they have something worthwhile to say and that they have the skills to communicate that message in an effective way. All the Writing Workshops present opportunities to honor student writing.

USING THE WRITING WORKSHOPS

The Writing Workshops are designed to help social studies teachers implement a structured writing program in their classes by taking students step by step through the writing process. Literary models written by Latinos and historians of the time period that students are studying are presented for writers to analyze. Directed reading questions point students to important historical details and exemplary literary elements in the writing models. During the prewriting step, questions about topic, audience, and purpose focus the writers' attention on the task at hand. Students learn prewriting techniques not only by explanation but also through examples. As students begin their first draft in the writing stage, guidelines assist them in choosing linguistic options and determining organization. Before students begin to revise, peers respond to student writing and help writers make improvements. Editing develops awareness of proper English usage by teaching proofreading. Finally, in postwriting students present their writing to others. The publishing activities offer social studies teachers ways to honor students' work. Finally, the forms on the following pages assist teachers, or even students, with different techniques for evaluating the final product.

WRITING WORKSHOP EVALUATION

Writer_____ Title _____

    Write comments about the content, organization, style, and spelling, usage, and mechanics in the space below.

Content

Well-done: _____

_____

_____

Needs Improvement: _____

_____

_____

Organization

Well-done: _____

_____

_____

Needs Improvement: _____

_____

_____

Style

Well-done: _____

_____

_____

Needs Improvement: _____

_____

_____

Spelling, Usage, Mechanics

Well-done: _____

_____

_____

Needs Improvement: _____

_____

_____

▲ WRITING WORKSHOP EVALUATION

Writer_____ Title _____

To evaluate a paper holistically, first read the paper. Then, with your first impression in mind, use this scoring guide as a basis for your assessment.

SCORE	CRITERIA
4	clear, concise sentences varied sentence structure specific or descriptive details special flair; uses imagination or makes thoughtful comments effective word choice good use of transitions writes to the topic well-organized excellent spelling, usage, mechanics other: _____
3	clear, concise sentences some detail, imagination, or thoughtful ideas writes to the topic some use of transitions mechanical or usage problems do not interfere adequate organization appropriate paragraphing other: _____
2	some incomplete sentences lacks organization partial development of the topic errors interfere with understanding faulty paragraphing other: _____
1	little or no organization short and underdeveloped wanders from the topic many mechanical problems other: _____
0	inappropriate illegible off the topic blank page

▲ WRITING WORKSHOP EVALUATION

Writer_____   Title _____

Rating: 5 = highest possible rating;   1 = lowest possible rating

AREAS	RATING	COMMENTS
CONTENT		
Content Soundness. Is the content thoughtful, factually accurate, logically valid, and otherwise sound?		
Interest. Is the paper interesting?		
Appropriateness. Is the content appropriate for the audience and purpose?		
Topic. Has the topic been narrowed accurately to suit the length and purpose of the paper?		
Main Idea. Is there a clear main idea or thesis statement?		
Support. Is there enough supporting evidence? Are there enough details?		
Introduction. Does the introduction catch the reader's attention? Is it effective?		
Conclusion. Does the conclusion contain a reminder of the main idea or thesis statement? Is it effective?		
Title. Is the title appropriate?		
ORGANIZATION		
Order. Is the content arranged logically and effectively?		
Unity. Are all the supporting ideas and details relevant to the main idea or thesis statement?		
Coherence. Are transitions used to connect ideas clearly?		
USAGE, MECHANICS, AND STYLE		
Clarity. Are all statements clear? Do the sentences read well?		
Sentence Style. Are all sentences sufficiently varied in length and structure?		
Correctness. Is the paper free of errors in usage, mechanics, and style?		
Legibility. Is the handwriting or typing legible?		
Appearance. Is the paper neat and clean? Has it been written or typed in the correct form?		

THE LATINO EXPERIENCE IN U.S. HISTORY • © Globe Fearon

▲ Unit 1 Workshop: Writing about Geography in History

In March 1493, when Columbus returned to Spain from his first voyage across the Atlantic, he wanted to convince people that he had discovered valuable lands that would enrich Spain. In this passage from a letter to Gabriel Sanchez, a member of the Spanish court, Columbus describes one of the islands he visited, which he named *La Española,* or Hispaniola.

Discover ◁
- **the specific details and images that make Columbus's description come alive**
- **the overall impression that his description creates**
- **how geographic themes are used in Columbus's description**

Look at the Model

> This island Hispaniola and all the other ones are exceedingly grandiose [magnificent], and this one in the extreme. There are harbors on the coastline that cannot be compared to any others I know in all Christendom, and plenty of good large rivers that are a marvel to see. Its lands are high and have a great many sierras [jagged mountain ranges] and soaring mountains . . . accessible [easy to reach] and full of all kinds of trees, so tall they seem to touch the sky; I have heard it said, moreover, that these trees never lose their leaves. . . . Some were in blossom, others with fruit, others yet at a different stage, according to the variety; and I could hear nightingales and other small birds of a thousand different kinds singing in the month of November. . . . On this island there are marvelous pine woods and vast fields; and there is honey, and many kinds of birds and a great diversity of fruits. This land also has many mines of metal, and people in uncountable number.
>
> Hispaniola is a marvel. Its sierras and mountains, its lowlands and meadows and its beautiful thick soil, are so apt for planting and sowing, for raising all kinds of cattle and for building towns and villages. As for the sea ports here, seeing is believing; and so also the many big rivers of good water, most of which carry gold. . . . [T]here are many spices and great mines of gold and other metals.
>
> —Letter from Christopher Columbus to Gabriel Sanchez, March 14, 1493

1. What details does Columbus provide about Hispaniola's geography—waterways, terrain, plant and animal life, natural resources, and population?

   _____

   _____

2. Descriptive writing uses images that tell us how something looks, sounds, smells, tastes, or feels to the touch. a) Find three visual images in Columbus's description. b) Where does he use an image that appeals to our sense of hearing?

   a) _____

   b) _____

3. After reading Columbus's description, what is your overall impression of Hispaniola?

   _____

   _____

4. How would you summarize Columbus's purpose in describing Hispaniola? Is he mainly interested in evoking the island's beauty, or is he trying to make another point? Explain.

   _____

   _____

Name _____ Date _____

▲ Prewriting

Choose Your Topic

How do you think an explorer from another time or planet would describe one of the places explored by the Spanish from 1000s to 1700s? Imagine that you are such an explorer and write a description of such an area as if you were seeing it for the first time.

Name the place you are going to describe here: _____

Who will be reading this description? Will it be included in a letter (like Columbus's), in a private journal or autobiography, in an article in the travel section of your newspaper, or in an official government report?

Identify your audience here: _____

What overall impression would you like your description to convey? If you have mixed feelings, you might

want to identify more than one impression: _____

What is the purpose of your description—to inform, explain, entertain, or amaze your readers? Are you also trying to persuade them to think or act a certain way? Identify your purpose (or purposes) here:

_____

The tone of your description—the attitude you take, the voice you use—will be determined by your choice of audience, your overall impression of the place, and your purpose. Will your audience respond better to formal or informal language?

Describe your tone here: _____

Take Notes

In good descriptive writing, you use your powers of observation to make a subject come alive for your audience. So before you begin writing, read about the place you are going to describe and use your imagination to write notes about everything you might see, hear, smell, taste, or touch. You can use details from your own experience and life. Include characteristics of the place you think a foreign visitor would most likely notice: its landscape, population, vegetation, architecture, economy, and social habits. Your notes do not have to be complete sentences; just jot down what strikes you as important. Some of Columbus's notes about Hispaniola might have looked like this:

> Water—harbors, plenty of large rivers (gold!)
>
> Land—sierras and mountains, soil good for planting and cattle, great mines
>
> Trees—all kinds, tall, never lose leaves, marvelous pine woods, fruit

Use the space below to write your own notes. Begin by jotting down a few broad categories. Then leave several lines of space under each category so that you can fill in important details. Try to include some vivid images that will catch your readers' attention.

_____

_____

_____

▲ Writing

Your First Draft

Use this space to write a first draft of your description. Do not worry about spelling, punctuation, and other mistakes right now. (You will have a chance to revise later.) As you write, refer to your prewriting notes—but feel free to include any new ideas that occur to you, or to discard any notes that no longer seem important. The guidelines on the left side of the page will help you organize your draft.

Identify the place you are writing about.

_____

_____

Write a sentence or two that sum up your overall impression of the place.

_____

_____

_____

Add details about the physical and human characteristics of the place.

_____

_____

_____

Use descriptive words that appeal to your readers' senses. Help your readers picture the place you are describing. Also try to include some images that are *not* visual.

_____

_____

_____

_____

Do the images you have chosen reinforce the overall impression you want to convey?

_____

_____

Think about your purpose. Do you need to add more details to get your point across? Conclude by restating your main impression of the place. Include a statement about the importance of the period.

_____

_____

_____

_____

Name _____ Date _____

 ## Revising

Talk It Over

Choose a partner. Listen as your partner reads his or her description aloud twice. During the first reading, close your eyes and try to picture the place your partner is describing. After the second reading, jot down the answers to these questions:

1. Can you picture the place being described? Are you confused about any of its physical or human characteristics?

2. What overall impression of the place does the description convey?

3. What words could the writer add or change to make the description more concrete (specific) or vivid? Are there any dull or repetitive words that could be cut?

4. Can you suggest any changes in sentence structure that would improve the rhythm of the description? What changes in paragraph organization might strengthen the writing?

Now switch roles. Read your own paragraph aloud, and listen to your partner's comments.

Make the Changes

Reread your first draft and think about your partner's comments. Make any changes that you think will improve your description. Then copy your revised description onto a clean sheet of paper.

Editing

Review these proofreading marks to help you correct errors.

∧	add something	ⱳⱳ	add quotation marks
ℐ	delete something	⫟	new paragraph
≡	capitalize	/	lower case
⊙	make a period	ⓢⱷ	spell correctly
∧	add a comma	∾	transpose

Reread your description to check for errors in grammar, spelling, and punctuation. Then exchange papers with your partner and proofread each other's work. As you read the description, make a small check in the margin whenever you find an error. When you get your paper back, correct the mistakes your partner has found.

Postwriting

Evaluate Your Writing

If your description has many proofreading marks, copy it onto a clean sheet of paper before submitting it for final evaluation.

Publishing Your Writing

Illustrate your description and post the picture and description on the class bulletin board.

THE LATINO EXPERIENCE IN U.S. HISTORY • © Globe Fearon

▲ Unit 2 Writing Workshops: Stating Your Case

One of the first calls for a Latin American revolution against Spain came from a Peruvian Jesuit priest living in exile. In his *Letter to Spanish Americans* (see text pages 84–85), Juan Batiste Vizcardo y Guzmán set forth the reasons he believed the colonies should fight for their freedom from Spain.

Discover
- **the writer's main complaint against Spain**
- **the specific details that support his agreement**
- **the action the writer urges Spanish Americans to take**

Look at the Model

> Every law that opposes the universal well-being of those for whom it is made is an act of tyranny; to demand compliance [submission] is to force into slavery....
>
> Since men first began to organize themselves into society for their greater welfare, we are the only ones [whose] government obliges us to buy what we need at the highest prices and to sell our products at the lowest prices....
>
> ... Is it not a marvel that with enough gold and silver to almost satiate [satisfy] the universe, we barely possess the wherewithal [means] to cover our nakedness? What purposes do so many fertile lands serve if, besides lacking the instruments to work them, it is useless for us to produce anything more than for our own consumption [use]?...
>
> ... Let us renounce [reject] . . . a government which [because of its] remoteness cannot provide for us even a part of the advantages which all men should expect of the society of which they are members; this government which far from fulfilling its indispensable [essential] obligation to protect the liberty and security of his persons, persists in destroying them, and instead of making an effort to make us happy, heaps all kinds of calamities [misfortunes] upon us....
>
> The moment has arrived: let us seize it..., and tyranny will be immediately destroyed.
>
> —Juan Batiste Vizcardo y Guzmán *Letter to Spanish Americans* (London, 1801)

1. In this excerpt, what is the writer's main complaint against Spain?

_____

_____

2. What are some of the specific details he uses to support his argument?

_____

_____

3. What duty does the writer believe a government owes its people?

_____

_____

4. According to the writer, what should a society do when its government does not fulfill that duty? What consequence will result from that action?

_____

_____

Name _____   Date _____

▲ Prewriting

Choose Your Topic

Imagine that you are a *criollo*, a *mestizo*, or a Native American living in Latin America during the 1790s and you have decided to write an open letter expressing your views about the most important issue of the day: Spanish control of your homeland. Would you argue that Spanish rule should be immediately overthrown or would you propose some other solution? State your opinion here:

_____

Who will be reading your letter? Does your audience consist of other Spanish Americans who share your opinion but need to be inspired to take strong action? Or are you trying to reach Spanish Americans who disagree with you and must be persuaded to change their minds? Or are you hoping to convince the Spanish rulers that they must change their policies if they want to avoid a bloody revolution? Identify your audience here:

_____

Freewrite

Freewriting is a technique that can help you discover ideas about your subject. When you freewrite, you jot down whatever thoughts come to mind for a certain length of time or until you have filled a certain number of pages. You do not stop to change or even evaluate what you have written—you just write down whatever comes to mind. (If you cannot think of anything, keep repeating the same word until you discover something else to write.) Either freewrite for five minutes or until you have filled the space below.

_____

_____

_____

_____

_____

_____

_____

_____

_____

_____

After you have finished freewriting, wait several minutes and then evaluate what you have written. Add, cross out, or rewrite your freewriting ideas, keeping in mind your audience and purpose.

▲ Writing

Your First Draft

Use the guidelines on the left side of the page to help you write a first draft of your open letter. Do not worry about spelling, punctuation, grammar, and other mistakes right now. As you write, include ideas from your freewriting page and any other ideas that occur to you now.

Begin by stating your opinion about Spanish control of Latin America.

_____
_____
_____

Provide specific evidence—facts, statistics, examples, personal experiences—to support your position. Use your textbook or other reference books if necessary.

_____
_____
_____
_____

Use strong, vital language to state your case.

_____
_____

Organize your arguments in a logical order. Consider presenting your strongest argument last.

_____
_____
_____

Consider presenting the opposing position and then show why it is wrong or unworkable.

_____
_____
_____

State what action you believe should be taken, or what action might result, if Spain does not change its policies.

_____
_____
_____

Conclude with a strong emotional appeal designed to move your audience.

_____

Revising

Talk It Over

Work with a partner to revise your letter. Listen as your partner reads his or her letter aloud twice. During the first reading, see if you can follow the argument your partner is presenting. After the second reading, jot down answers to these questions:

1. What audience is the letter addressing?

2. What is the writer's opinion about the Spanish presence in Latin America? What course of action does the letter recommend or warn against?

3. Has the writer included enough evidence to support his or her opinion? Is that evidence presented in a clear, logical order?

4. How effective is the writer's use of language? Are there any dull words or repetitive passages that could be cut? How powerful is the letter's emotional appeal to readers?

Now switch roles. Read your letter aloud and listen to your partner's comments.

Editing

Review these proofreading marks to help you correct errors.

∧	add something	᭚᭚	add quotation marks
℘	delete something	❡	new paragraph
≡	capitalize	/	lower case
⊙	make a period	⑤ⓟ	spell correctly
⋀	add a comma	∽	transpose

Reread your letter to check for errors in spelling, capitalization, punctuation, and grammar. Then exchange papers with your partner and proofread each other's work. As you read your partner's letter, make a small check in the margin whenever you find an error. When you get your paper back, correct the mistakes your partner has found.

Postwriting

Evaluate Your Writing

If your description has many proofreading marks, copy it onto a clean sheet of paper before submitting it for final evaluation.

Publishing Your Writing

In small groups, read your letters aloud. Then discuss how you could combine the strongest arguments and emotional appeals from each letter into one group letter. Read this letter to the whole class or post it on a class bulletin board.

▲ Unit 3 Writing Workshops: Explaining a Historical Event

In writing about the past, the historian's purpose is usually to explain or clarify what happened and why. To do so, the historian must search for the truth about what happened and then present evidence to support that view. In the following passage, a contemporary historian explains how the famous myth of the Alamo is somewhat different from what actually occurred.

Discover ◁
- the main ideas of the passage
- the factual evidence the writer uses to support these main ideas
- the writer's interpretation of the historical event

Look at the Model

> It seems safe to suggest that the events of March 6, 1836, at the Alamo have contributed more to Mexican American schoolchildren's loss of self-esteem than any other historical episode. Children learn that thousands of Mexicans needlessly and wantonly [mercilessly] slaughtered some 175 Americans who courageously chose to die.
>
> The story of the Alamo was never so simple. . . . [N]ot all the defenders of the Alamo were Yankees. Nor did they choose to die. Although Colonel Travis's slogan was "Victory or Death," he clearly expected victory. "I believe this place can be maintained," he wrote, and from his first call for help, on February 23, through March 3, Travis expected more men to come to his assistance. At the beginning of the siege, Santa Anna had only some 600 troops. By the end of the siege, some 2,400 had arrived, not the 6,000 sometimes suggested. Most of the Mexican soldiers were bewildered Indian conscripts [draftees] who did not even speak Spanish. Woefully [sadly] ill-equipped, they were no match for superior Texas artillery and long rifles. Travis then had reason to remain confident of victory until toward the end, when it became clear that no help from fellow Texans would be forthcoming.
>
> —Walter Lord, "Myths and Realities of the Alamo" *The American West*

1. What is the main idea of the first paragraph of the passage?

   _____

   _____

2. **a.** What is the main idea of the second paragraph?

   _____

   _____

   b. What is the topic sentence that states this idea?

   _____

   _____

3. List three or more facts that the writer presents in support of this second main idea.

   _____

   _____

4. In explaining events, historians rely on facts, but they also present opinions—judgments and interpretations that are based on facts yet cannot be proved. How is this historian's interpretation of what happened at the Alamo different from the usual interpretation?

   _____

   _____

▲ Prewriting

Choose Your Topic

Imagine that you are a historian writing a paragraph about one of the events discussed in Unit 3. (For ideas, see Snapshot of the Times on pages 115, 127, and 136.) What event will you write about?

_____

As a historian, your main purpose will be **expository**—to explain or convey information about the event. But you may also have another purpose—to persuade your audience to accept your interpretation of what happened. (For example, perhaps you want to show that what really happened is different from what most people think happened.) If your purpose is also persuasive, state what you want your readers to believe:

_____

Think about your audience. Are you writing for other historians who already know a great deal about this event? Or are you addressing a general audience, whose knowledge may be limited, one-sided, or nonexistent? Identify your audience here:

_____

Make an Outline

Reread the discussion of the event that appears in Unit 3 and do any additional literary research you feel is necessary. Then organize your information by arranging it in either a formal or an informal outline. In a formal outline, you use an organized system of Roman numerals, regular numbers, and upper- and lower-case letters. In an informal outline, you just group together each main idea and its supporting details. A formal outline for the passage about the Alamo might look like this:

I. Standard interpretation of the Alamo
  A. 175 courageous Yankees who chose to die slaughtered by thousands of heartless Mexicans
  B. Interpretation contributed to Mexican American children's loss of self-esteem

II. Why story of Alamo not so simple
  A. Not all defenders Yankees
  B. Did not courageously choose to die
  C. Expected victory
    a. Thought more help would arrive
    b. Not that outnumbered—Santa Anna had 600 troops, then 2,400 arrived (not 6,000)
    c. Bewildered Indian conscripts, did not speak Spanish
    d. Mexicans ill-equipped, no match for Texas artillery and long rifles
    e. Not clear until end that no help was arriving

In the space below, state the main idea you will write about. (You do not have to write a complete topic sentence.) Then, on a separate sheet of paper, write a formal or an informal outline showing all the supporting details you will use to back up this main idea.

_____

_____

_____

▲ Writing

Your First Draft

Use your prewriting outline and the guidelines on this page to help you write the first draft of your paragraphs. Do not worry about spelling, punctuation, grammar, and other mistakes right now. Feel free to change the organization you established in your outline or to discard any points that no longer seem important.

Identify the event you are writing about.

_____

_____

Explain the significance of the event. (You may choose to save this explanation for the end of your paragraph.)

_____

_____

_____

Present how things happened, using chronological order. Use transition words such as *first*, *then*, and *later* so the order of events is clear to your audience.

_____

_____

_____

_____

Use strong action verbs to make the event come alive for your audience.

_____

_____ ___ ___

If you are trying to disprove another interpretation of the event, explain your purpose. Then provide factual evidence to support your conclusions. (You will also need to summarize the interpretation you disagree with.)

_____

_____

_____

_____

End you arguments with your strongest evidence.

_____

_____

Conclude your paper by restating your main idea, or with the significance of the event.

_____

_____

Revising

Talk It Over

Work with a partner to revise your first draft. Listen as your partner reads his or her paragraph aloud twice. During the first reading, try to understand your partner's explanation of the event. After the second reading, jot down the answers to these questions:

1. Has the writer made you understand exactly what happened? Is the order confusing?

2. What additional information might the writer include to make his or her explanation clearer?

3. If your partner is presenting an interpretation of the event, has he or she provided enough supporting evidence? Do you find the writer's interpretation convincing?

4. Can you suggest any changes in paragraph organization, sentence structure, or language that might strengthen your partner's writing?

Now switch roles. Read your own paragraph aloud and listen to your partner's comments.

Make the Changes

Reread your paragraph, remembering your partner's comments. Make any changes that you think will improve your explanation of the event. Then copy your revision onto a clean sheet of paper.

Editing

Review these proofreading marks to help you correct errors.

∧	add something	ⱲⱲ	add quotation marks
⸮	delete something	⁋	new paragraph
≡	capitalize	/	lower case
⊙	make a period	⑤	spell correctly
⋏	add a comma	∾	transpose

Reread your paragraph to check for errors in spelling, capitalization, punctuation, and grammar. Then exchange papers with your partner and proofread each other's work. As you read your partner's paragraph, make a small check in the margin whenever you find an error. When you get your paper back, correct the mistakes your partner has found.

Postwriting

Evaluate Your Writing

If your paragraph has many proofreading marks, copy it onto a clean sheet of paper before submitting it for final evaluation.

Publishing Your Writing

Organize your paragraphs into a class notebook. Group together those paragraphs that discuss the same event and then organize all the entries chronologically. Include a title page, a list of authors, and a table of contents. A volunteer can write a brief introduction.

▲ Unit 4 Writing Workshops: Analyzing a Historical Person

Poet, essayist, and revolutionary leader José Martí (see pages 172–176) is one of the towering figures in Cuban history. Here a contemporary historian analyzes how Martí both changed—and failed to change—life in Cuba.

Discover ◁
- **how the writer analyzes Martí's contribution to Cuban history**
- **the details that support the writer's analysis**
- **the writer's attitude toward Martí**

Look at the Model

> Cuba produced one of the great romantic figures of the hemisphere: José Martí. With a black general, Antonio Maceo, beside him Martí fought a civil war not only for the independence of Cuba, but for the true emancipation [liberation] of the African in the Americas. In his essay, "My Race," he argued that there were no races; men were alike in matters of the soul; their vices and virtues were the same in the African desert as in the Scottish cathedral. . . .
>
> The failure of Martí was that . . . Cuba remained a racist society, dominated like the rest of the Caribbean by colonialist political, social, and economic policies. Philosophy has not changed the world. Living conditions for blacks and mulattos, the laboring class of Cuba and the rest of the Caribbean, did not improve. In matters of health and nutrition they may actually have grown worse. . . .
>
> Earl Shorris, *Latinos: A Biography of the People* (New York, 1992)

1. In the first paragraph, what two goals does Shorris say that Martí was fighting for in Cuba?

   _____

   _____

2. According to the writer, what did Martí believe about people?

   _____

   _____

3. In the second paragraph, what does Shorris argue was Martí's great failure?

   _____

   _____

4. List one supporting detail that Shorris presents to back up each of his claims about Martí.

   a. _____

   b. _____

   c. _____

5. How would you describe the writer's attitude toward Martí?

   _____

   What words in this passage best convey that attitude?

   _____

▲ Prewriting

Choose Your Topic

Write one or two paragraphs analyzing the historical significance of one of the people discussed in Unit 4. Which person will you write about?

_____

Your audience will determine how much background information you need to include. You might be writing for historians who already know a great deal about this person, or for your classmates, whom you assume know only what they have read in the textbook. Perhaps you are writing for a general audience that may never have heard of this person. Identify your audience here:

_____

What do you think of this person? Is he or she a hero or a villain or something in between? Describe your attitude here:

_____

Make a Chart

To write your analysis, you will need to gather information on your subject by rereading the material in Unit 4 and by doing additional research at the library. Take notes as you read. Then, when you feel you have found enough information, organize your prewriting notes into a chart. Choose two or three headings that will help you structure your material.

If Earl Shorris had used a chart, two of his entries might have looked like this:

WHAT MARTÍ FAILED TO ACCOMPLISH	WHAT MARTÍ ACCOMPLISHED
Despite his moral influence and views on racial equality, Cuba remained a racist society.	Not only great political leader—also great thinker who had profound moral influence on Cuba.

Notice that this chart uses a simple format—two headings across the top with entries listed in vertical columns under each heading. There are many other ways to set up a chart—you might get some ideas by flipping through a news magazine or one of your textbooks.

Use the space below to take your notes. Then use a separate sheet of paper to arrange those notes into a chart.

_____

_____

_____

_____

_____

Name _____ Date _____

▲ Writing Your First Draft

Use this space to write a first draft of your analysis. Do not worry about spelling, capitalization, punctuation, and grammar right now. As you write, refer to your prewriting notes and chart. The guidelines on the left side of the page will also help you organize your ideas.

Identify the person you are writing about.

Depending on your audience, provide whatever background information you feel is necessary—either about the person or about the historical period.

Focus on why you think this person is an important figure in history. Consider both accomplishments and failures, strengths and weaknesses.

Include vivid adjectives and nouns to make this person come alive for your readers. Maybe quote or paraphrase from his or her writing.

Include enough evidence to support your main idea or ideas. Use facts to back up your opinions.

Let your audience know what your attitude is toward this person. If you have mixed feelings, explain why.

If you disagree with the usual analysis of this person, explain why.

Conclude by briefly restating your main idea or opinion about this person's importance.

Revising

Talk It Over

Work with a partner to revise your first draft. Listen as your partner reads his or her analysis aloud twice. During the first reading, try to follow your partner's train of thought. After the second reading, jot down the answers to these questions:

1. In the writer's opinion, why is this person important in history?

2. Did the writer include enough background information and supporting evidence?

3. Do you find the writer's analysis convincing? Why or why not?

4. Has the writer used vivid language? What words or phrases would you replace or cut?

5. Are the writer's ideas presented in a logical order? What changes in paragraph organization or sentence structure can you suggest?

Now switch roles. Read your own analysis aloud and listen to your partner's comments.

Make the Changes

Reread your first draft, remembering your partner's comments. Make any changes that you think will improve your analysis. Then copy your revision onto a clean sheet of paper.

Editing

Review these proofreading marks to help you correct errors.

∧	add something	ᐦᐦ	add quotation marks
⌿	delete something	℘	new paragraph
≡	capitalize	/	lower case
⊙	make a period	Ⓢ	spell correctly
∧	add a comma	∿	transpose

Reread your analysis to check for errors in spelling, punctuation, capitalization, and grammar. Then exchange papers with your partner and proofread each other's work. As you read your partner's analysis, make a small check in the margin whenever you find an error. When you get your paper back, correct the mistakes your partner has found.

Postwriting

Evaluate Your Writing

If your analysis has many proofreading marks, copy it onto a clean sheet of paper before submitting it for final evaluation.

Publishing Your Writing

Share your paper with other students who wrote about the same person. If anyone in the group suggests changes that you think will improve your writing, revise your analysis again. Then gather everyone's papers into a single group book. Decide on a title and then have a volunteer design a cover and title page. If possible, include a picture of the historical person who is the subject of your book.

Name _____ Date _____

 Unit 5 Writing Workshop: Writing an Oral History

The writer Victor Villeseñor grew up hearing tales from his grandmother and parents about their lives in Mexico and their escape during the Revolution. At the age of 30, Villeseñor decided to write an oral history of his family. First he taped more than 200 hours of conversations with his parents and other relatives. Then he traveled to Mexico to verify their stories. His nonfiction family epic *Rain of Gold* took him 15 years to complete.

In this passage, Villeseñor recounts a dramatic incident from his father's childhood. After a dangerous journey, 11-year-old Juan and his family have finally reached the train that will take them—and thousands of other refugees—north to the border. But just as the train starts to move, Juan and some other boys sneak off. They have made a bet to see who can wait the longest and be the last to run after the train and jump aboard. Finally, Juan is the only boy left—but he has waited too long. The train picks up speed and pulls out of sight.

Discover 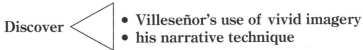 • **Villeseñor's use of vivid imagery**
• **his narrative technique**

Look at the Model

Juan's feet didn't hurt anymore and he ran up the tracks without once slowing down until the sun was long gone and the moon had come out. He went all night—walking and running—until he came out of the other side of the small red-rock hills. . . .

He ran, not stopping, not caring how much his bloody, swollen feet hurt or his throbbing head pained until, way up there in the distance in the darkish daybreak, he thought he saw the little flickering lights of a hundred campfires.

He slowed down, catching his breath, and he could hear people talking. He listened carefully as he came and then, up ahead. . . . He saw the train, the train he'd been after all this time. He began to sob . . . . He was going to be able to find his mother and family and not be lost forever and ever. . . .

One of the boys who'd raced with him saw him coming. "*Dos mio!* " said the startled boy. "You came the whole way on foot, Juan?"

But Juan couldn't hear the boy, much less see him. . . . His whole face, neck and shoulders were white from where the salty sweat had dried on his skin. He was falling, stumbling, gasping, crying as he came toward their fires, white-lipped and wide-eyed.

"Your mother," said the boy, "she said you'd catch us . . . "

—Victor Villeseñor, *Rain of Gold* (Houston, 1991)

1. Villeseñor uses vivid imagery to help the reader share Juan's experience. Find an image that appeals to each of these senses: sight, touch, and hearing.

   _____

   _____

2. What do you think of Villeseñor's style—writing his father's childhood memories as narrative that reads like fiction, not history?

   _____

   _____

3. What might have been different if Villeseñor had written his father's exact words?

   _____

   _____

Name _____ Date _____

▲ Prewriting

Choose Your Topic

Imagine that you have decided to write an oral history of your family or someone else's family. Interview a relative, neighbor, or friend about his or her life. Who will be the subject of your oral history?

_____

Briefly summarize the key facts you already know about this person's life. _____

_____

What additional information do you want to learn about this person? Is there a particular incident or period in this person's life that you would like to focus on?

_____

_____

Think about the technique you will use in writing your oral history. Will you tape-record the interview or take notes? Will you write your interview word for word or will you turn your subject's words into a more storylike, literary narrative? Will you write in the first person (using the pronoun *I*) or the third person (using the pronoun *he* or *she*)? Describe the technique you plan to use:

_____

Ask Questions

When journalists gather information for a story, they often look for answers to these questions: **Who? What? When? Where? Why?** and **How?** You may want to prepare for your interview by asking similar questions. Other questions will occur to you during the course of your conversation. Here are some questions that Villeseñor might have asked his father during an interview. (The answers to some of these questions are not included in this excerpt.)

Who? Who was with you on your journey to the United States? Whom did you meet along the way? Who were the boys you bet with? Who first spoke to you when you reached the train?

What? What happened during your race to catch the train? What happened after you caught up with it?

When? When did you leave your home in Mexico? When did the train incident happen? When did you finally arrive in the United States?

Where? Where did you live in Mexico? Where did you get on and off the train?

Why? Why did your family flee from Mexico? Why did you make the bet with those boys?

How? How did you survive during your run to catch the train? How long did the run take? How did you feel when you caught up with the train?

On a separate sheet of paper, write down at least five questions that you would like to ask during the interview. Leave several lines of space under each question so you can fill in the answers as you take notes during the interview or when you transcribe your tape afterward. As you ask questions, be sure to listen carefully to the answers without interrupting or acting impatient. You can ask follow-up questions when the person has finished talking. Remember that the best way to get someone to talk is to be a good listener.

▲ Writing

Your First Draft

The guidelines on this page will help you write a first draft of your oral history. Do not worry about spelling, punctuation, capitalization, and grammar right now. As you write, refer to your prewriting questions and notes. If you have recorded your interview, you may need to listen to the tape several times.

Include an introduction in which you identify and describe the person you are writing about, discussing his or her current situation and relation to you.

_____

_____

_____

Explain why you chose this person as the subject of your oral history. (Are you trying to learn more about your own family history, a particular period, or a country?

_____

_____

_____

Identify the focus of your oral history—for example, the person's childhood or a dramatic incident in his or her life.

_____

_____

_____

In the main part of your oral history, try to use this person's own words as much as possible. Use a consistent point of view (first person or third person).

_____

_____

_____

Use images that set the scene and help the reader understand what the person was experiencing. Include details that reveal his or her character.

_____

_____

_____

If you are focusing on an incident, build up suspense about what is going to happen next. Explain how the incident was resolved.

_____

_____

_____

End on a strong note. Use a quote that shows how the person feels about that period in his or her life. Or say what his or her recollections mean to you.

_____

_____

Revising

Talk It Over

Work with a partner to revise your first draft. Listen as your partner reads his or her oral history aloud twice. During the first reading, try to visualize the person your partner has interviewed. After the second reading, jot down the answers to these questions:

1. Did the writer tell a story? Did the narrative capture your interest? Were you bored?

2. Were you confused by any details? Did you want to know more about something—or less?

3. Did you get to know the person's way of talking? Would you use more direct quotations or tighten up any of the quotes? Does the writer use a consistent point of view?

4. What changes in organization can you suggest?

Now switch roles. Read your oral history aloud and listen to your partner's comments.

Make the Changes

Reread your first draft, remembering your partner's comments. Make any changes that you think will improve your oral history. Then copy your revision onto a clean sheet of paper.

Editing

Review these proofreading marks to help you correct errors.

∧	add something	ⱴⱴ	add quotation marks
℘	delete something	ℐ	new paragraph
≡	capitalize	/	lower case
⊙	make a period	ⓢ	spell correctly
⋀	add a comma	∩	transpose

Reread your oral history to check for errors in spelling, punctuation, capitalization, and grammar. Then exchange papers with your partner and proofread each other's work. As you read your partner's oral history, make a small check in the margin whenever you find an error. When you get your paper back, correct the mistakes your partner has found.

Postwriting

Evaluate Your Writing

If your oral history has many proofreading marks, copy it onto a clean sheet of paper before submitting it for final evaluation.

Publishing Your Writing

Display your oral history on a large sheet of poster board, along with photographs or drawings of the person—then and now. If possible, also display some mementos of the period, such as ticket stubs, old passports, clothing, letters, and newspaper clippings.

Name _____ Date _____

▲ Unit 6 Writing Workshop: Writing a Poem About a Historical Event

The poet and novelist Julia Alvarez was born in the Dominican Republic and moved to the United States at the age of 10. In this poem titled "How I Learned to Sweep," she writes about her response to an important historical event that dominated the news when she was a teenager. See if you can guess what she is writing about.

Discover
- **the poet's response to the event**
- **her use of rhythm and meter**
- **the poem's startling imagery and figures of speech**

Look at the Model

My mother never taught me sweeping. . . .
One afternoon she found me watching
TV. She eyed the dusty floor
boldly, and put a broom before
me, and said she'd like to be able
to eat her dinner off that table,
and nodded at my feet, then left.
I knew right off what she expected
and went at it. I stepped and swept;
the TV blared the news; I kept
my mind on what I had to do,
until in minutes, I was through.
Her floor was as immaculate [spotless]
as a just-washed dinner plate.
I waited for her to return
and turned to watch the President,
live from the White House, talk of war:
in the Far East our soldiers were
landing in their helicopters
into the jungle their propellers

swept like weeds seen underwater
While perplexing [confusing] shots were fired
from those beautiful green gardens
into which these dragonflies
filled with little men descended.
I got up and swept again
as they fell out of the sky.
I swept all the harder when
I watched a dozen of them die . . .
as if their dust fell through the screen
upon the floor I had just cleaned.
She came back and turned the dial;
The screen went dark. *That's beautiful,*
she said, and ran her clean hand through
my hair, and on, over the window-
sill, coffee table, rocker, desk,
and held it up— I held my breath—
That's beautiful, she said, impressed,
she hadn't found a speck of death.

—Julia Alvarez, "How I Learned to Sweep," from *Homecoming* (New York, 1984)

1. What event is the speaker watching on the news? How does she respond to what she sees?

_____

_____

2. Although the poem sounds conversational, it uses both **rhythm** and **meter**. Which lines rhyme exactly or approximately? Where do you hear a loose pattern of strong and weak beats?

_____

_____

3. Explain the **figure of speech** in line 24. What is the *duet* in line 30?

_____

_____

4. What startling comparison does the speaker make in the last line? Considering this line, what do you think the poem is really about?

_____

_____

▲ Prewriting

Choose Your Topic

Write a poem about a current issue or historical event that you feel strongly about. Choose an event that has local, national, or global importance. Identify the event here:

_____

Think about your audience. How familiar do you expect your readers to be with this event? Describe your audience here:

_____

What kind of poem will you write? Do you want to write a structured poem that has rhythm and meter? Or are you more comfortable writing free verse—poetry that tries to sound like ordinary speech and does not use a regular meter or rhyme scheme? Another possibility is to follow Julia Alvarez's example and use some rhythm and meter in a loose, unpredictable way. Identify your poetic form here:

_____

What tone will you use? Do you want to write a serious or a humorous poem? Will your voice be joyful or sad, impassioned or bitter, angry or mocking? Pick two or three words to describe your tone:

_____

Make a List

A good way to get started writing a poem is to make a list of images, figures of speech, or other details that come to mind when you think about your subject. Use all your senses and let your feelings influence the kinds of words you choose. Change your wording and try several variations. Remember that you cannot plan a poem the way you plan an essay. Many of your best ideas will come during the writing process.

If Judith Ortiz Cofer had made a list of images and figures of speech, it might have included these items (and variations):

- immaculate floor/like a just-washed dinner plate/floor as immaculate as . . .
- helicopter propellers swept like underwater weeds/weeds underwater
- dragonflies filled with little men/tiny men/minuscule men
- their dust fell through the screen/clean/cleaned
- couldn't find a speck of death/didn't find/hadn't found

Use the space below to write your own list. Continue onto a separate page if necessary.

_____

_____

_____

_____

When you have finished writing, check over your list and put a check next to the items you like best. Cross out anything you do not like.

▲ Writing

Your First Draft

The guidelines on this page will help you write a first draft of your poem. Do not worry about spelling and other mistakes right now. As you write, include ideas from your prewriting list and any other ideas that occur to you.

Begin with an interesting first line.

_____

_____

Use images that let the reader share your physical sensations and emotions. Include whatever information about the event you feel is necessary.

_____

_____

_____

If you use figures of speech, try to find fresh comparisons. Avoid flowery language.

_____

_____

_____

Create your rhythm by using pauses, repetition, and variations in line length.

_____

_____

Pay close attention to line breaks. They can indicate a natural pause in speech or a break in thought.

_____

_____

_____

If you are using rhyme, pick a **rhyme scheme**. Or will you use rhyme more loosely?

_____

_____

Another sound effect you can use is **alliteration**, the repetition of consonant sounds.

_____

_____

End with a line that leaves the reader with something to think about. Then write a title for the poem.

_____

_____

Revising

Talk It Over

Work with a partner to revise your first draft. Listen as your partner reads his or her poem aloud twice. During the first reading, close your eyes. After the second reading, jot down the answers to these questions:

1. What event is the poem about? Does the poet expect you to be familiar with this event? If not, is there enough background information?

2. Has the poet used strong images and original figures of speech? Are there any phrases that you would replace or cut?

3. If the poet has used rhyme or meter, does it sound forced or mechanical?

4. If the poem is written in free verse, does the rhythm sound natural? How could it be improved?

5. What do you think of the poem's subject matter and message?

Now switch roles. Read your own poem aloud and listen to your partner's comments.

Make the Changes

Reread your first draft, remembering your partner's comments. Make any changes that you think will improve your poem. Then copy your revision onto a clean sheet of paper.

Editing

Review these proofreading marks to help you correct errors.

∧	add something	ᵛᵛ	add quotation marks
ℓ	delete something	⁹ℱ	new paragraph
≡	capitalize	/	lower case
⊙	make a period	ⓢ	spell correctly
∧	add a comma	∿	transpose

Reread your analysis to check for errors in spelling, punctuation, capitalization, and grammar. (However, a poem does not always have to follow the usual rules for English.) Then exchange papers with your partner and proofread each other's work. As you read your partner's poem, make a small check in the margin whenever you find an error. When you get your paper back, correct the mistakes your partner has found.

Postwriting

Evaluate Your Writing

If your poem has many proofreading marks, copy it onto a clean sheet of paper before submitting it for final evaluation.

Publishing Your Writing

Stage a class reading and then display your work on a poetry bulletin board.

Name _____ Date _____

 Unit 7 Writing Workshop: Writing a Personal Narrative

In her memoir *Silent Dancing: A Partial Remembrance of a Puerto Rican Childhood*, the writer Judith Ortiz Cofer explores the meaning of her bilingual, bicultural childhood. She describes shuttling between a small town in Puerto Rico and Paterson, New Jersey, when she was growing up. In this excerpt from the essay "One More Lesson," Ortiz Cofer writes about her first school experience in Paterson. She was in the third grade and had forgotten all her English while living in Puerto Rico.

 **Discover**
- **the personal experience the writer is remembering**
- **how she felt about the experience and what she learned from it**
- **your own response to her experience**

Look at the Model

> I remember one day, soon after I joined the rowdy class, when our regular teacher was absent and Mrs. D., the sixth-grade teacher from across the hall, attempted to monitor both classes. She scribbled something on the chalkboard and went to her own room. I felt a pressing need to use the bathroom and asked Julio, the Puerto Rican boy who sat behind me, what I had to do to be excused. He said that Mrs. D. had written on the board that we could be excused by simply writing our names under the sign. I got up from my desk and started for the front of the room when I was struck on the head hard with a book. Startled and hurt, I turned around expecting to find one of the bad boys in my class, but it was Mrs. D. I faced. I remember her angry face, her fingers on my arms pulling me back to my desk, and her voice saying incomprehensible [not understandable] things to me in a hissing tone. Someone finally explained to her that I was new, that I did not speak English. I also remember how suddenly her face changed from anger to anxiety. But I did not forgive her for hitting me with that hardcover spelling book. Yes, I would recognize that book even now. It was not until years later that I stopped hating that teacher for not understanding that I had been betrayed [fooled] by a classmate, and my inability to read her warning on the board. I instinctively [without being taught] understood then that language is the only weapon a child has against the absolute power of adults.
>
> -Judith Ortiz Cofer, Silent Dancing: A Partial Remembrance of a Puerto Rican Girlhood (Houston, 1990)

1. Briefly summarize the experience Ortiz Cofer remembers in this narrative.

   _____

   _____

2. How did this incident make her feel—both at the time and later?

   _____

   _____

3. What did the writer learn from this experience and what concrete action did she take? How might this incident have contributed to her decision to become a writer?

   _____

   _____

4. What were your emotions as you read this narrative?

   _____

5. Do you think that an incident like this could happen today?

   _____

Name _____ Date _____

▲ Prewriting

Choose Your Topic

Write a personal narrative about an experience in your life that has affected you strongly. Choose an experience that you remember well and that you are willing to share with others. Briefly identify the experience here:

_____

A personal narrative is always informal in tone—but you need to make some other decisions about the voice you will use. Will your narrative be humorous or serious? Loving or angry? Nostalgic [sentimental] or bitter? Describe your tone here:

_____

Now consider your audience. Who will read your narrative—family, friends, strangers? Identify your audience here:

_____

Freewrite

Freewriting is a good technique for getting started on a personal narrative. The idea is to jot down whatever thoughts occur to you. Don't worry about spelling, grammar, capitalization, punctuation, or even paragraph organization. Keep your pen moving until you have filled a certain number of pages or written for a certain number of minutes. You can repeat a word if you get stuck. If Judith Ortiz Cofer had freewritten before she wrote about her third-grade experience, the first few lines might have looked something like this:

New Jersey, Paterson, Paterson, Paterson, third grade, back from Puerto Rico, forgot all my English. In a rowdy class. One day the teacher was absent—what was her name?—Mrs. D. from across the hall watched our class. Wrote something on the board and left. Couldn't read it, had to go to the bathroom. That Julio lied to me that RAT, said to just write my name on the board and leave. Mrs. D. threw a spelling book at my head, hardcover. Angry face, fingers pulling me back to my desk, hissing things I could not understand. Do I still hate her? Maybe.

Use the space below and any additional pages you need to freewrite for five minutes.

_____

_____

_____

_____

_____

After you have finished freewriting, wait a few minutes and then evaluate what you have written. Add whatever details or ideas occur to you and cross out unnecessary or repeated material. Number the sentences and phrases to improve the order.

Name _____ Date _____

▲ Writing

Your First Draft

The guidelines on this page will help you write a first draft of your personal narrative. Do not worry about spelling, punctuation, capitalization, and grammar right now. As you write, refer to your prewriting notes but also include any new ideas that occur to you.

Begin by setting the scene. Provide whatever background information you feel is necessary for your audience.

_____
_____
_____

Describe what happened using chronological order—the order in which events occurred.

_____
_____

Use an informal, conversational tone and the first-person point of view.

_____
_____

Include sensory details—clear images that help the reader share the sensations you experienced.

_____
_____

Also include details that reveal your thoughts and feelings. Were you happy, angry, embarrassed, scared? Do you still feel the same way?

_____
_____

Describe the people who appear in your personal narrative. Provide descriptive details that reveal both their appearance and character.

_____
_____

If you include dialogue, try to make it sound natural. Use varied and expressive verbs that convey the speaker's tone of voice with words such as _whispered, whined, shrieked, cooed, hissed, giggled._

_____
_____
_____

Conclude by discussing what the experience meant to you or means to you now. What did you learn? How did you change as a result?

_____
_____

Name _____ Date _____

 Revising

Talk It Over

Work with a partner to revise your first draft. Listen as your partner reads his or her personal narrative aloud twice. During the first reading, try to imagine what the experience was like. After the second reading, jot down the answers to these questions.

1. What are the time and setting of the experience?

2. Has the writer used the first-person point of view and an informal tone? If there is dialogue, does it sound as if real people are talking?

3. Are there images that help you share the feelings that the writer experienced?

4. Has the writer included details that describe his or her thoughts and feelings? Do you understand what the experiences meant to the writer?

5. Can you suggest any changes in word choice, sentence structure, or paragraph organization?

Now switch roles. Read your own narrative aloud and listen to your partner's comments.

Make the Changes

Reread your first draft, remembering your partner's comments. Make any changes that you think will improve your narrative. Then copy your revision onto a clean sheet of paper.

Editing

Review these proofreading marks to help you correct errors.

∧	add something	⩗⩗	add quotation marks
⌀	delete something	⁋	new paragraph
≡	capitalize	/	lower case
⊙	make a period	ⓢⓟ	spell correctly
⋏	add a comma	∿	transpose

Reread your analysis to check for errors in spelling, punctuation, capitalization, and grammar. Then exchange papers with your partner and proofread each other's work. As you read your partner's narrative, make a small check in the margin whenever you find an error. When you get your paper back, correct the mistakes your partner has found.

Postwriting

Evaluate Your Writing

If your narrative has many proofreading marks, copy it onto a clean sheet of paper before submitting it for final evaluation.

Publishing Your Writing

Your teacher will read several papers to the class without identifying the writers. As a class, discuss your responses to these narratives.

▲ Checklist for Writing A Research Paper

Writer _____ Title _____

Prewriting

Planning

_____ What are some subjects that might interest me? Which shall I choose as a topic?

_____ Is the topic narrow enough for one paper?

_____ Is the topic engaging enough to hold my interest?

Researching

_____ Where can I find information about my topic? Will a list help?

_____ What sources should I use (books, articles, encyclopedias, and so forth), and where do I find them?

_____ Do I have enough note cards to take down all important information?

_____ Have I made one bibliography card for each source I used?

_____ Do my note cards have complete source information?

    _____ Do I have the source title(s), author, and publication information as it will appear in my bibliography?

    _____ Have I recorded the library call number, if necessary, and page number where I found the information?

_____ Am I taking accurate research notes?

    _____ Did I use a new card for each new subject and source?

    _____ Have I placed a citation for the source and a page number on each note card?

    _____ Have I placed a subject heading on each card?

_____ Do I need to make an outline to organize my information?

    _____ What are my subtopics?

    _____ Have I organized my note cards by subtopic?

    _____ What is the best organization for my paper—chronological, spatial, order of importance, or developmental?

Writing

Drafting

_____ Do I have an introduction that includes my thesis statement?

_____ Is the body of my paper clear, unified, and coherent?

_____ Do I have a satisfactory conclusion where I restate my thesis and summarize my major points?

_____ Have I avoided plagiarism, presenting someone else's ideas as if they are my own?

▲ Checklist for Writing A Research Paper: (continued)

Writer _____ Title _____

Citing Sources

_____ Have I used at least three sources?

_____ Have I footnoted all information I have borrowed from other sources?

_____ Have I created a bibliography that follows proper form?

Revising

Polishing the Introduction

_____ Does my opening statement arouse interest and include enough background information so my audience can understand my thesis statement and the body paragraphs that follow?

_____ Is my purpose for writing clear in my thesis statement?

Polishing the Body

_____ Does the organization of my body paragraphs develop my thesis and its subtopics?

_____ Are the facts and details in each paragraph organized logically?

_____ Do I need transitional words or phrases to make my organization clearer?

_____ Have I cited all direct quotations and any other borrowed ideas in a consistent manner?

Polishing the Conclusion

_____ Does my conclusion restate my thesis and summarize my major points?

Polishing the Style

_____ Have I made my writing style interesting by varying sentence lengths and structure?

_____ Would illustrations, diagrams, maps, or charts improve my paper?

Checking for Sense

_____ Does my research paper make sense?

Editing

_____ Have I corrected all spelling errors, usage problems, and mechanical mistakes?

_____ Is the revised copy of my research paper neat and easy to read?

Postwriting

Final Polishing

_____ Do I have a title page that contains my name, the title of my paper, and any other information the teacher requires?

_____ Would a folder or cover help me make a good impression?

Using Maps with *The Latino Experience in U.S. History*

This chart lists mapping activities to give students practice with geographic elements in the study of Latino history. Each activity is correlated to one or more of the themes of geography and can be done by completing one of the four outline maps on pp. 284–287. Most activities can be completed using the text. Activities requiring additional research appear in italics.

	Map	Mapping Activity	Geographic Theme
Unit 1	The Americas	Native American Nations	location, movement
	The World	*Routes of Spanish Explorers*	movement, interaction
	Latin America	Route of Cortés	movement, place, region, interaction
	The Americas	Spanish possessions	location, place, region
Unit 2	Latin America	Spanish colonies	place, region, interaction
	Latin America	*Slave populations*	place, region
	The Americas	Wars of Independence	location, place, region, movement
Unit 3	The United States	Expansion	place, region, movement
	The Americas	Mexican War (1846–48)	region, movement
Unit 4	The United States	Expansion	place, region, movement
	The Americas	Immigration	movement, place, region
		U.S. Civil War in Southwest	movement, place, region
		The End of Slavery	region, movement
	Latin America	Cuban-Spanish-American-War	movement, place, region
Unit 5	The Americas	Immigration	movement, place, region
	Latin America	*Mexican Revolution*	movement, place, region
	United States	Latino population and the Dust Bowl	movement, interaction, region, place
Unit 6	The Americas	Immigration	movement, place, region
	The United States	Latino populations	movement, place, region
	Latin America	Countries	location, place, region
	The United States	Sites of civil rights encounters	place, movement
	The World	20th century wars and military conflicts	place, movement
		Express Yourself, Chapter 30 (p. 391)	movement, location
	Latin America	*Revolutions and Forms of Government*	region, movement
Unit 7	The Americas	Immigration	movement, place, region
	The United States	Latino populations	movement, place, region
		Cities with Latino populations	location, region
		Population changes	movement, regions
		Latino place names	location, region
	Latin America	Countries	location, place, region

OUTLINE MAP

The World

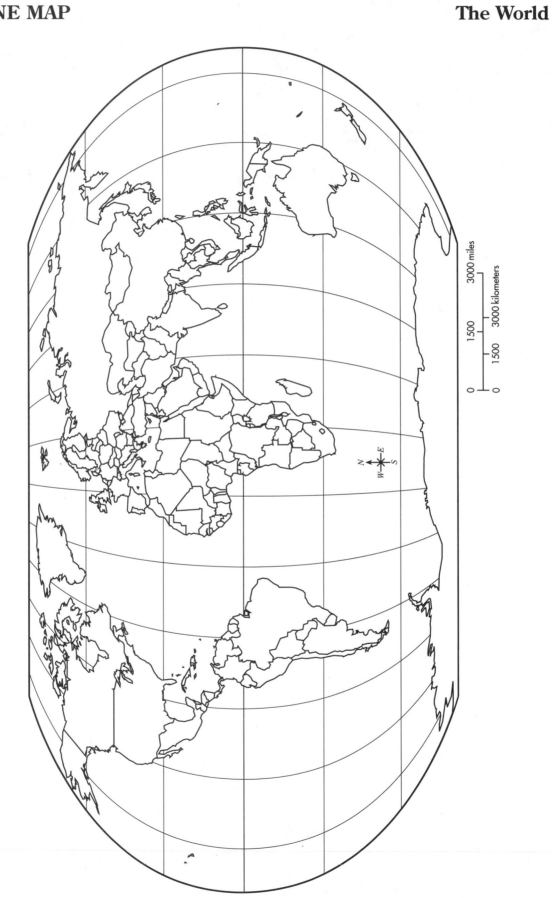

0   1.000 miles
0   1.000 kilometers

Present-day national borders
Rivers

Outline Map   Latin America

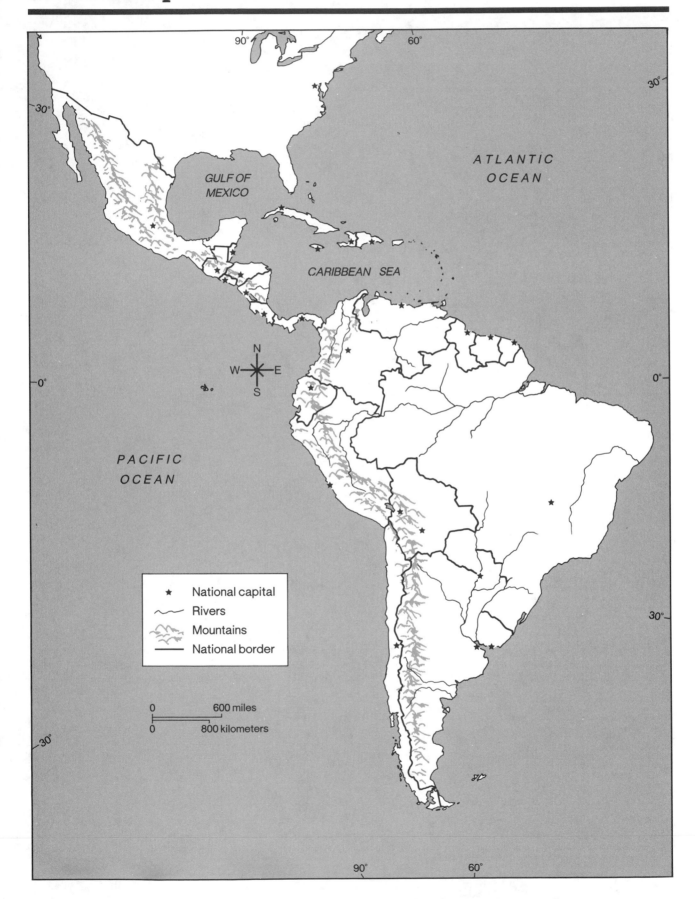

PACIFIC
OCEAN

GULF OF
MEXICO

CARIBBEAN SEA

ATLANTIC
OCEAN

★	National capital
～	Rivers
⁓	Mountains
—	National border

0   600 miles

0   800 kilometers

THE LATINO EXPERIENCE IN U.S. HISTORY • © Globe Fearon

Name _____ Date _____

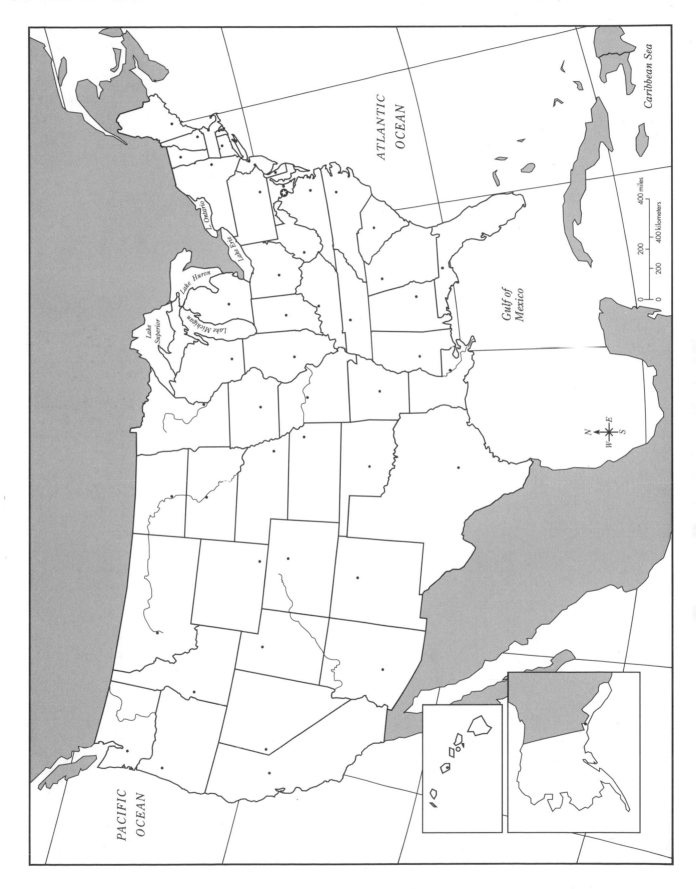

Caribbean Sea

ATLANTIC OCEAN

L. Ontario

Lake Erie

Lake Huron

Lake Michigan

Lake Superior

Gulf of Mexico

400 miles

400 kilometers

200

200

N
W — E
S

PACIFIC OCEAN